# GUIDE TO
# THE HYMNS AND TUNES
# OF AMERICAN METHODISM

# GUIDE TO
# THE HYMNS AND
# TUNES OF
# AMERICAN METHODISM

*COMPILED BY*
*SAMUEL J. ROGAL*

MUSIC REFERENCE COLLECTION, NUMBER 7

GREENWOOD PRESS
NEW YORK • WESTPORT, CONNECTICUT • LONDON

Library of Congress Cataloging-in-Publication Data

Rogal, Samuel J.
    Guide to the hymns and tunes of American Methodism.

    (Music reference collection, ISSN 0736-7740 ; no. 7)
    Bibliography: p.
    Includes indexes.
    1. Hymns, English—Dictionaries.  2. Methodist
Church—United States—Hymns—Dictionaries.  3. Hymns,
English—Bio-bibliography.  4. Hymns, English—
Indexes.  I. Title.  II. Series.
ML102.H95R6  1986      783.9      85-27114
ISBN 0-313-25123-1 (lib. bdg. : alk. paper)

Library of Congress Catalog Card Number: 85-27114
ISBN: 0-313-25123-1
ISSN: 0736-7740

First published in 1986

Greenwood Press, Inc.
88 Post Road West, Westport, Connecticut 06881

Printed in the United States of America

The paper used in this book complies with the
Permanent Paper Standard issued by the National
Information Standards Organization (Z39.48-1984).

10 9 8 7 6 5 4 3 2 1

# CONTENTS

This book is dedicated to
all singers of sacred song,
to all who achieve
spiritual uplift by raising their voices
to and for the Glory of God:

Onward, then, ye people,
Join our happy throng,
Blend with ours your voices,
In the triumph song;
Glory, laud, and honour
Unto Christ the King;
This through countless ages,
Men and angels sing.

Sabine Baring-Gould

# INTRODUCTION

O, for a thousand tongues to sing
My great Redeemer's praise;
The glories of my God and King,
The triumphs of His grace!

So begins the opening stanza of the initial piece of the 1878 Hymnal of
the Methodist Episcopal Church, with Tunes, the first significant revision, with music, of an "authorized" American Methodist hymnal (either
North or South) since thirty years previous.  Charles Wesley's image of
"a thousand tongues" singing the glories of God seems to have anticipa-
ted the denominational and liturgical struggles (not to mention those
of a social and political nature) within American Methodism that would
cause the denomination to remain divided for most of the nineteenth
century—and well into the century following.  More accurately, however,
the younger Wesley's lines forecast, in none too subtle terms, the extreme variety that would eventually come to characterize Methodist hymnody (North and South) in the United States, causing a host of problems
for the editors of its hymnals.  Those "thousand tongues" would eventually learn to sing in spiritual and theological harmony, but they would
have to achieve that end by turning the pages of hymnals that did not
always strike the same denominational or political chords.
     The popular and direct predecessors of the 1878 Hymnal—Collection
of Hymns for Public, Social, and Domestic Worship (Nashville, 1847);
Thomas Osmond Summers' Songs of Zion: A Supplement to the Hymn Book of
the Methodist Episcopal Church, South (Nashville, 1851); James Floy's
Hymns for the Use of the Methodist Episcopal Church (New York, 1849);
Sylvester Main and William C. Brown's Hymns for the Use of the Methodist Episcopal Church. With Tunes for Congregational Worship (New York,
1857)—had long suffered from negative criticism.  Worshipers, theolo-
gians, and church officials, Northern and Southern alike, viewed those
volumes as being little more than antiquated anthologies for the congregational poetry of Isaac Watts and John and Charles Wesley; as such,
those volumes failed to reflect and advance the heart and spirit of true
American Methodism.  For example, of the 1047 hymns in the 1847 Nashville Collection, 600 (or 57 percent) originated from the minds and
pens of the Wesleys, while the Nonconformist (or Independent) Watts had
authored 150 of the remainder.  In the North, the degree of dissatisfac-
tion with the editorial efforts of Floy bears evidence by the fact that
for the next thirty years, a steady stream of alternative hymnals pour-
ed forth.  Such hymnals as The Wesleyan Sacred Harp (Boston, 1855), The

Chorus (Philadelphia, 1856), Methodist Social Hymn Book (New York, 1856), Sacred Melodies for Social Worship (New York, 1859), The Heart and Voice (Philadelphia, 1865), New Hymn and Tune Book: An Offering of Praise for the Methodist Episcopal Church (New York, 1866) satisfied the hearts and voices of certain Northern congregations, while Summers' 1851 Songs of Zion, The New Hymn Book (Nashville, 1881), and the Hymn Book of the Methodist Episcopal Church, South (Nashville, 1889) accomplished the same purposes for Southern Methodists. Essentially, those hymnals emerged to become the order of the day, rivaling and even substituting for the official versions.

In the North, particularly, the new Methodist Hymnal of 1878 proclaimed the beginning of a new order for American Methodist hymnody. "It has . . . been a special aim," declared the hymnal committee of the General Conference of 1876, "to prepare a book which would so commend itself to the whole Church as to secure uniformity of use in all our congregations, thus becoming a strong additional bond of union as well as a powerful stimulus to worship" (Hymnal, 1878, vi). Certainly, few contemporaries could have argued with or even challenged the desire for union and uniformity, but hardly any American Methodist who could analyze a hymnal text could have found hard evidence for anything resembling "newness." The 1878 Hymnal offered 1117 hymns; yet, its committee of editors remained fixed to past practices and principles of selection. In retaining the 767 hymns from the 1849 hymnal of James Floy, the editors reinforced the grip of Isaac Watts, the Wesleys, and the general tradition of eighteenth-century England upon the hymnody of Methodism in the United States (Benson, The English Hymn, 290-303).

There exists little doubt that American Methodist hymnody had reached maturity and independence when, in 1902, the Conference of the Methodist Episcopal Church, South, directed its bishops to join their counterparts in the North in carrying forth a single hymnal project for both factions of the denomination. The result bore fruit some three years later with the publication of The Methodist Hymnal: 717 hymns, in contrast to the 1117 of the 1878 Northern volume and to the 918 selections of the Hymn Book of the Methodist Episcopal Church, South (1889). More important, of those 717 hymns, Only 129 (or 18 percent) bore the authorship of John or Charles Wesley, and the more than one-half million copies of the first printing transported a middle-groun "popular" hymnody to American Methodist sanctuaries. The cost of that popularity may best be understood by reading carefully the short preface to the 1905 Hymnal. In placing their stamp of approval upon the work of the editorial committee, the thirty-six bishops of both Churches could

> gladly note that the hymns of the Wesleys are given the prominence which justly belongs to them in any collection to be used by Methodists. But the book will be found to contain also the choicest work of the other hymn writers of the eighteenth century, namely, Doddridge, Watts, Cowper, Newton, Montgomery, and a very considerable number of new hymns selected from the ancient and modern treasuries of religious poetry. They are the expression of sound doctrine and healthful Christian experience, and it is believed will greatly enrich our worship and bring us into closer fellowship with believers in all lands and in all ages. (Hymnal, 1905, vi)

In the end, those same bishops underscored their desire that the new
hymnal "may everywhere supplant those unauthorized publications which
often teach what organized Methodism does not hold, and which, by exclu-
ding the nobler music of the earlier and later days, prevent the growth
of a true musical taste" (Hymnal, 1905, vii).  Without doubt, the 1905
volume served as an express reaction to the gospel songbooks of the Ira
David Sankey-Dwight Lyman Moody era (1873-1893), but the appeal to denominational unity proved its strongest sounding note.  Its editors ma-
nipulated their selections toward a definition of hymnodic taste; the
words and the music of those pieces represent American Methodism's united contribution united contribution to the aesthetic as well as to the
liturgical function of congregational song.  Although the book begins,
as did its predecessor, with Charles Wesley's "O for a thousand tongues
to sing," it nonetheless manages to ring a note of true American poetry,
of true American hymnody, with such lines as these, composed by John
Greenleaf Whittier and set to music (Elton) by Frederic C. Maker:

> Breathe through the heats of our desire
>    Thy coolness and Thy balm;
> Let sense be dumb, let flesh retire:
> Speak through the earthquake, wind, and fire,
>    O still small voice of calm!

Although the 1905 Hymnal would remain in common congregational use
for nearly a third of a century, it would not constitute American Methodism's most significant contribution  to the hymnody of this nation.
Specifically, almost a century following the publication in 1836 of
their first hymn collection, the American Methodists came forth with
what can easily be identified as their finest product—The Methodist Hymnal of 1935, which went through no less than twelve printings during its
initial year of publication (October 1935-October 1936).  To achieve
that high quality and widespread acceptance, the members of the joint
committee had appointed Robert Guy McCutchan (then Dean of the School of
Music at Depauw University, Greencastle, Indiana) as the general editor;
they had expanded the primary audience for the book to embrace the Methodist Episcopal Church, both North and South, and the Methodist Protestant Church—a connection that had originated in Leeds, England, in
1827, and whose American contingent had published editions of its own
hymnal in 1837, 1859, and 1871.  The joint commission also provided for
a section entitled "Songs of Salvation"—twenty-eight gospel songs written by such popular proponents of that genre as Fanny Jane Crosby, Annie
S. Hawks, and Erastus Johnson.  Ultimately, Dean McCutchan published a
handbook entitled Our Hymnody: A Manual of the Methodist Hymnal (1937),
issued, in part, to underscore the commission's attempt to inject a rea-
sonable degree of consistency into the denomination's attitude concerning congregational song.

One must not assume, however, that the 1945 Hymnal represented the
discarding of the traditional hymnody of Methodism, or that it stood as
the clarion call to gospel song.  Even the most superficial analysis of
the book reveals that the "Songs of Salvation" section (#227-#255) proved but a small concession to gospel song—a mere five percent!  Further-
more, although Dean McCutchan and his editors replaced Charles Wesley's
"O, for a thousand tongues to sing" with Bishop Reginald Heber's Anglican "Holy, holy, holy! Lord God Almighty!" as the opening hymn (Wesley's
piece became hymn #162), they continued to rely heavily, as had their
predecessors, upon the British Nonconformists of the eighteenth century.

In addition, they continued to pay reverence to the Wesleys and their
contemporaries, as well as to the Anglican poets and hymnodists of the
nineteenth century evangelical revival.  According to the prefatory note,
"The Joint Commission constantly held in mind the perpetuation of the
Wesley tradition, the varied desires of the Church, the different ages
of Church members, the continued valued of evangelism, and the emphasis
upon the application of the gospel to everyday life" (Hymnal, 1935, i).
In other words, the volume came forth as a grand liturgical compromise,
a tribute to the middle ground that characterized the denomination's theological and political considerations during those decades from World War
I to 1960.  "It is the devout hope of those who have had a part in its
preparation that the use of this, THE METHODIST HYMNAL, will unite our
people in corporate praise and devotion and enhance the musical ministry
of Methodism" (Hymnal, 1935, ii).
     The problem, of course, focused upon the emphasis placed by the edi-
tors of the 1935 Hymnal on "the application of the gospel to everyday
life."  As American society moved into the second half of the twentieth
century, the applications of 1935 began to fade; by 1960, the need for a
new hymnal became apparent.  Thus, in 1960, the General Conference of the
Methodist Church authorized its Commission on Worship to appoint a committee to revise the 1935 volume; that revision occupied four years of
work and resulted in a draft submitted to the 1964 Conference.  In terms
of recency and overall significance as applied to the history of hymnal
publications, a large portion of the laurel must go to the 1966 Methodist
Hymnal.  Essentially, the succinct third paragraph of its equally succinct preface identifies the purpose and the scope of the book:

> In the present hymnal, the Hymnal Committee desires
> to provide all Methodists with adequate aids to the
> worship of almighty God.  In brief, this revision
> /of the 1935 Hymnal/ attempts to do three things:
> (1) to draw upon the rich heritage of ecumenical
> hymnody, including our own Wesleyan tradition; (2)
> to bring to our people for use in worship a hymnal
> of sufficient diversity to allow for the variety of
> religious experiences, thus meeting the needs of the
> present age; and (3) to reach into the future with a
> hymnal that will serve the religious needs of the
> next generation.  We attempt to do for our genera-
> tion what our predecessors sought to do for theirs:
> to provide a hymnal that makes it possible for us
> to sing our common faith in Christ as Lord and Sa-
> vior (Hymnal, 1966, v).

     Indeed, the 1966 volume does well to echo those sentiments; it does
exist as a tribute to transition and conciliation, as a significant collection of hymnodic tradition and of general projection into the future
of American hymnody (and not, merely, into the future of Methodist hymnody).  It begins with a return to Charles Wesley's "O for a thousand
tongues to sing/My great Redeemer's praise" and ends with Daniel Roberts'
"God of our fathers, whose almighty hand/Leads forth in beauty all the
starry band"; at its center—much like a general assembly of all those
hymnodic generations referred to in the preface to this hymnal—reside
Folliet S. Pierpoint, Samuel Longfellow, Fanny Jane Crosby, John Masterman, Isaac Watts, Horatius Bonar, Philip Doddridge, Laurence Housman,
John Milton, Cecil Frances Alexander, Carleton C. Buck, Caroline Sandell-

Berg, Chao Tzu-Ch'en, William Walsam How, and a veritable legion of hymnodists (Methodist, non-Methodist, even non-Christian) who comprise the hymnic anthology of American Methodism in and for the middle and late twentieth century.

The publication of this Guide to the Hymns and Tunes of American Methodism finds the Methodist Hymnal of 1966 well into its twenty-first year, and those who follow the history and development of American hymnody realize full well the plans underway to publish its successor. In mid-May 1985, members of the Hymnal Revision Committee met in Nashville, Tennessee, to continue earlier discussions on that project tentatively labeled The United Methodist Book of Worship, to be published by the United Methodist Publishing House. The committee held its third meeting in October 1985; it has scheduled future sessions for 1986 (three) and 1987 (four) before the presentation of its report to the 1988 General Conference in St. Louis. Bishop Reuben P. Job chairs the committee, while Carlton R. Young, who edited the 1964/1966 Hymnal, will serve as the general editor of the project.

The problems confronting this committee differ radically from those with which its predecessors (from 1878 through 1935) struggled. Specifically, any editorial group preparing a hymnal for the 1990s and beyond (and there are several denominations hard at work at the task) cannot limit itself to the transitional considerations that tended to focus, principally, upon matching a particular hymn with the best possible hymn tune. To the contrary, the assembly of professors (of sacred music, homiletics, and theology) and professionals (church ministers and church musicians) must carefully direct its collective attention to the sensitive and emotional issues swarming about and within church sanctuaries of late twentieth-century United States. Those same issues will indeed affect the very form and the very function of congregational song in this nation. Thus, for Bishop Job's committee, decisions must come forth regarding

    *inclusive language

    *text-tune relationship and appropriateness

    *eighteenth-century Wesleyan hymns

    *hymns and tunes from popular or commercial but
        unofficial Methodist collections

    *ethnic and minority poems and songs

    *old favorites and even older standard pieces

    *hymns from previous official collections

    *hymns reflecting political positions (both
        national and global)

    *hymns reflecting social and economic issues

    *marketing the new hymnal, both within and
        without the Church

    *accommodating charismatic and evangelical
        groups

> *variations on the same volume: congregational
> edition, full music edition, supporting
> handbooks an d companions
>
> *arrangement of sections, as well as placement
> of hymns within sections
>
> *reliance upon alternate tunes (or setting forth
> suggestions for alternates)

Clearly, one can only speculate upon the results of what will be a long series of deliberations—of hymnological, musical, social, political, and linguistic compromise.  Those very deliberations, however, will produce at least one certainty: a significant percentage of the more than two thousand hymns and tunes listed in this Guide will find their way into an already overcrowded graveyard of discarded hymn texts and hymn tunes, while an equally significant number will have their texts altered beyond recognition.

Any guide to or catalogue of American Methodist hymnody prepared within the past century would not be sufficiently representative without the inclusion of hymns and hymn tunes from two important volumes: the 1911 Methodist Sunday School Hymnal and the 1954 Hymnal of the African Methodist Episcopal Church (A.M.E.).  The first volume stands as the product of the Board of Sunday Schools and emerged from the editorial committee's conviction that "our Sunday schools have suffered much from the very general use of books not especially designed or adapted to the needs and capacities of our youth" (Sunday School Hymnal, 1911, p. ii).  Actually, the editors og the 1878 Hymnal had set aside eighteen hymns for "Children and Youth" (#872-#889), but those merely paid a type of hymnodic lip service to a form that had not advanced appreciably since the early eighteenth century of Isaac Watts.  The compilers of the 1905 collection also included a section for "Children and Youth"—this one consisting of nineteen hymns (#672-#685) held together by the thin threads of the words "child" or "children."  For example, Bishop Reginald Heber's "By cool Siloam's shady rill" (#678) contains the word child in stanzas two and four only; stanza six (the last four lines of the hymn) reads,

> Dependent on thy bounteous breath,
> We seek thy grace alone,
> In childhood, manhood, age, and death,
> To keep us still thine own.

In other words, the piece functions as a children's hymn no more than Daniel C. Roberts' "God of our fathers, whose almighty hand" serves as a dedication to male parents.

Therefore, the reader of the 1911 Methodist Sunday School Hymnal discovers, without much surprise, that the volume exists, essentially, as an abbreviated version of the 1905 Hymnal, with the notable exception of such obvious children's songs as Gertrude Knox's "On the highway of the King,/Children's happy voices ring," the anonymous "Ring out the bells for Christmas,/The happy, happy day," Anne Shepherd's "Around the throne of God in heaven/Thousands of children stand," J.D. Hammond's "The whole wide world for Jesus!/This shall our watchword be."  The Methodist Board of Sunday Schools and its editors did not define, with any degree of clarity, the term "children's hymnody," nor does there appear, other than upon the title page, a clear identification of what constitu-

tes a legitimate Sunday school hymnal.  Again, the importance of the 1911
collection appears to be that it underscores the failure of the form to
have achieved any real identification.  The editors could only affirm
their conviction that "the Sunday schools will appreciate the best in
hymns and tunes, if they have a fair chance really to know the best"
(Sunday School Hymnal, 1911, p. ii).  In this instance, the "best" begins
with Charles Wesley's "Come, Thou Almighty King" and ends with Ebenezer
Elliott's "When wilt Thou save the people?"—neither of which was intended to be a children's hymn.

The African Methodist Episcopal Church issued its first hymn book
in 1818 under the editorship of Richard Allen, Daniel Coker, James Chap-
man, and Jacob Tapisco.  Various editions and revisions, most of those
without significant change, came forth at a fairly consistent rate between 1836 and 1872.  The Church produced substantive revisions of its
Hymnal in 1876, 1888, 1892, 1896, and 1940; a musical edition found its
way into the press in 1897.  Interestingly enough, Richard Allen's name
remained in all versions until 1954; that edition (the one analyzed for
this Guide), proved the Church's most distinctive hymnal, as well as the
"most voluminous ever published in the  history of the A.M.E. Church"
(A.M.E. Hymnal, p. 9).

The 1954 A.M.E. Hymnal reveals an interesting combination of traditional English hymnody of the eighteenth and nineteenth centuries—
Watts, Charles Wesley, John Newton, John Keble, Charlotte Elliott, et
al—and late nineteenth-century American gospel song: "Life is like a
mountain railroad,/With an engineer that's brave," "Nothing between my
soul and the Saviour," "I never can forget the day/I heard my mother
kindly say," "The name of Jesus is so sweet,/I love its music to repeat,"
and others that bear similar styles of imagery and language level.  That
combination becomes even more evident when one observes Joseph Addison's
eighteenth-century Spectator hymn, "The spacious firmament on high,/With
all the blue ethereal sky"—as set to Franz Joseph Haydn's "Creation"—
sleeping none too peacefully between Mrs. Lydia Baxter's "There is a gate
that stands ajar" (with tune by Silas Jones Vail) and Fanny J. Crosby's
"To the work! to the work! we are servants of God,/Let us follow the
path that our Master has trod" (with music by William Howard Doane).
Nonetheless, although the 1954 edition does represent conscientious at-
tempts to capture the spirit of middle twentieth-century American hymnody, it remains fairly close in content and organization to the 1935 Methodist Hymnal; clearly, the collection exists far apart from what we,
in the 1970s and 1980s, have come to know and recognize as the congregational and liturgical music of the Black Church.

# PURPOSE AND SCOPE
# OF THIS BOOK

The Guide to the Hymns and Tunes of American Methodism surveys the specifics of American Methodist hymnody, both texts and tunes, from 1878 through 1966—from approximately the middle of the nineteenth century to the middle of the twentieth. Principally, such a survey provides a number of answers to certain questions that arise periodically but consistently:

1. What hymn text has the denomination considered official, and for how long have certain texts remained in the official hymnals.

2. What hymn tunes have been associated with particular texts, and for what duration?

3. What tunes have remained the same but had their titles changed?

4. What specific authors of texts, as well as composers and arrangers of tunes, have traditionally been included in the denomination's hymnals? What authors, composers, and arrangers have been removed or added, and when?

5. What changes have been made by general editors in terms of placing (or numbering of) a specific hymn within a particular hymnal?

6. What are the general backgrounds of known authors, composers, and arrangers?

This book serves as a reference guide to six major hymnals representing the Methodist Church in the United States. As has been noted in the prefatory section, a new official hymnal will be published within the next twn years; I hope that this Guide will assist to expedite the work of the hymnal committee, especially as its members review the contents of past collections. Further, and in a more general, denominational sense, this Guide will allow historians and students of hymnody (both British and American) to hold on to the past for purposes of comparison, contrast, analysis, and (if for no other reason) simple information.
    The Guide has been arranged in six separate sections. In the first

section, the poets (or hymnodists) appear alphabetically, followed by
the opening lines of those of their hymns that appear in the six Methodist hymnals; the hymns also appear in alphabetical order by first word.
Then follow the reference designations to the hymnals (arranged chrono-
logically), hymn numbers within the collection, the identification of
the accompanying hymn tune, and the composer and/or arranger of that particular tune.  For example:

> ADDISON, JOSEPH
>    5.  How are Thy servants blest, O Lord!/How sure is
>         their defense
>        HMEC-1113.  Ortonville (Thomas Hastings)
>        MH (1905)-202.  Avon (Hugh Williams)
>        MH (1935)-71.  Praetorius (Harmoniae Scholae
>                  Gorlicensis, 1599)
>        MH (1966)-52.  Caithness (Scottish Psalter,
>                  1635)

In other words, Addison's "How are Thy servants blest, O Lord!" carries
the entry number 5 (since all items are indexed by entry number rather
than by page); it appears in the 1878 Hymnal as #1113, set to Thomas
Hastings' tune, "Ortonville"; in the 1905 Hymnal as #202, accompanied
with Hugh Wilson's "Avon"; in the 1935 Hymnal as #71, set to "Praetorius," from the Harmoniae Scholae Gorlicensis of 1599; and finally in the
1966 Hymnal, #52, set to the tune "Caithness," from the Scottish Psalter
of 1635.  According to this entry, Addison's "How are Thy servants blest,
O Lord!" does not appear in the 1911 Methodist Sunday School Hymnal or
in the 1954 A.M.E. Hymnal.  Finally, the reader will note, in the appro-
priate biographical sections, sketches of Addison, Hastings, and Wilson;
the index to composers and arrangers will lead to other tunes in Methodist hymnals by Hastings and Wilson, as well as from the Harmoniae Scholae Gorlicensis and the 1635 Scottish Psalter; the index to tune-names
will identify other hymns in Methodist hymnals set to Ortonville, Avon,
Praetorius, and Caithness.

Immediately preceding the main section of hymn entries, the table
of hymnals presents bibliographical data for each of the six collections;
the identifying abbreviation precedes each title.

The reader will find, following the table of hymnals, a list of
works consulted for the preparation of this Guide, as well as sources
for quotations and references in the prefatory essay.  The list will
serve, also, as a general bibliographical guide to the history and development of Methodist hymnody in the United States.

# TABLE OF HYMNALS

HMEC     HYMNAL OF THE METHODIST EPISCOPAL CHURCH. WITH TUNES.
Cincinnati: Hitchcock and Walden. New York: Nelson and
Phillipps. 1878. Editorial Committee: James M. Buckley,
Richard Wheatley, Erastus Wentworth, John N. Brown, Charles E. Hendrickson, Daniel A. Whedon, Calvin S. Harrington, William Rice, George Prentice, Charles F. Allen,
Francis D. Hemenway, William Hunter, Arthur Edwards, Jeremiah H. Bayliss, Charles H. Payne. Special Music Editors:
Eben Tourjee, Joseph Perry Holbrook. Contains 1117 hymns,
2 doxologies, 20 occasional pieces and chants, 9 indexes,
3 ritual orders (baptism, reception of members, the Lord's
Supper), "Preface to the Hymnal," "Address to the Members
and Friends of the Methodist Episcopal Church," "Preface
to the Hymnal with Tunes," Contents." Pp. 492 + viii. A
number of reprints, especially New York: Phillips and Hunt/
Cincinnati: Cranston and Stowe, 1887; New York: Hunt and
Eaton/Cincinnati: Cranston and Stowe, 1889. Hard cover;
measures 6" x 8¼".

MH (1905)    THE METHODIST HYMNAL. OFFICIAL HYMNAL OF THE METHODIST
EPISCOPAL CHURCH AND THE METHODIST EPISCOPAL CHURCH, SOUTH.
New York: Eaton and Mains. Cincinnati: Jennings and Gra-
ham. 1905. Joint Commission for the Preparation of a
Common Hymnal: D.A. Goodsell, S.F. Upham, C.M. Stuart, C.
M. Coburn, R.J. Cooke, C.S. Nutter, W.A. Quayle, H.G. Jack-
son, C.W. Smith, C.T. Winchester, J.M. Black (Methodist
Episcopal Church); E.E. Hoss, George B. Winton, H.M. Du
Bose, W.F. Tillett, Paul Whitehead, John M. Moore, Edwin
Mims, H.N. Snyder, F.S. Parker, James Campbell, R.T. Ker-
lin (Methodist Episcopal Church, South). Music Editors:
Karl Pomroy Harrington (Wesleyan University), Peter Christian Lutkin (Northwestern University). Contains 717 hymns,
10 doxologies, 20 chants and occasional pieces, 7 indexes,
the psalter, the ritual (baptism, reception of members,
the Lord's supper, matrimony, burial of the dead), "His-
toric Note," "Preface," "Classification." Pp. 655 + viii.
Hard cover; measures 5½" x 8¼".

MSSH     THE METHODIST SUNDAY SCHOOL HYMNAL. ISSUED UNDER THE AUSPI-
CES OF THE BOARD OF SUNDAY SCHOOLS OF THE METHODIST EPIS-

COPAL CHURCH. Edited by John R. Van Pelt, Ph.D., and Peter
C. Lutkin, Mus. D. New York and Cincinnati: The Methodist
Book Concern. 1911. Editorial Committee: Henry Spellmeyer,
Charles M. Stuart, William O. Shepard, Curtis E. Mogg, Frank
L. Brown, David G. Downey, Edgar Blake, John L. Nuelsen.
Contains 280 hymns, doxology, topical and first-line indexes,
"Exercises for the Opening and Closing Worship of the Sun-
day School," "Supplemental Selections for Use in Opening Ex-
ercises," "Prefatory Note." Pp. 312 + viii. Hard cover;
measures 5 5/8" x 8 3/16".

MH (1935)    THE METHODIST HYMNAL. OFFICIAL HYMNAL. THE METHODIST EPIS-
             COPAL CHURCH. THE METHODIST EPISCOPAL CHURCH, SOUTH. THE
             METHODIST PROTESTANT CHURCH. New York, Cincinnati, Chi-
             cago: The Methodist Book Concern. 1935. Editors: Robert
             Guy McCutchan and Van Denman Thompson, with assistance
             from Philip S. Waters. Commissions on the Revision: Wil-
             liam F. Anderson, Edwin Holt Hughes, Frederick D. Leete,
             H. Lester Smith, Titus Lowe, Henry Hitt Crane, Joseph M.
             Grey, Earl Enyeart Harper, John W. Langdale, Oscar Tho-
             mas Olson, Karl P. Harrington, Robert G. McCutchan, James
             R. Houghton, Howard Wilder Lyman, Albert Riemenschneider
             (Methodist Episcopal Church); Warren A. Candler, John M.
             Moore, Urban V.W. Darlington, Sam. R. Hay, A. Frank Smith,
             Nolan B. Harmon, Jr., Ivan Lee Holt, D.N. Hotchkiss,
             Fitzgerald S. Parker, Wilbur Fisk Tillett, Walter Kirk-
             land Greene, J. Abner Sage, Guy E. Snavely, Henry N. Sny-
             der, Charles C. Washburn (Methodist Episcopal Church,
             South); John C. Broomfield, Hugh Latimer Elderdice, Har-
             lan Luther Freeman, Charles Edward Forlines, J.W. Hawley,
             Eugene C. Makosky (Methodist Protestant Church). Con-
             tains 562 hymns, 2 "Wesley Graces," ritual music for the
             Holy Communion, 35 responses and sentences, 10 ancient
             hymns and canticles, ritual and responsive readings, 23
             indexes. Pp. 695 + iv. Hard cover; measures 5 11/16" x
             8½".

AMEH         A.M.E. HYMNAL. WITH RESPONSIVE-SCRIPTURE READINGS. ADAP-
             TED IN CONFORMITY WITH THE DOCTRINES AND USAGES OF THE
             AFRICAN METHODIST EPISCOPAL CHURCH. Published by the
             A.M.E. Sunday School Union. 1954. Editorial Committee:
             S.L. Greene, D. Ward Nichols, G.W. Baber, L.H. Hemingway,
             F.D. Jordan, Wallace M. Wright, A.L. Haskell, Harriett
             B. Wright, E.A. Selby. Contains 673 hymns, "Publisher's
             Word," order of service, baptism of infants, the Lord's
             supper, responses, readings, prayers, solemnization of
             matrimony, general dedicatory services, the burial ser-
             vices, "Methodist Hymnody" (an historical summary), re-
             sponsive readings, 4 indexes. Pp. 648. Hard cover; mea-
             sures 5 5/8" x 8 11/16".

MH (1966)    THE METHODIST HYMNAL. OFFICIAL HYMNAL OF THE METHODIST
             CHURCH. Nashville, Tennessee: The Methodist Publishing
             House. 1964, 1966. General Editor: Carlton R. Young.
             Chairs of the Hymnal subcommitees: Nolan B. Harmon
             (Texts), Earl E. Harper (Executive-Editorial), Will Hil-

debrand (Psalter and Ritual), Austin C. Lovelace (Tunes).
Contains 552 hymns.  "Preface," John Wesley's "Directions
for Singing (date: 1761), the order of worship, the psalter, "Canticles and Othee Acts of Praise," "Canticles
with Music," "Instructions on Chanting," "The Christian
Year," "General Aids to Worship," "Service Music for the
Order of Worship," the sacrament of baptism, confirmation
and reception into the Church, the Lord's supper or Holy
Communion, "Music for Holy Communion," 10 indexes.  Pp.
unnumbered (except for hymns) + xvi.  Hard cover; measures 8 3/4" x 5 7/8".

# SELECTED REFERENCES

Barkley, John M. (ed.). Handbook to the Church Hymnary, 3rd edition. London: Oxford University Press, 1979.

Benson, Louis Fitzgerald. The English Hymn: Its Development and Use in Worship. New York: George H. Doran Company, 1915.

---. The Hymnody of the Christian Church. New York: George H. Doran Company, 1927.

Bett, Henry. The Hymns of Methodism, 3rd edition. London: Epworth Press, 1945.

Brawley, Benjamin. History of the English Hymn. New York: Abingdon Press, 1932.

Christophers, S.W. Hymn Writers and Their Hymns. London: S.W. Partridge, 1866.

Dahle, John. Library of Christian Hymns, translated by M. Caspar Johnson. 3 volumes. Minneapolis: Augsburg Publishing House, 1924.

Diehl, Katharine Smith. Hymns and Tunes—An Index. New York and London: The Scarecrow Press, Inc., 1966.

Douglas, Winfred. Church Music in History and Practice. New York: Charles Scribner's Sons, 1937.

Duffield, Samuel W. English Hymns: Their Authors and History, 3rd edition, revised and corrected. New York: Funk and Wagnalls, 1888.

Foote, Henry Wilder. Three Centuries of American Hymnody. 1940; reprinted New York: Archon Books, 1968.

Frost, Maurice. English and Scottish Psalm and Hymn Tunes, c. 1543-1677. London: Oxford University Press, 1953.

--- (ed.). Historical Companion to Hymns Ancient and Modern. London: William Clowes and Sons, Ltd., 1962.

Gillman, Frederick John. The Evolution of the English Hymn. New York: Macmillan Company, 1935.

Goldhawk, Norman P. On Hymns and Hymn-Books. London: Epworth Press, 1983.

Hustad, Donald P. Dictionary-Handbook to Hymns for the Living Church. Carol Stream, Illinois: Hope Publishing Company, 1978.

Hymns Ancient and Modern. For Use in the Services of the Church. With Accompanying Tunes. Historical Edition. London: William Clowes and Sons, Limited, 1909.

Jefferson, H.A.L. Hymns in Christian Worship. New York: Macmillan Company, 1950.

Julian, John (ed.). A Dictionary of Hymnology. Setting forth the Origin and History of Christian Hymns of All Ages and Nations. Revised Edition, with Supplements. 2 volumes. London: John Murray, 1907.

Lightwood, James T. Hymn Tunes and their Story. London: Epworth Press, 1923.

Lovelace, John. "Hymnal Revision Committee Okays 240 'Probables' in Early Decisions." The United Methodist Reporter, 24 May 1985, p. 24, col. 4-6.

Manning, Bernard Lord. The Hymns of Wesley and Watts. London: Epworth Press, 1942.

Marks, Harvey B. The Rise and Growth of English Hymnody. London: Revell and Company, 1937.

McCutchan, Robert Guy. Hymns in the Lives of Men. New York: Abingdon-Cokesbury Press, 1945.

McDormand, Thomas, and Frederick S. Crossman. Judson Concordance to Hymns. Valley Forge, Pennsylvania: Judson Press, 1965.

Milgate, Wesley. Songs of the People of God. London: Collins Liturgical Publications, 1982.

Miller, Josiah. Singers and Songs of the Church. New York: Anson D.F. Randolph Company, 1875.

Parks, Edna. The Hymns and Hymn Tunes Found in the English Metrical Psalters. New York: Coleman-Ross Company, 1966.

Patrick, Millar. Four Centuries of Scottish Hymnody. London: Oxford University Press, 1949.

Phillips. C. Henry. The Singing Church. London: Faber, 1945.

Phillips, C.S. Hymnody, Past and Present. New York: Macmillan Company, 1937.

Rogal, Samuel J. The Children's Jubilee. A Bibliographical Survey of Hymnals for Infants, Youth, and Sunday Schools Published in Britain and America, 1665-1900. Westport, Connecticut, and London, England: Greenwood Press, 1983.

---. Sisters of Sacred Song: A Selected Listing of Women Hymnodists in Great Britain and America. New York and London: Garland Publishing, 1981.

Routley, Erik. A Panorama of Christian Hymnody. Collegeville, Minnesota: Liturgical Press, 1979.

---. An English-Speaking Hymnal Guide. Collegeville, Minnesota: Liturgical Press, 1979.

Sedgwick, Daniel. A Comprehensive Index of Names of Original Authors of Hymns, Versifiers of Psalms, and Translators of Several Languages. 2nd edition. London, 1863.

Selborne, Palmer Roundell, Earl of. Hymns: Their History and Development. London: Adam and Charles Black, 1892.

Stulken, Marilyn Kay. Hymnal Companion to the Lutheran Book of Worship. Philadelphia: Fortress Press, 1981.

Wordsworth, Christopher, and Henry Littlehales. The Old Service Book of the English Church. London: Methuen and Company, 1904.

# GUIDE TO
# THE HYMNS AND TUNES
# OF AMERICAN METHODISM

# THE HYMNS

ADAMS, JESSIE
1. I feel the winds of God today:/Today my sail I lift
    MSSH-162. Hardy Norseman (Norwegian Traditional)

ADAMS, JOHN GREENLEAF
2. Heaven is here, where hymns of gladness/Cheer the toilers'
    rugged way
    MH (1935)-461. Austrian Hymn (Franz Joseph Haydn)

ADAMS, SARAH FLOWER
3. Nearer, my God, to Thee,/Nearer to Thee
    HMEC-724. Bethany (Lowell Mason)
    MH (1905)-315. St. Edmund (Arthur Seymour Sullivan)
             Bethany (Lowell Mason)
    MSSH-180. Bethany (Lowell Mason)
    AMEH-32. Bethany (Lowell Mason)
    MH (1966)-263. Bethany (Lowell Mason)

ADEBESIN, BIODUN
4. Jesus, we want to meet/On this Thy holy day (translated from
    A.T. Olajida Olude)
    MH (1966)-487. Nigeria (A.T. Olajida Olude)

ADDISON, JOSEPH
5. How are Thy servants blest, O Lord!/How sure is their defense!
    HMEC-1113. Ortonville (Thomas Hastings)
    MH (1905)-202. Avon (Hugh Wilson)
    MH (1935)-71. Praetorius (Harmoniae Scholae Gorlicensis,
             1599)
    MH (1966)-52. Caithness (Scottish Psalter, 1635)
6. The Lord my pasture shall prepare,/And feed me with a shep-
    herd's care
    HMEC-180. Rakem (Isaac Baker Woodbury)
7. The spacious firmament on high,/With all the blue ethereal
    sky
    HMEC-138. Creation (Franz Joseph Haydn)
    MH (1905)-84. Creation (Franz Joseph Haydn)
    MH (1935)-66. Creation (Franz Joseph Haydn)
    AMEH-493. Creation (Franz Joseph Haydn)
    MH (1966)-43. Creation (Franz Joseph Haydn)
8. When all Thy mercies, O my God,/My rising soul surveys
    HMEC-160. Manoah (Etienne Henri Mehul and Franz Joseph
             Haydn)
    MH (1905)-105. Manoah (Etienne Henri Mehul and Franz
             Joseph Haydn)
    MH (1935)-542. Manoah (Etienne Henri Mahul and Franz
             Joseph Haydn)

AMEH-80.  Geneva (John Cole)
MH (1966)-70.  Winchester Old (George Kirbye)
9.  When rising from the bed of death,/O'erwhelmed with guilt and
      fear
    HMEC-412.  Grigg (Joseph Grigg)

ADKINS, LEON M.
    10.  "Go, make of all disciples."/We hear the call, O Lord
         MH (1966)-342.  Lancashire (Henry Smart)

ALEXANDER, CECIL FRANCIS
    11.  All things bright and beautiful,/All creatures great and
           small
         MSSH-262.  Keats (William Henry Monk)
         MH (1935)--447.  Royal Oak (English Traditional)
         MH (1966)-34.  Royal Oak (English Traditional)
    12.  Jesus call us o'er the tumult/Of our life's wild, restless
           sea
         MH (1905)-545.  Wilmot (Carl Maria von Weber)
                         Jude (William Herbert Jude)
         MSSH-140.  Jude (William Herbert Jude)
         MH (1935)-233.  Galilee (William Herbert Jude)
         AMEH-53.  Galilee (William Herbert Jude)
         MH (1966)-107.  Galilee (William Herbert Jude)
    13.  O happy home, where Thou art loved the dearest,/Thou loving
           Friend, and Saviour of our race (trans. from Carl Johann
           Philipp Spitta)
         MH (1905)-671.  Alverstroke (Joseph Barnby)
    14.  O Son of God, in glory crowned,/The Judge ordained of quick
           and dead!
         HMEC-1022.  Windsor (George Kirbye)
    15.  Once in royal David's city/Stood a lowly cattle shed
         MH (1935)-442.  Irby (Henry John Gauntlett)
    16.  Souls in heathen darkness lying,/Where no light has broken
           through
         HMEC-941.  Hamden (Lowell Mason)
    17.  There is a green hill far away,/Without a city wall
         MSSH-89.  The Green Hill (George Coles Stebbins)
         MH (1935)-135.  Meditation (John Henry Gower)
         AMEH-151.  Winchester (Unknown)
         AMEH-399.  Meditation (John Henry Gower)
         MH (1966)-414.  Windsor (William Damon's Booke of Musicke,
                           1591)
    18.  When wounded sore, the stricken soul/Lies bleeding and un-
           bound
         HMEC-320.  Cowper (Lowell Mason)
                    Cleansing Fountain (American Traditional)

ALEXANDER, JAMES WADDELL
    19.  Near the cross was Mary weeping,/There her mournful station
           keeping (trans. from Jacopone de Todi)
         MH (1905)-154.  Stabat Mater (H. Knight)
    20.  O sacred Head, now wounded,/With grief and shame weighed down
           (trans. from Paul Gerhardt)
         HMEC-222.  Munich (Felix Mendelssohn-Bartholdy)
                    Passion Choral (Hans Leo Hassler)

MH (1905)-151.  Munich (Felix Mendelssohn-Bartholdy )
                Passion Choral (Hans Leo Hassler)
MH (1935)-141.  Passion Choral (Hans Leo Hassler)
AMEH-113.  Gerhardt (John Henry Holbrook)
MH (1966)-418.  Passion Chorale (Hans Leo Hassler)

ALFORD, HENRY
    21.  Come, ye thankful people come,/Raise the song of harvest-
            home
            HMEC-1083.  St. George (Sir George Job Elvy)
            MH (1905)-717.  St. George's, Windsor (George Job Elvy)
            MSSH-272.  St. George (George Job Elvy)
            MH (1935)-545.  St. George's, Windsor (George Job Elvy)
            AMEH-357.  St. George's, Windsor (George Job Elvy)
            MH (1966)-522.  St. George's, Windsor (George Job Elvy)
    22.  Forth to the land of promise bound,/Our desert path we tread
            HMEC-1036.  Harris (Louis Devereaux)
    23.  Forward! be out watchword,/Steps and voices joined
            HMEC-564.  Elah (Franz Joseph Haydn)
            MH (1905)-384.  Vexillum (Henry Smart)
            MSSH-227.  Forward (Henry Smart)
    24.  My bark is wafted to the strand/By breath divine
            MH (1905)-451.  Middletown (Caleb Thomas Winchester, arr.
                            Karl Pomeroy Harrington)
    25.  Ten thousand times ten thousand,/In sparkling raiment bright
            HMEC-1062.  Alford (John Bacchus Dykes)
            MH (1905)-618.  Alford (John Bacchus Dykes)
            MH (1935)-531.  Alford (John Bacchus Dykes)
            AMEH-437.  Alford (John Bacchus Dykes)

ALINGTON, CYRIL A.
    26.  Good Christian men, rejoice and sing!/Now is the triumph of
            our King!
            MH (1966)-449.  Gelobt Sei Gott (Melchoir Vulpius)

ALLEN, JAMES
    27.  Sweet the moments, rich in blessing,/Which before the cross
            I spend
            HMEC-730.  Dulcetta (Ludwig van Beethoven)
            MH (1935)-143.  Dorrnance (Isaac Baker Woodbury)

ALLEN, JONATHAN
    28.  Sinners, will you scorn the message/Sent in mercy from above?
            HMEC-342.  Neander (Joachim Neander)
            AMEH-245.  Greenville (Jean Jacques Rousseau)

ALLEN, WILLIS BYRD
    29.  The great world was weary and turned from the light;/The
            sinful were tired of sinning and slept
            MSSH-65.  In the Same Country (George A. Burdett)
                      In the Same Country (John Henry Gower)

ALWOOD, J.K.
    30.  O they tell me of a home far beyond the skies,/O they tell me
            of a home far away

AMEH-577.  O They Tell Me of a Home (J.K. Alwood)

AMIS, LEWIS B.
31.  Jehovah, God who dwelt of old/In temples made with hands
MH (1905)-665.  Temple (Maro Lummis Bartlett)

ANDERSON, MARIA FRANCES
32.  Our country's voice is pleading,/Ye men of God arise!
HMEC-933.  Webb (George James Webb)

ANSTICE, JOSEPH
33.  Lord! how happy should we be,/If we could leave our cares to
Thee
MH (1905)-519.  Meribah (Lowell Mason)

ARKWRIGHT, JOHN STANHOPE
34.  O valiant hearts, who to your glory came/Through dust of
conflict and thro' battle flame
MH (1935)-495.  Langran (James Langran)

ARLOTT, JOHN
35.  God, whose form is all creation,/Take the gratitude we give
MH (1966)-514.  Sankey (Ira David Sankey)

AUBER, HARRIET
36.  Bright was the guiding star that led,/With mild, benignant
ray
HMEC-300.  Melody (I.P. Cole)
37.  Ere mountains reared their forms sublime,/Or heaven and earth
in order stood
HMEC-132.  Hamburg (Lowell Mason)
38.  Hasten, Lord, the glorious time,/When, beneath Messiah's sway
HMEC-937.  Eltham (Lowell Mason)
MH (1905)-637.  St. Bees (John Bacchus Dykes)
39.  How blest the children of the Lord,/Who, walking in His sight
HMEC-902.  Hebron (Lowell Mason)
40.  O God, our strength, to Thee our song/With grateful hearts
we raise
HMEC-33.  Arlington (Thomas Augustine Arne)
41.  On Thy Church, O Power divine,/Cause Thy glorious face to
shine
HMEC-779.  Rosefield (Henri Abraham Caesar Malan)
42.  Our blest Redeemer, ere He breathed/His tender, last farewell
HMEC-280.  Elizabethtown (George Kingsley)
MH (1905)-189.  St. Cuthbert (John Bacchus Dykes)
MSSH-109.  St. Cuthbert (John Bacchus Dykes)
MH (1935)-177.  St. Cuthbert (John Bacchus Dykes)
43.  This is the day the Lord hath made:/O earth, rejoice, rejoice
and sing
HMEC-76.  Merton (Henry Kemble Oliver)
44.  With joy we hail the sacred day,/Which God has called His own
HMEC-74.  Merton (Henry Kemble Oliver)
MH (1905)-65.  Mount Calvary (Robert Prescott Stewart)
45.  With stately towers and bulwarks strong,/Unrivaled and alone
HMEC-764.  St. Ann's (William Croft)

BABCOCK, MALTBIE DAVENPORT
    46.  Be strong!/We are not here to play, to dream, to drift
          MSSH-229. Fortitude (David Stanley Smith)
          MH (1935)-300. Fortitude (David Stanley Smith)
    47.  This is my Father's world,/And to my listening ears
          MH (1935)-72. Terra Beata (Franklin L. Sheppard)
          MH (1966)-45. Terra Beata (Franklin L. Sheppard)

BACON, LEONARD
    48.  O God, beneath Thy guiding hand/Our exiled fathers crossed
          the sea
          MH (1935)-493. Duke Street (John Hatton)
          MH (1966)-550. Duke Street (John Hatton)
    49.  Though now the nations sit beneath/The darkness of o'er-
          spreading death
          HMEC-925. Promise (Francois Hippolite Barthelemon)

BAKER, SIR HENRY WILLIAMS
    50.  How welcome was the call,/And sweet the festal lay
          HMEC-1107. Dennis (Hand George Naegelli)
    51.  O God of love, O King of peace,/Make wars throughout the
          world to cease
          HMEC-1102. Mendon (German Traditional)
          MH (1905)-705. Brookfield (Thomas Bishop Southgate)
          MH (1935)-511. Theodore (Peter Christian Lutkin)
    52.  O perfect life of love!/All, all is finished now
          MH (1905)-155. Aber (William Henry Monk)
    53.  O praise our God to-day,/His constant mercy bless
          HMEC-891. Boylston (Lowell Mason)
    54.  O what, if we are Christ's,/Is earthly shame or loss?
          HMEC-638. Selvin (Lowell Mason)
    55.  The King of love my Shepherd is,/Whose goodness faileth never
          MH (1905)-136. Dominus Regit Me (John Bacchus Dykes)
          MSSH-184. Dominus Regit Me (John Bacchus Dykes)
          MH (1935)-353. Dominus Regit Me (John Bacchus Dykes)
          MH (1966)-67. Dominus Regit Me (John Bacchus Dykes)

BAKER, THEODORE
    56.  We gather together to ask the Lord's blessing!/He chastens
          and hastens His will to make known (trans. from a Nether-
          lands folk hymn)
          MH (1935)-20. Kremser (Edward Kremser)
          AMEH-16. Kremser (Edward Kremser)
          MH (1966)-59. Kremser (Edward Kremser)

BAKEWELL, JOHN
    57.  Hail, Thou once despised Jesus!/Hail, Thou Galilean King!
          HMEC-246. Autumn (Francois Hoppolite Barthelemon)
          MH (1905)-171. Autumn (Francois Hippolite Barthelemon)
          MH (1935)-166. Autumn (Francois Hippolite Barthelemon)
          AMEH-114. Autumn (Francois Hippolite Barthelemon)

MH (1966)-454.  In Babilone (Traditional Dutch melody)

BALL, WILLIAM C.
    58.  Little voices through the temple stealing,/Little hymns to
           God the Father sing
           MSSH-37.  Little Voices (Horace Alden Miller)
    59  Praise the King of heaven,/Call upon His name
           MSSH-34.  Praise the King of Heaven (Frank Moore Jeffery)

BALLENTINE, WILLIAM G.
    60.  God save America!/New world of glory
           AMEH-581.  Russian Hymn (Alexis Feodorovitch Lvov)

BANKS, GEORGE LINNAEUS
    61.  I live for those who love me,/For those I know are true
           MSSH-239.  Guthrie (from a Tyrolese air)

BARBAULD, ANNA LAETITIA
    62.  Again, the Lord of life and light/Awakes the kindling ray
           HMEC-77.  Merton (Henry Kemble Oliver)
    63.  How blest the righteous when he dies!/When sinks a weary soul
           to rest
           HMEC-982.  Ashwell (Lowell Mason)
           MH (1905)-582.  Zephyr (William Batchelder Bradbury)
    64.  Praise to God, annointed praise,/For the love that crowns our
           days!
           HMEC-1084.  St. George (Sir George Job Elvy)
    65.  When as returns this solemn day,/Man comes to meet his Maker,
           God
           AMEC-36.  Zephyr (William Batchelder Bradbury)

BARBER, MARY ANN SERRETT
    66.  Prince of Peace, control Thy will;/Bid this struggling heart
           be still
           HMEC-463.  Aletta (William Batchelder Bradbury)
           MH (1905)-337.  Aletta (William Batchelder Bradbury)
           MH (1935)-216.  Aletta (William Batchelder Bradbury)

BARING-GOULD, SABINE
    67.  Now the day is over,/Night is drawing nigh
           MH (1905)-59.  Merrial (Joseph Barnby)
           MSSH-48.  Merrial (Joseph Barnby)
           MH (1935)-53.  Merrial (Joseph Barnby)
           AMEH-54.  Merrial (Joseph Barnby)
           MH (1966)-495.  Merrial (Joseph Barnby)
    68.  Onward, Christian soldiers!/Marching as to war
           HMEC-563.  Onward/Christian Victor (Arthur Seymour Sulli-
               van)
           MH (1905)-383.  St. Gertrude (Arthur Seymour Sullivan)
           MSSH-214.  St. Gertrude (Arthur Seymour Sullivan)
           MH (1935)-280.  St. Gertrude (Arthur Seymour Sullivan)
           AMEH-191.  St. Gertrude (Arthur Seymour Sullivan)
           MH (1966)-305.  St. Gertrude (Arthur Seymour Sullivan)
    69.  Through the night of doubt and sorrow/Onward goes the pilgrim
           band (trans. from Bernhardt Severin Ingemann)

MH (1905)-567.  Lux Eoi (Arthur Seymour Sullivan)

BARNES, CHARLES W.
    70.  Commit thy way,/And day by day
        MSSH-172.  Delaware (Harriet F. Grove)

BARRATT, ALFRED
    71.  'Tis our festal day, Lord Jesus,/And we bring our sweetest
          song
        MSSH-268.  Festal Day (Leonard Parker)
    72.  We are the Saviour's army,/Marching 'neath the flag of truth
        MSSH-220.  The Saviour's Army (Charles Jessop)

BARTON, BERNARD
    73.  Lamp of our feet, whereby we trace/Our path when wont to
          stray
        MH (1905)-205.  Barton (Unknown)
        MH (1966)-368.  Evan (William Henry Havergal, arr. Lowell
              Mason)
    74.  Walk in the light! so shalt thou know/That fellowship of love
        HMEC-507.  Manoah (Etienne Henri Mehul and Franz Joseph
              Haydn)
        MH (1905)-361.  Manoah (Etienne Henri Mehul and Franz
              Joseph Haydn)
        MH (1935)-378.  Manoah (Etienne Henri Mehul and Franz
              Joseph Haydn)
        MH (1966)-403.  Manoah (Etienne Henri Mehul and Franz
              Joseph Haydn)
    75.  We journey through a vale of tears,/By many a cloud o'ercast
        HMEC-620.  Gould (John Edgar Gould)
        MH (1905)-447.  Gouda (Berthold Tours)

BATEMAN, CHRISTIAN HENRY
    76.  Come, Christians, join to sing/Alleluia! Amen!
        MH (1966)-77.  Spanish Hymn (Benjamin Carr)

BATEMAN, HENRY
    77.  Light of the world! whose kind and gentle care/Is joy and
          rest
        MH (1905)-505.  Cochran (Uzziah Christopher Burnap)

BATES, KATHARINE LEE
    78.  Dear God, our Father, at Thy knee confessing/Our sins and
          follies, close in Thine embrace
        MH (1935)-361.  Deeper Life (Lindsay Bartholomew Longacre)
    79.  O beautiful for spacious skies,/For amber waves of grain
        MSSH-279.  America the Beautiful (Horatio Parker)
        MH (1935)-491.  Materna (Samuel Augustus Ward)
        AMEH-378.  Materna (Samuel Augustus Ward)
        MH (1966)-543.  Materna (Samuel Augustus Ward)
    80.  The Kings of the East are riding/Tonight to Bethlehem
        MH (1935)-101.  Wallace (Clarence Grant Hamilton)

BATHURST, WILLIAM HILEY
    81.  Before Thy mercy-seat, O Lord, /Behold, Thy servants stand

HMEC-61.  Belmont (Samuel Webb)
82.  Holy Spirit, from on high,/O'er us bend a pitying eye
AMEH-198.  Horton (Xavier Schnyder von Wartensee)
83.  How sweet the hour of closing day,/When all is peaceful and
serene
HMEC-980.  Rest (William Batchelder Bradbury)
84.  Jesus, Thy Church, with longing eyes,/For Thine expected
coming waits
HMEC-928.  Appleton (William Boyce)
85.  O for a faith that will not shrink,/Though pressed by every
foe
HMEC-667.  Maitland (George N. Allen)
MH (1905)-424.  Heber (George Kingsley)
MH (1935)-270.  Arlington (Thomas Augustine Arne)
AMEH-329.  Manoah (Giaochino Antonio Rossini)
MH (1966)-142.  Pisgah (J.C. Lowry)
86.  O for that flame of living fire,/Which shone so bright in
saints of old!
HMEC-274.  Melcombe (Samuel Webbe)
MH (1905)-187.  Melcombe (Samuel Webbe)
87.  Why should our tears in sorrow flow/When God recalls His own
HMEC-971.  China (Timothy Swan)
MH (1905)-591.  Green Hill (Albert Lister Peace)

BAX, CLIFFORD
88.  Turn back, O man, forswear thy foolish ways,/Old now is
earth, and none may count her days
MH (1966)-475.  Geneva (Genevan Psalter, 1551)

BAXTER, LYDIA
89.  Take the name of Jesus with you,/Child of sorrow and woe
HMEC-653.  Precious Name (William Howard Doane)
MH (1905)-508.  Precious Name (William Howard Doane)
MH (1935)-253.  Precious Name (William Howard Doane)
AMEH-173.  Precious Name (William Howard Doane)
MH (1966)-87.  Precious Name (William Howard Doane)
90.  There is a gate that stands ajar,/And through its portals
gleaming
AMEH-492.  There Is a Gate That Stands Ajar (Silas Jones
Vail)

BAXTER, RICHARD
91.  Lord, it belongs not to my care/Whether I die or live
HMEC-669.  Cooling (Alonzo Judson Abbey)
MH (1905)-470.  St. Agnes (John Bacchus Dykes)
MH (1935)-516.  St. Agnes (John Bacchus Dykes)
MH (1966)-218.  Horsley (William Horsley)

BAYLY, ALBERT F.
92.  Lord, whose love through humble service/Bore the weight of
human need
MH (1966)-479.  Beecher (John Zundel)

BEACH, CURTIS
93.  O how glorious, full of wonder/Is Thy name o'er all the earth
MH (1966)-41.  Hymn to Joy (Ludwig van Beethoven)

BEDDOME, BENJAMIN
- 94. And must I part with all I have,/My dearest Lord, for Thee?
    AMEH-654.  Without tune
- 95. Buried beneath the yielding wave,/The great Redeemer lies
    AMEH-320.  Dundee (Scottish Psalter, 1615)
- 96. Come, Holy Spirit, come,/With energy divine
    HMEC-285.  State Street (Jonathan Call Woodman)
    MH (1905)-182.  Thatcher (George Frederick Handel)
- 97. Did Christ o'er sinners weep,/And shall our cheeks be dry?
    HMEC-405.  Owen (Joseph Emerson Sweetser)
    MH (1905)-276.  Monsell ( Joseph Barnby)
    AMEH-240.  Laban (Lowell Mason)
- 98. Father of mercies, bow Thine ear,/Attentive to our earnest
        prayer
    HMEC-819.  Griswold (Unknown)
- 99. God's holy law transgressed,/Speaks nothing but despair
    HMEC-314.  State Street (Jonathan Call Woodman)
- 100. How great the wisdom, power, and grace,/Which in redemption
        shine!
    HMEC-315.  Azmon (Carl Gotthelf Glaser, arr. Lowell Mason)
    MH (1905)-8.  Marlow (John Chetham)
    AMEH-418.  Cambridge (John Randall)
- 101. Our few revoking years,/How swift they glide away!
    HMEC-950.  Frome (Hugh Bond)
- 102. Prayer is the breath of God in man,/Returning whence it
        came
    HMEC-706.  Salome (Ludwig van Beethoven)
- 103. 'Tis faith supports my feeble soul/In times of deep distress
    AMEH-658.  Without tune
- 104. Witness, ye men and angels, now,/Before the Lord we speak
    HMEC-466.  Barley (William Tans'ur)

BEEBE, VELMA V.
- 105. O linger not!/The sun leaps high
    MSSH-144.  O Linger Not (Peter Christian Lutkin)

BENNARD, GEORGE
- 106. On a hill far away stood an old rugged cross,/The emblem of
        suff'ring and shame
    AMEH-402.  The Old Rugged Cross ( George Bennard)
    MH (1966)-228.  The Old Rugged Cross (George Bennard)

BENNETT, SANFORD FILMORE
- 107. There's a land that is fairer than day,/And by faith we can
        see it afar
    AMEH-575.  Sweet By and By (Joseph Philbrick Webster)

BENSON, LOUIS FITZGERALD
- 108. For the bread, which Thou hast broken;/For the wine, which
        Thou hast poured
    MH (1935)-412.  Agape (Charles John Dickinson)
    MH (1966)-314.  Kingdom (V. Earle Copes)
- 109. Near the cross her vigil keeping,/Stood the mother, worn with
        weeping
    MH (1935)-138.  Stabat Mater (French church melody)

110. O Thou whose feet have climbed life's hill,/And trod the
        path of youth
        MH (1935)-559.  St. Magnus (Jeremiah Clark)
111. The light of God is falling/Upon life's common way
        MH (1935)-468.  Laufer (Emily Swan Perkins)

BETHAM-EDWARDS, MATILDA BARBARA
112. God makes my life a little light/Within the world to glow
        MH (1935)-450.  Capel (English traditional)

BETHUNE, GEORGE WASHINGTON
113. It is not death to die,--/To leave this weary road (trans.
        from Abraham Henri Caesar Malan)
        HMEC-993.  Capello (Lowell Mason)
        MH (1905)-585.  Greenwood (Joseph Emerson Sweetser)
114. There is no name so sweet on earth,/No name so dear in
        heaven
        MSSH-79.  The Blessed Name (William Batchelder Bradbury)
115. When time seems short and death is near,/And I am pressed
        by doubts and fear
        HMEC-333.  Rakem (Isaac Baker Woodbury)
        MH (1905)-296.  Selena (Isaac Baker Woodbury)

BICKERSTETH, EDWARD HENRY
116. O brothers, lift your voices,/Triumphant songs to raise
        MSSH-238.  Brothers' Voices (Henry Johnson Storer)
117. O God, the Rock of Ages,/Who evermore hast been
        MH (1905)-18.  Greenland (Franz Joseph Haydn)
        AMEH-69.  Miriam (Joseph Perry Holbrook)
118. Peace, perfect peace, in this dark world of sin?/The blood
        of Jesus whispers peace within
        MH (1905)-528.  Pax Tecum (George Thomas Caldbeck)
        MH (1935)-354.  Pax Tecum (George Thomas Caldbeck)
        MH (1966)-229.  Song 46 (Orlando Gibbons)
119. Stand, soldier of the cross,/Thy high allegiance claim
        MH (1935)-413.  Festal Song (William Henry Walter)
120. "'Till He come:" O let the words/Linger on the trembling
        chords
        HMEC-845.  Nassau (Johann Rosenmuller)
        MH (1905)-240.  Nassau (Johann Rosenmuller)

BURDSALL, RICHARD
121. The voice of free grace cries, "Escape to the mountain:/For
        Adam's lost race Christ hath opened a fountain. . . ."
        HMEC-330.  Scotland (John Clarke)

BLACKIE, JOHN STUART
122. Angels holy, high and lowly,/Sing the praises of the Lord!
        MSSH-9.  Windermere (Frederick Charles Maker)

BLACKLOCK, THOMAS
123. Come, O my soul, in sacred lays,/Attempt thy great Creator's
        praise
        HMEC-133.  Luton (George Burder)
        MH (1905)-23.  Park Street (Frederick Marco Antonio
                                Venua)

AMEH-9.  Woodworth (William Batchelder Bradbury)

BLAISDELL, JAMES ARNOLD
  124.  Beneath the forms of outward rite/Thy supper, Lord, is spread
        MH (1966)-321.  Perry (Leo Sowerby)

BLANCHARD, FERDINAND Q.
  125.  O Child of lowlt manger birth/On whose low cry the angels
           wait
        AMEH-109.  Eaton (George Whitefield Chadwick)

BLANDLY, E.W.
  126.  I can hear my Saviour calling,/I can hear my Saviour calling
        AMEH-339.  Where He Leads Me (J.S. Norris)

BLISS, PHILIP PAUL
  127.  "Almost persuaded," now to believe,/"Almost persuaded,"
           Christ to receive
        MSSH-119.  Almost Persuaded (Philip Paul Bliss)
        AMEH-250.  Almost Persuaded (Philip Paul Bliss)
  128.  Brightly beams our Father's mercy/From His lighthouse ever
           more
        MH (1935)-254.  Lower Lights (Philip Paul Bliss)
        AMEH-255.  Let the Lower Lights Be Burning (Philip Paul
                     Bliss)
        MH (1966)-148.  Lower Lights (Philip Paul Bliss)
  129.  I am so glad that our Father in heav'n/Tells of His love
           in the Book He has giv'n
        AMEH-553.  Jesus Loves Me (Philip Paul Bliss)
  130.  I will sing of my Redeemer,/And His wonderful love to me
        MSSH-11.  My Redeemer (James McGranahan)
  131.  Sing them over again to me,/Wonderful words of life
        AMEH-208.  Wonderful Words of Life (Philip Paul Bliss)
        MH (1966)-109.  Words of Life (Philip Paul Bliss)
  132.  The whole world was lost in the darkness of sin;/The Light
           of the world is Jesus
        MSSH-120.  The Light of the World (Philip Paul Bliss)
  133.  'Tis the promise of God, full salvation to give/Unto him who
           on Jesus His Son will believe
        AMEH-508.  'Tis the Promise of God (Philip Paul Bliss)
  134.  "Whosoever heareth," shout, shout the sound!/Spread the
           blessed tidings all the world around
        AMEH-261.  Whosoever Will (Philip Paul Bliss)

BODE, JOHN ERNEST
  135.  Jesus, I have promised/To serve Thee to the end
        MH (1905)-350.  Angel's Story (Arthur Henry Mann)
        MSSH-152.  Angel's Story (Arthur Henry Mann)
        MH (1935)-226.  Angel's Story (Arthur Henry Mann)
        AMEH-313.  Angel's Story (Arthur Henry Mann)
        MH (1966)-164.  Angel's Story (Arthur Henry Mann)

BOEHM, ANTHONY WILHELM
  136.  Of Him who did salvation bring,/I could forever think and
           sing

        HMEC-327.  Rockingham (Lowell Mason)
        MH (1935)-188.  Rockingham (Lowell Mason)

BONAR, HORATIUS
   137.  A few more years shall roll,/A few more seasons come
        HMEC-957.  Shawmut (Lowell Mason)
        MH (1905)-578.  Chalvey (Leighton George Hayne)
   138.  Beyond the smiling and the weeping,/I shall be soon
        MH (1905)-627.  Beyond (Karl Pomeroy Harrington)
   139.  Far down the ages now,/Much of her journey done
        AMEH-668.  Without tune
   140.  Go, labor on; spend and be spent,/Thy joy to do the Father's
       will
        HMEC-603.  Illinois (Jonathan Spilman)
        MH (1905)-399.  Illinois (Jonathan Spilman)
        MH (1935)-292.  Ernan (Lowell Mason)
        AMEH-448.  Ernan (Lowell Mason)
   141.  Here, O my Lord, I see Thee face to face;/Here would I touch
       and handle things unseen
        MH (1905)-237.  Penitentia (Edward Dearle)
        MH (1935)-415.  Penitentia (Edward Dearle)
        MH (1966)-326.  Adoro Te (Thirteenth-century Benedictine
               plainsong)
        MH (1966)-327.  Penitentia (Edward Dearle)
   142.  I heard the voice of Jesus say,/"Come unto me and rest. . ."
        HMEC-426.  Truman (Joseph Perry Holbrook)
        MH (1905)-304.  Vox Dilecti (John Bacchus Dykes)
               Truman (Joseph Perry Holbrook)
        MH (1935)-210.  Vox Dilecti (John Bacchus Dykes)
               Truman (Joseph Perry Holbrook)
        AMEH-149.  Downs (Lowell Mason)
        AMEH-348.  I Heard the Voice of Jesus Say (English tra-
               ditional)
        AMEH-543.  Evan (William Henry Havergal)
        MH (1966)-117.  Vox Dilecti (John Bacchus Dykes)
   143.  I lay my sins on Jesus,/The spotless Lamb of God
        HMEC-754.  St. Hilda (Justin Heinrich Knecht)
        MH (1905)-488.  St. Hilda (Justin Heinrich Knecht)
        MH (1935)-230.  St. Hilda (Justin Heinrich Knecht)
   144.  I was a wandering sheep,/I did not love the fold
        HMEC-434.  Morris (John Black)
        MH (1905)-300.  Pastor Bonus (Alfred James Caldicott)
   145.  Make haste, O man, to live,/For thou so soon must die
        HMEC-576.  Boylston (Lowell Mason)
        MH (1905)-390.  St. George (Henry John Gauntlett)
   146.  No, not despairingly/Come I to Thee
        MH (1905)-453.  Kedron (Ann Baird Spratt)
        MH (1935)-333.  Kedron (Ann Baird Spratt)
   147.  Now in parting, Father, bless us;/Saviour, still Thy peace
       bestow
        HMEC-855.  Autumn (Francois Hippolyte Barthelemon)
   148.  O Love of God, how strong and true,/Eternal, and yet ever
       new
        MH (1905)-83.  Martham (John Henry Maunder)

149.  Rejoice and be glad!/The Redeemer is come!
        MSSH-121.  Rejoice and Be Glad (John J. Husband)
150.  Rest for the toiling hand,/Rest for the anxious brow
        HMEC-994.  Capello (Lowell Mason)
        AMEH-463.  Dover (Aaron Williams)
151.  Still one in life and one in death,/One in our hope of rest
        above
        HMEC-796.  Linwood (Gioacchimo Rossini)
152.  Thy way, not mine, O Lord,/However dark it be!
        HMEC-655.  Jewett (Carl Maria von Weber, arr. Joseph Perry
                Holbrook)
        MH (1905)-527.  Blessed Home (John Stainer)
153.  Upward where the stars are burning,/Silent, silent in their
        turning
        AMEH-187.  Bonar (John Baptiste Calkin)
154.  What a Friend we have in Jesus,/All our sins and griefs to
        bear!
        HMEC-728.  What a Friend We Have in Jesus (Charles Crozat
                Converse)
155.  When the weary, seeking rest,/To Thy goodness flee
        MH (1905)-509.  Intercession New (William Hutchins Call-
                cott)

BONAR, JANE CATHERINE LUNDIE
    156.  Fade, fade, each earthly joy;/Jesus is mine
            HMEC-741.  Fade, Fade, Each Earthly Joy (Theodore Edson
                    Perkins)

BORTHWICK, JANE LAURIE
    157.  Be still, my soul: the Lord is on thy side;/Bear patiently
            the cross of grief and pain (trans. from Katharina von
            Schlegel)
            MH (1935)-73.  Finlandia (Jean Sibelius)
            AMEH-358.  Finlandia (Jean Sibelius)
            MH (1966)-209.  Finlandia (Jean Sibelius)
    158.  God calling yet! shall I not hear?/Earth's pleasures shall I
            still hold dear? (trans. from Gerhard Tersteegan)
            HMEC-352.  Ingham (Lowell Mason)
            MH (1905)-252.  Rivaulx (John Bacchus Dykes)
            MH (1935)-185.  Federal Street (Henry Kemble Oliver)
            MH (1966)-105.  Federal Street (Henry Kemble Oliver)
    159.  Jesus, still lead on,/Till our rest be won (trans. from
            Nicolaus Ludwig von Zinzendorf)
            MH (1935)-336.  Seelenbrautigam (Adam Drese)
    160.  My Jesus, as Thou wilt;/O may Thy will be mine (trans. from
            Benjamin Schmolke)
            HMEC-654.  Jewett (Carl Maria von Weber, arr. Joseph
                    Perry Holbrook)
            MH (1905)-524.  Jewett (Carl Maria von Weber, arr. Joseph
                    Perry Holbrook)
            MH (1935)-330.  Jewett (Carl Maria von Weber)
            AMEH-401.  Jewett (Carl Maria von Weber)
            MH (1966)-167.  Munich (Gessanbuch, Meiningen, 1693)

BOTTOME, FRANCIS

161.  O spread the tidings round,/Wherever man is found
  AMEH-504.  O Spread the Tidings (William J. Kirkpatrick)

BOURNE, WILLIAM ST. HILL
162.  Christ, who once among us/As a child did dwell
  MH (1905)-683.  St. Hill (John Stainer)
  MSSH-18.  St. Hill (John Stainer)

BOWIE, WALTER RUSSELL
163.  Lord Christ, when first Thou cam'st to men,/Upon a cross,
   they bound Thee
  MH (1966)-355.  Kirken Den Er Et Gammelt Hus (Ludwig
          Matthias Lindeman)
164.  O holy city, seen of John,/Where Christ, the Lamb, doth
   reign
  MH (1935)-474.  Ford Cottage (Frederick Charles Maker)
  MH (1966)-481.  Morning Song (Wyeth's _Repository of Sacred
        Song_, 1813)

BOWLY, MARY PETERS
165.  O Lord, while we confess the worth/Of this the outward seal
  HMEC-829.  Serenity (William Vincent Wallace)

BOWRING, SIR JOHN
166.  Earth's transitory things decay;/Its pomps, its pleasures,
   pass away
  HMEC-978.  Bristol (Edward Little White)
167.  God is love: His mercy brightens/All the path in which we
   rove
  HMEC-150.  Wellesley (Lizzie S. Tourjee)
  MH (1905)-88.  Ascham (Edmund Sardinson Carter)
        Dulcetta (Ludwig van Beethoven)
  MH (1935)-75.  Stuttgart (_Psalmodia Sacra_, Gotha, 1715)
  AMEH-68.  Bowring (Unknown)
  MH (1966)-63.  Stuttgart (Henry John Gauntlett)
168.  How sweetly flowed the gospel sound/From lips of gentleness
   and grace
  HMEC-328.  Rockingham (Lowell Mason)
  MH (1905)-290.  St. Boniface (Joseph Barnby)
169.  In the cross of Christ I glory,/Towering o'er the wrecks of
   time
  HMEC-204.  Rathburn (Ithmar Conkey)
  MH (1905)-143.  Asbury (Claude Wallace Harrington)
         Rathburn (Ithmar Conkey)
  MSSH-87.  Rathburn (Ithmar Conkey)
  MH (1935)-149.  Rathburn (Ithmar Conkey)
  AMEH-105.  Rathburn (Ithmar Conkey)
  AMEH-160.  Layton (J.T. Layton)
  MH (1966)-416.  Rathburn (Ithmar Conkey)
170.  Upon the Gospel's sacred page/The gathered beams of ages
   shine
  HMEC-290.  Dover (Aaron Williams)
  MH (1905)-199.  Holborn Hill (_St. Alban's Tune Book_,
        1865)
171.  Watchman, tell us of the night,/What its signs of promise are

```
            HMEC-935.  Watchman (Lowell Mason)
            MH (1905)-636.  St. George's, Windsor (George Job Elvy)
                            Watchman (Lowell Mason)
            MH (1935)-485.  Watchman (Lowell Mason)
            MH (1966)-358.  Aberystwyth (Joseph Parry)
```

BRACE, SETH COLLINS
```
     172.  Mourn for the thousands slain,/The youthful and the strong
            HMEC-890.  Boylston (Lowell Mason)
            MH (1905)-698.  Owen (Joseph Emerson Sweetser)
```

BRACKENBURY, ROBERT CARR
```
     173.  My son, know thou the Lord,/Thy father's God obey
            HMEC-360.  Capello (Lowell Mason)
```

BRECK, MRS. FRANK A.
```
     174.  Face to face with Christ, my Saviour,/Face to face--what
            will it be?
            AMEH-455.  Face to Face (Grant Colfax Tullar)
```

BREWER, LEIGH RICHMOND
```
     175.  Long years ago o'er Bethlehem's hills/Was seen a wondrous
            thing
            MH (1935)-99.  Weinacht (Karl Pomeroy Harrington)
```

BRIDGES, MATTHEW
```
     176.  Crown Him with many crowns,/The Lamb upon His throne
            HMEC-257.  Diademata (George Job Elvy)
            MH (1905)-179.  Diademata (George Job Elvy)
            MSSH-107.  Diademata (George Job Elvy)
            MH (1935)-170.  Diademata (George Job Elvy)
            AMEH-20.  Diademata (George Job Elvy)
            MH (1966)-455.  Diademata (George Job Elvy)
     177.  My God, accept my heart this day,/And make it always Thine
            HMEC-468.  Barby (William Tans'ur)
            MH (1905)-369.  St. Marguerite (Edward Charles Walker)
     178.  Rise, glorious Conqueror, rise/Into Thy native skies
            HMEC-229.  Dort (Lowell Mason)
            MH (1905)-161.  Dort (Lowell Mason)
            MSSH-102.  Dort (Lowell Mason)
```

BRIDGES, ROBERT SEYMOUR
```
     179.  Ah, holy Jesus, how hast Thou offended,/That man to judge
            Thee hath in hate pretended? (trans. from Johann Her-
            mann)
            MH (1966)-412.  Herzliebster Jesu (Johann Cruger)
     180.  O splendor of God's glory bright,/O Thou that bringest light
            from light (trans. from Ambrose of Milan)
            MH (1966)-29.  Wareham (William Knapp)
```

BRIGGS, GEORGE WALLACE
```
     181.  Christ is the world's true light,/Its captain of salvation
            MH (1966)-408.  Surette (Katherine K. Davis)
     182.  God hath spoken by His prophets,/Spoken His unchanging Word
            MH (1966)-460.  Ebenezer (Thomas John Williams)
```

BROMEHEAD, JOSEPH
    183.  Jerusalem, my happy home!/Name ever dear to me!
          HMEC-1044.  Newbold (George Kingsley)
          MH (1905)-608.  Lambeth (Wilhelm August Schultheis)

BROOKE, STOPFORD AUGUSTUS
    184.  It fell upon a summer day,/When Jesus walked in Galilee
          MH (1935)-443.  Childhood (Students' Hymnal, University
                          of Wales, 1923)

BROOKS, CHARLES TIMOTHY, and JOHN SULLIVAN DWIGHT
    185.  God bless our native land!/Firm may she ever stand
          MH (1905)-703.  America (Henry Carey)
          MSSH-275.  America (Henry Carey)
          MH (1935)-490.  America (Henry Carey)
          AMEH-482.  America (Henry Carey)
          (See also under DWIGHT, JOHN SULLIVAN)

BROOKS, PHILLIPS
    186.  God hath sent His angels to the earth again,/Bringing joyful
             tidings to the sons of men
          MSSH-97.  Easter Angels (James Cutler Dunn Parker)
    187.  O little town of Bethlehem,/How still we see thee lie!
          MH (1905)-121.  St. Louis (Lewis Henry Redner)
                    Bethlehem (Joseph Barnby)
          MSSH-68.  St. Louis (Lewis Henry Redner)
          MH (1935)-100.  St. Louis (Lewis Henry Redner)
          AMEH-96.  St. Louis (Lewis Henry Redner)
          MH (1966)-381.  St. Louis (Lewis Henry Redner)

BROOKS, R.T.
    188.  Thanks to God whose word was spoken,/In the deed that made
             the earth
          MH (1966)-18.  Lauda Anima (John Goss

BROWN, PHOEBE HINSDALE
    189.  I love to steal awhile away/From every cumbering care
          HMEC-709.  Woodstock (Deodatus Dutton, Jr.)
          MH (1905)-498.  Woodstock (Deodatus Dutton, Jr.)
          MH (1935)-55.  Woodstock (Deodatus Dutton, Jr.)
    190.  O Lord, Thy work revive,/In Zion's gloomy hour
          HMEC-771.  Amantus (William Augustus Muhlenberg)

BROWNE, SIMON
    191.  And now, my soul, another year/Of thy short life is past
          MH (1905)-570.  Green Hill (Albert Lister Peace)
    192.  O how can they look up to heaven,/And ask for mercy there
          MH (1905)-696.  Olney (Charles Francis Gounod, arr. John
                        Frederick Bridge)

BROWNING, ELIZABETH BARRETT
    193.  Of all the thoughts of God that are/Borne inward into souls
             afar
          MH (1905)-541.  Pater Omnium (Henry James Ernest Holmes)
    194.  Since without Thee we do no good,/And with Thee do no ill
          MH (1905)-504.  Abiding Grace (John Spencer Camp)

BROWNLIE, JOHN
    195.  The King shall come when morning dawns,/And light triumphant
           breaks (trans. from the Greek)
           MH (1966)-353.  St. Stephen (William Jones)

BRYANT, WILLIAM CULLEN
    196.  As shadows cast by cloud and sun,/Flit o'er the summer grass
           HMEC-907.  Ernan (Lowell Mason)
    197.  Dear ties of mutual succor bind/The children of our feeble
           race
           HMEC-905.  Ernan (Lowell Mason)
           MH (1905)-689.  Bartholdy (Felix Mendelssohn-Bartholdy)
    198.  Deem not that they are blest alone/Whose day a peaceful te-
           nor keep
           HMEC-627.  Dwight (Joseph Perry Holbrook)
           MH (1905)-456.  St. Barbara (Peter Christian Lutkin)
    199.  Look from Thy sphere of endless day,/O God of mercy and of
           might!
           HMEC-929.  Appleton (William Boyce)
           MH (1905)-644.  St. Boniface (Joseph Barnby)
    200.  Mighty One, before whose face/Wisdom had her glorious seat
           HMEC-881.  Sweet Story (English traditional)
    201.  O Thou, whose own vast temple stands,/Built over earth and
           sea  (see 202 below)
           HMEC-869.  Dundee (Guillaume Franc)
    202.  Thou, whose unmeasured temple stands,/Built over earth and
           sea (See 201 above)
           MH (1905)-659.  Dundee (Scottish Psalter, 1615)
           MH (1935)-549.  Dundee (Scottish Psalter, 1615)
           MH (1966)-345.  Dundee (Scottish Psalter, 1615)
    203.  When doomed to death, the apostle lay/At night in Herod's
           dungeon cell
           HMEC-900.  Hebron (Lowell Mason)
    204.  When the blind suppliant in the way,/By friendly hands to
           Jesus led
           HMEC-201.  Ames (Sigismund Neukomm, arr. Lowell Mason)

BUCK, CARLTON C.
    205.  O Lord, may church and home combine/To teach Thy perfect way
           MH (1966)-520.  St. Peter (Alexander Robert Reinagle)

BUCKOLL, HENRY JAMES
    206.  Come, my soul, thou must be waking;/Now is breaking (trans.
           from Friedrich Rudolph Ludwig von Canitz)
           MH (1935)-30.  Haydn (Franz Joseph Haydn)
           MH (1966)-258.  Haydn (Franz Joseph Haydn)

BUELL, HARRIET E.
    207.  My Father is rich in houses and lands,/He holds the wealth
           of the world in His hands!
           AMEH-84.  My Father Is Rich (John B. Sumner)

BULFINCH, STEPHAN GREENLEAF
    208.  Hail to the Sabbath day!/The day divinely given
           HMEC-87.  Lisbon (Daniel Read)

MH (1905)-66.  Schumann (Robert Schumann)
AMEH-228A.  Lisbon (Daniel Read)

BULLOCK, WILLIAM
209.  In grief and fear to Thee, O Lord,/We now for succor fly
HMEC-1095.  Zelzah (German melody)

BUNTING, WILLIAM MACLARDIE
210.  Rites cannot change the heart,/Undo the evil done
HMEC-830.  Serenity (William Vincent Wallace)

BUNYAN, JOHN
211.  He who would valiant be/'Gainst all disaster
MH (1905)-265.  Monk's Gate (English traditional)
MH (1966)-155.  St. Dunstan's (Charles Winfred Douglas)

BURDER, GEORGE
212.  Come, ye that know and fear the Lord,/And raise your souls
above)
AMEH-67.  Warwick (Samuel Stanley)

BURGESS, GEORGE
213.  The harvest dawn is near,/The year delays not long
HMEC-579.  Leighton (Henry Wellington Greatorex)
214.  While o'er the deep Thy servants sail,/Send Thou, O Lord,
the prosperous gale
HMEC-1111.  Gratitude (Thomas Hastings)

BURKE, CHRISTIAN
215.  Lord of life and King of glory,/Who didst deign a child to
be
MH (1935)-426.  Sicilian Mariners' Hymn (Sicilian melody)
MH (1966)-517.  Sicilian Mariners' Hymn (Sicilian melody)

BURLEIGH, WILLIAM HENRY
216.  From lips divine, like healing balm/To hearts oppressed and
torn
HMEC-671.  Cooling (Alonzo Judson Abbey)
217.  Lead us, O Father, in the paths of peace;/Without Thy guiding
hand we go astray
MH (1905)-475.  Burleigh (Joseph Barnby)
MH (1935)-271.  Burleigh (Joseph Barnby)
MH (1966)-269.  Langran (James Langran)
218.  Still will we trust, though earth seem dark and dreary,/And
the heart faint beneath His chastening rod
MH (1905)-486.  Diadema (Joseph Barnby)

BURNS, JAMES DRUMMOND
219.  At Thy feet, our God and Father,/Who hast blessed us all our
days
MH (1935)-37.  St. Asaph (William Samuel Bambridge)
MH (1966)-498.  St. Asaph (William Samuel Bambridge)
220.  Hushed was the evening hymn,/The temple courts were dark
MH (1905)-674.  Samuel ( Arthur Seymour Sullivan)
MSSH-173.  Samuel (Arthur Seymour Sullivan)

MH (1935)-451. Samuel (Arthur Seymour Sullivan)
221. Still with Thee, O my God,/I would desire to be
MH (1905)-525. Rhodes (Charles Warwick Jordan)
222. Thou, Lord, art love, and everywhere/Thy name is brightly shown
AMEH-8. Belmont (William Gardiner)

BURROWES, ELISABETH
223. God of the ages, by whose hand/Through years long past our lives were led
MH (1966)-206. Rockingham (Lowell Mason)
Mason (Lowell Mason)

BURTON, HENRY
224. Break, day of God, O break,/Sweet light of heavenly skies
MH (1935)-504. Darwall (John Darwall)
225. O King of kings, O Lord of hosts, whose throne is lifted high/Above the nations of the earth, the armies of the sky
MH (1905)-714. Rex Regum (John Stainer)
226. There's a light upon the mountains,/And the day is at the spring
MH (1935)-123. Mt. Holyoke (Maurice L. Wostenholm)

BURTON, JOHN
227. Holy Bible, book divine,/Precious treasure, thou art mine
MSSH-113. Pleyel's Hymn (Ignace Josef Pleyel)
228. O Thou that hearest prayer,/Attend our humble cry
HMEC-282. Zebulon (Lowell Mason)
229. Saviour, while my heart is tender,/I would yield that heart to Thee
MSSH-146. Brocklesby (Charlotte Alington Barnard)

BUTLER, CHARLES J.
230. I was once far away from the Savior,/And as vile as a sinner could be
AMEH-527. I Was Once Far Away from the Savior (Charles J. Butler)
231. Since Christ my soul from sin set free,/This world has been a Heav'n to me
AMEH-500. 'Tis Heaven (James M. Black)

BUTTRESS, JOHN
232. Hail, sacred truth! whose piercing rays/Dispel the shades of night
HMEC-298. Burlington (John Freckleton Burrows)

BYRNE, MARY E.
233. Be Thou my Vision, O Lord of my heart;/Naught be all else to me, save as Thou art (trans. from the Old Irish)
MH (1966)-256. Slave (Traditional Irish melody)

BYROM, JOHN
234. Christians, awake! salute the happy morn/Whereon the Saviour of the world was born

MH (1935)-93.  Yorkshire (John Wainright)

CAMERON, WILLIAM
    235.  When the last trumpet's awful voice/This rending earth shall
          shake
          HMEC-989.  Mount Auburn (George Kingsley)

CAMPBELL, JANE MONTGOMERY
    236.  We plow the fields and scatter/The good seed on the land
          (trans. from Matthias Claudius)
          HMEC-1086.  St. James (Unknown)
          MH (1905)-716.  St. Anselm (Joseph Barnby)
          MH (1935)-544.  St. Anselm (Joseph Barnby)
          AMEH-196.  Matthias Claudius/Dresden (Johann Abraham
                    Peter Schultz)
          MH (1966)-513.  Wir Pflugen (Johann Abraham Peter Schultz)

CAMPBELL, MARGARET COCKBURN
    237.  Praise ye Jehovah! praise the Lord most holy,/Who cheers the
          contrite, girds with strength the weak
          MH (1905)-20.  Praise (Karl Pomeroy Harrington)

CAMPBELL, ROBERT
    238.  At the Lamb's high feast we sing/Praise to our victorious
          King (trans. from the Roman Breviary)
          HMEC-847.  Innocents (William Henry Monk)
    239.  They come, God's messengers of love,/They come from realms
          of peace above
          HMEC-167.  Zephyr (William Batchelder Bradbury)

CARLYLE, JOSEPH D.
    240.  Lord, when we bend before Thy throne,/And our confessions
          pour
          HMEC-60.  Belmont (Samuel Webbe)

CARNEY, JULIA A. FLETCHER
    241.  Little drops of water,/Little drops of sand
          MSSH-199.  Rhodes (Unknown)
                  Gott Ein Vater (Friedrich Silcher)
    242.  Think gently of the erring one;/O let us not forget
          MH (1905)-699.  St. Mark (Henry John Gauntlett)

CARTER, DELLA A.
    243.  O the great joy that I find in His service,/Working for Jesus
          from day unto day
          AMEH-322.  O the Great Joy That I Find (Della A. Carter)

CARTER, R. KELSO
    244.  Standing on the promises of Christ my King,/Through eternal
          ages let His praises ring
          MH (1966)-221.  Promises (R. Kelso Carter)

CARY, PHOEBE
   245.  One sweetly solemn thought/Comes to me o'er and o'er
         HMEC-1053.  Cary (Levi Franklin Snow)
         MH (1905)-620.  Cary (Levi Franklin Snow)
         MH (1935)-515.  Dulce Domum (Robert Ambrose)

CASWELL, EDWARD
   246.  Earth has many a noble city;/Bethlehem, thou dost all excel
         (trans. from Aurelius Clemens Prudentius)
         MH (1966)-405.  Stuttgart (Henry John Gauntlett)
   247.  I love, I love Thee, Lord most high!/Because Thou first hast
         loved me (trans. from the seventeenth-century Latin)
         AMEH-417.  Retreat (Thomas Hastings)
   248.  Jesus, the very thought of Thee/With sweetness fills the
         breast (trans from Bernard of Clairvaux)
         HMEC-700.  Holy Cross (Unknown)
         MH (1905)-533.  Sawley (James Walch)
                 Holy Cross (Unknown, arr. James Clifft
                             Wade)
         MSSH-166.  Sawley (James Walch)
         MH (1935)-348.  St. Agnes (John Bacchus Dykes)
         AMEH-122.  St. Agnes (John Bacchus Dykes)
         MH (1966)-82.  St. Agnes (John Bacchus Dykes)
   249.  My God, I love Thee, not because/I hope for heaven thereby
         (trans. from Francis Xavier)
         MH (1905)-483.  St. Bernard (John Richardson)
         MH (1935)-214.  Molleson (Douglas Fletcher)
   250.  Now doth the sun ascend the sky,/And wake creation with its
         ray (trans. from Ambrose of Milan)
         HMEC-107.  Evening Hymn (Thomas Tallis)
   251.  O come, all ye faithful, triumphantly sing!/Come, see in the
         manger the angels' dread King! (trans. from the Latin)
         MH (1905)-125.  Portuguese Hymn (Unknown)
   252.  O Jesus, King most wonderful,/Thou Conqueror renowned (trans.
         from Bernard of Clairvaux)
   253.  O Jesus, Thou the beauty art/Of angel-worlds above
         HMEC-702.  Holy Cross (Unknown)
   254.  O Thou pure light of souls that love,/True joy of every
         human breast (trans. from the eighth-century Breviary)
         HMEC-687.  Retreat (Thomas Hastings)
   255.  When morning gilds the skies,/My heart awakening cries
         (trans. from the German)
         MH (1905)-32.  Laudes Domini (Joseph Barnby)
         MSSH-2.  Laudes Domini (Joseph Barnby)
         MH (1935)-31.  Laudes Domini (Joseph Barnby)
         AMEH-11.  Laudes Domini (Joseph Barnby)
         MH (1966)-91.  Laudes Domini (Joseph Barnby)

CAWOOD, JOHN
   256.  Almighty God, Thy word is cast/Like seed upon the ground
         HMEC-301.  Melody (I.P. Cole)
   257.  Hark! what mean those holy voices,/Sweetly sounding through
         the skies?
         HMEC-188.  Wilmot (Carl Maria von Weber)
         MH (1905)-109.  St. Oswald (John Bacchus Dykes)

CENNICK, JOHN
    258.  Be present at our table, Lord;/Be here and everywhere adored
            MH (1966)-518.  Old 100th (Louis Bourgeois)
    259.  Children of the heavenly King,/As we journey let us sing
            HMEC-720.  Vienna (William Henry Havergal)
            MH (1905)-547.  Vienna (Justin Heinrich Knecht)
            MSSH-27.  Vienna (Justin Heinrich Knecht)
            MH (1935)-326.  Pleyel's Hymn (Ignace Josef Pleyel)
            MH (1966)-300.  Pleyel's Hymn (Ignace Josef Pleyel)
    260.  Jesus, my all, to heaven is gone,/He whom I fix my hopes
           upon
            HMEC-450.  Darley (W.H.W. Darley)
            MH (1905)-306.  Duane Street (George Coles)
            MH (1935)-189.  Duane Street (George Coles)
            AMEH-652.  Without tune
    261.  Thou dear Redeemer, dying Lamb,/I love to hear of Thee
            HMEC-697.  Emmons (Friedrich Burgmuller)
            MH (1905)-532.  Emmons (Friedrich Burgmuller)

CHADWICK, JOHN WHITE
    262.  It singeth low in every heart,/We hear it each and all
            MSSH-259.  Auld Lang Syne (Scottish traditional)
            MH (1935)-521.  Auld Lang Syne (William Shield)
            AMEH-583.  Auld Lang Syne (William Shield)

CHANDLER, JOHN
    263.  Above the clear blue sky,/In heav'n's bright abode
            MSSH-20.  Children's Voices Edward John Hopkins)
    264.  Blest Spirit, one with God above,/Thou source of life and
           holy love (trans. from the Latin)
            HMEC-129.  All Saints (William Knapp)
    265.  O Christ, who hast prepared a place/For us around Thy throne
           of grace (trans. from Santolius Victorinus)
            HMEC-49.  Hebron (Lowell Mason)
    266.  The royal banner is unfurled,/The cross is reared on high
           (trans. from Venantius Fortunatus)
            HMEC-219.  Hermon (Lowell Mason)

CHANDLER, JOHN, and LOUIS FITZGERALD BENSON
    267.  O splendor of God's glory bright,/From light eternal bring-
           ing light (trans. from Ambrose of Milan)
            MH (1935)-38.  Wareham (William Knapp)

CHARLES, ELIZABETH RUNDLE
    268.  Is thy cruse of comfort failing?/Rise and share it with a
           friend
            MSSH-207.  Newman (Carl Fowler Price)
    269.  Lo, the day, the day of life!/Day of unimagined light (trans.
           from Peter Gonella of Tortona)
            HMEC-1026.  Charles (James Parker)
    270.  Never further than Thy cross:/Never higher than Thy feet
            HMEC-205.  Aletta (William Batchelder Bradbury)
            MH (1905)-144.  Aletta (William Batchelder Bradbury)
            MH (1935)-146.  Aletta (William Batchelder Bradbury)
            MH (1966)-430.  Canterbury (Orlando Gibbons)

271.  The morning kindles all the sky,/The heavens resound with
           anthems high (trans. from St. Ambrose of Milan)
           HMEC-233.  Lowry (Joseph Emerson Sweetser)

CHATFIELD, ALLEN WILLIAM
   272.  Lord Jesus, think on me,/And purge away my sin (trans. from
           Synesius of Cyrene)
           MH (1966)-284.  Southwell (Damon's Psalmes, 1579)

CHESTERTON, GILBERT KEITH
   273.  O God of earth and altar,/Bow down and hear our cry
           MH (1966)-484.  King's Lynn (arr. Ralph Vaughan Williams)

CHORLEY, HENRY FOTHERGILL
   274.  God, the All-Terrible! Thou who ordainest/Thunder Thy cla-
           rion, and lightning Thy sword
           HMEC-1092.  Russian Hymn (Alexis Feodorovitch Lvov)
           MH (1905)-707.  Russian Hymn (Alexis Feodorovitch Lvov)
           MH (1966)-544.  Russian Hymn (Alexis Feodorovitch Lvov)

CHORLEY, HENRY FOTHERGILL, and JOHN ELLERTON
   275.  God the Omnipotent! King, who ordainest/Thunder Thy clarion,
           the lightning Thy sword
           MH (1935)-505.  Russian Hymn (Alexis Feodorovitch Lvov)

CLARK, ALEXANDER
   276.  Heav'nly Father, bless me now;/At the cross of Christ I bow
           MH (1935)-304.  Seymour (Carl Maria von Weber)
           MH (1966)-95.  Aus der Tiefe (Martin Herbat)

CLARKE, JAMES FREEMAN
   277.  Brother, hast thou wandered far/From thy Father's happy
           home
           HMEC-906.  Ernan (Lowell Mason)

CLEMENTS, JOHN R.
   278.  In the land of fadeless day/Lies the "city four-square,"/
           It shall never pass away
           AMEH-456.  In the Land of Fadeless Day (Hart Pease Danks)

CLEPHANE, ELIZABETH CECELIA
   279.  Beneath the cross of Jesus/I fain would take my stand
           MH (1935)-144.  St. Christopher (Frederick Charles Maker)
           AMEH-130.  St. Christopher (Frederick Charles Maker)
           MH (1966)-417.  St. Christopher (Frederick Charles Maker)
   280.  There were ninety and nine that safely lay/In the shelter
           of the fold
           MH (1935)-247.  The Ninety and Nine (Ira David Sankey)

CLOUGH, SAMUEL O'MALEY
   281.  I have a Saviour, He's pleading in glory,/A dear, loving
           Saviour, tho' earth-friends be few
           MH (1935)-237.  I Am Praying for You (Ira David Sankey)
           AMEH-342.  I Am Praying for You (Ira David Sankey)

CODNER, ELIZABETH
  (Misprint, in HMEC and MH (1905) for CONDER, ELIZABETH; see under
    290 below)

COGHILL, ANNA LOUISE WALKER
  282.  Work, for the night is coming,/Work through the morning
          hours
            MH (1905)-422.  Work Song (Lowell Mason)
            MSSH-201.  Work Song (Lowell Mason)
            MH (1935)-293.  Work Song (Lowell Mason)
            AMEH-263.  Work Song (Lowell Mason)

COKE, THOMAS
  283.  My hope, my all, my Saviour Thou,/To Thee, lo, now my soul
          I bow!
            HMEC-624.  Fillmore (Jeremiah Ingalls)

COLLYER, ROBERT
  284.  Unto Thy temple, Lord, we come/With thankful hearts to wor-
          ship Thee
            AMEH-225.  Mendon (Samuel Dyer)

COLLYER, WILLIAM BENGO
  285.  Assembled at Thy great command,/Before Thy face, dread King,
          we stand
            HMEC-922.  Arnheim (Samuel Holyoke)
  286.  Great God! what do I see and hear!/The end of things crea-
          ted! (trans. from Bartholomaus Ringwaldt)
            HMEC-1028.  Judgment Hymn (Joseph Klug's Gesangbuch,
              1535)
  287.  Haste, traveler, haste! the night comes on,/And many a shin-
          ing hour is gone
            HMEC-354.  Ingham (Lowell Mason)
            MH (1905)-251.  Clolata (W. St. Clair Palmer)
  288.  Return, O wanderer, return,/And seek thy Father's face
            HMEC-370.  Balerma (Richard Simpson)
            MH (1905)-255.  Woodworth (William Batchelder Bradbury)
            MH (1935)-195.  Woodworth (William Batchelder Bradbury)
  289.  When on the brink of death/My trembling soul shall stand
            HMEC-997.  Tioga (Thomas Hastings)

CONDER, ELIZABETH
  290.  Lord, I hear of show'rs of blessing,/Thou art scatt'ring
          full and free
            HMEC-384.  Even Me (William Batchelder Bradbury)
            MH (1905)-346.  Even Me (William Batchelder Bradbury)
            AMEH-259.  Even Me (William Batchelder Bradbury)

CONDER, EUSTACE ROGERS
  291.  Ye fair green hills of Galilee/That girdle quiet Nazareth
            MH (1935)-124.  Stella (Henri Frederick Hemy)

CONDER, JOSIAH
  292.  Day by day the manna fell:/O to learn this lesson well
            MH (1905)-438.  Munus (John Baptiste Calkin)

293. How shall I follow Him I serve?/How shall I copy Him I love?
     MH (1905)-339.  Germany (Ludwig van Beethoven)
294. Many creatures have fled/Since our Saviour broke the bread
     HMEC-844.  Nassau (Johann Rosenmuller)
295. Oh holy, holy Lord!/Thou God of hosts, by all adored
     HMEC-10.  Old Hundred (Guillame Franc)
296. The Lord is King! lift up thy voice,/O earth, and all ye
     heavens rejoice!
     HMEC-134.  Luton (George Burder)
     MH (1905)-90.  Church Triumphant (James William Elliott)

COOK, JOSEPH SIMPSON
297. Gentle Mary laid her Child/Lowly in a manger
     MH (1935)-107.  Tempus Adest Floridum (arr. Ernest Mac
                     Millan)
     MH (1966)-395.  Tempus Adest Floridum (arr. Ernest Mac
                     Millan)

COOMBS, CHARLES WHITNEY
298. Long years ago o'er Bethlehem's hills/Was seen a wondrous
     thing
     MH (1905)-120.  Festgesang (Alfred Wathall)
                     Weihnacht (Karl Pomeroy Harrington)

COOPER, JOHN
299. Father of heaven, whose love profound/A ransom for our souls
     hath found
     HMEC-35.  Mainzer (Joseph Mainzer)

COPELAND, BENJAMIN
300. Christ's life our code, His cross our creed,/Our common,
     glad confession be
     MH (1905)-138.  Copeland (Karl Pomeroy Harrington)
     MH (1935)-331.  Copeland (Karl Pomeroy Harrington)
301. Our fathers' God to Thee we raise,/In cheerful song, our
     grateful praise
     MH (1905)-713.  Puritan (Henry Morton Durham)
                     Theodore (Peter Christian Lutkin)
     MH (1935)-494.  Theodore (Peter Christian Lutkin)

COPENHAVER, LAURA SCHERER
302. Heralds of Christ, who bear the King's commands,/Immortal
     tidings in your mortal hands
     MH (1935)-482.  National Hymn (George William Warren)
     MH (1966)-406.  National Hymn (George William Warren)

COPPIN, L.J.
303. A song, I'll sing to you, of men both good and true,/Who
     labored, battling for the right
     AMEH-613.  Henderson (Robert Lowry)

COSIN, JOHN
304. Come, Holy Ghost, our souls inspire,/And lighten with ce-
     lestial fire (trans. from Gregory the Great)
     HMEC-273.  Chesterfield (Thomas Haweis)

AMEH-207.  Seymour (Carl Maria von Weber)
MH (1966)-467.  Veni Creator (<u>Vesperale</u> <u>Romanum</u>, 1848)

COSTER, GEORGE THOMAS
305.  King of the City Splendid./Eternal in the height
MH (1935)-473.  City of Light (Arthur Vennell Coster)
306.  March on, O soul, with strength!/Like those strong men of old
MH (1935)-264.  Arthur's Seat (John Goss)
MH (1966)-243.  Arthur's Seat (John Goss)

COTTERILL, JANE BOAK
307.  O Thou, who hast at Thy command/The hearts of all men in Thy hand
HMEC-459.  Percy (Henry Percy Smith)
MH (1905)-341.  Maryton (Henry Percy Smith)

COTTERILL, THOMAS
308.  Dread Jehovah! God of nations!/From Thy temple in the skies
MH (1905)-709.  Asham (Edmund Sardinson Carter)
309.  Eternal Spirit, God of truth,/Our contrite hearts inspire
HMEC-281.  Elizabethtown (George Kingsley)
AMEH-199.  Maitland (George Nelson Allen)
310.  Help us, O Lord, Thy yoke to wear,/Delighting in Thy perfect will
HMEC-904.  Ernan (Lowell Mason)
MH (1905)-691.  Hesperus (Henry Williams Baker)
311.  In memory of the Saviour's love,/We keep the sacred feast
HMEC-838.  Simpson (Louis Spohr)
MH (1935)-413.  Salzburg (Johann Michael Haydn)
MH (1966)-319.  Salzburg (Johann Micharl Haydn)
312.  Our God is love; and all His saints/His image bear below
HMEC-783.  Cornell (John Henry Cornell)
MH (1905)-552.  Cornell (John Henry Cornell)

COWPER, FRANCES MARIA MADAN
313.  My span of life will soon be done,/The passing moments say
HMEC-664.  Heber (George Kingsley)
MH (1905)-426.  Nox Praecessit (John Baptiste Calkin)

COWPER, WILLIAM
314.  A glory gilds the sacred page,/Majestic like the sun
MH (1905)-198.  Burlington (John Freckleton Burrowes)
MH (1935)-388.  Burlington (John Freckleton Burrowes)
315.  Far from the world, O Lord, I flee,/From strife and tumult far
HMEC-713.  Woodstock (Deodatus Dutton, Jr.)
316.  God moves in a mysterious way/His wonders to perform
HMEC-161.  Manoah (Etienne Henri Mehul and Franz Joseph Haydn)
MH (1905)-96.  Dundee (Scottish Psalter, 1615)
MH (1935)-68.  Dundee (Scottish Psalter, 1615)
AMEH-81.  Dundee (Christopher Tye)
AMEH-221.  Devizes (Isaac Tucker)
MH (1966)-215.  Dundee/French (Scottish Psalter, 1615)

317. God of my life, to Thee I call;/Afflicted, at Thy feet I
        fall
        HMEC-625.  Fillmore (Jeremiah Ingalls)
318. Hark, my soul! it is the Lord;/'Tis thy Saviour,--hear His
        word
        HMEC-552.  Hall (Wartemburg melody)
        MH (1905)-307.  Solitude (Lewis Thomas Downes)
        MSSH-145.  St. Bees (John Bacchus Dykes)
        AMEH-257.  St. Bees (John Bacchus Dykes)
        AMEH-426.  Pleyel's Hymn (Ignace Josef Pleyel)
        AMEH-671.  Without tune
319. Hear what God the Lord hath spoken:/O my people, faint and
        few
        HMEC-777.  Austria (Franz Joseph Haydn)
        MH (1905)-211.  Crucifix (Henry Smart)
320. In holy contemplation,/We sweetly then pursue
        HMEC-641.  Endsleigh (Salvatore Ferretti)
321. Jesus, where'er Thy people meet,/There they behold Thy
        mercy-seat
        HMEC-44.  Malvern (Lowell Mason)
        MH (1905)-37.  Wescott (Joseph Barnby)
                       Malvern (Lowell Mason)
        MH (1935)-24.  Malvern (Lowell Mason)
        MH (1966)-98.  Malvern (Lowell Mason)
322. My former hpes are fled;/My terror now begins
        HMEC-308.  Shawmut (Lowell Mason)
323. My Lord, how full of sweet content,/I pass my years in
        banishment (trans. from Jeanne Guyon)
        HMEC-696.  Rolland (William Batchelder Bradbury)
        MH (1905)-518.  Alsace (Ludwig van Beethoven)
        MH (1935)-334.  Hamburg (arr. Lowell Mason)
324. O for a closer walk with God,/A calm and heavenly frame
        HMEC-549.  Church (Joseph Perry Holbrook)
        MH (1905)-492.  Ruth (Lorin Webster)
                        Naomi (Hans George Naegeli)
        MH (1935)-228.  Naomi (Hans George Naegeli)
        AMEH-143.  Avon (Hugh Wilson)
        AMEH-174.  Zerah (Lowell Mason)
        MH (1966)-268.  Naomi (Hans George Naegeli)
325. Sometimes a light surprises/The Christian while he sings
        MH (1905)-454.  Bentley (John Hullah)
        MH (1935)-351.  Petition (Franz Joseph Haydn)
        MH (1966)-231.  Llanfyllin (Traditional Welsh melody)
326. The Spirit breathes upon the word,/And brings the truth to
        sight
        AMEH-201.  Maitland (George Nelson Allen)
327. There is a fountain filled with blood/Drawn from Immanuel's
        veins
        HMEC-319.  Cowper (Lowell Mason)
                   Cleansing Fountain (American traditional)
        MH (1905)-291.  Cowper (Lowell Mason)
                        Cleansing Fountain (American traditional)
        MH (1935)-140.  Cleansing Fountain (American Traditional)
        AMEH-235.  Cleansing Fountain Lowell Mason)
        MH (1966)-421.  Cleansing Fountain (American folk melody)

328.  What glory gilds the sacred page!/Majestic, like the sun
          (Variation of 314 above)
          HMEC-296.  Burlington (John Freckleton Burrowes)
329.  What various hindrances we meet/In coming to a mercy-seat!
          HMEC-690.  Sweet Hour of Prayer (William Batchelder
                            Bradbury)
          MH (1905)-496.  Linwood (Gioacchino Antonio Rossini)
          AMEH-186.  Venn (George Job Elvy)

COX, CHRISTOPHER CHRISTIAN
    330.  Silently the shades of evening/Gather round my lowly door
          HMEC-115.  Stockwell (Darius Eliot Jones)
          MH (1905)-52.  Stockwell (Darius Eliot Jones)
          AMEH-57.  Stockwell (Darius Eliot Jones)

COX, FRANCES ELIZABETH
    331.  Sing praise to God who reigns above,/The God of all crea-
              tion (trans. from Johann Jakob Schutz)
          MH (1935)-355.  Mit Freuden Zart (Bohemian Brethren's
                            Gesangbuch, 1566)
          MH (1966)-4.  Mit Freuden Zart (Bohemian Brethren's
                            Gesangbuch, 1566)

COX, SAMUEL K.
    332.  Lord, Thou hast promised grace for grace/To all who daily
              seek Thy face
          MH (1905)-347.  Belleville (Peter Christian Lutkin)

COXE, ARTHUR CLEVELAND
    333.  How beauteous were the marks divine,/That in Thy meekness
              used to shine
          HMEC-202.  Ames (Sigismund Neukomm, arr. Lowell Mason)
          MH (1905)-127.  Canonbury (Robert Schumann)
          MH (1935)-116.  Canonbury (Robert Schumann)
          MH (1966)-80.  Windham (Daniel Reed)
    334.  In the silent midnight watches,/List--thy bosom door!
          HMEC-376.  In the Silent Midnight Watches (Hubert Platt
                            Main)
                      Wood End (G.P. Merrick)
    335.  O where are kings and empires now,/Of old that went and
              came?
          HMEC-763.  St. Ann's (William Croft)
          MH (1905)-214.  St. Ann's (William Croft)
          MH (1935)-384.  St. Ann's (William Croft)
          MH (1966)-308.  St. Ann's (William Croft)
    336.  Saviour, sprinkle many nations,/Fruitful let Thy sorrows be
          HMEC-944.  Faben (John Henry Wilcox)

CRABBE, GEORGE
    337.  Pilgrim, burdened with thy sin,/Come the way to Zion's gate
          HMEC-346.  Horton (Xavier Schnyder von Wartensee)

CREWDSON, JANE
    338.  O Thou, whose bounty fills my cup/With every blessing meet!
          MH (1905)-531.  Belmont (William Gardiner)

CROLY, GEORGE
    339.  Spirit of God! descend upon my heart;/Wean it from earth,
               through all its pulses move
               MH (1905)-197.  Emilie (John Wesley Baume)
               MH (1935)-179.  Morecombe (Frederick Coak Atkinson)
               AMEH-17.  Morecombe (Frederick Coak Atkinson)

CROSS, ADA CAMBRIDGE
    340.  The dawn of God's dear Sabbath/Breaks o'er the earth again
               MH (1905)-72.  St. Anselm (Joseph Barnby)

CROSS, ALLEN EASTMEN
    341.  Jesus, kneel beside me/In the dawn of day
               MH (1935)-308.  Eudoxia (Sabine Baring-Gould)

CROSSWELL, WILLIAM
    342.  Lord, lead the way the Saviour went,/By lane and cell ob-
               scure
               HMEC-897.  Return (Theodore Freelinghuysen Seward)

CRUM, J.M.C.
    343.  Now the green blade riseth from the buried grain,/Wheat
               that in dark earth many days has lain
               MH (1966)-441.  French Carol (Traditional French carol)

CUMMINS, JAMES JOHN
    344.  Shall hymns of grateful love/Thro' heav'n's high arches
               ring
               MH (1905)-26.  Darwall (John Darwall)

CUNIGGIM, MAUDE MERRIMON
    345.  O living Christ, chief Corner Stone/Of God's great temple
               Thou
               MH (1935)-547.  Arlington (Thomas Augustine Arne)
               MH (1966)-349.  St. Peter's (Alexander Robert Reinagle)

CUNNINGHAM, JOHN WILLIAM
    346.  From Calvary a cry was heard,/A bitter and heart-rending
               cry
               HMEC-209.  Germany (Ludwig van Beethoven)

CUSHING, WILLIAM ORCUTT
    347.  Ring the bells of heaven!/There is joy today
                AMEH-540.  Ring the Bells of Heaven (George Frederick
                     Root)
    348.  When He cometh, when He cometh/To make up His jewels
               MSSH-261.  Jewels (George Frederick Root)

CUTTER, WILLIAM
    349.  She loved her Saviour, and to Him/Her costliest present
               brought
               HMEC-896.  Return (Theodore Freelinghuysen Seward)
               MH (1905)-694.  Parker (Karl Pomeroy Harrington)

DAVIES, SAMUEL
    350.  Lord, I am Thine, entirely Thine,/Purchased and saved by
            blood divine
            HMEC-460.  Sessions (Luther Orlando Emerson)
            MH (1905)-342.  Sessions (Luther Orlando Emerson)
            MH (1935)-224.  Sessions (Luther Orlando Emerson)

DAVIS, FRANK M.
    351.  Saviour, lead me, lest I stray,/Gently lead me all the way
            AMEH-368.  Saviour, Lead Me (Frank M. Davis)

DAVIS, OZORA STEARNS
    352.  At length there dawns the glorious day/By prophets long
            foretold
            MH (1935)-469.  St. Michel's (from Hymns and Psalms,
                  1789)
            MH (1966)-189.  Clonmel (Traditional Irish melody)
    353.  We bear the strain of earthly care,/But bear it not alone
            MH (1935)-471.  Azmon (Carl Gotthelf Glaser)
            MH (1966)-202.  Shepherds' Pipes (Annabeth McClelland
                  Gay)

DAVIS, WILLIAM T.
    354.  To Thee, O God, whose guiding hand/Our fathers led across
            the sea
            HMEC-1105.  Duke Street (John Hatton)

DEARMER, PERCY
    355.  Book of books, our people's strength,/Statesman's, tea-
            cher's, hero's treasure
            MH (1935)-390.  Dessau/Liebster Jesu (Johann Rudolph
                  Ahle)
            MH (1966)-370.  Liebster Jesu (Johann Rudolph Ahle)
    356.  Father, we praise Thee, now the night is over;/Active and
            watchful, stand we all before Thee (trans. from
            Gregory the Great)
            MH (1966)-504.  Christe Sanctorum (French church melody)
    357.  Life is good, for God contrives it,/Deep on deep its wonder
            lies
            MH (1935)-160.  Trefaenan (Welsh traditional)
    358.  To the Name that is salvation,/Praise and homage let us pay
            MH (1935)-79.  Oriel (Kaspar Ett)
    359.  Welcome, day of the Lord, the first and best of the seven,/
            Day whereon Christ arose, brought us the promise of
            life
            MH (1935)-395.  Welcome (Rowland Leach)
    360.  When by fear my heart is daunted,/Thou dost hold be in Thy
            hand
            MH (1935)-319.  Tantum Ergo (Samuel Webbe)

DEAS, EDWARD C.
    361.  We are happy as we sing to-day,/Praises to our Lord and King
            AMEH-382.  Praise Jehovah (Edward C. Deas)

DECK, JAMES GEORGE

362.  Jesus, Thy Name I love,/All other names above
          AMEH-352.  Jesus, My Lord (Joseph Perry Holbrook)

DEEMS, CHARLES FORCE
   363.  I should not want: in deserts wild/Thou spread'st Thy table
             for Thy child
          MH (1905)-436.  Clolata (W. St. Clair Palmer)

DENHAM, DAVID
   364.  'Mid scenes of confusion and creature complaints,/To find
             at the banquet of mercy there's room
          HMEC-1054.  The Saint's Home (Sir Henry Rowley Bishop)

DENNY, SIR EDWARD
   365.  Light of the lowly pilgrim's heart,/Star of the coming day
          HMEC-914.  Newbold (George Kingsley)
   366.  What grace, O Lord, and beauty shone/Around Thy steps be-
             low!
          HMEC-196.  Noel (Lowell Mason)
          MH (1905)-126.  Denny (Lowell Mason)
          MH (1935)-115.  This Endris Nyght (Old English carol)
          AMEH-135.  Spohr (Louis Spohr)

DEXTER, HENRY MARTIN
   367.  Shepherd of tender youth,/Guiding in love and truth (trans.
             from Clement of Alexandria)
          HMEC-885.  Tivoli (Edward John Hopkins)
          MH (1905)-672.  Dort (Lowell Mason)
          MH (1935)-429.  Kirby Bedon (Edward Bunnett)
          MH (1966)-86.  Hinman (Austin C. Lovelace)

DICKINSON, CHARLES ALBERT
   368.  Blessed Master, I have promised,/Hear my solemn vow
          MH (1935)-223/  Bullinger (Ethelbert William Bullinger)

DICKSON, DAVID
   369.  Jerusalem, my happy home!/Name ever dear to me
          AMEH-471.  Shining Shore (George Frederick Root)

DIX, WILLIAM CHATTERTON
   370.  As with gladness men of old/Did the guiding star behold
          HMEC-182.  Dix (William Henry Monk)
          MSSH-77.  Dix (William Henry Monk)
          MH (1935)-90.  Dix (Conrad Kocker)
          MH (1966)-397.  Dix (Conrad Kocker)
   371.  Beauteous are the flowers of earth,/Flowers we bring with
             holy mirth
          MH (1905)-673.  Children's Offerings (John Stainer)
          MSSH-266.  Children's Offerings (John Stainer)
   372.  "Come unto me, ye weary,/And I will give you rest."
          MH (1905)-295.  Savoy Chapel (John Baptiste Calkin)
          MH (1935)-194.  Meirionydd (Welsg hymn melody)
   373.  Hallelujah! sing to Jesus!/His the sceptre, His the throne
          MH (1905)-176.  Carlton (Joseph Barnby)
   374.  To Thee, O Lord, our hearts we raise/In hymns of adoration
          MH (1966)-524.  Norse Air (arr. William J. Kirkpatrick)

375.  What Child is this, who, laid to rest,/On Mary's lap is
      sleeping?
      MH (1905)-67.  What Child Is This (Old English traditio-
                     nal)
      MH (1935)-109.  Greensleeves (Old English traditional)
      MH (1966)-385.  Greensleeves (Old English traditional)

DOANE, GEORGE WASHINGTON
376.  Fling out the banner! let it float/Skyward and seaward, high
      and wide
      MH (1905)-639.  Doane (John Baptiste Calkin)
      MSSH-244.  Waltham (John Baptiste Calkin)
      MH (1935)-502.  Doane (John Baptiste Calkin)
377.  Softly now the light of day/Fades upon our sight away
      HMEC-117.  Mercy (Louis Moreau Gottschalk, arr. Edwin
                     Pond Parker)
      MH (1905)-53.  Mercy (Louis Moreau Gottschalk, arr. Edwin
                     Pond Parker)
      MSSH-50.  Mercy (Louis Moreau Gottschalk, arr. Edwin Pond
                     Parker)
      MH (1935)-47.  Mercy (Louis Moreau Gottschalk, arr.
                     Edwin Pond Parker)
      AMEH-56.  Seymour (Carl Maria von Weber)
      MH (1966)-494.  Mercy (Louis Moreau Gottschalk, arr.
                     Edwin Pond Parker)
378.  Thou art the way:--to Thee alone/From sin and death we flee
      HMEC-318.  St. Bernard (London Tune Book, 1875)
      MH (1905)-133.  St. Bernard (John Richardson)
      MH (1935)-332.  St. Bernard (John Richardson)
      MH (1966)-75.  St. Bernard (John Richardson)

DOANE, WILLIAM CROSWELL
379.  Ancient of days, who sittest enthroned in glory,/To Thee
      all knees are bent
      MH (1905)-76.  Ancient of Days (John Albert Jeffery)
      MH (1935)-59.  Ancient of Days (John Albert Jeffery)
      AMEH-233.  Ancient of Days (John Albert Jeffery)
      MH (1966)-459.  Ancient of Days (John Albert Jeffery)

DOBELL, JOHN
380.  Now is the accepted time,/Now is the day of grace
      HMEC-361.  Capello (Lowell Mason)

DODDRIDGE, PHILIP
381.  And will the great eternal God/On earth establish His abode?
      HMEC-867.  Mendon (German traditional)
      MH (1905)-663.  Miller (Carl Philip Emmanuel Bach, arr.
                     Edward Miller)
382.  And will the judge descend?/And must the dead arise?
      AMEH-25.  Greenwood (Joseph Emerson Sweetser)
      AMEH-655.  Without tune
383.  Awake, my soul, stretch every nerve,/And press with vigour
      on
      HMEC-594.  Arlington (Thomas Augustine Arne)
      MH (1905)-396.  Christmas (Heorge Frederick Handel)

MSSH-203.  Christmas (George Frederick Handel)
MH (1935)-359.  Christmas  (George Frederick Handel)
AMEH-278.  Henry (Sylvanus Billings Pond)
AMEH-**664**.  Without tune
MH (1966)-249.  Christmas (George Frederick Handel)

384. Awake, my soul, to meet the day;/Unfold thy drowsy eyes
HMEC-96.  Peterboro' (Ralph Harrison)
AMEH-194.  Maitland (George Nelson Allen)

385. Awake, ye saints, and raise your eyes,/And raise your voices high
HMEC-948.  Frome (Hugh Pond)

386. Beset by snares on every hand,/In life's uncertain path I stand
MH (1905)-425.  Hebron (Lowell Mason)

387. Do not I love Thee, O my Lord?/Then let me nothing love
MH (1905)-338.  Howard (Elizabeth Howard Cuthbert)

388. Eternal Source of every joy,/Well may Thy praise our lips enjoy
HMEC-1082.  Southwell (Herbert Stephen Irons)
MH (1905)-715.  All Saints (William Knapp)

389. Father of all, Thy care we bless,/Which crowns our families with peace
MH (1905)-670.  Maryton (Henry Percy Smith)

390. Father of mercies, send Thy grace,/All-powerful from above
HMEC-894.  Invitation (Thomas Hastings)

391. God of my life, through all my days/My grateful powers shall sound Thy praise
HMEC-692.  Welton (Henri Abraham Caesar Malan)
MH (1905)-322.  Welton (Henri Abraham Caesar Malan)
AMEH-387.  Ward (arr. Lowell Mason)

392. Great God, we sing that mighty hand/By which supported still we stand
MH (1935)-539.  Federal Street (Henry Kemble Oliver)
MH (1966)-509.  Wareham (William Knapp)

393. Grace! 'tis a charming sound,/Harmonious to the ear
HMEC-321.  Silver Street (Isaac Smith)
AMEH-423.  Dover (Thomas Williams)

394. Great Source of being and of love!/Thou waterest all the worlds above
HMEC-774.  Appleton (William Boyce)

395. Hark the glad sound! the Saviour comes!/The Saviour promised long
HMEC-185.  Antioch (George Frederick Handel)
MH (1905)-108.  Nativity (Henry Lakee)

396. How gentle God's commands!/How kind His precepts are!
HMEC-176.  Dennis (Hans George Naegeli)
MH (1905)-100.  Dennis (Hans George Naegeli)
MH (1935)-69.  Dennis (Hans George Naegeli)
AMEH-82.  Dennis (Hans George Naegeli)
MH (**1966**)-53.  Dennis (Hans George Naegeli)

397. How rich Thy bounty, King of kings!/Thy favors, how divine
MH (1905)-224.  St. Gabriel (Henry Wellington Greatorex)

398. How swift the torrent rolls/That bears us to the sea
HMEC-958.  Shawmut (Lowell Mason)
MH (1905)-580.  Aber (William Henry Monk)

399. Jesus, I love Thy charming name,/'Tis music to mine ear
    AMEH-650.  Without tune
400. Jesus, my Lord, how rich Thy grace,/Thy bounties how com-
    plete!
    HMEC-893.  Invitation (Thomas Hastings)
    MH (1905)-406.  Eagley (James Walch)
401. Let Zion's watchmen all awake,/And take the alarm they give
    HMEC-823.  Coronation (Oliver Holden)
    MH (1905)-223.  Cornell (John Henry Cornell)
    MH (1935)-399.  Arlington (Thomas Augustine Arne)
    MH (1966)-335.  Arlington (Thomas Augustine Arne)
402. Lord of the Sabbath, hear our woes,/On this day, in Thy
    house
    HMEC-78.  Overberg (Johann Christian Heinrich Rink)
    MH (1905)-73.  Martham (John Henry Maunder)
403. My gracious Lord, I won Thy right/To every service I can pay
    HMEC-605.  Federal Street (Henry Kemble Oliver)
    MH (1905)-336.  Holborn Hill (St. Alban Tune Book, 1865)
    MH (1935)-257.  Holborn Hill (St. Alban Tune Book, 1865)
404. O happy day that fixed my choice/On Thee, my Saviour and my
    God!
    HMEC-447.  Rockingham (Lowell Mason)
    MH (1905)-312.  Happy Day (Edward Francis Rimbault)
    MH (1935)-212.  Happy Day (Edward Francis Rimbault)
    AMEH-350.  Happy Day (Edward Francis Rimbault)
    MH (1966)-128.  Hebron (Lowell Mason)
405. Rich are the joys that cannot die,/With God laid up in
    store
    HMEC-903.  Hebron (Lowell Mason)
406. See, Israel's gentle Shepherd stands/With all-engaging
    charms
    HMEC-827.  Serenity (William Vincent Wallace)
    MH (1905)-230.  Serenity (William Vincent Wallace)
    MSSH-407.  Meditation (John Henry Gower)
    MH (1966)-312.  Meditation (John Henry Gower)
407. Sing, O ye ransom'd of the Lord,/Your great Deliv'rer sing
    AMEH-327.  Manoah (Giachino Antonio Rossini)
408. Sovereign of all the worlds on high,/Allow my humble claim
    HMEC-429.  Burlington (John Freckleton Burrowes)
409. The King of heaven His table spreads,/And blessings crown
    the board
    HMEC-834.  Dundee (Guillaume Franc)
    MH (1905)-233.  Dundee (Guillaume Franc)
    MH (1935)-409.  Dundee (Guillaume Franc)
    MH (1966)-325.  Dundee (Guillaume Franc)
410. The Saviour, when to Heaven He rose,/In splendid triumph
    o'er His foes
    HMEC-812.  Migdol (Lowell Mason)
411. Tomorrow, Lord, is Thine,/Lodged in Thy sovereign hand
    MH (1905)-253.  Mornington (Garret Colley Wellesley,
        Earl of Mornington)
412. What though the arm of conquering death/Does God's own house
    invade?
    MH (1905)-592.  Mear (Unknown)
413. Ye golden lamps of heaven, farewell,/With all your feeble

        light
        HMEC-1034. Harris (Louis Devereaux)
414.  Ye servants of the Lord,/Each in his office wait
        MH (1905)-429. Laban (Lowell Mason)

DIDGE, MARY MAPES
415.  Can a little child like me,/Thank the Father fittingly?
        MSSH-35. Thanksgiving (William Kipp Bassford)

DORSEY, THOMAS A.
416.  Precious Lord take my hand,/Lead me on, let me stand
        AMEH-333. Precious Lord Take My Hand (E.C. Deas)

DRAPER, WILLIAM HENRY
417.  All creatures of our God and King,/Lift up your voice and
            with us sing (trans. from St. Francis of Assisi)
        MH (1935)-65. Lasst uns Erfreuen (Geistliche Kirchenge-
                        sang, 1623)
        MH (1966)-60. Lasst uns Erfreuen (Geistliche Kirchenge-
                        sang, 1623)

DRYDEN, JOHN
418.  Creator Spirit! by whose aid/The world's foundations first
            were laid (trans. from Rabanus Maurus)
        MH (1905)-194. St. Catherine (J.G. Walton)

DUFFIELD, GEORGE, JR.
419.  Stand up, stand up for Jesus,/Ye soldiers of the cross
        HMEC-567. Webb (George James Webb)
        MH (1905)-386. Webb (George James Webb)
        MSSH-202. Stand Up for Jesus (Adam Geibel)
                    Webb (George James Webb)
        MH (1935)-283. Geibel (Adam Geibel)
        MH (1966)-248. Webb (George James Webb)

DUNCAN, MARY LUNDIE
420.  Jesus, tender Shepherd, hear me;/Bless Thy little lamb to-
            night
        MH (1935)-452. Dijon (Old German melody)
421.  Lo! round the throne, a glorious band,/The saints in count-
            less myriads stand
        HMEC-1040. Park Street (Frederick Marc Antonio Venua)

DUNN, ROBINSON PORTER
422.  We sinners, Lord, with earnest heart,/With sighs and
            prayers and tears (trans. from Bernard of Clairvaux)
        HMEC-408. Parsons (Samuel Hubbard)

DWIGHT, JOHN SULLIVAN, and CHARLES TIMOTHY BROOKS
423.  God bless our native land!/Firm may she ever stand
        HMEC-1090. America (Henry Carey)
        (See also under BROOKS, CHARLES TIMOTHY)

DWIGHT, TIMOTHY
424.  I love Thy kingdom, Lord,/The house of Thine abode
        HMEC-770. Amantus (William Augustus Muhlenberg)

                    MH (1905)-208.  St. Thomas (Aaron Williams)
                    MSSH-114.  St. Thomas (Aaron Williams)
                    MH (1935)-379.  St. Thomas (Aaron Williams)
                    AMEH-35.  St. Thomas (Aaron Williams)
                    MH (1966)-294.  St. Thomas (Aaron Williams)
           425.  Shall man. O God of light and life,/Forever molder in the
                    grave?
                    HMEC-981.  Rest (William Batchelder Bradbury)
                    MH (1905)-596.  Rosedale (George Frederick Root)
           426.  While life prolongs its precious light,/Mercy is found, and
                    peace is given
                    HMEC-349.  Wells (Israel Holdroyd)
                    MH (1905)-254.  St. Cross (John Bacchus Dykes)

DYER, SIDNEY
           427.  Work, for the night is coming,/Work thro' the morning hours
                    HMEC-565.  Work Song (Lowell Mason)

EASTBURN, JAMES W.
           428.  O holy, holy, holy Lord,/Bright in Thy deeds and in Thy
                    name
                    HMEC-137.  Uxbridge (Lowell Mason)

ECKING, SAMUEL
           429.  Peace, troubled soul, thou need'st not fear;/Thy great Pro-
                    vider still is near
                    HMEC-164.  Hamburg (Lowell Mason)

EDGAR, MARY S.
           430.  God, who touchest earth with beauty,/Make my heart anew
                    MH (1966)-273.  Bullinger (Ethelbert William Bullinger)

EDMESTON, JAMES
           431.  Little travelers Zionward,/Each one entering into rest
                    HMEC-879.  New Brunswick (John Black)
           432.  Roll on, thou mighty ocean!/And, as thy billows flow
                    HMEC-931.  Missionary Hymn (Lowell Mason)
           433.  Saviour, breathe an evening blessing,/Ere repose our spirits
                    seal
                    HMEC-116.  Stockwell (Darius Eliot Jones)
                    MH (1905)-55.  Evening Prayer (George Coles Stebbins)
                    MSSH-47.  Evening Prayer (George Coles Stebbins)
                    MH (1935)-50.  Evening Prayer (George Coles Stebbins)
                    AMEH-513.  Evening Hymn (George Coles Stebbins)
                    MH (1966)-496.  Stuttgart (Psalmodia Sacra, Gotha, 1715)
           434.  Sweet is the light of Sabbath eve,/And soft the sunbeams
                    lingering there
                    HMEC-80.  Overberg (Johann Christian Heinrich Rink)
           435.  When shall the voice of singing/Flow joyfully along
                    HMEC-934.  Webb (George James Webb)

ELA, DAVID HOUGH

436.  The chosen three, on mountain height,/While Jesus bowed in
         prayer
       HMEC-198.  Noel (Lowell Mason)
       MH (1905)-129.  Boardman (Charles Jefferys, arr. George
                     Kingsley)

ELLERTON, JOHN
437.  Again, the morn of gladness,/The morn of light is here
       MSSH-36.  Redcrest (Peter Christian Lutkin)
438.  Behold us, Lord, a little space/From daily tasks set free
       HMEC-597.  St. Agnes (John Bacchus Dykes)
       MH (1905)-394.  St. Agnes (John Bacchus Dykes)
       MH (1935)-459.  St. Agnes (John Bacchus Dykes)
       MH (1966)-549.  Dumfermline (Scottish Psalter, 1615)
439.  Now the labourer's task is o'er;/Now the battle day is past
       MH (1935)-526.  Requiescat (John Bacchus Dykes)
440.  Saviour, again to Thy dear name we raise,/With one accord,
         our parting hymn of praise
       HMEC-94.  Eventide (William Henry Monk)
       MH (1905)-38.  Ellers (Edward John Hopkins)
       MSSH-40.  Ellers (Edward John Hopkins)
       MH (1935)-29.  Ellers (Edward John Hopkins)
       AMEH-42.  Benediction (Edward John Hopkins)
       MH (1966)-236.  Ellers (Edward John Hopkins)
441.  The day Thou gavest, Lord, is ended,/The darkness falls at
         Thy behest
       MH (1905)-60.  St. Clement (Clement Cotterill Schole-
                          field)
       MH (1935)-54.  St. Clement (Clement Cotterill Schole-
                          field)
       AMEH-21.  St. Clement (Clement Cotterill Scholefield)
       MH (1966)-500.  Commandments (Louis Bourgeois)
442.  The Lord be with us each day/His blessings we receive
       MH (1935)-28.  Belmont (William Gardiner)
443.  This is the day of light;/Let there be light to-day
       HMEC-86.  Lisbon (Daniel Read)
       MH (1935)-397.  Dominica (Herbert Stanley Oakeley)
444.  Welcome, happy morning! age to age shall say:/Hell to-day
             is vanquished, heaven is won today (Trans. from
             Venantius Fortunatus)
       HMEC-231.  Baptiste (John Baptise Calkin)
       MH (1905)-166.  Baptiste (John Baptiste Calkin)
       MSSH-95.  Happy Morning (John Baptiste Calkin)
       MH (1935)-161.  Hermes (Frances Ridley Havergal)
       MH (1966)-452.  Hermes (Frances Ridley Havergal)

ELLIOTT, CHARLOTTE
445.  Christian, seek not yet repose,/Cast thy dreams of ease
         away
       MH (1905)-494.  Vigilate (William Henry Monk)
446.  Just as I am, without one plea,/But that Thy blood was shed
         for me
       HMEC-393.  Woodworth (William Batchelder Bradbury)
       MH (1905)-272.  Dunston ( Joseph Barnby)
                     Woodworth (William Batchelder Bradbury)

MSSH-125.  Woodworth (William Batchelder Bradbury)
MH (1935)-198.  Woodworth (William Batchelder Bradbury)
AMEH-226.  Woodbury (William Batchelder Bradbury)
Just As I Am (Katherine L. Smith)
MH (1966)-119.  Woodworth (William Batchelder Bradbury)
447.  My God, is any hour so sweet,/From blush of morn to evening star
HMEC-752.  The Hour of Prayer (John Bacchus Dykes)
MH (1905)-501.  Almsgiving (John Bacchus Dykes)
448.  My God, my Father, while I stray/Far from my home, on life's rough way
MH (1905)-521.  Hanford (Arthur Seymour Sullivan)
MH (1935)-306.  Hanford (Arthur Seymour Sullivan)
449.  O Holy Saviour, Friend unseen,/Since on Thine arm Thou bid'-st me lean
MH (1905)-478.  Flemming (Friederich Ferdinand Flemming)
MSSH-194.  Flemming (friederich Ferdinand Flemming)
MH (1935)-327.  Flemming (Friederich Ferdinand Flemming)
MH (1966)-144.  Flemming (Friederich Ferdinand Flemming)
450.  With tearful eyes I look around;/Life seems a dark and stormy sea
HMEC-363.  Hamburg (Lowell Mason)

ELLIOTT, EBENEZER
451.  When wilt Thou save the people?/O God of mercy, when?
MSSH-280.  Commonwealth (Josiah Booth)

ELLIOTT, EMILY ELIZABETH STEELE
452.  Thou didst leave Thy throne and Thy kingly crown,/When Thou camest to earth for me
MH (1905)-122.  Elliott (Timothy Richard Matthews)
MSSH-78.  Margaret (Timothy Richard Matthews)
MH (1935)-95.  Margaret (Timothy Richard Matthews)
AMEH-98.  Veni (Timothy Richard Matthews)

ELLSWORTH, W.W.
453.  Saviour! hear us, we pray,/Keep us safe through this day
MSSH-42.  Brahms (arr. Peter Christian Lutkin)
AMEh-31.  Lucy (Johannes Brahams)

ESLING, CATHERINE WATTERMAN
454.  Come unto me, when shadows darkly gather,/When the sad heart is weary and distressed
HMEC-642.  Henley (Lowell Mason)
MH (1905)-462.  Henley (Lowell Mason)
MH (1935)-350.  Adrian (Thomas Franklin Rinehart)

EVANS, CARA B.
455.  The love of Christ contraineth;/O let the watchword ring
MSSH-241.  St. Helena (Edwin S. Soley)

EVANS, JONATHAN
456.  Come, Thou soul-transforming Spirit,/Bless the sower and the seed
HMEC-55.  Greenville (Jean Jacques Rousseau)

457.  Hark! the voice of love and mercy/Sounds aloud from Calvary
        HMEC-224.  Calvary (Samuel Stanley)
        AMEH-123.  Adele (J.M. North)

EVANS, WILLIAM EDWIN
  458.  Come, O Thou God of grace,/Dwell in this holy place
        MH (1905)-661.  Italian Hymn (Felice Giardini)
        MH (1935)=550.  Italian Hymn (Felice Giardini)
        MH (1966)-352.  Italian Hymn (Felice Giardini)

EVEREST, CHARLES WILLIAM
  459.  "Take up thy cross," the Saviour said,/"If thou wouldst my
        disciple be. . . ."
        HMEC-601.  Illinois (Jonathan Spilman)
        MH (1905)-433.  Germany (Ludwig van Beethoven)
        MH (1935)-260.  Germany (Ludwig van Beethoven)
        AMEH-10A.  Woodworth (William Batchelder Bradbury)
        AMEH-64.  Germany (Ludwig van Beethoven)
        MH (1966)-160.  Germany (Ludwig van Beethoven)

FABER, FREDERICK WILLIAM
  460.  Faith of our fathers! living still/In spite of dungeon,
        fire, and sword
        HMEC-608.  St. Catherine (Henri Frederick Hemi)
        MH (1905)-415.  St. Catherine (Henri Frederick Hemi)
        MSSH-117.  St. Catherine (Henri Frederick Hemi)
        MH (1935)-256.  St. Catherine (Henri Frederick Hemi)
        AMEH-435.  St. Catherine (Henri Frederick Hemi)
        MH (1966)-151.  St. Catherine (Henri Frederick Hemi)
  461.  Hark, hark, my soul! angelic songs are swelling/O'er earth's
        green fields and ocean's wave-beat shore
        HMEC-1070.  Angels' Song (John Bacchus Dykes)
        MH (1905)-621.  Pilgrims (Henry Smart)
                 Angels' Song (John Bacchus Dykes)
        MH (1935)-532.  Pilgrims (Henry Smart)
        AMEH-136.  Pilgrims (Henry Smart)
  462.  I worship Thee, most gracious God,/And all Thy ways adore
        MH (1905)-480.  Holy Trinity (Joseph Barnby)
        MH (1935)-328.  Abergele (John Ambrose Lloyd)
  463.  My God, how wonderful Thou art,/Thy majesty how bright
        HMEC-147.  Stephens (William Jones)
        MH (1905)-86.  St. Stephen (William Jones)
  464.  O come and mourn with me awhile;/O come ye to the Saviour's
        side
        MH (1905)-152.  St. Cross (John Bacchus Dykes)
        MH (1935)-134.  St. Cross (John Bacchus Dykes)
        AMEH-312.  St. Cross (John Bacchus Dykes)
  465.  O God, Thy power is wonderful,/Thy glory passing bright
        HMEC-125.  Bemerton (Henry Wellington Greatorex)
        MH (1905)-87.  Barnby (Joseph Barnby)
  466.  O how the thought of God attracts/And draws the heart from
        earth
        HMEC-509.  Manoah (Etienne Henri Mehul and George Frede-

rick Handel)
    MH (1905)-363.  Sawley (James Walch)
    MH (1935)-374.  Sawley (James Walch)
467.  O it is hard to work for God,/To rise and take His part
    HMEC-596.  St. Agnes (John Bacchus Dykes)
    MH (1905)-442.  Dalehurst (Arthur Cottman)
468.  O paradise! o paradise!/Who doth not crave for rest?
    HMEC-1071.  Paradise (Joseph Barnby)
    MH (1905)-622.  Paradise (John Bacchus Dykes)
                Paradise (Joseph Barnby)
469.  There is a wideness in Gid's mercy,/Like the wideness of
      the sea
    HMEC-149.  Wellesley (Lizzie S. Tourjee)
    MH (1905)-98.  Cross of Jesus (John Stainer)
               Wellesley (Lizzie S. Tourjee)
    MSSH-141.  Wellesley (Lizzie S. Tourjee)
    AMEH-243.  Wellesley (Lizzie S. Tourjee)
    MH (1935)-75.  Wellesley (Lizzie S. Tourjee)
    MH (1966)-69.  In Babilone (Julius Rontgen)
470.  Workmen of God! O lose not heart,/But learn what God is
    like
    HMEC-591.  Winchester Old (from Thomas Este's Whole
               Booke of Psalmes)
    MH (1905)-392.  Nativity (Hanry Laher)

FARRAR, FREDERIC WILLIAM
471.  In the field with their flocks abiding,/They lay on the
    dewy ground
    HM (1905)-117.  Chope (Richard Robert Chope)
    MSSH-72.  In the Field (Henry John Farmer)

FARRINGTON, HARRY WEBB
472.  I know not how that Bethlehem's Babe/Could in the Godhead
    be
    MH (1935)-112.  Shirleyn (Earl Enyeart Harper)
    AMEH-309.  Shirleyn (Earl Enyeart Harper)
    MH (1966)-123.  Shirleyn (Earl Enyeart Harper)
473.  O God, Creator, in whose hand/The rolling planets lie
    MH (1935)-555.  Byrd (Rob Roy Perry)

FAWCETT, JOHN
474.  Blest be the tie that binds/Our hearts in Christian love
    HMEC-797.  Dennis (Hans George Naegelli)
    MH (1905)-556.  Dennis (Hans George Naegelli)
    MSSH-118.  Dennis (Hans George Naegelli)
    MH (1935)-416.  Dennis (Hans George Naegelli)
    AMEH-446.  Boylston (Lowell Mason)
    MH (1966)-306.  Dennis (Hans George Naegelli, arr. Lowell
               Mason)
475.  How precious is the book divine,/By inspiration given!
    HMEC-297.  Burlington (John Freckleton Burrowes)
    MH (1905)-201.  Burlington (John Freckleton Burrowes)
476.  Infinite excellence,/Thou glorious Prince of grace!
    HMEC-31.  Andrews (John Black)
477.  Lord, dismiss us with Thy blessing,/Fill our hearts with

      joy and peace
     HMEC-52.  Greenville (Jean Jacques Rousseau)
     MH (1905)-39.  Eton (Joseph Barnby)
              Greenville (Jean Jacques Rousseau)
     MSSH-39.  Sicilian Mariners (Sicilian melody)
     MH (1935)-26.  Sicilian Mariners (Sicilian melody)
     AMEH-524.  Sicilian Mariners (Sicilian melody)
     MH (1966)-165.  Sicilian Mariners (Sicilian melody)
478.  Our sins on Christ were laid;/He bore the mighty load
     HMEC-312.  Shawmut (Lowell Mason)
479.  Religion is the chief concern/Of ,ortals here below
     MH (1905)-314.  Green Hill (Albert Lister Peace)
480.  Sinners, the voice of God regard;/'Tis mercy speaks to-day
     HMEC-371.  Balerma (Richard Simpson)
     MH (1905)-246.  Nox Praecessit (John Baptiste Calkin)
481.  Thy presence, gracious God, afford;/Prepare us to receive
       Thy word
     HMEC-39.  Miller (Carl Philip Emmanuel Bach, arr. Edward
            Miller)
482.  Thy way is in the sea;/Thy paths we cannot trace
     HMEC-174.  Haydn (Franz Joseph Haydn)

FEATHERSTONE, WILLIAM R.
   483.  My Jesus, I love Thee,/I know Thou art mine
       MSSH-196.  My Jesus I Love Thee (Adoniram Judson Gordon)
       AMEH-434.  Gordon (Adoniram Judson Gordon)
       MH (1966)-166.  Gordon (Adoniram Judson Gordon)

FINDLATER, SARAH BORTHWICK
   484.  O happy home, where Thou art loved the dearest,/Thou loving
          Friend, and Saviour of our race (trans. from Carl Jo-
          hann Philip Spitta)
       MH (1935)-427.  Alverstroke (Joseph Barnby)
   485.  Rejoice, all ye believers,/And let your lights appear
          (trans. from Laurentiut Laurenti)
       AMEH-106.  Lancashire (Henry Smart)

FLOWERDEW, ALICE
   486.  Fountain of mercy, God of love,/How rich Thy bounties are!
       HMEC-1081.  Southwell (Herbert Stephen Irons)

FORD, DAVID EVERARD
   487.  How vain is all beneath the skies!/How transient every
          earthly bliss!
       HMEC-960.  Seasons (Ignace Pleyel)
   488.  Vain are all terrestrial pleasures;/Mixed with dross the
          purest gold
       HMEC-647.  Ellesdie (Johann Christian Wolfgang Amadeus
            Mozart)

FOSDICK, HARRY EMERSON
   489.  God of grace and God of glory,/On Thy people pour Thy power
       MH (1935)-279.  Cwm Rhondda (John Hughes)
       AMEH-284.  Cwm Rhondda (John Hughes)
       MH (1966)-470.  Cwm Rhondda (John Hughes)

FOSTER, CATHERINE
    490.  Dread Jehovah! God of nations!/From Thy temple in the skies
          HMEC-1091.  Wilmot (Carl Maria von Weber)

FOX, WILLIAM JOHNSON
    491.  Flung to the heedless winds,/Or on the waters cast (trans.
          from Martin Luther)
          HMEC-911.  Ibstone (Maria Tiddeman)

FRANCIS, BENJAMIN
    492.  Great King of glory, come,/And with Thy favor crown
          HMEC-865.  Murray (Unknown)
          MH (1905)-656.  Christ Church (Charles Steggall)
    493.  Praise the Saviour, all ye nations,/Praise Him, all ye hosts
          above
          MH (1905)-649.  Harwell (Lowell Mason)

FRAZIER, PHILIP
    494.  Many and great, O God, are Thy things,/Maker of earth and
          sky (paraphrase from an American folk hymn)
          MH (1966)-40.  Lacquiparle (American folk hymn)

FRECKLETON, THOMAS WESLEY
    495.  O God, who workest hitherto,/Working in all we see
          AMEH-447.  Eagley (James Walch)
    496.  The toil of brain, or heart, or hand,/Is man's appointed
          lot
          MH (1905)-414.  Service (Lorin Webster)

FRIZZELLE, J. WELLINGTON
    497.  Cross of Jesus, cross of love,/Emblem of my King above
          MSSH-88.  Messiah (Louis Joseph Ferdinand Herold)

FROTHINGHAM, OCTAVIUS BROOKS
    498.  Thou, Lord of hosts, whose guiding hand/Has brought us here
          before Thy face
          AMEH-449.  Bromley (Jeremiah Clark)

FRY, CHARLES W.
    499.  I have found a friend in Jesus,/He's everything to me
          AMEH-355.  The Lily of the Valley (E. Hanks)

GABRIEL, CHARLES H.
    500.  Low in a manger--dear little Stranger,/Jesus, the wonder-
          ful Savior was born
          AMEH-547.  Low in a Manger (Charles H. Gabriel)

GAMBOLD, JOHN
    501.  O tell me no more of this world's vain store,/The time for
          such trifles with me now is o'er
          HMEC-758.  Kelbrook (John Riley)

GANSE, HERVEY DODDRIDGE
    502. Jesus, one word from Thee/Fills my sad soul with peace
        HMEC-634. Olmutz (Lowell Mason)
    503. Thou who like the wind dost come,/Come to me, but ne'er de-
        part
        HMEC-283. Marth (Joseph Perry Holbrook)

GATES, ELLEN HUNTINGTON
    504. I will sing you a song of that beautiful land,/The faraway
        home of the soul
        MSSH-255. Home of the Soul (Philip Phillips)
        MH (1935)-525. Home of the Soul (Philip Phillips)

GIBBONS, THOMAS
    505. Arise, my soul, on wings sublime,/Above the vanities of
        time
        HMEC-530. Janes (Johann Christian Wolfgang Amadeus
               Mozart)
    506. Great God, the nations of the earth/Are by creation Thine
        HMEC-910. Hummel (Heinrich Christian Zeuner)
        MH (1905)-645. Hummel (Heinrich Christian Zeuner)
    507. When Jesus dwelt in mortal clay,/What were His works, from
        day to day
        MH (1905)-695. Alsace (Ludwig van Beethoven)

GILBERT, EVA O.B.
    508. Waving and tossing through field and glen,/Billows of shin-
        ing gold
        MSSH-206. The Song of the Gleaners (Karl Pomeroy Har-
               rington)

GILDER, RIXHARD WATSON
    509. God of the strong, God of the weak,/Lord of all lands and
        our own land
        MH (1935)-457. Godwin (William Godwin Blanchard)
    510. Thro' love to light!/O wonderful the way
        AMEH-561. Through Love to Light (Jean Sibelius)
    511. To Thee, Eternal Soul, be praise!/Who, from of old to our
        own days
        MH (1905)-14. Gilder (Anne Oldberg)
               Worship (Karl Pomeroy Harrington)
        MH (1935)-10. Worship (Karl Pomeroy Harrington)

GILL, THOMAS HORNBLOWER
    512. Break, new-born year, on glad eyes break!/Melodious voices
        move!
        MH (1905)-572. Greeting (Alfred George Wathall)
    513. Lord! when I all things would possess,/I crave but to be
        Thine
        MH (1905)-343. Faith (John Bacchus Dykes)
    514. Not only when ascends the song,/And soundeth sweet the
        word
        MH (1905)-520. Ascending Song (Alfred George Wathall)
    515. The glory of the spring how sweet!/The new-born life how
        glad!

MSSH-264. The Glory of the Spring (Horatio Parker)
516. We come unto our fathers' God,/Their Rock is our salvation
MH (1935)-385. Luther (Geistliche Lieder, 1535)
MH (1966)-58. Nun Freut Euch (Klug's Gesangbuch, Wittenberg, 1535)

GILLMAN, FREDERICK JOHN
517. God send us men whose aim 'twill be/Not to defend some ancient creed
MH (1966)-191. Kedron (Pilsbury's United States Harmony, 1799)

GILMAN, SAMUEL
518. This child we dedicate to Thee,/O God of grace and purity
(trans. from Joachim Neander)
HMEC-832. Ward (Lowell Mason)
MH (1905)-232. Maryton (Henry Percy Smith)

GILMORE, JOSEPH HENRY
519. He leadeth me! O blessed thought!/ O words with heavenly comfort fraught!
HMEC-622. He Leadeth Me (William Batchelder Bradbury)
MH (1905)-489. He Leadeth Me (William Batchelder Bradbury)
MSSH-177. He Leadeth Me (William Batchelder Bradbury)
MH (1935)-242. He Leadeth Me (William Batchelder Bradbury)
AMEH-288. He Leadeth Me (William Batchelder Bradbury)
MH (1966)-217. He Leadeth Me (William Batchelder Bradbury)

GILMOUR, H.L.
520. My soul in sad exile was out on life's sea,/So burdened with sin and distress
AMEH-374. My Soul in Sad Exile (George D. Moore)

GLADDEN WASHINGTON
521. Behold a Sower! from afar/He goeth forth with might
MH (1935)-391. Bethlehem (Gottfried Wilhelm Fink)
522. O Master, let me walk with Thee/In lowly paths of service free
MH (1905)-411. Canonbury (Robert Schumann)
Maryton (Henry Percy Smith)
MSSH-236. Maryton(Henry Percy Smith)
MH (1935)-259. Maryton (Henry Percy Smith)
AMEH-440. Maryton (Henry Percy Smith)
MH (1966)-170. Maryton (Henry Percy Smith)

GOADBY, FREDERICK WILLIAM
523. O Thou, whose hand hath brought us/Unto this joyful day
MH (1935)-551. Webb (George James Webb)

GORDON, GEORGE ANGIER
524. O Will of God beneath our life,/The sea beneath the wave
MH (1935)-78. Magnus (Jeremiah Clark)

GOUGH, BENJAMIN
525. Jesus, full of love divine,/I am Thine and Thou art mine

HMEC-488.  Onido (Ignace Pleyel)
526.  The joyful morn is breaking,/The brightest morn of earth
    MSSH-69.  Christmas Morn (Edward John Hopkins)

GOULD, HANNAH FLAGG
527.  Day of God, thou blessed day,/At thy dawn the grave gave
    way
    HMEC-90.  Dijon ( German evening hymn)
528.  O Thou, who hast spread out the skies,/And measured the
    depths of the sea
    HMEC-1110.  Desire ("J.B.")

GRAEFF, FRANK E.
529.  Does Jesus care when my heart is pained/Too deeply for
    mirth and song
    AMEH-454.  Does Jesus Care? (J. Lincoln Hall)

GRANT, SIR ROBERT
530.  By Thy birth, and Thy tears;/By Thy human griefs and fears
    HMEC-417.  Toplady (Thomas Hastings)
    MH (1905)-280.  Gethsemane (Richard Redhead)
    MH (1935)-207.  Gethsemane (Richard Redhead)
    MH (1966)-113.  Redhead (Richard Redhead)
531.  Lord od earth, Thy forming hand/Well this beauteous frame
    hath planned
    MH (1905)-469.  Maidstone (Walter Bond Gilbert)
532.  O worship the King all-glorious above,/And gratefully sing
    His wonderful love
    HMEC-140.  Lyons (Johann Michael Haydn)
    MH (1905)-106.  Lyons (Johann Michael Haydn)
    MSSH-10.  Lyons (Johann Michael Haydn)
    MH (1935)-4.  Lyons (Johann Michael Haydn)
    AMEH-271.  Lyons (Johann Michael Haydn)
    MH (1966)-473.  Lyons (Johann Michael Haydn)
533.  Saviour, when, in dust, to Thee/Low we bend the adoring
    knee
    HMEC-723.  Spanish Hymn (Unknown)
            Blumenthal (Jacob Blumenthal)
    MH (1905)-500.  Spanish Hymn (Unknown)
            Blumenthal (Jacob Blumenthal)
534.  The starry firmament on high,/And all the glories of the
    sky
    HMEC-293.  Uxbridge (Unknown)
    MH (1905)-203.  Alstone (Christopher Edwin Willing)
535.  The mercy heard my infant prayer;/Thy love, with all a mo-
    ther's care
    HMEC-658.  Ganges (S. Chandler)
536.  When gathering clouds around I view,/and days are dark,
    and friends are few
    MH (1905)-134.  St. Petersburg (Dimitri Stepanovich
                 Bortniansky)

GRAY, JAMES M.
537.  O listen to our wondrous story,/Counted once among the
    lost (trans. from the Welsh)

MSSH-132.  Listen to Our Story (William Owen)

GREG, SAMUEL
    538.  Slowly, slowly dark'ning/The evening hours roll on
        MH (1905)-464.  Implicit Trust (Alfred George Wathal)
    539.  Stay, Master, stay upon this heavenly hill;/A little longer,
           let us linger still
        MH (1935)-122.  Yorkshire (John Wainwright)
        AMEH-519.  Yorkshire (John Wainright)

GRIGG, JOSEPH
    540.  Behold a stranger at the door!/He gently knocks, has knocked
           before
        MH (1905)-249.  Bera (John Edgar Gould)
        MH (1935)-196.  Bera (John Edgar Gould)
        AMEH-239.  Federal Street (Henry Kemble Oliver)
    541.  Jesus, and shall it ever be,/A mortal man ashamed of Thee?
        HMEC-604.  Federal Street (Henry Kemble Oliver)
        MH (1905)-443.  Federal Street (**Henry Kemble Oliver**)
        MH (1935)-258.  Federal Street (Henry Kemble Oliver)
        AMEH-45.  Federal Street (Henry Kemble Oliver)

GROBEL, KENDRICK
    542.  O Guide to every child of Thine,/To untamed colt, the bridle
           (trans. from Clement of Alexandria)
        MH (1966)-84.  Nun Freut Euch (Josef Klug's <u>Gesangbuch</u>,
                      Wittenberg, 1535)

GROSE, HOWARD B.
    543.  Give of your best to the Master;/Give of the strength of
           your youth
        AMEH-539.  Give of Your Best (Mrs. Charles Barnard)

GUITERMAN, ARTHUR
    544.  Bless the four corners of this house,/And be the lintel blest
        MH (1935)-433.  Home (Van Denman Thompson)

GURNEY, DOROTHY FRANCES BLOOMFIELD
    545.  O perfect Love, all human thought transcending,/Lowly we
           kneel in prayer before Thy throne
        MH (1905)-668.  O Perfect Love (Joseph Barnby)
        MH (1935)-431.  O Perfect Love (Joseph Barnby)
        MH (1966)-333.  O Perfect Love (Joseph Barnby)

GURNEY, JOHN HAMPDEN
    546.  Great King of nations, hear our prayer,/While at Thy feet we
           fall
        HMEC-1094.  Zelzah (German melody)
        AMEH-585.  St. Agnes (John Bacchus Dykes)
    547.  Lord, as to Thy dear cross we flee,/And pray to be forgiven
        HMEC-590.  Winchester Old (from Thomas Este's <u>Whole Booke</u>
                of Psalmes)

HALL, CHRISTOPHER NEWMAN
    548.  Friend of sinners! Lord of Glory!/Lowly, Mighty! Brother,
           King!
           MH (1905)-130.  Weston (John Edward Roe)

HALL, ELVINA MABLE
    549.  I hear the Saviour say, "Thy strength indeed is small;/Child
           of weakness, watch and pray. . . ."
           AMEH-483.  Jesus Paid It All (John T. Grape)

HAMILTON, MARY C.D.
    550.  Lord, guard and guide the men who fly/Through the great spa-
           ces of the sky
           MH (1966)-541.  Hesperus (Henry Baker)

HAMMOND, J. DEMPSTER
    551.  The whole wide world for Jesus!/This shall our watchword be
           MSSH-237.  The Whole Wide World (John Henry Maunder)

HAMMOND, WILLIAM
    552.  Awake and sing the song/Of Moses and the Lamb
           HMEC-4.  Silver Street (Isaac Smith)
           AMEH-294.  St. Thomas (Unknown)
    553.  Lord, we come before Thee now,/At Thy feet we humbly bow
           HMEC-21.  Pleyel's Hymn (Ignace Pleyel)
           MH (1905)-35.  Pleyel's Hymn (Ignace Pleyel)

HANKEY, CATHERINE
    554.  I love to tell the story,/Of unseen things above
           HMEC-756.  I Love To Tell the Story (William Gustavus
                Fischer)
           MH (1905)-544.  Hankey (William Gustavus Fischer)
           MSSH-128.  Hankey (William Gustavus Fischer)
           MH (1935)-249.  Hankey (William Gustavus Fischer)
           AMEH-254.  I Love To Tell the Story (William Gustavus
                Fischer)
           MH (1966)-149.  Hankey (William Gustavus Fischer)
    555.  Tell me the old, old story,/Of unseen things above
           MSSH-124.  Tell Me the Old, Old Story (William Howard
                Doane)

HANNAN, F. WATSON
    556.  O God, my powers are Thine;/So may my service be
           MSSH-235.  Teacher's Dedication Hymn (Frank Moore Jef-
                fery)

HARBAUGH, HENRY
    557.  Jesus, I live to Thee,/The loveliest and the best
           HMEC-500.  Greenwood (Joseph Emerson Sweetser)
           MH (1935)-335.  Lake Enon (Isaac Baker Woodbury)

HARKNESS, GEORGIA
    558.  Hope of the world, Thou Christ of great compassion,/Speak to
           our fearful hearts by conflict rent
           MH (1966)-161.  Vicar (V. Earle Copes)

HARLOW, S. RALPH
    559.  O young and fearless prophet of an ancient Galilee:/Thy life
          is still a summons to serve humanity
          MH (1935)-266.  Blairgowrie (John Bacchus Dykes)
          MH (1966)-173.  Blairgowrie (John Bacchus Dykes)

HARMER, SAMUEL YOUNG
    560.  In the Christian's home in glory/There remains a land of
          rest
          AMEH-462.  Rest for the Weary (William McDonald)

HARRELL, COSTEN J.
    561.  Eternal God and sovereign Lord,/By men and heavenly hosts
          MH (1966)-351.  Germany (William Gardiner)

HART, JOSEPH
    562.  Come, Holy Spirit, come,/Let Thy bright beams arise
          MSSH-108.  Chiselhurst (Joseph Barnby)
          AMEH-204.  Dover (Aaron Williams)
    563.  Come, ye sinners, poor and needy,/Weak and wounded, sick and
          sore
          HMEC-340.  Greenville (Jean Jacques Rousseau)
                   Albyn (John Black)
          MH (1905)-259.  Eton (Joseph Barnby)
                   Greenville (Jean Jacques Rousseau)
          MH (1935)-187.  Greenville (Jean Jacques Rousseau)
          MH (1966)-104.  Pleading Savior (Christian Lyre, 1830)
    564.  Glory to God on high,/Our peace is made with heaven
          HMEC-841.  Prayer (Leonard Marshall)
    565.  O for a glance of heavenly day,/To take this stubborn heart
          away
          HMEC-396.  Rose Hill (Joseph Emerson Sweetser)
          MH (1905)-274.  Hursley (Peter Ritter, arr. William Henry
                   Monk)
          AMEH-161.  Hursley (Franz Joseph Haydn)
    566.  Once more we come before our God;/Once more His blessing ask
          HMEC-29.  Andrews (John Black)
          MH (1905)-33.  St. Agnes (John Bacchus Dykes)
    567.  Prayer is appointed to convey/The blessings God designs to
          give
          HMEC-689.  Sweet Hour of Prayer (William Batchelder Brad-
                   bury)
          MH (1905)-502.  Uxbridge (Lowell Mason)
          AMEH-442.  Hursley (from the German)
    568.  That doleful night before His death,/The Lamb, for sinners
          slain
          HMEC-840.  Simpson (Louis Spohr)
          AMEH-237.  Jerusalem (Charles F. Roper)
    569.  This God is the God we adore,/Our faithful, unchangeable
          friend
          HMEC-143.  David (George Frederick Handel)
    570.  Vain Man, thy fond pursuits forbear;/Repent, thine end is
          nigh
          HMEC-365.  Mear (Aaron Williams)

HASKELL, ANTONIO L.

571. Be still, and let the spirit speak,/Forego the worldly strain
        AMEH-443.  Be Still (Antonio L. Haskell)

HASKELL, JULIA SIMPSON
    572.  Over the ocean wave, far, far away,/There the poor heathen
            live, waiting for the day
            AMEH-569.  Over the Ocean (William Batchelder Bradbury)

HASTINGS, HORACE LORENZO
    573.  Shall we meet beyond the river,/Where the surges cease to
            roll?
            AMEH-472.  Shall We Meet? (Elihu S. Rice)

HASTINGS, THOMAS
    574.  Delay not, delay not, O sinner, draw near,/The waters of
            life are now flowing for thee
            HMEC-336.  Expostulation (Josiah Hopkins)
    575.  Gently, Lord, O gently lead us/Through this gloomy vale of
            tears
            HMEC-646.  Ellesdie (Johann Christian Wolfgang Amadeus
                         Mozart
            MH (1905)-319.  Sardis (Ludwig van Beethoven)
    576.  Hail to the brightness of Zion's glad morning!/Joy to the
            lands that in darkness have lain!
            HMEC-912.  Ibstone (Maria Tiddeman)
            MH (1935)-488.  Wwsley (Lowell Mason)
            AMEH-210.  Wesley (Lowell Mason)
    577.  He that goeth forth with weeping,/Bearing precious seed in
            love
            AMEH-159.  Layton (J.T. Layton)
    578.  How tender is Thy hand,/O Thou most gracious Lord!
            HMEC-177.  Dennis (Hans George Naegelli)
    579.  Jesus, while our hearts are bleeding/O'er the spoils that
            death has won
            HMEC-1002.  Talmar (Isaac Baker Woodbury)
    580.  Lord, I would come to Thee,/A sinner all defiled
            AMEH-659.  Without Tune
    581.  Saviour, hear us, through Thy merit;/Lowly bending at Thy
            feet
            AMEH-158.  Layton (J.T. Layton)
    582.  Saviour, I look to Thee/Be not Thou far from me
            AMEH-180.  Olivet (Lowell Mason)

HATCH, EDWIN
    583.  Breathe on me, Breath of God,/Fill me with life anew
            MH (1905)-196.  Burleigh (John Baptiste Calkin)
            MH (1935)-180.  Trentham (Robert Jackson)
            AMEH-18.  Trentham (Robert Jackson)
            MH (1966)-133.  Trentham (Robert Jackson)

HATFIELD, EDWIN FRANCIS
    584.  'Tis Thine alone, almighty name,/To raise the dead to life
            HMEC-895.  Invitation (Thomas Hastings)

HAVERGAL, FRANCES RIDLEY
    585.  Another year is dawning,/Dear Master, let it be

MH (1905)-571.  Sylvester (John Spencer Camp)
MSSH-263.  Flotow (Friedrich von Flotow)
MH (1935)-534.  Bremen (Melchoir Vulpius)
586.  From glory unto glory!/Be this our joyous song
MH (1905)-573.  St. Colomb (William Stevenson Hoyt)
587.  Golden harps are sounding,/Angel voices ring
MH (1905)-175.  Hermas (Frances Ridley Havergal)
MSSH-100.  Hermas (Frances Ridley Havergal)
588.  I am trusting Thee, Lord Jesus,/Trusting only Thee
MSSH-185.  Bullinger (Ethelbert William Bullinger)
589.  I could not do without Thee,/O Saviour of the lost
MH (1905)-353.  Magdalena (John Stainer)
590.  I gave my life for thee,/My precious blood I shed
MSSH-131.  I Gave My Life (Philip Paul Bliss)
AMEH-536.  What Hast Thou Done for Me? (Philip Paul Bliss)
591.  Lord, speak to me that I may speak/In living echoes of Thy
tone
MH (1905)-410.  Gratitude (Paul Ami Isaac David Bost)
MSSH-230.  Gratitude (Paul Ami Isaac David Bost)
MH (1935)-460.  Gratitude (Paul Ami Isaac David Bost)
MH (1966)-195.  Canonbury (Robert Schumann)
592.  Master, speak! Thy servant heareth,/Waiting for Thy gracious
word
MH (1935)-221.  Amen, Jesus Han Skal Raade (Anton Peter
Berggreen)
AMEH-274.  Amen, Jesus Han Skal Raade (Anton Peter Berg-
green)
593.  Singing for Jesus, our Saviour and King,/Singing for Jesus,
the Lord whom we love
MSSH-14.  Bromham (Timothy Richard)
594.  Take my life and let it be/Consecrated, Lord, to Thee
MH (1905)-348.  Consecration (Unknown)
Messiah (Louis Joseph Ferdinand Herold,
arr. George Kingsley)
MSSH-200.  Consecration (Unknown)
MH (1935)-225.  Messiah (Louis Joseph Ferdinand Herold,
arr. George Kingsley)
AMEH-242.  Ellingham (Nathaniel S. Godfrey)
AMEH-535.  Take My Life ( William Batchelder Bradbury)
MH (1966)-187.  Messiah (Louis Joseph Ferdinand Herold,
arr. George Kingsley)
595.  Tell it out among the heathen that the Lord is King;/Tell it
out!
MH (1905)-634.  Tell It Out (Ira David Sankey)
596.  True-hearted, whole-hearted, faithful and loyal,/King of our
lives, by Thy grace we will be
MH (1905)-420.  Two-Hearted, Whole-Hearted (George Coles
Stebbins)
MSSH-224.  Two-Hearted, Whole-Hearted (George Coles Steb-
bins)
MH (1935)-255.  Two-Hearted, Whole-Hearted (George Coles
Stebbins)
MH (1966)-179.  Two-Hearted, Whole-Hearted (George Coles
Stebbins)
597.  Who is on the Lord's side?/Who will serve the King?
MSSH-226.  Armageddon (John Goss)

HAWEIS, HUGH REGINALD
598.   The Homeland! O the Homeland!/The land of souls freeborn!
            MH (1905)-615.   Homeland (Arthur Seymour Sullivan)
            MH (1935)-530.   Homeland (Arthur Seymour Sullivan)

HAWEIS, THOMAS
599.   Dark was the night, and cold the ground/On which the Lord
            was laid
            AMEH-125.   Melvin (Unknown)
            AMEH-126.   Sorrow (Samuel W. Beazley)
600.   Enthroned on high, almighty Lord,/The Holy Ghost send down
            HMEC-270.   Chesterfield (Thomas Haweis)
601.   From the cross uplifted high/Where the Saviour deigns to die
            HMEC-338.   Rosefield (Henri Abraham Caesar Malan)
602.   Great Spirit, by whose mighty power/All creatures live and
            move
            HMEC-271.   Chesterfield (Thomas Haweis)
603.   Thou from whom all goodness flows,/I lift my soul to Thee
            HMEC-619.   Gould (John Edgar Gould)

HAWKS, ANNIE SHERWOOD
604.   I need Thee every hour,/Most gracious Lord
            HMEC-760.   I Need Thee Every Hour (Robert Lowry)
            MH (1905)-506.   I Need Thee Every Hour (Robert Lowry)
            MSSH-154.   I Need Thee Every Hour (Robert Lowry)
            MH (1935)-232.   I Need Thee Every Hour (Robert Lowry)
            AMEH-338.   I Need Thee Every Hour (Robert Lowry)
            MH (1966)-265.   I Need Thee Every Hour (Robert Lowry)

HAY, JOHN
605.   Defend us, Lord, from every ill;/Strengthen our hearts to do
            Thy will
            MH (1905)-403.   Joshua (Peter Christian Lutkin)
                             Grostette (Henry Wellington Greatorex)
606.   Not in dumb resignation/We lift our hands on high
            MH (1935)-467.    Llangloffan (from Hymnau a Thonau,
                             1865)

HAYWARD, THOMAS
607.   Welcome, delightful morn,/Thou day of sacred rest
            MH (1905)-67.   Warsaw (Thomas Clark)
                             Lischer (Friedrich Schneider)
            MH (1935)-394.   Lischer (Friedrich Schneider)

HEARN, MARIANNE FARNINGHAM
608.   Just as I am, Thine own to be,/Friend of the young, who lo-
            vest me
            AMEH-227.   Just As I Am (Joseph Barnby)
            MH (1966)-169.   Just As I Am (Joseph Barnby)
609.   We hope in Thee, O God!/The day wears on to night
            MH (1905)-328.   Resignation (Moses Smith Cross)
            MH (1935)-365.   Resignation (Moses Smith Cross)

HEATH, GEORGE
610.   My soul, be on thy guard;/Ten thousand foes arise

HMEC-581.  Laban (Lowell Mason)
MH (1905)-493.  Leighton (Henry Wellington Greatorex)
            Laban (Lowell Mason)
MH (1935)-277.  Laban (Lowell Mason)
AMEH-266.  Laban (Lowell Mason)
MH (1966)-246.  Laban (Lowell Mason)

HEBER, REGINALD
611.  Beneath our feet, and o'er our head,/Is equal warning given
      HMEC-373.  Faithful (Samuel Parkman Tuckerman)
612.  Bread of the world in mercy broken,/Wine of the soul in mer-
      cy shed
      MH (1905)-238.  Eucharistic Hymn (John Sebastian Bach
                      Hodges)
      MH (1935)-414.  Eucharstic Hymn (John Sebastian Bach
                      Hodges)
      MH (1966)-320.  Eucharistic Hymn (John Sebastian Bach
                      Hodges)
      MH (1966)-322.  Sri Lampang (Thailand folk melody)
      MH (1966)-323.  Rendez a' Dieu (Louis Bourgeois)
613.  Brightest and best of the sons of the morning,/Dawn on our
      darkness, and lend us Thine aid
      HMEC-186.  Hanover (Johann Christian Wolfgang Amadeus
                 Mozart)
      MH (1905)-114.  Morning Star (James P. Harding)
      MSSH-76.  Morning Star (James P. Harding)
      MH (1935)-119.  Morning Star (James P. Harding)
      MH (1966)-400.  Morning Star (James P. Harding)
614.  By cool Siloam's shady rill/How sweet the lily grows!
      HMEC-875.  Siloam (Isaac Baker Woodbury)
      MH (1905)-678.  Siloam (Isaac Baker Woodbury)
615.  From Greenland's icy mountains,/From India's coral strand
      HMEC-930.  Missionary Hymn (Lowell Mason)
      MH (1905)-655.  Missionary Hymn (Lowell Mason)
      MSSH-249.  Missionary Hymn (Lowell Mason)
      MH (1935)-484.  Missionary Hymn (Lowell Mason)
      AMEH-216.  Missionary Hymn (Lowell Mason)
616.  God, that madest earth and heaven,/Darkness and light
      MSSH-52.  Ar Hyd y Nos (Welsh traditional)
      MH (1935)-43.  Ar Hyd y Nos (Welsh traditional)
      MH (1966)-497.  Ar Hyd y Nos (Welsh traditional)
617.  Holy, holy, holy, Lord God, Almighty!/Early in the morning
      our song shall rise to Thee
      HMEC-136.  Nicaea (John Bacchus Dykes)
      MH (1905)-78.  Nicaea (John Bacchus Dykes)
      MSSH-3.  Nicaea (John Bacchus Dykes)
      MH (1935)-1.  Nicaea (John Bacchus Dykes)
      MH (1966)-26.  Nicaea (John Bacchus Dykes)
618.  Hosanna to the living Lord!/Hosanna to the incarnate Word
      HMEC-71.  Oilead (Etienne Henri Mehul)
619.  Lord of mercy and of might,/Of mankind the life and light
      HMEC-387.  Grey (F.R. Grey)
620.  O God, by whom the seed is given,/By whom the harvest blest
      HMEC-62.  Belmont (Samuel Webbe)
621.  The Son of God goes forth to war,/A kingly crown to gain
      MH (1905)-416.  Cutler (Henry Stephen Cutler)

MSSH-221. Cutler (Henry Stephen Cutler)
MH (1935)-285. All Saints, New (Henry Stephen Cutler)
AMEH-307. All Saints, New (Henry Stephen Cutler)
MH (1966)-419. All Saints, New (Henry Stephen Cutler)
622. Thou art gone to the grave; but we will not deplore thee,/
     Though sorrows and darkness encompass the tomb
     HMEC-999. Frederick (George Kingsley)
623. When through the torn sail the wild tempest is streaming,/
     When o'er the dark wave the red lightning is gleaming
     HMEC-1114. Sullivan (Arthur Seymour Sullivan)

HEDGE, FREDERICK HENRY
624. A mighty fortress is our God,/A bulwark never failing
     (trans. from Martin Luther)
     HMEC-166. Fortress (Martin Luther)
     MH (1905)-101. Ein' Feste Burg (German Chorale, Martin
                    Luther)
     MSSH-22. Ein' Feste Burg (German Chorale, Martin Luther)
     MH (1935)-67. Ein' Fese Burg (German Chorale, Martin
                    Luther)
     MH (1966)-20. Ein' Feste Burg (Martin Luther)
625. "It is finished!" Man of Sorrows!/From Thy cross our frail-
     ty borrows
     MH (1935)-139. Christi Mutter (Corner's Gesangbuch,
                    1625)

HEGINBOTHOM, OTTIWELL
626. Now let my soul, eternal King,/To Thee its grateful tribute
     bring
     HMEC-294. Uxbridge (Lowell Mason)
627. Yes, I will bless Thee, O my God,/Through all my fleeting
     days
     HMEC-705. Roscoe (Edward Little White)

HEMANS, FELICIA DOROTHEA
628. Come to the land of peace;/From shadows come away
     HMEC-1052. Vigil (St. Alban's Tune Book)
629. Calm on the bosom of thy God,/Fair spirit, rest thee now!
     HMEC-988. Mount Auburn (George Kingsley)
630. Lowly and solemn be/Thy children's cry to Thee
     HMEC-1005. Our Father (Edward Little White)
631. O Thou, who in the olive shade,/When the dark hour came on
     HMEC-618. Caddo (William Batchelder Bradbury)

HENLEY, JOHN
632. Children of Jerusalem/Sang the praises of Jesus' name
     MSSH-30. Infant Praises (from John Curwen's Tune Book,
              1842)

HENRY, S.M.I.
633. I know my heav'nly Father knows/The storms that would my way
     oppose
     AMEH-520. He Knows (Edwin Othello Excell)

HERBERT, GEORGE

634.  Let all the world in every corner sing:/My God and King!
        MH (1935)-8.  All the World (John Porter)
        MH (1966)-10.  All the World (Robert Guy McCutchan)
635.  Teach me, my God and King,/In all things Thee to see
        MH (1905)-417.  Mornington (Garret Colley Wellesley, Earl
                  of Mornington)
        MH (1935)-320.  Mornington (Garret Colley Wellesley, Earl
                  of Mornington)

HERVEY, JAMES
  636.  Since all the varying scenes of time/God's watchful eye sur-
          veys
        HMEC-615.  St. Augustine (John Black)

HERZOG, JOHN F.
  637.  In mercy, Lord, remember me,/Through all the hours of night
        HMEC-114.  Kentucky (Jeremiah Ingalls)
                   Evan (William Henry Havergal)

HEWITT, ELIZA E.
  638.  More about Jesus, I would know,/More of His grace to others
          show
        AMEH-530.  More about Jesus (John R. Sweney)
  639.  There's sunshine in my soul today,/More glorious and bright
        AMEH-580.  Sunshine (John R. Sweney)

HICKSON, WILLIAM EDWARD
  640.  Now to heaven our prayer ascending,/God speed the right
        MSSH-253.  Weimar (German Melody)

HIGGINSON, THOMAS WENTWORTH
  641.  To Thine eternal arms, O God,/Take us, Thine erring children
          in
        AMEH-439.  Sympathy (Henry Basford)

HILLHOUSE, AUGUSTUS LUCAS
  642.  Trembling before Thine awful throne,/O Lord, in dust my sins
          I own
        HMEC-444.  Samson (George Frederick Handel)

HINE, STUART K.
  643.  O Lord my God!/When I in awesome wonder (trans. from Carl
          Boberg)
        MH (1966)-17.  O Store Gud (Swedish folk melody)

HODDER, EDWIN
  644.  Thy word is like a garden,Lord,/With flowers bright and
          fair
        MSSH-111.  Bethlehem (Gottfried Wilhelm Fink)

HODGES, GEORGE SAMUEL
  645.  Hosanna we sing, like the children dear,/In the olden days
          when the Lord lived here
        MSSH-15.  Hosanna We Sing (John Bacchus Dykes)

HOFFMAN, ELISHA ALBRIGHT
    646.  Down at the cross where my Saviour died,/Down where for
             cleansing from sin I cried
             AMEH-501.  Down at the Cross (John Hart Stockton)
    647.  Have thy affections been nail'd to the cross?/Is thy heart
             right with God?
             AMEH-347.  Is Thy Heart Right with God? (Elisha Albright
                        Hoffman)
    648.  What a fellowship, what a joy divine,/Leaning on the Ever-
             lasting Arms!
             AMEH-188.  Leaning on Jesus (Anthony J. Showalter)

HOLDEN, OLIVER
    649.  They who seek the throne of grace,/Find that throne in
             every place
             HMEC-717.  Hendon (Henri Abraham Caesar Malan)
             MH (1905)-515.  Evelyn (Emma Louise Ashford)

HOLLAND, HENRY SCOTT
    650.  Judge eternal, throned in splendor,/Lord of lords and King
             of kings
             MH (1966)-546.  Tantum Ergo (Samuel Webb the elder)

HOLLAND, JOSIAH GILBERT
    651.  There's a song in the air!/There's a star in the sky!
             MH (1905)-112.  Stella (Alfred George Wathall)
                            Christmas Song (Karl Pomeroy Harrington)
                            Kolding (Peter Christian Lutkin)
             MSSH-73.  Christmas Song (Karl Pomeroy Harrington)
             MH (1935)-98.  Christmas Song (Karl Pomeroy Harrington)
             MH (1966)-380.  Christmas Song (Karl Pomeroy Harrington)

HOLMES, JOHN HAYNES
    652.  O God, whose smile is in the sky,/Whose path is in the sea
             AMEH-65.  St. Agnes (John Bacchus Dykes)
    653.  The voice of God is calling/Its summons unto men
             MH (1935)-454.  Meirionydd (Welsh hymn melody)
             MH (1966)-200.  Meirionydd (Welsh hymn melody, William
                            Lloyd)

HOLMES, OLIVER WENDELL
    654.  Lord of all being! throned afar,/Thy glory flames from sun
             to star
             HMEC-135.  Luton (George Burder)
             MH (1905)-82.  Keble (John Bacchus Dykes)
             MH (1935)-62.  Keble (John Bacchus Dykes)
             MH (1966)-64.  Louvan (Virgil Corydon Taylor)
    655.  O love divine, that stooped to share/Our sharpest pang, our
             bitterest tear!
             HMEC-629.  Dwight (Joseph Perry Holbrook)
             MH (1905)-457.  Zephyr (William Batchelder Bradbury)
             MH (1935)-273.  Hesperus/Quebec (Henry Baker)
             MH (1966)-270.  Hesperus (Henry Baker)
    656.  The gracious God whose mercy lends/The light of home, the
             the smile of friends

> MH (1905)-669.  Mendon (German traditional)
> MH (1935)-432.  Riminaton (Francis Duckworth)

HOOD, EDWIN PAXTON
    657.  Jesus lives, and Jesus leads,/Though the way be dreary
          MSSH-106.  Faversham (Josiah Booth)

HOPKINS, JOHN HENRY, JR.
    658.  We three kinqs of Orient are,/Bearinq gifts we traverse afar
          MSSH-75.  Three Kings of Orient  (John Henry Hopkins, Jr.)
          MH (1935)-102.  Three Kings of Orient (John Henry Hopkins,
                Jr.)
          MH (1966)-402.  Three Kinqs of Orient (John Henry Hopkins,
                Jr.)

HOPKINS, JOSIAH
    659.  O turn ye, O turn ye, for why will ye die,/When God in great
          mercy is coming so nigh?
          HMEC-335.  Expostulation (Josiah Hopkins)

HOPPER, EDWARD
    660.  Jesus, Saviour, pilot me/Over life's tempestuous sea
          MH (1905)-482.  Jesus, Saviour, Pilot Me (John Edgar
                Gould)
          MSSH-164.  Jesus, Saviour, Pilot Me (John Edgar Gould)
          MH (1935)-269.  Pilot (John Edgar Gould)
          AMEH-290.  Pilot (John Edgar Gould)
          MH (1966)-247.  Pilot (John Edgar Gould)

HOPPS, JOHN PAGE
    661.  Father, lead me day by day,/Ever in Thine own sweet way
          MSSH-191.  Posen (Georg Christoph Strattner)
          MH (1935)-437.  Orientis Partibus (Pierre de Corbeil)
          AMEH-555.  Orientis Partibus (Pierre de Corbeil)
    662.  We praise Thee, Lord, for hours of bliss,/For days of quiet
          rest
          MH (1905)-550.  St. John's, Westminster (James Turle)

HORNE, CHARLES SYLVESTER
    663.  For the might of Thine arm we bless/Thee, our God, our fa-
          ther's God
          MH (1935)-492.  Cormac (Irish traditional)
          MH (1966)-534.  Cormac (Irish traditional)

HOSMER, FREDERICK LUCIAN
    664.  From age to age they gather, all the brave of heart and
          strong,/In the strife of truth and error, of the right
          against the wrong
          AMEH-377.  Battle Hymn of the Republic (William Steffe)
    665.  I little see, I little know,/Yet can I fear no ill
          MH (1905)-450.  Fellowship (Alfred George Wathall)
    666.  Not always on the mount may we/Rapt in the heavenly vision
          be
          MH (1905)-477.  Intercession Old (Latin melody, arr. John
                Bacchus Dykes)
    667.  O Thou, in all Thy might so far,/In all Thy love so near

MH (1905)-484.  Racine  (Peter Christian Lutkin)
MH (1966)-12.  Richmond (Thomas Haweis)
668.  "Thy Kingdom come," on bended knee/The passing ages pray
    MH (1935)-463.  Irish (A Collection of Hymns and Sacred
                          Poems, Dublin, 1749)
669.  We cannot think of them as dead/Who walk with us no more
    MH (1935)-423.  St. Flavian (Day's Psalter, 1562)

HOSS, ELIJAH EMBREE
    670.  O God, great Father, Lord, and King!/Our children unto Thee
          we bring
        MH (1905)-231.  Baptism (Peter Christian Lutkin)

HOUSMAN, LAURENCE
    671.  Father eternal, Ruler of creation,/Spirit of life, which
          moved ere form was made
        MH (1966)-469.  Geneva (Genevan Psalter, 1551)
    672.  Honor and glory, power and salvation/Be in the highest unto
          Him who reigneth
        MH (1935)-16.  Coelites Plaudant (Rouen church melody)

HOW, WILLIAM WALSHAM
    673.  For all the saints who from their labors rest,/Who Thee by
          faith before the world confessed
        MH (1905)-430.  Sarum (Joseph Barnby)
        MH (1935)-527.  Sarum (Joesph Barnby)
                        Sine Nomine (Ralph Vaughan Williams)
        MH (1966)-536.  Sine Nomine (Ralph Vaughan Williams)
        MH (1966)-537.  Sarum (Joseph Barnby)
    674.  Lord Jesus, when we stand afar/And gaze upon Thy holy cross
        HMEC-213.  Eucharist (Isaac Baker Woodbury)
        MH (1905)-145.  Beloit (Carl Gottlieb Reissiger)
    675.  O holy Lord, content to fill/In lowly home the lowliest
          place
        MSSH-81.  Brookfield (Thomas Bishop Southgate)
    676.  O Jesus, crucified for man,/O Lamb, all glorious on Thy
          throne
        MH (1905)-326.  Sefton (John Baptiste Calkin)
        AMEH-110.  Beloit (Carl Gottlieb Reissiger)
    677.  O Jesus, Thou art standing/Outside the fast-closed door
        MH (1905)-282.  St. Hilda (Justin Heinrich Knecht and Ed-
                        ward Husband)
        MSSH-139.  St. Hilda (Justin Heinrich Knecht and Edward
                   Husband)
        MH (1935)-197.  St. Hilda (Justin Heinrich Knecht and Ed-
                        ward Husband)
        AMEH-118.  St. Hilda (Justin Heinrich Knecht and Edward
                   Husband)
        MH (1966)-108.  St. Hilda (Justin Heinrich Knecht and Ed-
                        ward Husband)
    678.  O Word of God incarnate,/O Wisdom from on high
        MH (1905)-200.  Magdalena (John Stainer)
        MH (1935)-386.  Munich (Felix Mendelssohn-Bartholdy)
        AMEH-531.  Aurelia (Samuel Sebastian Wesley)
        MH (1966)-372.  Munich (Felix Mendelssohn-Bartholdy)

679.  Summer suns are glowing/Over land and sea
    MSSH-267.  Ruth (Samuel Smith)
680.  We give Thee but Thine own,/Whate'er the gift may be
    HMEC-892.  Boylston (Lowell Mason)
    MH (1905)-688.  Chiselhurst (Joseph Barnby)
    MH (1935)-456.  Schumann (from Cantica Laudis, 1850)
    MH (1966)-181.  Schumann (from Cantica Laudis, 1850)

HOWE, JULIA WARD
681.  Mine eyes have seen the glory of the coming of the Lord;/He
    is tramping out the vintage where the grapes of wrath
    are stored
    MSSH-278.  Battle Hymn of the Republic (John William
        Steffe)
    AMEH-376.  Battle Hymn of the Republic (John William
        Steffe)
    MH (1966)-545.  Battle Hymn of the Republic (John William
        Steffe)

HOYLE, R. BIRCH
682.  Thine is the glory,/Risen, conquering Son (trans. from Ed-
    mond L. Budry)
    MH (1966)-450.  Judas Maccabeus (George Frederick Han-
        del)

HUDSON, RALPH E.
683.  My life, my love, I give to Thee,/Thou Lamb of God, who died
    for me
    AMEH-515A.  My Life, My Love (C.R. Dunbar)

HUNTER, JOHN
684.  Dear Master, in whose life I see/All that I would, but fail
    to be
    MH (1935)-376.  Hursley (Katholisches Gesangbuch, 1774)
    MH (1966)-254.  Hursley (Katholisches Gesangbuch, 1774)

HUNTER, WILLIAM
685.  My heavenly home is bright and fair:/Nor pain nor death can
    enter there
    HMEC-1072.  Going Home (Wiliam McDonald)
    MH (1905)-628.  Going Home (William Miller, arr. Hubert
        Platt Main)
686.  The Great Physician now is near,/The sympathizing Jesus
    MSSH-127.  Great Physician (John Hart Stockton)
    AMEH-360.  Great Physician (John Hart Stockton)
687.  Who shall forbid our chastened woe,/Our tears of love to
    start?
    HMEC-986.  Mount Auburn (George Kingsley)

HUNTINGTON, DE WITT C.
688.  O think of the home over there,/By the side of the river of
    light
    AMEH-578.  The Home over There (Tullius C. O'Kane)

HUNTINGTON, FREDERICK DAN

689.  There is no night in heaven;/In that blest world above
          HMEC-1049.  Greek Hymn (Joseph Perry Holbrook)
          AMEH-469.  St. Thomas (George Frederick Handel)

HUSSEY, JENNIE EVELYN
    690.  King of my life, I crown Thee now,/Thine shall the glory be
          AMEH-620.  King of My Life (William J. Kirkpatrick)

HUTCHINSON, ALBERT H.
    691.  For all the blessings of the year,/For all the friends we
              hold so dear
          MH (1935)-456.  Oldbridge (Robert Newton Ouaile)
          AMEH-119.  Oldbridge (Robert Newton Ouaile)
          MH (1966)-525.  Childhood (Henry Walford Davies)

HUTTON, JAMES
    692.  My opening eyes with rapture see/The dawn of this returning
              day
          HMEC-83.  Rockingham (Lowell Mason)

HYDE, ANN BEADLEY
    693.  Say, sinner, hath a voice within/Oft whispered to thy secret
              soul
          HMEC-353.  Ingham (Lowell Mason)

HYDE, WILLIAM DE WITT
    694.  Creation's Lord, we give Thee thanks/That this world is in-
              complete
          AMEH-219.  Rockingham Old (Edward Miller)

IRONS, WILLIAM JOSIAH
    695.  Father of love, our Guide and Friend,/O lead us gently on
          HMEC-614.  St. Augustine (John Black)
    696.  Sing with all the sons of glory./Sing the resurrection song!
          HMEC-225.  Summerside (John Black)
          MH (1905)-160.  Hymn of Joy (Ludwig van Beethoven)
          MH (1935)-150.  Hymn of Joy (Ludwig van Beethoven)
          AMEH-394.  Hymn of Joy (Ludwig van Beethoven)
          MH (1966)-440.  Hymn of Joy (Ludwig van Beethoven)

JACKSON, NINA B.
    697.  Thy way, O Lord, not mine,/Thy will be done, not mine
          AMEH-184.  Thy Way (E.C. Deas)

JACKSON, SAMUEL
    698.  Though all the world my choice deride,/Yet Jesus shall my
              portion be (trans. from Gerhard Tersteegen)
          HMEC-695.  Rolland (William Batchelder Bradbury)

JACOBI, JOHN CHRISTIAN
    699.  Holy Ghost, dispel our sadness;/Pierce the clouds of nature's
           night (trans. from Paul Gerhardt)
        HMEC-265.  Fulton (William Batchelder Bradbury)
        MH (1905)-192.  Light of the World (Friedrich Heinrich
                    Hummel)
        MH (1966)-132.  Hyfrydol (Rowland Hugh Prichard)

JENKINS, TUDOR
    700.  When mother love makes all things bright,/When joy comes
           with the morning light
        AMEH-134.  Rachel (E.M. Wren)

JERVIS, THOMAS
    701.  With joy we lift our eyes/To those bright realms above
        HMEC-43.  Waugh (Ralph Harrison)

JOHNS, JOHN
    702.  Come, kingdom of our God,/Sweet reign of light and love
        AMEH-445.  St. Thomas (Aaron Williams)

JOHNSON, ERASTUS
    703.  O sometimes the shadows are deep,/And rough seems the path
           to the goal
        MH (1905)-434.  The Rock of Refuge (William Gustavus
                    Fischer)
        MH (1935)-245.  The Rock of Refuge (William Gustavus
                    Fischer)
        AMEH-496.  The Rock of Refuge (William Gustavus Fischer)
        MH (1966)-245.  The Rock of Refuge (Wiiliam Gustavus
                    Fischer)

JOHNSON, SAMUEL
    704.  City of God, how broad and far/Outspread thy walls sublime
        MH (1905)-209.  Bracondale (Josiah Booth)
        MH (1935)-420.  Grafenberg (Johann Cruger)
    705.  Life of ages, richly poured,/Love of God, unspent and free
        MH (1935)-405.  Orientis Partibus (Pierre de Corbeil)

JONES, CHARLES P.
    706.  When judgment day is drawing nigh,/Where shall I be?
        AMEH-506.  Where Shall I Be? (Charles P. Jones)

JONES, EDITH
    707.  Father, who art alone/Our helper and our stay
        MH (1935)-554.  Samuel (Arthur Seymour Sullivan)

JONES, EDMUND
    708.  Come, humble sinner, in whose breast/A thousand thoughts re-
           volve
        HMEC-369.  Balerma (Richard Simpson)
        MH (1905)-260.  Balerma (Richard Sompson)

JUDKIN, THOMAS JAMES
    709.  Enthroned in Jesus now/Upon His heavenly seat

HMEC-253. Langton (Charlotte Streatfeild)
710. Holy Spirit, Fount of blessing,/Ever watchful, ever kind
HMEC-266. Fulton (William Batchelder Bradbury)

JUDSON, ADONIRAM
711. Our Father, God, who art in heaven,/All hallowed be Thy name
HMEC-716. Woodstock (Deodatus Dutton, Jr.)

JULIAN, JOHN
712. O God of God! O Light of Light!/Thou Prince of Peace, Thou
King of kings
MH (1905)-15. Liddon (John Albert Jeffery)

KEBLE, JOHN
713. Blest are the pure in heart,/For they shall see our God
HMEC-501. Greenwood (Joseph Emerson Sweetser)
MH (1905)-360. Greenwood (Joseph Emerson Sweetser)
MH (1935)-369. Greenwood (Joseph Emerson Sweetser)
MH (1966)-276. Franconia (Johann Balthasar Koenig, arr.
William Havergal)
714. Lord, in Thy name Thy servants plead,/And Thou hast sworn to
hear
HMEC-1080. Southwell (Herbert Stephen Irons)
715. New every morning is the love/Our wakening and uprising
prove
HMEC-103. Hursley (Peter Ritter, arr. William Henry
Monk)
MH (1905)-42. Canonbury (Robert Schumann)
MSSH-43. Canonbury (Robert Schumann)
MH (1935)-35. Melcombe (Samuel Webbe)
MH (1966)-499. Melcombe (Samuel Webbe)
716. Sun of my soul, Thou Saviour dear,/It is not night if Thou
be near
HMEC-102. Hursley (Peter Ritter, arr. William Henry
Monk)
MH (1905)-47. Hursley (Peter Ritter, arr. William Henry
Monk)
MSSH-46. Hursley (Peter Ritter, arr. William Henry
Monk)
MH (1935)-56. Hursley (Peter Ritter, arr. William Henry
Monk)
AMEH-49. Hursley (Peter Ritter, arr. William Henry Monk)
MH (1966)-502. Hursley (Peter Ritter, arr. William Henry
Monk)

KELLY, THOMAS
717. Arise, ye saints, arise!/The Lord our Leader is
HMEC-577. Leighton (Henry Wellington Greatorex)
718. Come, ye saints, look here and wonder;/See the place where
Jesus lay
MH (1905)-226. Summerside (John Black)
719. Hark, ten thousand harps and voices/Sound the note of praise
above!

MH (1905)-177. Harwell (Lowell Mason)
MSSH-99. Harwell (Lowell Mason)
MH (1935)-167. Harwell (Lowell Mason)
AMEH-156. Harwell (Lowell Mason)

720. Hark! the notes of angels singing,/"Glory, glory, to the Lamb!"
HMEC-58. Rathbun (Ithmar Conkey)

721. In Thy name, O Lord, assembling,/We, Thy people, now draw near
HMEC-54. Greenville (Jean Jacques Rousseau)

722. Look, ye saints, the sight is glorious,/See the Man of sorrows now
HMEC-249. Coronation (Oliver Holden)
MH (1905)-169. Regent Square (Henry Smart)
MH (1935)-165. Cwm Rhondda (John Hughes)
AMEH-100. Victor's Crown (Horatio William Parker)
MH (1966)-453. Bryn Calfaria (William Owen)

723. O where is now that glowing love/That marked our union with the Lord?
HMEC-561. Warren (Vrigil Corydon Taylor)

724. On the mountain's top appearing,/Lo! the sacred herald stands
HMEC-767. Zion (Thomas Hastings)
MH (1905)-647. Zion (Thomas Hastings)
AMEH-213. Zion (Thomas Hastings)

725. The head that once was crowned with thorns,/Is crowned with glory now
HMEC-256. Heber (George Kingsley)
MH (1905)-173. Laud (John Bacchus Dykes)
MH (1935)-163. St. Magnus (Jeremiah Clark)
MH (1966)-458. St. Magnus (Jeremiah Clark)
AMEH-2. St. Magnus (Jeremiah Clark)

726. The Lord is risen indeed;/The grave hath lost its prey
HMEC-235. Rialto (George Frederick Root)
MH (1905)-157. Rialto (George Frederick Root)
AMEH-383. Wright (M.T. Sterling)

727. We sing the praise of Him who died,/Of Him who died upon the cross
HMEC-208. Germany (Ludwig can Beethoven)

728. Zion stands with hills surrounded,/Zion, kept by power divine
HMEC-768. Zion (Thomas Hastings)
MH (1905)-212. Eton College (Joseph Barnby)

KEMPTHORNE, JOHN
729. Praise the Lord! ye heavens. adore Him;/Praise Him, angels, in the height
HMEC-57. Rathbun (Ithmar Conkey)

KEN, THOMAS
730. All praise to Thee, my God, this night,/For all the blessings of the light!
MH (1935)-51. Tallis' Canon/Evening Hymn (Thomas Tallis)
MH (1966)-493. Tallis' Canon/Evening Hymn (Thomas Tallis)

731. Awake, my soul, and with the sun/Thy daily stage of duty run

HMEC-106. Evening Hymn (Thomas Tallis)
MH (1905)-44. Morning Hymn (Francois Hippolyte Barthele-
mon)
MH (1935)-34. The Morning Watch (Carl Fowler Price)
AMEH-442A. Hursley (from the German)
MH (1966)-180. Tallis' Canon (Thomas Tallis)
732. Glory to Thee, my God, this night,/For all the blessings of
the light (variant of 730 above)
HMEC-105. Evening Hymn (Thomas Tallis)
MH (1905)-49. Evening Hymn (Thomas Tallis)

KENNEDY, BENJAMIN HALL
733. Ask ye what great thing I know/That delights and stirs me
so? (trans. from Johann Christoph Schwedler)
MH (1935)-147. Hendon (Henri Abraham Caesar Malan)
MH (1966)-124. Hendon (Henri Abraham Caesar Malan)
734. Children of the Heavenly King,/As we journey, let us sing
(trans. from Johann Christoph Schwedler)
AMEH-334. Hendon (Henri Abraham Caesar Malan)

KENNEDY, GERALD H.
735. God of love and God of power,/Grant us in this burning hour
MH (1966)-153. Unser Herrscher (Joachim Neander)

KERR, HUGH THOMPSON
736. God of our life, through all the circling years,/We trust in
Thee
MH (1966)-47. Sandon (Charles Henry Purday)

KETHE, WILLIAM
737. All people that on earth do dwell,/Sing to the Lord with
cheerful voice
HMEC-11. Old Hundreth (Guillaume Franc)
MH (1905)-16. Old Hundreth (Guillaume Franc)
MH (1935)-13. Old Hundreth (Genevan Psalter)
AMEH-515. Old Hundreth (Genevan Psalter)
MH (1966)-21. Old 100th (Louis Bourgois)

KEY, FRANCIS SCOTT
738. O say, can you see by the dawn's early light,/What so proud-
ly we hailed at the twilight's last gleaming
MSSH-277. National Anthem (John Stafford Smith)
AMEH-584. National Anthem (John Stafford Smith)

KIDDER, MARY ANN
739. Lord, I care not for riches,/Neither silver nor gold
AMEH-326. Is My Name Written There? (Frank M. Davis)

KILLINGHALL, JOHN
740. In every trying hour/My soul to Jesus dies
AMEH-475. Gerar (Lowell Mason)

KIMBALL, HARRIET McEWAN
741. Pour Thy blessings, Lord, like showers,/On these barren
lives of ours
MH (1905)-693. Hollingside (John Bacchus Dykes)

742.   Wider and wider yet/The gates of the nations swing
          MSSH-240.  Vogl (John H. Wigmore)

KING, JOHN
   743.   When, His salvation bringing,/To Zion Jesus came
          HMEC-883.  Miriam (Joseph Perry Holbrook)
          MSSH-84.  Amsterdam (Berthold Tours)
          MH (1935)-129.  Tours (Berthold Tours)

KINGSLEY, CHARLES
   744.   From Thee all skill and science flow,/All pity, care, and
             love
          MH (1935)-462.  Grafenberg (Joseph Cruger)
          MH (1966)-485.  Massachusetts (Katherine K. Davis)

KIPLING, RUDYARD
   745.   Father in heaven who lovest all,/O help Thy children when
             they call
          MH (1935)-294.  Germany (Ludwig van Beethoven)
   746.   God of our fathers, known of old,/Lord of our far-flung
             battle line
          MH (1905)-710.  Magdalen (John Stainer)
          MH (1935)-497.  Melita (John Bacchus Dykes)

KIRKPATRICK, WILLIAM J.
   747.   I've wandered far away from God,/Now I'm coming home
          AMEH-340.  Lord, I'm Coming Home (William J. Kirkpatrick)

KNIGHT, CAMILLA J.
   748.   Hear the chiming Easter bells,/Their joyous music ringing
          MSSH-90.  Hear the Chiming Easter Bells (John Henry
                       Gower)
                    Hear the Chiming Easter Bells (George A. Bur-
                       dett)

KNOWLES, JAMES DAVIS
   749.   O God, through countless worlds of light/Thy power and
             glory show
          HMEC-870.  Dundee (Guillaume Franc)

KNOWLTON, MISS H.O.
   750.   Pass the word along the line;/Tell it, friend to friend
          MSSH-232.  Dunbar (John H. Maunder)

KNOX, GERTRUDE L.
   751.   On the highway of the King,/Children's happy voices sing
          MSSH-269.  Highway of the King (Mrs. R.R. Forman)

KOMMER, J. THURLOW
   752.   Sing out your hallelujas,/Ye ransomed of the Lord!
          MSSH-11.  Albany (George Edgar Oliver)

LANEY, THOMAS J.
    753.  'Tis a sweet and glorious thought that comes to me,/I'll
           live on, yes, I'll live on
              AMEH-544.  'Tis a Sweet and Glorious Thougt (Thomas J.
                    Laney)

LANIER, SIDNEY
    754.  Into the woods my Master went,/Clean forspent, forspent
              MH (1935)-132.  Lanier (Peter Christian Lutkin)

LARCOM, LUCY
    755.  Draw Thou my soul, O Christ,/Closer to Thine
              MH (1935)-297.  St. Edmund (Arthur Seymour Sullivan)
              MH (1966)-188.  St. Edmund (Arthur Seymour Sullivan)

LATHBURY, MARY ARTEMISIA
    756.  Break Thou the bread of life,/Dear Lord, to me
              MH (1905)-325.  Bread of Life (William Fisk Sherwin)
              MSSH-112.  Bread of Life (William Fisk Sherwin)
              MH (1935)-387.  Bread of Life (William Fisk Sherwin)
              AMEH-164.  Bread of Life (William Fisk Sherwin)
              MH (1966)-369.  Bread of Life (William Fisk Sherwin)
    757.  Day is dying in the west;/Heaven is touching earth with rest
              MH (1905)-57.  Evening Praise (William Fisk Sherwin)
              MSSH-49.  Evening Praise (William Fisk Sherwin)
              MH (1935)-44.  Chatauqua/Evening Praise (William Fisk
                    Sherwin)
              AMEH-58.  Chatauqua/Evening Praise (William Fisk Sherwin)
              MH (1966)-503.  Chatauqua/Evening Praise (William Fisk
                    Sherwin)
    758.  O Shepherd of the nameless fold,/The blessed church to be
              MH (1966)-304.  Norse Air (arr. William J. Kirkpatrick)

LAUFER, CALVIN WEISS
    759.  O Thou eternal Christ of God,/Ride on! Ride on! Ride on!
              MH (1935)-130.  Percival-Smith (Calvin Weiss Laufer)
              MH (1966)-482.  Llangloffan (Traditional Welsh melody)
    760.  We thank Thee, Lord, Thy paths of service lead/To blazoned
            heights and down the slopes of need
              MH (1935)-458.  Field (Calnin Weiss Laufer)
              MH (1966)-203.  Field (Calvin Weiss Laufer)

LEESON, JANE ELIZABETH
    761.  Gracious Saviour, gentle Shepherd,/Little ones and dear to
            Thee
              HMEC-889.  Gaylord (Joseph Perry Holbrook)
    762.  Saviour, teach me day by day,/Love's sweet lesson to obey
              MH (1905)-676.  Percivals (Unknown)
              MSSH-171.  Ferrier (John Bacchus Dykes)
              MH (1935)-449.  Innocents (The Parish Choir, 1850)
              MH (1966)-162.  Orientis Partibus (Medieval French melo-
                    dy)

LELAND, JOHN
    763.  The day is past and gone,/The evening shades appear
              HMEC-113.  Kentucky (Jeremiah Ingalls)

              AMEH-391.  Silver Street (Isaac Smith)
              AMEH-665.  Without tune

LENTE, EMMA A.
    764.  Come, weary travelers, come from the by-ways;/Come to the
           right way that leads unto God
           MSSH-133.  The Way (George A. Burdett)

LEWIS, HOWELL ELVET
    765.  Friend of the home: as when in Galilee/The mothers brought
           their little ones to Thee
           MH (1935)-406.  Ffigysbren (Welsh hymn melody)

LITTLEDALE, RICHARD FREDERICK
    766.  Come down, O love divine,/See Thou this soul of mine (trans.
           from Bianco da Siena)
           MH (1966)-466.  Down Ampney (Ralph Vaughan Williams)

LITTLEFIELD, MILTON SMITH
    767.  Come, O Lord, like morning sunlight,/Making all life new
           and free
           MH (1935)-33.  Trust (Felix Mendelssohn-Bartholdy)
    768.  O Son of man, Thou madest known,/Through quiet work in shop
           and home
           MH (1935)-121.  Brookfield (Thomas Bishop Southgate)
           AMEH-241.  Rachel (E.M. Wren)
           MH (1966)-197.  Canonbury (Robert Schumann)

LITTLEWOOD, WILLIAM EDENSOR
    769.  There is no love like the love of Jesus,/Never to fade or
           fail
           MSSH-159.  Love of Jesus (Theodore Edson Perkins)

LIVINGSTONE, JOHN H.
    770.  My soul, with humble fervor raise/To God the voice of grate-
           ful praise
           HMEC-449.  Rockingham (Lowell Mason)

LLOYD, WILLIAM FREEMAN
    771.  "My times are in Thy hand:"/My God, I wish them there
           HMEC-637.  Eelvin (Lowell Mason)
           MH (1905)-449.  Monsell (Joseph Barnby)
           MH (1935)-322.  Ferguson (George Kingsley)

LOGAN, JOHN
    772.  Go forth, ye heralds, in my name,/Sweetly the gospel trumpet
           sound
           HMEC-810.  Migdol (Lowell Mason)
           AMEH-410.  Duke Street (John Hatton)

LONGFELLOW, SAMUEL
    773.  Again as evening's shadow falls,/We gather in these hallowed
           walls
           HMEC-109.  Hebron (Lowell Mason)
           MH (1905)-48.  Abends (Herbert Stanley Oakeley)

MH (1935)-42.  Abends (Herbert Stanley Oakeley)
774.  Go forth to life, O child of earth!/Still mindful of Thy
       heav'nly birth
      MH (1935)-296.  Rhys (Rhys Thomas)
775.  God of the earth, the sky, the sea,/Maker of all above
      MH (1966)-36.  Germany (William Gardiner's Sacred Melo-
              dies, 1815)
776.  God's trumpet wakes the slumbering world;/Now, each man to
       his post!
      MSSH-215.  Trumpet Call (Peter Christian Lutkin)
      MH (1935)-262.  Corwin (Joseph W. Lerman)
777.  Holy Spirit, Truth divine!/Dawn upon this soul of mine
      HMEC-263.  Fulton (William Batchelder Bradbury)
      MH (1935)-173.  Mercy (Louis Moreau Gottschalk)
      AMEH-166.  Haven (Edwin Henry Lamare)
      MH (1966)-135.  Canterbury (Orlando Gibbons)
778.  I look to Thee in every need,/And never look in vain
      MH (1905)-473.  Wessex (Edward John Hopkins)
      MH (1935)-325.  O Jesu (Hirschberg Gesangbuch, 1741)
      MH (1966)-219.  O Jesu (Hirschberg Gesangbuch, 1741)
779.  Now, on land and sea descending,/Brings the night its peace
       profound
      MH (1935)-45.  Vesper Hymn/Bortaniansky (Dimitri Stepa-
              novich Bortniansky)
      AMEH-489.  Vesper Hymn/Bortniansky (Dimitri Stepanovich
              Bortniansky)
      MH (1966)-505.  Vesper Hymn/Bortniansky (Dimitri Stepa-
              novich Bortniansky)
780.  O God, Thou giver of all good;/Thy children live by daily
       food
      MH (1966)-515.  Puer Nobis Nascitus (Michael Praetorius)
781.  O still in accents sweet and strong/Sounds forth the ancient
       word
      HMEC-598.  St. Agnes (John Bacchus Dykes)
      MH (1905)-395.  Mount Calvary (Robert Prescott Stewart)
      MH (1935)-289.  Mount Calvary (Robert Prescott Stewart)
782.  One holy Church of God appears,/Through every age and race
      MH (1966)-296.  St. Stephen (William Jones)

LONGSTAFF, WILLIAM D.
   783.  Take time to be holy,/Speak oft with the Lord
      MH (1935)-251.  Holiness (George Coles Stebbins)
      AMEH-304.  Holiness (George Coles Stebbins)
      MH (1966)-266.  Holiness (George Coles Stebbins

LOWELL, JAMES RUSSELL
   784.  Once to every man and nation/Comes the moment to decide
      MH (1935)-263.  Ton-y-Botel (Welsh hymn melody)
      MH (1966)-242.  Ebenezer (Thomas John Williams)

LOWRY, ROBERT
   785.  Low in the grave He lay--Jesus my Saviour!/Waiting the com-
       ing day--Jesus, my Lord!
      AMEH-129.  Low in the Grave (Robert Lowry)
      MH (1966)-444.  Christ Arose (Robert Lowry)
   786.  Shall we gather at the river/Where bright angel feet have

        trod

        AMEH-459.  Shall We Gather at the River? (Robert Lowry)

787.  What  can wash away my sin?/Nothing but the blood of Jesus

        AMEH-510.  What Can Wash Away My Sin? (Robert Lowry)

LUKE, JEMIMA

    788.  I think, when I read that sweet story of old,/When Jesus was
          here among men

        HMEC-880.  Sweet Story (English traditional)

        MH (1905)-682.  Athens (Greek traditional)

        MSSH-82.  Davenant (Unknown)

            East Horndon (English traditional)

        MH (1935)-440.  Sweet Story (William Batchelder Bradbury)

        AMEH-550.  Sweet Story (William Batchelder Bradbury)

        AMEH-567.  Davenant (Unknown)

LYNCH, THOMAS TOKE

    789.  Gracious Spirit, dwell with me!/I, myself, would gracious
          be

        MH (1905)-195.  Palgrave (H. de la Haye Blackith)

    790.  Lift up your heads, rejoice,/Redemption draweth nigh

        AMEH-112.  Blessed Home (John Stainer)

LYON, P.H.B.

    791.  O God, before whose altar/The stars like tapers burn

        MH (1966)-486.  Llangloffan (Traditional Welsh melody)

LYTE, HENRY FRANCIS

    792.  Abide with me! Fast falls the eventide!/The darkness dee-
          pens--Lord, with me abide!

        HMEC-93.  Eventide (William Henry Monk)

        MH (1905)-50.  Eventide (William Henry Monk)

        MSSH-53.  Eventide (William Henry Monk)

        MH (1935)-520.  Eventide (William Henry Monk)

        AMEH-52.  Eventide (William Henry Monk)

        MH (1966)-289.  Eventide (William Henry Monk)

    793.  Jesus, I my cross have taken,/All to leave, and follow Thee

        HMEC-643.  Ellesdie (Johann Christian Wolfgang Amadeus
                  Mozart)

        MH (1905)-458.  Ellesdie (Johann Christian Wolfgang
                  Amadeus Mozart)

        MH (1935)-261.  Ellesdie (Johann Christian Wolfgang
                  Amadeus Mozart)

        AMEH-314.  Ellesdie (Johann Christian Wolfgang Amadeus
                  Mozart)

        AMEH-533.  Zundel (John Zundel)

        MH (1966)-251.  Ellesdie (The Christian Lyre, 1830)

    794.  My spirit on Thy care,/Blest Saviour, I recline

        HMEC-635.  Olmutz (Lowell Mason)

    795.  Praise, my soul, the King of heaven;/To His feet thy tri-
          bute bring

        HMEC-734.  Regent Square (Henry Smart)

        MH (1935)-77.  Regent Square (Henry Smart)

        AMEH-305.  Regent Square (Henry Smart)

        MH (1966)-66.  Regent Square (Henry Smart)

    796.  Praise the Lord, His glories show,/Saints within His courts

below
    HMEC-27.  Monkland (John B. Wilkes)
797.  The leaves, around me falling,/Are preaching of decay
    HMEC-1088.  Righini (Vincenzo Righini)
798.  There is a safe and secret place/Beneath the wings divine
    HMEC-158.  Dundee (Guillaume Franc)


MACDUFF, JOHN ROBERT
    799.  Christ is coming! let creation/Bid her groans and travail
        cease
        HMEC-1016.  Pilgrimage (Unknown)
        MH (1905)-602.  Eton College (Joseph Barnby)
    800.  Jesus wept!/those tears are over,/But His heart is still the
        same
        MH (1905)-132.  St. Joseph (Henry Heathcate Statham)

MACE, FRANCES LAUGHTON
    801.  Only waiting, till the shadows/Are a little longer grown
        HMEC-644.  Ellesdie (Johann Christian Wolfgang Amadeus
            Mozart)

MACKAY, J.B.
    802.  Is there any one can help us, one who understands our
        hearts,/When the thorns of life have pierced them till
        they bleed
        AMEH-512.  Is There Anyone Can Help Us? (J.B. Mackay)

MACKAY, MARGARET
    803.  Asleep in Jesus! blessed sleep,/From which none ever wakes
        to weep!
        HMEC-979.  Rest (William Batchelder Bradbury)
        MH (1905)-583.  Caryl (Peter Christian Lutkin)
                Rest (William Batchelder Bradbury)
        AMEH-485.  Asleep in Jesus (William Batchelder Bradbury)

MACKAY, WILLIAM PATON
    804.  We praise Thee, O God, for the Son of Thy love!/For Jesus
        who died, and is now gone above
        AMEH-46.  Revive Us Again (John J. Husband)

MACKELLAR, THOMAS
    805.  Book of grace and book of glory,/Gift of God to age and
        youth
        MSSH-110.  Star of Peace (Lowell Mason)

MACLEOD, NORMAN
    806.  Courage, brother! do not stumble,/Though thy path be dark
        as night
        MH (1905)-513.  Barony (Arthur Seymour Sullivan)
        MSSH-182.  Barony (Arthur Seymour Sullivan)
        MH (1935)-298.  Courage, Brother (Arthur Seymour Sulli-
            van)

MANN, NEWTON, and MAX LANDSBERG
807.    Praise to the living God!/All praised be His name (trans.
            from Daniel ben Judah
            MH (1966)-30.  Leoni (Meyer Lyon)

MANT, RICHARD
808.    Round the Lord, in glory seated,/Cherubim and seraphim
            HMEC-56.  Rathbun (Ithmar Conkey)

MARCH, DANIEL
809.    Hark the voice of Jesus calling,/"Who will go and work to-
            day?"
            HMEC-607.  Federal Street (Henry Kemble Oliver)
            MH (1905)-402.  Lox Eoi (Arthur Seymour Sullivan)
            MSSH-205.  Lux Eoi (Arthur Seymour Sullivan)
            MH (1935)-288.  Ellesdie (Johann Christian Wolfgang Ama-
                deus Mozart
            AMEH-214.  Here I Am (Charles A. Tindley)

MARCUM, J.R.
810.    Thou hast been iur guide this day,/Thou hast led us all the
            way
            AMEH-55.  Chautauqua (William Fisk Sherwin)

MARCY, ELIZABETH EUNICE
811.    Out of the depths to Thee I cry,/Whose fainting footsteps
            trod
            HMEC-665.  Heber (George Kingsley)
            MH (1905)-427.  Naomi (Hans George Naegeli)

MARLATT, EARL
812.    "Are ye able," said the Master,/"To be crucified with me?"
            MH (1935)-268.  Beacon Hill (Henry Silverstone Mason)
            AMEH-452.  Beacon Hill (Henry Silverstone Mason)
            MH (1966)-413.  Beacon Hill (Henry Silverstone Mason)
813.    Spirit of life, in this new dawn,/Give us the faith that fol-
            lows on
            MH (1935)-178.  Maryton (Henry Percy Smith)
            MH (1966)-462.  Maryton (Henry Percy Smith)

MARRIOTT, JOHN
814.    Thou, whose almighty word/Chaos and darkness heard
            HMEC-913.  Ibstone (Maria Tiddeman)
            MH (1905)-629.  Righini (Vincenzo Righini)
            MH (1935)-480.  Righini (Vincenzo Righini)
            MH (1966)-480.  Dort (Lowell Mason)

MARSDEN, JOSHUA
815.    Go, ye messengers of God;/Like the beams of morning, fly
            HMEC-939.  Eltham (Lowell Mason)
            MH (1905)-640.  Culford (Edward John Hopkins)

MARTIN, CIVILLA D.
816.    Be not dismayed, whate'er betide,/God will take care of you
            MSSH-168.  God Cares (W. Stillman Martin)

AMEH-79.  Martin (W. Stillman Martin)
MH (1966)-207.  Martin (W. Stillman Martin)
817.  Why should I feel discouraged,/Why should the shadows come
AMEH-516.  Why Should I Feel Discouraged? (Charles H. Gabriel)

MARTIN, W.C.
818.  I trust in God wherever I may be,/Upon the land or on the
rolling sea
AMEH-502.  I Trust in God (Charles H. Gabriel)
819.  The name of Jesus is so sweet,/I love its music to repeat
AMEH-490.  The Name of Jesus (Edmund S. Lorenz)
820.  Where He may lead me I will go,/For I have learned to trust
Him so
AMEH-521.  Where He May Lead Me (James M. Black)

MASEFIELD, JOHN
821.  Sing, men and angels, sing/For God our Life and King
MH (1935)-152.  Masefield (John Porter)

MASON, MARY JANE
822.  Saviour, who died for me,/I give myself to Thee
HMEC-742.  Fade, Fade, Each Earthly Joy (Theodore Edson Perkins)

MASON, JOHN
823.  Now from the altar of our hearts,/Let warmest thanks arise
HMEC-99.  Warwick (Samuel Stanley)
MH (2905)-46.  Parker (Karl Pomeroy Harrington)

MASON, WILLIAM
824.  Again returns the day of holy rest/Which, when He made the
world
AMEH-591.  Pax Dei (John Bacchus Dykes)

MASSIE, RICHARD
825.  Christ Jesus lay in death's strong bands/For our offences
given (trans. from Martin Luther)
MH (1966)-438.  Christ Lag In Todesbanden (Johann Walther's
Geistliches Gesangbuchlein, Witten-
berg, 1524)
826.  I know no life divided,/O Lord of life, from Thee (trans.
from Carl Johann P. Spitta)
HMEC-755.  St. Hilda (Justin Heinrich Knecht)
MH (1905)-467.  Bentley (John Hullah)

MASTERMAN, JOHN HOWARD BERTRAM
827.  Lift up your hearts, O King of kings,/To brighter hopes and
kindlier things
MH (1935)-472.  Samson (George Frederick Handel)
MH (1966)-194.  Deus Tuorum Militum (Grenoble Antiphoner,
1868)

MATHESON, GEORGE
828.  Make me a captive, Lord,/And then I shall be free

            MH (1935)-367.  Leominster (George William Martin)
            MH (1966)-184.  Diademata (George Job Elvy)
    829.  O Love that wilt not let me go,/I rest my weary soul in Thee
            MH (1905)-481.  Margaret (Albert Lister Peace)
            MSSH-189.  Margaret (Albert Lister Peace)
            MH (1935)-318.  Margaret (Albert Lister Peace)
            AMEH-286.  Margaret (Albert Lister Peace)
            MH (1966)-234.  Margaret (Albert Lister Peace)

MATHESON, GREVILLE
    830.  O friend of souls! how blest the time/When in Thy love I
            rest (trans. from Wolfgang Chrsitoph Dessler)
            HMEC-613.  St. Augustine (John Black)

MATTHIAS, JOHN B.
    831.  I saw a way-worn trav'ler/In tattered garments clad
            AMEH-526.  Deliverance Will Come (John B. Matthias)

MAUDE, MARY FAWLER
    832.  Thine forever!--God of love,/Hear us from Thy throne above
            HMEC-465.  Fisk (Calvin S. Harrington)

MAXWELL, MARY HAMLIN
    833.  God hath said, "Forever blessed/Thou who seek me in their
            youth. . . ."
            HMEC-873.  Saviour, Like a Shepherd (William Batchelder Brad-
                        bury)

McCHEYNE, ROBERT MURRAY
    834.  When this passing world is done, When has sunk yon gleaming
            sun
            HMEC-1079.  Gethsemane (Richard Redhead)

McCOMB, WILLIAM
    835.  Chief of sinners though I be,/Jesus shed His blood for me
            HMEC-441.  Repose (Joseph Perry Holbrook)

McCONNELL, CLAUDIA
    836.  Oh! God we lift our hearts to Thee,/May praise be not in
            vain
            AMEH-148.  Metropolitan (John T. Layton)

McDANIEL, RUFUS H.
    837.  What a wonderful change in my life has been wrought!/Since
            Jesus came into my heart!
            AMEH-491.  What a Wonderful Change (Charles H. Gabriel)

McDONALD, WILLIAM
    838.  I am coming to the cross;/I am poor, and weak, and blind
            MH (1905)-351.  I Am Coming to the Cross (William Gustavus
                            Fischer)
            MH (1935)-246.  I Am Coming to the Cross (William Gustavus
                            Fischer)
            MH (1966)-116.  I Am Coming to the Cross (William Gustavus
                            Fischer)

McGREGOR, ERNEST FRANK
838. Lift high the trumpet song today!/From Olivet to Calvary
    MH (1935)-131. Suomi (Finnish cavalry march

McWHOOD, LEONARD BEECHER
840. All people of the earth,/Share but one common birth
    MH (1935)-508. Hymn of Nations (Leonard Beecher McWhood)

MEDLEY, SAMUEL
841. Awake, my soul, to joyful lays,/And sing thy great Redeemer's
    praise)
    MH (1905)-539. All Saints (William Knapp)
                   Loving-Kindness (William Caldwell)
    AMEH-142. Loving Kindness (William Caldwell)
842. I know that my Redeemer lives;/What joy the blest assurance
    gives
    HMEC-242. Ortonville (Thomas Hastings)
    MH (1905)-168. Truro (Charles Burney)
    MH (1935)-329. Truro (Charles Burney)
    MH (1966)-445. Truro (Charles Burney)
843. Mortals awake, with angels join,/And chant the solemn lay
    HMEC-193. Christmas (George Frederick Handel)
844. O could I speak the matchless worth,/O could I sound the
    glories forth
    HMEC-743. Ariel (Lowell Mason)
    MH (1905)-540. Ariel (Lowell Mason)
    MSSH-24. Ariel (Lowell Mason)
    MH (1935)-168. Ariel (Lowell Mason)
    AMEH-152. Ariel (Lowell Mason)
    MH (1966)-168. Ariel (Lowell Mason)
845. O what amazing words of grace/Are in the gospel found
    HMEC-323. Hummel (Heinrich Christopher Zeuner)
    MH (1905)-292. Hummel (Heinrich Christopher Zeuner)
    AMEH-419. Cambridge (John Randall)

MERRICK, JAMES
846. Author of good, we rest on Thee;/Thine ever watchful eye
    HMEC-617. Caddo (William Batchelder Bradbury)

MERRILL, WILLIAM PIERSON
847. Not alone for mighty empire,/Stretching far o'er land and
    sea
    MH (1935)-543. Hyfrydol (Rowland Hugh Prichard)
848. Rise up, O men of God!/Have done with lesser things
    MH (1935)-267. Festal Song (William Henry Walter)
                   Oxnam (Robert Gut McCutchan)
    AMEH-421. Festal Song (William Henry Walter)
    MH (1966)-174. Festal Song (William Henry Walter)

MIDLANE, ALBERT
849. "All things are ready," come,/Come to the supper spread
    HMEC-357. Olney (Lowell Mason)
850. News for little children!/Hark! how sweet the sound
    MSSH-122. Midlane (Thomas H. Smithers)
851. There's a Friend for little children,/Above the bright blue
    sky

MH (1905)-680. Edengrove (Samuel Smith)
MSSH-33. Edengrove (Samuel Smith)

MILES, C. AUSTIN
852. I come to the garden alone,/While the dew is still on the
roses
AMEH-498. In the Garden (C. Austin Miles)

MILLER, EMILY HUNTINGTON
853. Enter the temple, glorious King!/And write Thy name upon its
shrine
HMEC-862. Hursley (Peter Ritter, arr. William Henry Monk)
854. "God of all comfort," calm and fair,/Stretch the broad plains
beneath Thine eye
MSSH-29. God of All Comfort (Lucy Rider Meyer)
855. I love to hear the story/Which angel voices tell
HMEC-886. Tivoli (Edward John Hopkins)
856. Tell the blessed tidings,/Children of the King
MH (1905)-652. Deva (Edward John Hopkins)
MH (1935)-445. Deva (Edward John Hopkins)

MILLIGAN, JAMES LEWIS
857. There's a voice in the wilderness crying,/A call from the
ways untrod
MH (1935)-503. Hereford (Francis Donaldson Heins)
MH (1966)-362. Hereford (Francis Donaldson Heins)

MILMAN, HENRY HART
858. Bound up on th' accursed tree,/Faint and bleeding, who is
He?
AMEH-157. Spanish Hymn (Benjamin Carr)
859. Ride on, ride on in majesty!/Hark! all the tribes Hosanna
cry
MH (1905)-150. St. Drostane (John Bacchus Dykes)
MSSH-85. Winchester New (Musikalisches Handbuch, 1690)
MH (1935)-125. St. Drostane (John Bacchus Dykes)
MH (1966)-425. The King's Majesty (Graham George)

MILTON, JOHN
860. How lovely are Thy dwellings, Lord,/From noise and trouble
free!
HMEC-769. Zion (Thomas Hastings)
861. Let us with a gladsome mind,/Praise the Lord for He is kind
HMEC-145. Dix (William Henry Monk)
MH (1935)-81. Innicents (The Parish Choir, 1850)
MH (1966)-61. Innicents (The Parish Choir, 1850)
862. The Lord will come and not be slow;/His footsteps cannot err
HMEC-468. Newbold (George Kingsley)
MH (1905)-642. Eagley (James Walch)
MH (1966)-468. Old 107th (Genevan Psalter, 1547)

MOMENT, JOHN JAMES
863. Men and children everywhere,/With sweet music fill the air!
MH (1966)-11. Rock of Ages (Hebrew traditional)

MONOD, THEODORE
    864.  O the bitter shame and sorrow,/That a time could ever be
           MH (1905)-380.  Tetworth (George Munsell Garrett)
           MH (1935)-215.  St. Jude (Charles John Vincent)

MONSELL, JOHN SAMUEL BEWLEY
    865.  Awake! glad soul! awake! awake!/Thy Lord has risen long
           HMEC-232.  Colman (George Kingsley)
           MSSH-93.  Spes Coelestis (W.A. Smith)
           AMEH-102.  Arlington (Thomas Augustine Arne)
    866.  Fight the good fight with all thy might,/Christ is thy stren-
          gth, and Christ thy right
           MH (1905)-409.  Pentecost (William Boyd)
           MSSH-218.  Pentecost (William Boyd)
           MH (1935)-286.  Pentecost (William Boyd)
           MH (1966)-240.  Grace Church, Gananoque (Graham George)
           MH (1966)-241.  Pentecost (William Boyd)
    867.  God is love, by Him upholden/Hang the glorious orbs of light
           MSSH-7.  Regent Square (Henry Smart)
           MH (1966)-62.  Wylde Green (Peter Cutts)
    868.  Laboring and heavy laden,/Wanting help in time of need
           HMEC-732.  Dulcetta (Ludwig van Beethoven)
    869.  Light of the world, we hail Thee,/Flushing the eastern skies
           MH (1935)-114.  Salve Domine (Lawrence White Watson)
           AMEH-48.  Salve Domine (Lawrence White Watson)
           MH (1966)-398.  Complainer (William Walker)
    870.  Lord of the living harvest/That whitens o'er the plain
           HMEC-808.  Clare (Hubert Platt Main)
           MH (1905)-219.  Blairgowrie (John Bacchus Dykes)
           MH (1935)-401.  Missionary Hymn (Lowell Mason)
    871.  My head is low, my heart is sad,/My feet with travel torn
           HMEC-548.  Dedham (William Gardiner)
    872.  O Love, divine and golden,/Mysterious depth and height
           MH (1935)-430.  Blairgowrie (John Bacchus Dykes)
    873.  O Love divine and tender!/That through our homes doth move
           HMEC-1106.  Bolton (John Walsh)
    874. O my God, how Thy salvation/Fills my soul with peace and joy
           HMEC-729.  What a Friend We Have in Jesus (Charles Cro-
                    zat Converse)
    875.  O'er the distant mountains breaking,/Comes the redeeming
          dawn of day
           HMEC-1015.  Pilgrimage (Unknown)
    876.  On our way rejoicing,/As we homeward move
           MSSH-26.  St. Alban (Franz Joseph Haydn)
    877.  Sing to the Lord of harvest!/Sing songs of love and praise!
           HMEC-1085.  St. James (Unknown)
    878.  To Thee, O dear, dear Saviour!/My spirit turns for rest
           MH (1905)-324.  Savoy Chapel (John Baptiste Calkin)
    879.  What grace, O Lord, and beauty shone/Around Thy steps below
           MH (1966)-178.  Christus, Der Ist Mein Leben (Melchoir
                    Vulpius)

MONTGOMERY, JAMES
    880.  According to Thy gracious word,/In meek humility
           HMEC-836.  Dundee (Guillaume Franc)

MH (1905)-234.  St. John's Westminster (James Turle)
MH (1935)-410.  St. John's Westminster (James Turle)
AMEH-323.  Moore (Samuel Webbe)
MH (1966)-316.  Tallis' Ordinal (Thomas Tallis)
881.  Almighty Spirit, now behold/A world by sin destroyed
HMEC-916.  Newbold (George Kingsley)
882.  Angels from the realms of glory,/Wing your flight o'er all
the earth
HMEC-189.  Helmsley (Thomas Olivers)
MH (1905)-113.  Regent Square (Henry Smart)
MSSH-74.  Regent Square (Henry Smart)
MH (1935)-87.  Regent Square (Henry Smart)
AMEH-99.  Regent Square (Henry Smart)
MH (1966)-382.  Regent Square (Henry Smart)
883.  Be known to us in breaking bread,/But do not then depart
MH (1935)-408.  Dundee (Scottish Psalter)
MH (1966)-313.  St. Flavian (Day's Psalter, 1562)
884.  Behold the Christian warrior stand/In all the armour of his
God
HMEC-599.  Missionary Chant (Heinrich Christopher Zeuner)
MH (1905)-397.  Missionary Chant (Heinrich Christopher
Zeuner)
885.  Bright and joyful is the morn,/For to us a Child is born
HMEC-191.  Herald Angels (Felix Mendelssohn-Bartholdy)
886.  Come at the morning hour,/Come, let us kneel and pray
HMEC-750.  Whitefield (Edward Miller)
887.  Come in, thou blessed of the Lord,/Stranger nor foe art thou
HMEC-781.  Hermon (Lowell Mason)
888.  Come to Calvary's holy mountain,/Sinners ruined by the fall
HMEC-341.  Neander (Joachim Neander)
AMEH-336.  Regent Square (Henry Smart)
889.  Daughter of Zion, from the dust/Exalt thy fallen head
HMEC-909.  Hummel (Heinrich Christopher Zeuner)
890.  Father of all our mercies, Thou/In whom we move and live
AMEH-660.  Without tune
891.  Father of eternal grace,/Glorify Thyself in me
HMEC-464.  Aletta (William Batchelder Bradbury)
892.  "Forever with the Lord!"/Amen, so let it be!
HMEC-1050.  Vigil (St. Alban's Tune Book)
MH (1905)-625.  Vigil (Giovanni Paisiello)
AMEH-467.  St. Thomas (George Frederick Handel)
893.  Friend after friend departs:/Who hath not lost a friend?
HMEC-1009.  Requiem (Thomas Hastings)
MH (1905)-587.  Bath (William Henry Cooke)
894.  Go to dark Gethsemane,/Ye that feel the tempter's power
HMEC-223.  Gethsemane (Richard Redhead)
MH (1966)-434.  Redhead (Richard Redhead)
895.  God is my strong salvation;/What foe have I to fear?
HMEC-639.  Aurelia (Samuel Sebastian Wesley)
MH (1905)-448.  Jerusalem (John Stainer)
Aurelia (Samuel Sebastian Wesley)
MSSH-198.  Aurelia (Samuel Sebastian Wesley)
MH (1935)-324.  Aurelia (Samuel Sebastian Wesley)
MH (1966)-211.  Wedlock (The Sacred Harp, 1844)
896.  God is our refuge and defense;/In trouble our unfailing aid
HMEC-168.  St. Peter (from a German chorale)

MH (1905)-97. St. Peter (from a German chorale)

897. Grant me within Thy courts a place,/Among Thy saints a seat
HMEC-660. Clinton (Joseph Perry Holbrook)

898. Hail to the Lord's anointed,/Great David's greater son
HMEC-181. St. James (Johann Lindemann)
MH (1905)-650. Ellacombe (German traditional)
MSSH-59. Ellacombe (German traditional)
MH (1935)-85. Ellacombe (German traditional)
MH (1966)-359. Ellacombe (German traditional)

899. Hark! the song of jubilee;/Loud as mighty thunders roar
HMEC-938. Eltham (Lowell Mason)
MH (1905)-646. St. George's, Windsor (George Job Elvy)

900. Hosanna! be the children's song,/To Christ, the children's
King
HMEC-882. Colman (George Kingsley)
MH (1905)-679. Hummel (Heinrich Christopher Zeuner)

901. In the hour of trial, Jesus, plead for me;/Lest by base de-
nial, I depart from Thee
MH (1905)-431. Penitence (Spencer Lane)
MH (1935)-274. Penitence (Spencer Lane)
AMEH-147. Penitence (Spencer Lane)
MH (1966)-237. Penitence (Spencer Lane)

902. Lord, God, the Holy Ghost!/In this accepted hour
HMEC-286. State Street (Jonathan Call Woodman)

903. Lord, let me know mine end,/My days, how brief their date
HMEC-959. Shawmut (Lowell Mason)

904. Lord of hosts! to Thee we raise/Here a house of prayer and
praise
HMEC-858. Regent Square (Henry Smart)

905. Lord, teach Thy servants how to pray/With reverence and with
fear
AMEH-433. Coventry (Unknown)

906. Millions within Thy courts have met,/Millions this day before Thee bowed
HMEC-79. Overberg (Johann Christian Heinrich Rink)

907. Not here, as to the prophet's eye,/The Lord upon His throne
appears
HMEC-40. Miller (Carl Philip Emmanuel Bach, arr. Edward
Miller)

908. O for the death of those/Who slumber in the Lord!
HMEC-990. Owen (Joseph Emerson Sweetser)

909. O God, Thou art my God alone;/Early to Thee my soul shall
cry
HMEC-693. Welton (Henri Abraham Caesar Malan)

910. O Spirit of the living God,/In all Thy plenitude of grace
HMEC-276. Melcombe (Samuel Webbe)
MH (1905)-188. Keble (John Bacchus Dykes)
AMEH-416. Retreat (Thomas Hastings)

911. O where shall rest be found,/Rest for the weary soul?
HMEC-358. Capello (Lowell Mason)
MH (1905)-250. Ferniehurst(from The Church Hymnal)
AMEH-648. Dover (Aaron Williams)

912. O who, in such a world as this,/Could bear his lot of pain
HMEC-663. Heber (George Kingsley)

913. Our heavenly Father, hear/The prayer we offer now
AMEH-390. Silver Street (Isaac Smith)

914. Out of the depths of woe,/To Thee, O Lord, I cry
     HMEC-403.  Owen (Joseph Emerson Sweetser)
915. Pour out Thy spirit from on high;/Lord, Thine ordained ser-
     vants bless
     MH (1966)-337.  Herr Jesu Christ, Mein Leben Licht (Hymno-
                            dus Sacer, 1625)
916. Prayer is the soul's sincere desire,/Uttered or unexpressed
     HMEC-710.  Woodstock (Deodatus Dutton, Jr.)
     MH (1935)-303.  Camp Meeting (American traditional)
     AMEH-185.  Heber (George Kingsley)
     MH (1966)-252.  Shaddick (Bates G. Burt)
917. Rest from thy labor, rest,/Soul of the just, set free!
     HMEC-992.  Owen (Joseph Emerson Sweetser)
918. Servant of God, well done!/Rest from thy loved employ
     MH (1905)-597.  Nearer Home (Isaac Baker Woodbury, arr.
                            Arthur Seymour Sullivan)
     AMEH-463.  Dover (Aaron Williams)
919. Servants of God, in joyful lays,/Sing ye the Lord Jehovah's
     praise
     HMEC-68.  Duke Street (John Hatton)
920. Songs of praise the angels sang,/Heaven with hallelujahs
     rang
     HMEC-24.  Monkland (John B. Wilkes)
921. Sow in the morn thy seed;/At eve hold not thy hand
     HMEC-575.  Boylston (Lowell Mason)
     MH (1905)-389.  Veni (John Stainer)
922. Spirit, leave thy house of clay;/Lingering dust, resign thy
     breath!
     HMEC-1000.  Leavitt (Joseph Perry Holbrook)
923. Stand up, and bless the Lord,/Ye people of His choice
     HMEC-5.  Silver Street (Isaac Smith)
     MH (1935)-39.  Old 134th/St. Michael (Genevan Psalter,
                            1551)
     MH (1966)-16.  St. Michael (William Crotch)
924. Thank and praise Jehovah's name;/For His mercies, firm and
     sure
     HMEC-25.  Monkland (John B. Wilkes)
925. The glorious universe around,/The heavens with all their
     train
     HMEC-788.  Hummel (Heinrich Christopher Zeuner)
926. The God of harvest praise;/In loud thanksgiving raise
     HMEC-1087.  Righini (Vincenzo Righini)
927. The Lord is my Shepherd, no want shall I knoe;/I feed in
     green pastures, safe-folded  I rest
     HMEC-179.  Portuguese Hymn (John Francis Wade)
     MH (1905)-104.  Good Shepherd (Joseph Barnby)
                            Judea (John Bacchus Dykes)
     AMEH-76.  Poland (Thomas Koschat)
928. The tempter to my soul hath siad,/"There is no help in God
     for thee"
     HMEC-165.  Hamburg (Lowell Mason)
929. This stone to Thee in faith we lay;/To Thee this temple,
     Lord, we build
     HMEC-861.  Duke Street (John Hatton)
930. Thither the tribes repair,/Where all are wont to meet
     HMEC-89.  Thatcher (George Frederick Handel)

931. Thy word, Almighty Lord,/Where'er it enters in
     HMEC-288. Dover (Aaron Williams)
932. We bid thee welcome in the name/Of Jesus, our exalted Head
     MH (1905)-226. Keble (John Bacchus Dykes)
933. What is the thing of greatest price,/The whole creation
     round?
     MH (1905)-243. Burlington (John Freckleton Burrowes)
934. When on Sinai's top I see/God descend, in majesty
     HMEC-206. Aletta (William Batchelder Bradbury)
935. While through this world we roam,/From infancy to age
     HMEC-1048. Greek Hymn (Joseph Perry Holbrook)

MOORE, THOMAS
936. Come, ye disconsolate, where'er ye languish;/Come to the
     mercy-seat, fervently kneel
     HMEC-683. Come, Ye Disconsolate (Samuel Webbe)
     MH (1905)-526. Come, Ye Disconsolate (Samuel Webbe)
     MH (1935)-312. Consolation (Samuel Webbe)
     AMEH-232. Consolation (Samuel Webbe)
     MH (1966)-103. Consolator (Samuel Webbe, Sr.)
937. O Thou who driest the mourner's tear,/How dark this world
     would be
     HMEC-611. Naomi (Hans George Naegeli, arr. Lowell Mason)
     MH (1905)-522. Elm (John Varley Roberts)

MORE, HENRY
938. On all the earth Thy Spirit shower;/the earth in righteous-
     ness renew
     HMEC-268. Fulton (William Batchelder Bradbury)

MORRIS, MRS. C.H.
939. If you are tired of the load of your sin,/Let Jesus come in
     to your heart
     AMEH-344. Let Jesus Come into Your Heart (Mrs. C.H. Mor-
         ris)
940. Of Jesus' love that sought me,/When I was lost in sin
     AMEH-453. Sweeter As the Years Go By (Mrs. C.H. Morris)

MORRIS, GEORGE PERKINS
941. Man dieth and wasteth away,/And where is he?--Hark! from the
     skies
     HMEC-1012. Vernon (from the German)

MORRIS, S.S.
942. Hush! Hush! My soul be calm and still./Come blessed Saviour
     enter in
     AMEH-612. Hush! Hush! My Soul (E.C. Deas)

MORRISON, JOHN
943. Come, let us to the Lord our God/With contrite hearts re-
     turn
     HMEC-551. Church (Joseph Perry Holbrook)
944. The people that in darkness sat/A glorious light have seen
     MH (1966)-361. Caithness (Scottish Psalter, 1635)
945. The race that long in darkness pined/Have seen a glorious
     Light

AMEH-91.  Zerah (Lowell Mason)
946.  To us a Child of hope is born,/To us a Son is given
HMEC-184.  Antioch (George Frederick Handel)

MOTE, EDWARD
947.  My hope is built on nothing less/Than Jesus' blood and righ-
teousness
HMEC-421.  Evanston (Joseph Perry Holbrook)
MH (1905)-330.  The Solid Rock (William Batchelder Brad-
bury)
MSSH-163.  The Solid Rock (William Batchelder Bradbury)
MH (1935)-244.  The Solid Rock (William Batchelder Brad-
bury)
AMEH-393.  The Solid Rock (William Batchelder Bradbury)
MH (1966)-222.  The Solid Rack (William Batchelder Brad-
bury)

MOULE, HANDLEY CARR GLYN
948.  Lord and Saviour, true and kind/Be the Master of my mind
MH (1935)-560.  Boyce/Sharon (William Boyce)

MOULTRIE, GERARD
949.  We march, we march to victory,/With the cross of the Lord before us
MH (1905)-418.  The Good Fight (Joseph Barnby)
MSSH-223.  The Good Fight (Joseph Barnby)

MUHLENBERG, WILLIAM AUGUST
950.  I would not live alway; I ask not to stay/Where storm after
storm rises dark o'er the way
HMEC-998.  Frederick (George Kingsley)
MH (1905)-584.  Frederick (George Kingsley)
Goshen (Unknown)
951.  King of kings, and wilt Thou deign/O'er this wayward heart
to reign?
HMEC-945.  Horton (Xavier Schnyder Wartensee)
952.  Like Noah's weary dove,/That soared the earth around
HMEC-388 (F.R. Grey)
953.  Saviour, who Thy flock art feeding/With the Shepherd's
kindest care
HMEC-888.  Gaylord (Joseph Perry Holbrook)
MSSH-156.  St. Oswald (John Bacchus Dykes)
954.  Shout the glad tidings, exultingly sing,/Jerusalem triumphs,
Messiah is King!
MH (1905)-119.  Avison (Charles Avison)

MULHOLLAND, ROAS
955.  Give me, O Lord, a heart of grace,/A voice of joy, a shining
face
AMEH-514.  Brookfield (Thomas Bishop Southgate)

MUND, E.D.
956.  Amid the trials which I met,/Amid the thorns that pierce my
feet
AMEH-514.  Amid the Trials (Edmund S. Lorenz)

MURRAY, ROBERT
  957.  From ocean unto ocean/Our land shall own Thee Lord
        MH (1935)-476.  Lancashire (Henry Smart)

NEALE, JOHN MASON
  958.  All glory, laud, and honor/To Thee, Redeemer, King  (trans.
        Theodulph of Orleans)
        MH (1905)-31.  St. Theodulph (Melchoir Teschner)
        MSSH-84.  St. Theodulph (Melchoir Teschner)
        MH (1935)-128.  St. Theodulph (Melchoir Teschner)
        AMEH-403.  St. Theodulph (Melchoir Teschner)
        MH (1966)-424.  St. Theodulph (Melchoir Teschner)
  959.  Art thou weary, art thou languid,/Art thou sore distressed?
        MH (1905)-293.  Stephanos (Henry Williams Baker)
                  Bullinger (Ethelbert William Bullinger)
        MSSH-129.  Bullinger (Ethelbert William Bullinger)
        MH (1935)-193.  Stephanos (Henry Williams Baker)
        MH (1966)-99.  Stephanos (Henry Williams Baker)
  960.  Brief life is here our portion;/Brief sorrow, short-lived
        care (trans. from Bernard of Cluny)
        HMEC-1059.  Gauntlett (Henry John Gauntlett)
                  Webb (George James Webb)
  961.  Christ is made the sure Foundation,/Christ the Head and Cor-
        ner Stone (trans. from the Latin)
        HMEC-856.  Regent Square (Henry Smart)
        MH (1905)-662.  Regent Square (Henry Smart)
        AMEH-571.  Regent Square (Henry Smart)
        MH (1966)-298.  Regent Square (Henry Smart)
  962.  Christian, dost thou see them,/On the holy ground (trans.
        from Andrew of Crete)
        HMEC-1047.  Greek Hymn (Joseph Perry Holbrook)
        MH (1905)-616.  St. Andrew of Crete (John Bacchus Dykes)
                  Greek Hymn (Joseph Perry Holbrook)
        MSSH-183.  Greek Hymn (Joseph Perry Holbrook)
        MH (1935)-275.  St. Andrew of Crete (John Bacchus Dykes)
                  Greek Hymn (Joseph Perry Holbrook)
        MH (1966)-238.  Walda (Lloyd A. Pfautsch)
  963.  Come, ye faithful, raise the strain/Of triumphant gladness
        (trans. from John of Damascus)
        MH (1905)-163.  St. Kevin (Arthur Seymour Sullivan)
        MSSH-94.  St. Kevin (Arthur Seymour Sullivan)
        MH (1935)-151.  St. Kevin (Arthur Seymour Sullivan)
        MH (1966)-446.  St. Kevin (Arthur Seymour Sullivan)
        MH (1966)-448.  Ave Virginum (Leisentritt's Gesanbuch,
                  (1584)
  964.  Creator of the stars of night,/Thy people's everlasting
        light
        MH (1966)-78.  Conditor Alme (arr. Charles Winfred Doug-
                las)
  965.  For thee, O dear, dear country,/Mine eyes their vigils keep
        (trans. from Bernard of Cluny)
        HMEC-1060.  Bernard (Joseph Perry Holbrook)
        MH (1905)-614.  Rutherford (Cretien D'Urhan, arr. Edward
                Francis Rimbault)
                St. Geprge's, Bolton (James Walch)

966. Good Christian men, rejoice,/With heart and soul and voice
      (trans. from the Latin)
      MH (1935)-110.  In Dulce Jubilo (arr. Charles Winfred
                      Douglas)
      MH (1966)-391.  In Dulce Jubilo (arr. Charles Winfred
                      Douglas)
967. Jerusalem the golden,/With milk and honey blest (trans. from
      Bernard of Cluny)
      HMEC-1061.  Ewing (Alexander Ewing)
      MH (1905)-612.  Ewing (Alexander Ewing)
      MSSH-257.  Ewing (Alexander Ewing)
      MH (1935)-529.  Ewing (Alexander Ewing)
      AMEH-579.  Ewing (Alexander Ewing)
      MH (1966)-303.  Ewing (Alexander Ewing)
968. Joy dawned again on Easter Day,/The sun shone out with fai-
      rer ray (trans. from the Latin)
      MH (1935)-157.  Splendour/Puer Nobis Nascitur (Michael
                      Praetorius)
969. Lift up, lift up your voices now!/The whole wide world re-
      joices now
      AMEH-133.  Waltham (John Baptiste Calkin)
970. O come, O come, Emmanuel,/And ransom captive Israel (trans.
      from the Latin antiphon)
      MSSH-54.  Gounod (Charles Francois Gounod)
      MH (1935)-83.  Veni Immanuel (Ancient plain song, 13th
                     century)
      MH (1966)-354.  Veni Immanuel (Ancient plain song, 13th
                      century)
971. O happy band of pilgrims,/If onward ye will tread (trans.
      from Joseph of the Stadium)
      HMEC-640.  Aurelia (Samuel Sebastian Wesley)
      MSSH-197.  Vulpius (Melchoir Vulpius)
                 Felix (Felix Mendelssohn-Bartholdy, arr. Peter
                 Christian Lutkin)
972. O Lord of hosts, whose glory fills/The bounds of the eternal
      hills
      HMEC-859.  Duke Street (John Hatton)
      MH (1905)-658.  Alsace (Ludwig van Beethoven)
973. O sons and daughters, let us sing!/The King of heaven, the
      glorious King (trans. from Jean Tisserand)
      MH (1966)-451.  O Filii et Filiae (French carol)
974. O wondrous type!/O vision fair/Of glory that the Church
      shall share (trans. from the Sarum Breviary)
      HMEC-199.  Ames (Sigismund Neukomm, arr. Lowell Mason)
975. The day is past and over;/All thanks, O Lord, to Thee (trans.
      from Anatolius)
      MH (1935)-52.  Du Friedenfurst, Herr Jesu Christ (Bartho-
                     lomaus Gesius)
      MH (1966)-491.  Du Friedenfurst, Herr Jesu Christ (Bar-
                      tholomaus Gesius)
976. The day of resurrection!/Earth, tell it out abroad (trans.
      from John of Damascus)
      HMEC-230.  Mendebras (Lowell Mason)
      MH (1905)-164.  Rotterdam (Berthold Tours)
      MSSH-98.  Rotterdam (Berthold Tours)
      MH (1935)-159.  Rotterdam (Berthold Tours)

AMEH-108.  Lancashire (Henry Smart)
AMEH-395.  Rotterdam (Berthold Tours)
MH (1966)-437.  Lancashire (Henry Smart)
977.  The world is very evil,/The times are waxing late (trans.
      from Bernard of Cluny)
          HMEC-1058.  Rimbault (Charles D'Urhan, arr. Edward Fran-
                      cis Rimbault)

NEALE, JOHN MASON, and HENRY WILLIAMS BAKER
    978.  Of the Father's love begotten,/Ere the worlds began to be
          (trans. from Aurelius Clemens Prudentius)
              MH (1966)-357.  Divinum Mysterium (arr. Charles Winfred
                              Douglas)

NEEDHAM, JOHN
    979.  Rise, O my soul, pursue the paths/By ancient worthies trod
              MH (1905)-404.  Peterboro (Ralph Harrison)

NELSON, DAVID
    980.  My days are gliding swiftly by,/And I, a pilgrim stranger
              AMEH-470.  Shining Shore (George Frederick Root)

NEVIN, EDWIN HENRY
    981.  Always with us, always with us;--/Words of cheer and words
          of love
              HMEC-731.  Dulcetta (Ludwig van Beethoven)

NEWHALL, CHARLES STEDMAN
    982.  Jesus, Master, when today/I meet along the crowded way
              MH (1935)-470.  Beloit (Carl Gottlieb Reissiger)

NEWMAN, JOHN HENRY
    983.  Lead, kindly Light, amid the encircling gloom,/Lead Thou me
          on!
              HMEC-682.  Lux Benigna (John Bacchus Dykes)
              MH (1905)-460.  Lux Benigna (John Bacchus Dykes)
              MSSH-169.  Lux Benigna (John Bacchus Dykes)
              MH (1935)-514.  Lux Benigna (John Bacchus Dykes)
                              Sandon (Charles Henry Purday)
              AMEH-274.  Lead Kindly Light (John Bacchus Dykes)
              MH (1966)-272.  Lux Benigna (John Bacchus Dykes)
    984.  Praise to the Holiest in the height,/And in the depth we
          praise
              HMEC-207.  Dyer (Harvey C. Camp)
    985.  Unveil, O Lord, and on us shine/In glory and in grace
              HMEC-708.  Salome (Ludwig van Beethoven)

NEWTON, JOHN
    986.  Amazing grace! how sweet the sound,/That saved a wretch like
          me!
              HMEC-427.  Truman (Joseph Perry Holbrook)
              MH (1905)-309.  Simpson (Louis Spohr)
              MH (1935)-209.  Amazing Grace (Early American melody)
              AMEH-450.  Heber (George Kingsley)
              AMEH-457A.  Amazing Grace (Early American melody)
              MH (1966)-92.  Amazing Grace (Early American melody)

987. Approach, my soul, the mercy seat,/Where Jesus answers
        prayer
        MH (1905)-285. Soho (Joseph Barnby)
988. Behold the throne of grace;/The promise calls us near
        HMEC-498. Greenwood (Joseph Emerson Sweetser)
989. Come, my soul, thy suit prepare,/Jesus loves to answer
        prayer
        HMEC-718. Hendon (Henri Abraham Caesar Malan)
        MH (1905)-507. Hendon (Henri Abraham Caesar Malan)
990. Day of judjment, day of wonders!/Hark! the trumpet's awful
        sound
        HMEC-1029. Brest (Lowell Mason)
991. Dear Shepherd of Thy people, hear;/Thy presence now display
        MH (1935)-313. Somerset (William Henry Hewlett)
992. Glorious things of Thee are spoken,/Zion city of our God
        HMEC-776. Austria (Franz Joseph Haydn)
        MH (1905)-210. Austria (Franz Joseph Haydn)
        MSSH-115. Austria (Franz Joseph Haydn)
        MH (1935)-382. Austria (Franz Joseph Haydn)
        AMEH-12. Austria (Franz Joseph Haydn)
        MH (1966)-293. Austria (Franz Joseph Haydn)
993. Great Shepherd of Thy people, hear;/Thy presence now display
        (variant of #991 above)
        AMEH-420. Cambridge (John Randall)
994. How sweet the name of Jesus sounds/In a believer's ear!
        HMEC-316. St. Bernard (London Tune Book, 1875)
        MH (1905)-137. Holy Cross (James Clifft Wade)
        MSSH-21. St. Peter's, Oxford (Alexander Robert Reinagle)
        MH (1935)-347. Holy Cross (James Clifft Wade)
        AMEH-145. Evan (William Henry Havergal)
        AMEH-276. Elizabethtown (George Kingsley)
        MH (1966)-81. St. Peter (Alexander Robert Reinagle)
995. How tedious and tasteless the hours/When Jesus no longer I
        see!
        HMEC-747. Contrast (Lewis Edson)
        MH (1905)-538. Contrast (Lewis Edson)
        MH (1935)-349. Contrast (Lewis Edson)
        AMEH-231. DeFleury (Lewis Edson)
        AMEH-528. DeFleury (Lewis Edson)
996. In evil long I took delight,/Unawed by shame and fear
        HMEC-423. Evan (William Henry Havergal)
        AMEH-361. St. Agnes (John Bacchus Dykes)
997. Joy is fruit that will not grow/In nature's barren soil
        MH (1905)-546. Elizabethtown (George Kingsley)
        MH (1935)-357. Elizabethtown (George Kingsley)
998. Let worldly minds the world pursue;/It has no charms for me
        HMEC-516. Bridgman (Ludwig van Beethoven, arr. George
                                Kingsley)
999. Lord, I cannot let Thee go,/Till a blessing Thou bestow
        MH (1905)-514. Seymour (Carl Maria von Weber)
1000. May the grace of Christ our Saviour,/And the Father's bound-
        less love
        HMEC-53. Greenville (Jean Jacques Rousseau)
        MH (1905)-40. Sardis (Ludwig van Beethoven)
        MH (1935)-27. Sardis (Ludwig van Beethoven)
        MH (1966)-334. Stuttgart (Henry John Gauntlett)

1001. Now may He  who from the dead/Brought the Shepherd of the
        sheep
        HMEC-23.  Pleyel's Hymn (Ignace Pleyel)
1002. One there is above all others,/Well deserves the name of
        Friend
        MH (1905)-174.  Sanctuary (John Bacchus Dykes)
1003. Safely through another week,/God has brought us on our way
        MH (1905)-69.  Sabbath Morn (Lowell Mason)
        MH (1935)-393.  Sabbath Morn (Lowell Mason)
        MH (1966)-489.  Sabbath Morn (Lowell Mason)
1004. Sweet was the time when first I felt/The Saviour's pardoning
        blood
        HMEC-546.  Dedham (William Gardiner)
1005. Though troubles assail and dangers affright,/Though friends
        should  all fail, and foes all unite
        HMEC-141.  Lyons (Franz Joseph Haydn)
        MH (1905)-92.  Cobern (Henry John Gauntlett)
1006. While we pray for pardoning grace,/Through the dear Redee-
        mer's name
        HMEC-88.  Sabbath Morn (Lowell Mason)
1007. While, with ceaseless course, the sun/Hasted through the
        former year
        HMEC-956.  Benevento (Samuel Webbe)
        MH (1905)-574.  Benevento (Samuel Webbe)

NICHOL, HENRY ERNEST
    1008. Hark to the sound of voices!/Hark to the trams of feet
            MSSH-228.  Marching beneath the Banner (Henry Ernest Ni-
                chol)
    1009. We've a story to tell to the nations/That shall turn their
            hearts to the right
            MSSH-248.  Message (Henry Ernest Nichol)
            MH (1935)-501.  Message (Henry Ernest Nichol)
            MH (1966)-410.  Message (Henry Ernest Nichol)

NICHOLSON, JAMES
    1010. Lord Jesus, I long to be perfectly whole;/I want Thee for
            ever, to live in my soul
            AMEH-529.  Whiter Than Snow (William Gustavus Fischer)

NICKENS, J.T.
    1011. Thy thoughts concerning me, O God,/Are precious and divine
            AMEH-83.  Alleyne (J.T. Nickens)

NOEL, BAPTISTE WRIOTHESLEY
    1012. Jesus, the Lord of glory, died/That we may never die
            HMEC-255.  Heber (George Kingsley)
    1013. There's not a bird with lonely nest,/In pathless wood or
            mountain crest
            AMEH-75.  Wilmar (George Moss)

NOEL, CAROLINE MARIA
    1014. At the name of Jesus/Every knee shall bow
            MH (1966)-76.  King's Weston (Ralph Vaughan Williams)

NOEL, GERARD THOMAS
    1015.  If human kindness meets return,/And owns the grateful tie
           HMEC-839.  Simpson (Louis Spohr)
           MH (1905)-236.  Gerard (Arthur Seymour Sullivan)
    1016.  When musing sorrow weeps the past,/And mourns the present
           pain
           MH (1905)-455.  Beatitudo (John Bacchus Dykes)

NORTH, FRANK MASON
    1017.  Jesus, the calm that fills my breast,/No other heart than
           mine can give
           MH (1905)-549.  Waratah (Moses Smith Cross)
    1018.  O Master of the working world,/Who has the nations in Thy
           heart
           MH (1935)-480.  Melita (John Bacchus Dykes)
           MH (1966)-407.  Melita (John Bacchus Dykes)
    1019.  The world's astir!/The clouds of storm
           MH (1935)-562.  All Saints, New (Henry Stephen Cutler)
    1020.  Where cross the crowded ways of life,/Where sound the cries
           of race and clan
           MH (1905)-423.  Germany (Ludwig van Beethoven)
           MSSH-233.  Germany (Ludwig van Beethoven)
           MH (1935)-465.  Germany (Ludwig van Beethoven)
           AMEH-269.  Germany (Ludwig van Beethoven)
           MH (1966)-204.  Germany (Ludwig van Beethoven)

NUTTER, CHARLES
    1021.  Joy, joy, immortal joy!/The Lord is risen to reign
           MSSH-101.  Easter Joy (Peter Christian Lutkin)
    1022.  Our God is the sunshine gay,/And in the darkening shade
           MSSH-32.  Our God is the Sunshine Gay (Frank Moore Jef-
               fery)

OAKEY, EMILY SULLIVAN
    1023.  I am so glad that our Father in heaven/Tells of His love on
           the Book He has given
           MH (1935)-435.  Gladness (Philip Paul Bliss)

OAKELEY, FREDERICK
    1024.  O come, all ye faithful,/Joyful and triumphant (trans. from
           the Latin)
           MSSH-71.  Adeste Fideles/Portugues Hymn (John F. Wade's
               Cantus Diversi, 1751)
           MH (1935)-96.  Adeste Fideles/Portuguese Hymn (John F.
               Wade's Cantus Diversi, 1751)
           AMEH-88.  Adeste Fideles/Portuguese Hymn (John F. Wade's
               Cantus Diversi, 1751)
           MH (1966)-386.  Adeste Fideles (John F. Wade)

OATMAN, JOHNSON, JR.
    1025.  How to reach the masses, men of every birth?/For an answer
           Jesus gave a key
           AMEH-324.  Lift Him Up (B.B. Beall)

OGDEN, WILLIAM A.
    1026.  I've a message from the Lord, Hallelujah!/The message unto
            you I'll give
            AMEH-509.  I've a Message from the Lord

OLIVERS, THOMAS
    1027.  O Thou God of my salvation,/My Redeemer from all sin
            HMEC-733.  Regent Square (Henry Smart)
            MH (1905)-25.  Regent Square (Henry Smart)
    1028.  The God of Abraham praise,/All praises be His name (see
            also 1029 and 1030)
            MH (1935)-5.  Leoni(Hebrew "Yigdal," arr. Lowell Mason)
    1029.  The God of Abraham praise,/At whose supreme command (see
            also 1028 and 1030)
            MH (1905)-4.  Leoni (Hebrew "Yigdal," arr. Lowell Mason)
            MSSH-23.  Leoni (Hebrew "Yogdal," arr. Lowell Mason)
    1030.  The God of Abrah'm praise,/Who reigns enthroned above (see
            also 1028 and 1029)
            HMEC-1075.  Leoni (Meyer Leoni)
            AMEH-22.  Leoni (Meyer Leoni)
    1031.  The God who reigns on high/The great Archangels sing (va-
            riant of 1028-1030)
            HMEC-1077.  Leoni (Meyer Leoni)
    1032.  Though nature's strength decay,/And earth and hell with-
            stand
            HMEC-1076.  Leoni (Meyer Leoni)

OLSON, ERNEST WILLIAM
    1033.  Children of the heavenly Father/Safely in His bosom gather
            (trans. from Caroline Vilhelmina Sandell Berg)
            MH (1966)-521.  Tryggare Kan Ingen Vara (Swedish melody)

OPIE, AMELIA
    1034.  There seems a voice in every gale,/A tongue in every flower
            HMEC-122.  Oxford (William Coombs)
    1035.  We have heard a joyful sound: Jesus saves!/Tell the mes-
            sage all around: Jesus saves!
            MSSH-126.  Jesus Saves (William J. Kirkpatrick)

OXENHAM, JOHN
    1036.  In Christ there is no East or West,/In Him no South or
            North
            MH (1935)-507.  St. Peter (Alexander Robert Reinagle)
            MH (1966)-192.  St. Peter (Alexander Robert Reinagle)
    1037.  'Mid all the traffic of the ways--/Turmoils without, with-
            in
            MH (1935)-341.  St. Agnes (John Bacchus Dykes)
            MH (1966)-225.  Horsley (William Horsley)

P., F.B., and WILLIAM PRID
    1038.  O mother dear, Jerusalem!/When shall I come to thee
            MH (1905)-610.  Materna (Samuel Augustus Ward)
            MSSH-258.  Materna (Samuel Augustus Ward)

PAGE, KATE STEARNS
    1039.  We, Thy people, praise Thee,/God of every nation!

MH (1966)-6.  St. Anthony's Chorale (Franz Joseph Haydn,
arr. Edith Lovell Thomas)

PALGRAVE, FRANCIS TURNER
1040.  Star of morn and even,/Sun of highest heaven
MSSH-45.  Rogers Park (Robert W. Vasey)

PALMER, HORATIO RICHMOND
1041.  Yield not to temptation,/For yielding is sin
MSSH-187.  Yield Not (Horatio Richmond Palmer)
AMEH-582.  Yield Not (Horatio Richmond Palmer)

PALMER, RAY
1042.  And is there, Lord, a rest,/For weary souls designed
HMEC-1055.  Haverhill (Lowell Mason)
1043.  Come, Holy Ghost, in love,/Shed on us from above (trans.
from Robert II, King of France)
HMEC-284.  New Haven (Thomas Hastings)
MH (1905)-184.  Bethel (John Henry Cornell)
Olivet (Lowell Mason)
MH (1935)-176.  Olivet (Lowell Mason)
1044.  Eternal Father, Thou hast said,/That Christ all glory shall
obtain
HMEC-921.  Arnheim (Samuel Holyoke)
1045.  Jesus, these eyes have never seen/That radiant form of
Thine
HMEC-714.  Woodstock (Deodatus Dutton, Jr.)
MH (1905)-537.  Radiance (Joseph Smith)
1046.  Jesus, Thy joy of loving hearts!/Thou Fount of Life! Thou
Light of men! (trans. from Bernard of Clairvaux)
HMEC-691.  Welton (Henri Abraham Caesar Malan)
MH (1905)-536.  Westcott (Joseph Barnby)
MH (1935)-345.  Rimington (Francis Duckworth)
MH (1966)-329.  Rockingham/Mason (Lowell Mason)
1047.  My faith looks up to Thee,/Thou Lamb of Calvary
HMEC-762.  Olivet (Lowell Mason)
New Haven (Thomas Billings)
MH (1905)-334.  Bethel (John Henry Cornell)
Olivet (Lowell Mason)
MSSH-176.  Olivet (Lowell Mason)
MH (1935)-213.  Olivet (Lowell Mason)
AMEH-179.  Olivet (Lowell Mason)
MH (1966)-143.  Olivet (Lowell Mason)
1048.  O bread to pilgrims given,/O food that angels eat (trans.
from the Latin)
HMEC-849.  Innocents (William Henry Monk)
1049.  O Christ, our King, Creator, Lord,/Saviour of all who trust
Thy word (trans. from Gregory the Great)
HMEC-240.  Ware (George Kingsley)
1050.  With Thine own pity, Savior, see!/The thronged and darken-
ing way!
MH (1966) 340.  Grafenberg (Johann Cruger)

PARK, JOHN EDGAR
1051.  We would see Jesus; lo!/His star is shining

MH (1935)-113.  Cushman (Herbert B. Turner)
MH (1966)-90.  Cushman (Herbert B. Turner)

PARK, ROSWELL
1052.  Jesus spreads His banner o'er us,/Cheers our famished
          souls with food
          HMEC-853.  Autumn (Francois Hippolyte Berthelemon)
          MH (1905)-235.  Autumn (Francois Hippolyte Barthelemon)
          MH (1935)-411.  Autumn (Francois Hippolyte Barthelemon)
          MH (1966)-331.  Autumn (Francois Hippolyte Barthelemon)

PARKER, EDWIN POND
1053.  Lord, as we Thy Name profess,/May our hearts Thy love con-
          fess
          MH (1935)-295.  Savannah (London Foundery Collection,
                    1742)
1054.  Master, no offering/Costly and sweet
          MH (1935)-464.  Love's Offering (Edwin Pond Parker)

PARKER, WILLIAM HENRY
1055.  Holy Spirit, hear us;/Help us while we sing
          AMEH-556.  Ernstein (James Frederick Swift)
1056.  Tell me the stories of Jesus I love to hear;/Things I would
          ask Him to tell me
          MH (1935)-441.  Stories of Jesus (Frederic  Arthur Chal-
                    linor)
          AMEH-150.  Stories of Jesus (Frederic Arthur Challinor)
          MH (1966)-88.  Stories of Jesus (Frederic Arthur Challi-
                    nor)

PARKIN, CHARLES
1057.  See the morning sun ascending,/Radiant in the eastern sky
          MH (1966)-7.  Unser Herrscher (Joachim Neander)

PARTRIDGE, SYBIL F. (SISTER MARY XAVIER)
1058.  Lord, for tomorrow and its needs/I do not pray
          MSSH-178.  Vincent (Horatio Richmond Palmer)
          MH (1935)-314.  Vincent (Horatio Richmond Palmer)
          AMEH-486.  Vincent (Horatio Vincent Palmer)

PEABODY, WILLIAM BOURN OLIVER
1059.  Behold the western evening light!/It melts in deepening
          gloom
          HMEC-974.  Ditson (Unknown)
1060.  Who is thy neighbor? He whom thou/Hast power to aid or
          bless
          HMEC-898.  Return (Theodore Freelinghuysen Seward)
          MH (1905)-690.  Dalehurst (Arthur Cottman)

PEACOCK, JOHN
1061.  Behold, what condescending love/Jesus on earth displays!
          HMEC-828.  Serenity (William Vincent Wallace)

PENNEFATHER, WILLIAM
1062.  Jesus, stand among us/In Thy risen power

AMEH-560. Vesper (Frederick A. Mann)

PENNEWELL, ALMER T.
    1063. So lowly doth the Savior ride/A paltry borrowed beast
        MH (1966)-422. Epworth Church (V. Earle Copes)

PERKINS, B.J.
    1064. Another soldier gone/To get a great reward
        AMEH-661. Without tune

PERRONET, EDWARD
    1065. All hail the power of Jesus' name!/Let angels prostrate
        fall
        HMEC-248. Coronation (Oliver Holden)
        MH (1905)-180. Coronation (Oliver Holden)
                    Miles' Lane (William Shrubsole)
        MSSH-103. Miles' Lane (William Shrubsole)
                 Coronation (Oliver Holden)
        MH (1935)-164. Coronation (Oliver Holden)
                    Miles' Lane (William Shrubsole)
                    Diadem (James Ellor)
        AMEH-3. Coronation (Oliver Holden)
        AMEH-4. Diadem (James Ellor)
        AMEH-438. Miles' Lane (William Shrubsole)
        MH (1966)-71. Coronation (Oliver Holden)
        MH (1966)-72. Diadem (William Ellor)
        MH (1966)-73. Miles' Lane (William Shrubsole)

PHELPS, SYLVANUS DRYDEN
    1066. Saviour, Thy dying love/Thou gavest me,/Nor should I aught
        withhold
        MH (1905)-349. Something for Jesus (Robert Lowry)
        MSSH-188. Something for Jesus (Robert Lowry)
        MSSH (1935)-219. Something for Jesus (Robert Lowry)
        AMEH-318. Something for Jesus (Robert Lowry)
        MH (1966)-177. Something for Jesus (Robert Lowry)

PHILLIPS, HARRIET
    1067. We bring no glittering treasures,/No gems from earth's
        deep mine
        HMEC-884. Miriam (Joseph Perry Holbrook)

PIERPONT, FOLLIOTT SANDFORD
    1068. For the beauty of the earth,/For the beauty of the skies
        MH (1905)-28. Dix (Conrad Kocher)
        MSSH-19. Dix (Conrad Kocher)
        MH (1935)-18. Dix (Conrad Kocher)
        AMEH-517. Dix (Conrad Kocher)
        MH (1966)-35. Dix (Conrad Kocher)

PIERPONT, JOHN
    1069. O Thou to whom, in ancient time,/The lyre of Hebrew bards
        was strung
        HMEC-36. Mainzer (Joseph Mainzer)
        MH (1905)-12. Doane (John Baptiste Calkin)

1070.  On this stone, now laid with prayer,/Let Thy Church rise
         strong and fair
         HMEC-857.  Regent Square (Henry Smart)
         MH (1905)-657.  Nuremberg (Johann Rudolf Ahle)
         MH (1935)-548.  Pleyel's Hymn (Ignace Josef Pleyel)
         MH (1966)-348.  Pleyel's Hymn (Ignace Joseph Pleyel)

PIERSON, ARTHUR TAPPAN
   1071.  Can it be right for me to go/On this dark, uncertain way?
         AMEH-353.  Can It Be Right? (Philip Paul Bliss)

PIERSON, HARRIET H.
   1072.  Go forth in shining armor to conquer in the strife,/For he
         that overcometh shall win the crown of life
         MSSH-234.  Victor Mundi (George A. Burdett)

PIGGOTT, WILLIAM CHARTER
   1073.  For those we love within the veil,/Who once were comrades
         of our way
         MH (1935)-425.  Meyer/Es Ist Kein Tag (Johann David Me-
                           yer)

PLUMPTRE, EDWARD HAYES
   1074.  Rejoice, ye pure in heart!/Rejoice, give thanks and sing!
         MH (1905)-421.  Marion (Arthur Henry Messiter)
         MH (1935)-358.  Marion (Arthur Henry Messiter)
         AMEH-51.  Marion (Arthur Henry Messiter)
         MH (1966)-233.  Merion (Arthur Henry Messiter)
   1075.  Thine arm, O Lord, in days of old/Was strong to heal and
         save
         AMEH-1099.  Palestrina (Giovanni Petri Aloysius Pales-
                       trina)

POLLARD, ADELAIDE ADDISON
   1076.  Have Thine own way, Lord! Have Thine own way!/Thou art the
         Potter, I am the clay
         AMEH-441.  Have Thine Own Way, Lord (George Coles Steb-
                     bins)
         MH (1966)-154.  Adelaide (George Coles Stebbins)

POLLOCK, THOMAS BENSON
   1077.  Jesus, with Thy Church abide;/Be her Saviour, Lord, and
         Guide
         MH (1935)-380.  Litany/Hervey (Frederick Alfred John Her-
                           vey)
         MH (1966)-311.  Canterbury (Orlando Gibbons)

POPE, ALEXANDER
   1078.  Vital spark of heavenly flame,/Quit, O quit this mortal
         frame)
         HMEC-969.  Venetia (Traditional English melody)

POTT, FRANCIS
   1079.  Angel voices, ever singing/Round Thy throne of light
         MH (1905)-27.  Angel Voices (Arthur Seymour Sullivan)

     MSSH-8.  Angel Voices (Arthur Seymour Sullivan)
     MH (1935)-15.  Angel Voices (Arthur Seymour Sullivan)
     MH (1966)-2.  Angel Voices (Arthur Seymour Sullivan)
  1080.  The strife is o'er, the battle done,/The victory of life is
      won (trans. from the Latin)
     MSSH-92.  Victory (Giovanni Pierluigi Palestrina)
     MH (1935)-156.  Victory (Giovanni Pierluigi Palestrina)
     AMEH-132.  Conqueror (Giovanni Pierluigi Palestrina)
     MH (1966)-447.  Victory (Giovanni Pierluigi Palestrina)
  1081.  The year is gone, beyond recall,/With all its hopes and
      fears (trans. from the Poictiers Breviary)
     HMEC-949.  Frome (Hugh Bond)

POTTER, THOMAS JOSEPH
  1082.  Brightly gleams our banner,/Pointing to the sky
     MH (1905)-681.  St. Theresa (Arthur Seymour Sullivan)
     MSSH-28.  St. Theresa (Arthur Seymour Sullivan)
     MH (1935)-446.  St. Theresa (Arthur Seymour Sullivan)

POUNDS, JESSIE H. BROWN
  1083.  Somewhere the sun is shining,/Somewhere the songbirds dwell
     AMEH-458.  Somewhere the Sun Is Shining (J.S. Fearis)

PRENTISS, ELIZABETH PAYSON
  1084.  More love to Thee, O Christ,/More love to Thee!
     HMEC-725.  More Love to Thee (William Howard Doane)
     MH (1905)-317.  More Love to Thee (William Howard Doane)
     MSSH-165.  More Love to Thee (William Howard Dpane)
     MH (1935)-364.  More Love to Thee (William Howard Doane)
     AMEH-315.  More Love to Thee (William Howard Doane)
     MH (1966)-185.  More Love to Thee (William Howard Dpane)

PROCTER, ADELAIDE ANNE
  1085.  I do not ask, O Lord, that life may be/A pleasant road
     MH (1905)-542.  Orono (Karl Pomeroy Harrington)
  1086.  My God, I thank Thee, Who hast made/The earth so bright
     MH (1905)-29.  Wentworth (Frederick Charles Maker)
     MH (1935)-9.  Wentworth (Frederick Charles Maker)
        Fowler (Robert Guy McCutchan)
     MH (1966)-50.  Wentworth (Frederick Charles Maker)
  1087.  The shadows of the evening hours/Fall from the darkening
      sky
     MH (1905)-62.  St. Leonard (Henry Hiles)
     MH (1935)-46.  St. Leonard (Henry Hiles)
     AMEH-23.  St. Leonard (Henry Hiles)

PRYNNE, GEORGE RUNDLE
  1088.  Jesus, meek and gentle,/Son of God most high
     MH (1905)-685.  Moore (Karl Pomeroy Harrington)

PIPER, MARY
  1089.  "We shall see Him," in our nature,/Seated on His lofty
      throne
     HMEC-247.  Scudamore (Richard Robert Chope)

RAFFLES, THOMAS
    1090.  Blest hour, when mortal man retires/To hold communion with
           his God
           HMEC-45.  Malvern (Lowell Mason)
    1091.  High in yonder realm of light/Dwell the raptured saints
           above
           HMEC-1067.  Beulah (Elam Ives, Jr.)
    1092.  Sovereign Ruler, Lord of all,/Prostrate at Thy feet I fall
           HMEC-380.  Pleyel's Hymn (Ignace Josef Playel)

RAMSEY, WILL M.
    1093.  'Tis the story grand and true,/Of the Lord who died for you
           AMEH-189.  Ring It Out with a Shout (Carrie I. Booker)

RANKIN, JEREMIAH EAMES
    1094.  God be with you till we meet again!/By His counsels guide,
           uphold you
           MH (1905)-564.  God Be with You (William Gould Tomer)
           MSSH-41.  Rankin (William Gould Tomer)
           MH (1935)-557.  God Be with You (William Gould Tomer)
           AMEH-444.  God Be with You (William Gould Tomer)
           MH (1966)-539.  God Be with You (William Gould Tomer)
           MH (1966)-540.  Randolph (Ralph Vaughan Williams)

RAWNSLEY, HARDWICKE DRUMMOND
    1095.  Father, whose will is life and good/For all of mortal
           breath
           MH (1935)-478.  Tallis' Ordinal (Thomas Tallis)
    1096.  O God, whose will is life and good/For all of mortal breath
           (Variation of 1095)
           MH (1966)-411.  Tallis' Ordinal (Thomas Tallis)

RAWSON, GEORGE
    1097.  And will the mighty God,/Whom heaven cannot contain
           HMEC-499.  Greenwood (Joseph Emerson Sweetser)
           AMEH-26.  Greenwood (Joseph Emerson Sweetser)
    1098.  By Christ redeemed, in Christ restored,/We keep the memory
           adored
           HMEC-850.  Nauford (Arthur Seymour Sullivan)
           MH (1905)-239.  Hanford (Arthur Seymour Sullivan)

RAYMOND, ROSSITER WORTHINGTON
    1099.  Far out on the desolate billow/The sailor sails the sea
           MSSH-192.  Salutas (Friedrich Silcher)

REDDICK, D.W.
    1100.  Jesus, I love and praise and adore,/His blood atoned for me
           AMEH-367.  Jesus I Love and Praise Thee (D.W. Reddick)

REED, ANDREW
    1101.  Hear, O sinner, mercy hails you,/Now with sweetest voice
           she calls
           HMEC-343.  Neander (Joachim Neander)
    1102.  Holy Ghost, with light divine,/Shine upon this heart of

      mine

HMEC-267.  Fulton (William Batchelder Bradbury)

MH (1905)-185.  Fisk (Calvin Sears Harrington)

AMEH-197.  Mercy (Louis Moreau Gottschalk, arr. Edwin Pond Parker)

AMEH-205.  Seymour (Carl Maria von Weber)

1103.  I would be Thine: O take my heart,/And fill it with Thy love

HMEC-409.  Bemmerton (Henry Wellington Greatorex)

1104.  Spirit Divine, attend our prayer,/And make our hearts Thy home

HMEC-278.  St. Martin's (William Tans'ur)

MH (1905)-190.  Lambeth (William August Schulthes)

MH (1966)-461.  Ballerma (Francois Hippolyte Barthelemon)

REED, E.M.G.

1105.  Infant holy, Infant lowly,/For His bed a cattle stall (paraphrase from a Polish carol)

MH (1935)-105.  W Zlobie Lezy (Polish carol, arr. E.M.G. Reed)

MH (1966)-396.  W Zlobie Lezy (Polish carol, arr. E.M.G. Reed)

REED, ELIZABETH

1106.  O do not let the word depart,/And close thine eyes against the light

AMEH-262.  O Why Not To-Night? (J. Calvin Bushey)

REES, BRYN AUSTIN

1107.  Have faith in God, my heart,/Trust and be unafraid

MH (1966)-141.  Franconia (Johann Balthasar Koenig)

RICE, CAROLINE LAURA

1108.  Wilt Thou hear the voice of praise/Which the little children raise

HMEC-878.  New Brunswick (John Black)

MH (1905)-675.  Children's Praise (Joseph Barnby)

RICHARDS, LAURA E.

1109.  The little flowers came through the ground/At Easter time, at Easter time

MSSH-96.  Easter Time (Robert W. Vasey)

RICHARDSON, CHARLOTTE

1110.  O God, to Thee we raise our eyes;/Calm resignation we implore

HMEC-632.  Zephyr (William Batchelder Bradbury)

RILEY, ATHELSTANE

1111.  Ye watchers and ye holy ones,/Bright seraphs, cherubim and thrones

MH (1935)-6.  Lasst uns Erfreuen (from the Geistliche Kirchengesang, 1623)

MH (1966)-19.  Lasst uns Erfreuen (from the Geistliche Kirchengesang, 1623)

ROBBINS, HOWARD CHANDLER
     1112.   And have the bright immensities/Received our risen Lord
               MH (1966)-456.  Halifax (George Frederick Handel)

ROBERTS, DANIEL CRANE
     1113.   God of our fathers, whose almighty hand/Leads forth in beau-
               ty all the starry band
               MH (1905)-704.  National Hymn (George William Warren)
               MSSH-276.  National Hymn (George William Warren)
               MH (1935)-496.  National Hymn (George William Warren)
               AMEH-47.  National Hymn (George William Warren)
               MH (1966)-552.  National Hymn (George William Warren)

ROBERTS, THOMAS
     1114.   My Shepherd's mighty aid,/His dear redeeming love
               HMEC-761.  Browne (Mary Ann Browne)

ROBINS, GURDON
     1115.   There is a land mine eye hath seen/In visions of enraptured
               thought
               HMEC-1041.  Park Street (Frederick Marc Antoine Venua)

ROBINSON, GEORGE
     1116.   One sole baptismal sign,/One Lord below, above
               HMEC-800.  St. Ebbe (Richard Redhead)
            MH (1905)-559.  Samuel (Arthur Seymour Sullivan)
     1117.   When to the exiled seer were given/Those raptured views of
               highest heaven
               HMEC-864.  St. Faith (Unknown)

ROBINSON, RICHARD HAYES
     1118.   Holy Father, cheer our way/With Thy love's perpetual ray
               MH (1905)-56.  Vesperi Lux (John Bacchus Dykes)

ROBINSON, ROBERT
     1119.   Come, Thou Fount of every blessing,/Tune my heart to sing
               Thy grace
               HMEC-726.  Nettleton (John Wyeth)
               MH (1905)-19.  Nettleton (John Wyeth)
               MH (1935)-23.  Nettleton (John Wyeth)
               AMEH-153.  Nettleton (John Wyeth)
               MH (1966)-93.  Nettleton (John Wyeth)
     1120.   Mighty God! while angels bless Thee,/May a mortal lisp Thy
               name?
               HMEC-148.  Wellesley (Lizzie S. Tourjee)
               MH (1905)-85.  Carlton (Joseph Barnby)

ROMINGER, CHARLES H.
     1121.   Thou art, O Christ, the light and life/Of all my soul's as-
               piring hope
               MSSH-158.  Rominger (T. Stanley Skinner)

ROOT, GEORGE FREDERICK
     1122.   Come to the Saviour, make no delay;/Here in His word He's
               shown us the way

AMEH-422.  Come to the Saviour (George Frederick Root)

ROSCOE, JANE
    1123.  Thy will be done! I will not fear/The fate provided by Thy
           love
          HMEC-628.  Dwight (Joseph Perry Holbrook)

ROSCOE, WILLIAM
    1124.  Great God! beneath whose piercing eye/The earth's extended
           kingdoms lie
          HMEC-1103.  Duke Street (John Hatton)
          MH (1905)-708.  Deventer (Berthold Tours)

ROSSETTI, CHRISTINA GEORGINA
    1125.  In the bleak midwinter,/Frosty wind made moan
          MH (1935)-104.  Cranham (Gustav Holst)
          MH (1966)-376.  Cranham (Gustav Holst)
    1126.  Love came down at Christmas,/Love all lovely
          MH (1935)-94.  Garton (Irish traditional)
          MH (1966)-375.  Garton (Irish traditional)
    1127.  The shepherds had an angel,/The wise men had a star
          MH (1935)-436.  May Song (Traditional English carol)
          AMEH-554.  May Song (Traditional English carol)

ROUS, FRANCIS
    1128.  The Lord's my Shepherd, I'll not want:/He makes me down to
           lie
          HMEC-156.  Belmont (Samuel Webbe)

ROWLAND, MAY
    1129.  Come! Peace of God, and dwell again on earth,/Come, with
           calm that hailed Thy Prince's birth
          MH (1935)-510.  PAX (Lily Rendle)
    1130.  The day is slowly wending/Toward its silent ending
          MH (1935)-57.  Vesper Hymn/Rendle (Lily Rendle)
          MH (1966)-506.  Vesper Hymn/Rendle (Lily Rendle)
    1131.  Where the great ships passing cleave the ocean wave,/Where
           the lonely fishers nearer dangers brave
          MH (1935)-556.  Mariners (Lily Rendle)

RUMBAUGH, VIDA
    1132.  The righteous one shall be forever blest,/Their joyful, fai-
           thful hearts obey (trans. from the Thai)
          MH (1966)-214.  Sri Lampang (Thailand folk hymn)

RUSSELL, ARTHUR TOZER
    1133.  Let all together praise our God/Upon His lofty throne (trans.
           from Nicolaus Hermann)
          MH (1966)-389.  Lobt Gott, Ihr Christen (Nicolaus Hermann)

RYDEN, ERNEST EDWIN
    1134.  How blessed is this place, O Lord,/Where Thou art worshiped
           and adored
          MH (1966)-350.  Kent (John Friedrich Lampe)

RYLAND, JOHN
    1135.  Lord, I delight in Thee,/And on Thy care depend
            HMEC-175.  Haydn (Franz Joseph Haydn)

RYLE, JOHN C.
    1136.  No gospel like this feast/Spread for Thy Church by Thee
            HMEC-843.  Prayer (Leonard Marshall)


SAMMIS, JAMES H.
    1137.  When we walk with the Lord/In the night of His Word
            AMEH-518.  Trust and Obey (Daniel B. Towner)
            MH (1966)-223.  Trust and Obey (Daniel B. Towner)

SARGENT, LUCIUS MANLIUS
    1138.  Bondage and death the cup contains;/Dash to the earth the
            poisoned bowl!
            HMEC-901.  Hebron (Lowell Mason)

SCOTT, CLARA H.
    1139.  Open my eyes, that I may see/Glimpses of truth Thou hast
            for me
            AMEH-503.  Open My Eyes (Clara H. Scott)
            MH (1966)-267.  Open My Eyes (Clara H. Scott)

SCOTT, ELIZABETH
    1140.  Awake, ye saints, awake!/And hail this sacred day
            HMEC-73.  Warsaw (Thomas Clark)
    1141.  See how the morning sun/Pursues his shining way
            HMEC-112.  Kentucky (Jeremiah Ingalls)

SCOTT, ROBERT B.Y.
    1142.  O day of God, draw nigh/In beauty and in power
            MH (1966)-477.  St. Michael (Genevan Psalter, 1551)

SCOTT, THOMAS
    1143.  Hasten, sinner, to be wise!/Stay not for the morrow's sun
            HMEC-345.  Horton (Xavier Schnyder von Wartensee)
            MH (1905)-248.  Pleyel's Hymn (Ignace Josef Pleyel)
                            Horton (Xavier Schnyder von Wartensee)

SCOTT, SIR WALTER
    1144.  The day of wrath, that dreadful day,/When heaven and earth
            shall pass away!
            HMEC-1017.  Grace Church (Ignace Josef Pleyel)
            MH (1905)-603.  Irae (Joseph Barnby)
    1145.  When Israel of the Lord beloved,/Out from the land of bon-
            dage came
            HMEC-163.  Hamburg (Lowell Mason)
            MH (1905)-95.  Melcombe (Samuel Webbe)

SCRIVEN, JOSEPH
    1146.  What a Friend we have in Jesus,/All our sins and griefs to

bear!
MH (1905)-551.  Converse (Charles Crozat Converse)
MSSH-153.  Converse (Charles Crozat Converse)
MH (1935)-240.  Converse (Charles Crozat Converse)
AMEH-190.  Converse (Charles Crozat Converse)
MH (1966)-261.  Converse (Charles Crozat Converse)

SEAGRAVE, ROBERT
1147.  Rose, my soul, and stretch thy wings,/Thy better portion
       trace
       HMEC-1068.  Amsterdam (James Nares)
       MH (1905)-623.  Amsterdam (James Nares)
       MH (1935)-524.  Amsterdam (James Nares)
       MH (1966)-474.  Amsterdam (James Nares)

SEARS, EDMUND HAMILTON
1148.  Calm on the listening-ear of night,/Come heaven's melodious
       strains
       HMEC-195.  Carol (Richard Storrs Willis)
1149.  It came upon the midnight clear,/That glorious song of old
       HMEC-194.  Carol (Richard Storrs Willis)
       MH (1905)-110.  Carol (Richard Storrs Willis)
       MSSH-63.  Carol (Richard Storrs Willis)
       MH (1935)-92.  Carol (Richard Storrs Willis)
       AMEH-89.  Carol (Richard Storrs Willis)
       MH (1966)-390.  Carol (Richard Storrs Willis)

SELLERS, ERNEST O.
1150.  The Word is a lamp to my feet,/A light to my path alway
       AMEH-209.  Thy Word Have I Hid (Ernest O. Sellers)

SEYMOUR, AARON CROSSLY HOBART
1151.  Jesus, immortal King, arise;/Assert Thy rightful sway
       HMEC-908.  Hummel (Heinrich Christopher Zeuner)
       MH (1905)-632.  Evanston (Karl Pomeroy Harrington)

SHACKFORD, JOHN W.
1152.  O Thou who art the Shepherd/Of all the scattered sheep
       MH (1966)-201.  Munich (Gessanbuch, Meininger, 1693)

SHAW, KNOWLES
1153.  Sowing in the morning, sowing seeds of kindness,/Sowing in
       the noontide and the dewy eves
       AMEH-538.  Bringing in the Sheaves (George A. Minor)

SHEPHERD, ANNE HOULDITCH
1154.  Around the throne of God in heaven/Thousands of children
       stand
       MSSH-256.  Children's Praises (Henry E. Matthews)

SHEPHERD, THOMAS
1155.  Must Jesus bear the xross alone,/And all the world go free?
       HMEC-666.  Maitland (George Nelson Allen)
       MH (1905)-428.  Maitland (George Nelson Allen)
       MH (1935)-276.  Maitland (George Nelson Allen)

AMEH-279. Maitland (George Nelson Allen)
MH (1966)-183. Maitland (George Nelson Allen)

SHERWIN, WILLIAM FISK
1156. Sound the battle cry,/See the foe is nigh
AMEH-225. The Battle Cry (William Fisk Sherwin)

SHILLITO, EDWARD
1157. Away with gloom, away with doubt!/With all the morning
stars we sing
MH (1935)-158. Blairgowrie (Robert George Thompson)

SHIRLEY, SELINA, COUNTESS OF HUNTINGDON
1158. When Thou, my righteous Judge, shall come/To take Thy ransomed people home
HMEC-1027. Charles (James Parker)

SHRUBSOLE, WILLIAM, JR.
1159. Arm of the Lord, awake, awake!/Put on thy strength, the
nations shake
HMEC-920. Migdol (Lowell Mason)
1160. When, streaming from the eastern skies,/The morning light
salutes mine eyes
HMEC-110. Hebron (Lowell Mason)
Yoakley (William Yoakley)

SHURTLEFF, ERNEST WARBURTON
1161. Lead on, O King eternal,/The day of march has come
MH (1905)-408. Lancashire (Henry Smart)
MSSH-219. Lancashire (Henry Smart)
MH (1935)-278. Lancashire (Henry Smart)
AMEH-283. Lancashire (Henry Smart)
MH (1966)-478. Lancashire (Henry Smart)

SHUTTLEWORTH, HENRY CARY
1162. Father of men, in whom are one/All humankind beneath Thy
sun
MH (1935)-418. Llangoedmore (Welsh hymn melody)

SIGOURNEY, LYDIA HUNTLEY
1163. Blest Comforter divine,/Let rays of heavenly love
HMEC-287. Ontario (London Tune Book, 1875)
1164. Go to thy rest, fair child!/Go to thy dreamless land
HMEC-1008. The Long Home (Sir Arthur Seymour Sullivan)
1165. Labourers of Christ, arise,/And gird you for the toil
HMEC-578. Leighton (Henry Wellington Greatorex)
1166. The prodigal, with streaming eyes,/From folly just awake
HMEC-414. Grigg (Joseph Grigg)

SILL, EDWARD ROWLAND
1167. Send down Thy truth, O God:/Too long the shadows frown
MH (1935)-181. Garden City (Horatio William Parker)
AMEH-19. Garden City (Horatio William Parker)

SIMPSON, WILLIAM JAMES SPARROW

1168.  Cross of Jesus, cross of sorrow,/Where the blood of Christ
       was shed
          MH (1966)-426.  Charlestown (Stephen Jenks' American Com-
                               piler of Sacred Harmony, 1803)

SINCLAIR, GLADYS HYATT
   1169.  O God, that midst the parted sea/Thine own did keep
          MSSH-170.  Minnewaska (William J. Kirkpatrick)
                     The Parted Sea (Henry Johnson Storer)

SLADE, MARY B.C.
   1170.  From all the dark places/Of earth's heathen races
          MH (1905)-633.  The Kingdom Coming (Rigdon McCoy McIn-
                               tosh)
          MSSH-243.  The Kingdom Coming (Rigdon McCoy McIntosh)
          MH (1935)-483.  The Kingdom Coming (Rigdon McCoy McIn-
                               tosh)

SLEEPER, WILLIAM T.
   1171.  Out of my bondage, sorrow and night,/Jesus, I come, Jesus I
          come
          MSSH-142.  Out of My Bondage (George Coles Stebbins)
          AMEH-345.  Out of My Bondage (George Coles Stebbins)

SLEIGHT, MARY B.
   1172.  Hark! the voice of Jesus calling,/"Follow Me, follow Me."
          MSSH-135.  Follow Me (Horatio Richmond Palmer)

SMALL, JAMES GRINDLY
   1173.  I've found a Friend; oh such a Friend!/He loved me ere I
          knew Him
          MSSH-147.  I've Found a Friend (George Coles Stebbins)
          MH (1935)-241.  Friend (George Coles Stebbins)
          AMEH-111.  Constance (Arthur Seymour Sullivan)
          MH (1966)-163.  Friend (George Coles Stebbins)

SMITH, SIR JAMES EDWARD, M.D.
   1174.  Praise waits in Zion, Lord, for Thee:/Thy saints adore Thy
          holy Name
          HMEC-67.  Duke Street (John Hatton)
   1175.  When Power divine, in mortal form,/Hushed with a word the
          raging storm
          HMEC-630.  Zephyr (William Batchelder Bradbury)

SMITH, SAMUEL FRANCIS
   1176.  Lord of our life, God whom we fear,/Unknown, yet known; un-
          seen, yet near
          MH (1905)-503.  Louvan (Virgil Corydon Taylor)
          MH (1935)-307.  Louvan (Virgil Corydon Taylor)
   1177.  My country! 'tis of thee,/Sweet land of liberty
          HMEC-1089.  America (Henry Carey)
          MH (1905)-702.  America (Henry Carey)
          MSSH-274.  America (Henry Carey)
          MH (1935)-489.  America (Henry Carey)
          AMEH-481.  America (Henry Carey)
          MH (1966)-547.  America (Thesaurus Musicus, 1744)

1178.  Softly fades the twilight ray/Of the holy Sabbath day
   HMEC-92.  Dijon (German evening hymn)
   MH (1905)-74.  Holley (George Hews)
   MH (1935)-398.  Holley (George Hews)
1179.  The morning light is breaking!/The darkness disappears
   HMEC-932.  Webb (George James Webb)
   MH (1905)-653.  Webb (George James Webb)
   MSSH-246.  Webb (George James Webb)
   MH (1935)-487.  Webb (George James Webb)
   AMEH-215.  Webb (James George Webb)
1180.  Today the Saviour calls;/Ye wand'rers, come
   AMEH-244.  Today (Lowell Mason)

SMITH, WALTER CHALMERS
  1181.  Immortal, invisible, God only wise,/In light inaccessible
     hid from our eyes
    MH (1935)-64.  Joanna (Van Denman Thompson)
    MH (1966)-27.  St. Denio (Welsh melody)
  1182.  One thing I of the Lord desire,/For all my path miry hath
     been
    AMEH-285.  A Clean Heart (Fred H. Byshe)

SMYTHE, EDWIN
  1183.  Lord, dismiss us with Thy blessing,/Bid us now depart in
     peace
    HMEC-59.  Rathbun (Ithmar Conkey)

SOULE, HELOISE
  1184.  Let heaven highest praises bring,/And earth her songs of
     gladness sing (trans. from Bonaventura)
    MSSH-105.  Bonaventura (John Henry Gower)

SPAFFORD, HORATIO GATES
  1185.  When peace like a river, attendeth my way/When sorrows,
     like sea-billows, roll
    AMEH-189.  It Is Well Worth My Soul (Philip Paul Bliss)

STAMMERS, JOSEPH
  1186.  Breast the wave, Christian,/When it is strongest
    MSSH-211.  Onward (William C. Filby)

STANLEY, ARTHUR PENRHYN
  1187.  Day of wrath, O dreadful day!/When this world shall pass
     away (trans. from Thomas of Celano)
    HMEC-1023.  Reynoldstone (Timothy Richard Matthews)
    MH (1905)-599.  Reynoldstone (Timothy Richard Matthews)
  1188.  He is gone; a cloud of light/Has received Him from our sight
    MH (1905)-170.  Stanley (Joseph Barnby)
  1189.  O Master, it is good to be/High on the mountain here with
     Thee
    HMEC-200.  Ames (Sigismund Neukomm, arr. Lowell Mason)
    MH (1905)-131.  Hayes (Ludwig van Beethoven)

STEAD, LOUISA M.R.
  1190.  'Tis sweet to trust in Jesus,/And take Him at His word
    MH (1966)-208.  Trust in Jesus (William J. Kirkpatrick)

STEELE, ANNE
1191. Alas! what hourly dangers rise,/What snares beset my way
       AMEH-117. Warwick (Samuel Stanley)
1192. Almighty Maker of my frame,/Teach me the measure of my days
       HMEC-962. Seasons (Ignace Josef Pleyel)
1193. Come, let our souls adore the Lord,/Whose judgments yet de-
      lay
       HMEC-1096. Zelzah (German melody)
1194. Come, Thou Desire of all Thy saints,/Our humble strains at-
      tend
       HMEC-64. Marlow (John Chetham)
       AMEH-115. Warwick (Samuel Stanley)
1195. Come, ye that love the Saviour's name,/And joy to make it
      known
       HMEC-63. Marlow (John Chetham)
       MH (1905)-34. Laud (John Bacchus Dykes)
1196. Deep are the wounds which sin has made;/Where shall the sin-
      ner find a cure?
       HMEC-306. Louvan (Virgil Corydon Taylor)
1197. Far from these scenes of night,/Unbounded glories rise
       HMEC-1051. Vigil (St. Alban's tune book)
       AMEH-468. St. Thomas (George Frederick Handel)
1198. Father of mercies, in Thy word/What endless glory shines!
       HMEC-299. Melody (I.P. Cole)
       MH (1935)-389. Grafenberg (Johann Cruger)
       AMEH-385. St. Martin's (William Tans'ur)
       MH (1966)-367. Tallis' Ordinal (Thomas Tallis)
1199. Father, whate'er of earthly bliss/Thy sovereign will denies
       HMEC-610. Naomi (Hans George Naegeli, arr. Lowell Mason)
       MH (1905)-523. Naomi (Hans George Naegeli (arr. Lowell
                 Mason)
1200. Great Ruler of the earth and skies,/A word of Thine almighty
      breath
       HMEC-1101. Mendon (German traditional)
1201. How helpless nature lies,/Unconscious of her load!
       HMEC-309. Shawmut (Lowell Mason)
1202. Jesus demands this heart of mine,/Demands my love, my joy,
      my care
       AMEH-392. Silver Street (Isaac Smith)
1203. Jesus, Thou Source divine,/Whence hope and comfort flow!
       HMEC-313. State Street (Jonathan Call Woodman)
1204. Lord, how shall sinners dare/Look up to Thine abode
       HMEC-252. Carlisle (Charles Lockhart)
1205. Lord of my life, O may Thy praise/Employ my noblest powers
       HMEC-100. Warwick (Samuel Stanley)
1206. My God, my Father, blissful name,/O may I call Thee mine!
       AMEH-62. Naomi (Lowell Mason)
1207. O Thou, whose mercy hears/Contrition's humble sigh
       HMEC-553. Hall (Wartemburg melody)
1208. The Saviour! O what endless charms/Dwell in that blissful
      sound
       HMEC-325. Cambridge (John Randall)
1209. Thou Refuge of my soul,/On Thee, when sorrows rise
       HMEC-674. Schumann (Robert Schumann)
1210. The gracious presence, O my God,/All that I wish contains

HMEC-661.  Clinton (Joseph Perry Holbrook)
1211.  To Jesus, our exalted Lord,/The name by heaven and earth
           adored
       HMEC-852.  St. Alban (Unknown)

STEELE, HARRIET BINNEY
    1212.  Children, loud hosannas singing,/Hymned Thy praise in olden
             time
           HMEC-874.  Saviour, Like a Shepherd (William Batchelder
                      Bradbury)

STENNET, JOSEPH
    1213.  Another six days' work is done;/Another Sabbath is begun
             (Variant of 1214)
           MH (1905)-70.  Brookfield (Thomas Bishop Southgate)
    1214.  Return, my soul, enjoy thy rest;/Improve the day thy God
             hath blest (Variant of 1213)
           HMEC-504.  Rockingham (Lowell Mason)

STENNET, SAMUEL
    1215.  Had I the gift of tongues,/Great God, without Thy grace
           HMEC-504.  St. Thomas (George Frederick Handel)
    1216.  Majestic sweetness sits enthroned/Upon the Saviour's brow
           HMEC-241.  Ortonville (Thomas Hastings)
           MH (1905)-135.  Ortonville (Thomas Hastings)
           MH (1935)-220.  Ortonville (Thomas Hastings)
           AMEH-154.  Ortonville (Thomas Hastings)
           MH (1905)-135.  Ortonville (Thomas Hastings)
           AMEH-154.  Ortonville (Thomas Hastings)
           MH (1966)-83.  Ortonville (Thomas Hastings)
    1217.  On Jordan's stormy banks I stand,/And cast a wishful eye
           HMEC-1038.  Varina (Johann Christian Heinrich Rink)
           MH (1905)-617.  Beatitude (John Bacchus Dykes)
           MH (1935)-523.  Varina (George Frederick Root)
           AMEH-572.  On Jordan's Stormy Banks (Robert M. McIntosh)
           MH (1966)-291.  Promised Land (American folk melody)
    1218.  Prostrate, dear Jesus, at Thy feet/A guilty rebel lies
           AMEH-362.  Arlington (Thomas Augustine Arne)
    1219.  The counsels of redeeming grace/The sacred leaves unfold
           HMEC-295.  Burlington (John Freckleton Burrowes)
    1220.  Thy life I read, my gracious Lord,/With transport all di-
             vine
           HMEC-987.  Mount Auburn (George Kingsley)
    1221.  "'Tis finished!" so the Saviour cried,/And meekly bowed His
             head and died
           HMEC-218.  Olives' Brow (William Batchelder Bradbury)
           MH (1905)-149.  Westcott (Joseph Barnby)
           AMEH-120.  Westcott (Joseph Barnby)
    1222.  What majesty and grace/Through all the gospel shine!
           HMEC-322.  Silver Street (Isaac Smith)
           AMEH-424.  Dover (Thomas Williams)

STERNE, COLIN (see under NICHOL, HENRY ERNEST)

STERNHOLD, THOMAS
    1223.  The Lord descended from above,/And bowed the heavens most

HMEC-152.  Tappan (George Kingsley)

STOCKER, JOHN
1224.  Gracious Spirit, Love divine,/Let Thy light within me shine!
HMEC-262.  Fulton (William Batchelder Bradbury)
AMEH-206.  Seymour (Carl Maria von Weber)

STOCKING, JAY THOMAS
1225.  O Master Workman of the race,/Thou Man of Galilee
MH (1935)-118.  St. Michael's (Franz Joseph Haydn)
MH (1966)-171.  St. Michael's (William Gawler's Hymns
and Psalms, 1788)

STOCKTON, JOHN HART
1226.  Come, every soul by sin oppressed,/There's mercy with the
Lord
MH (1905)-261.  Stockton (John Hart Stockton)
MH (1935)-184.  Stockton (John Hart Stockton)
AMEH-248.  Stockton (John Hart Stockton)
MH (1966)-101.  Stockton (John Hart Stockton)

STONE, LLOYD
1227.  This is my song, O God of all the nations,/A song of peace
for lands afar and mine
MH (1966)-542.  Finlandia (Jean Sibelius)

STONE, SAMUEL JOHN
1228.  The Church's one foundation/Is Jesus Christ her Lord
MH (1905)-207.  Aurelia (Samuel Sebastian Wesley)
MSSH-116.  Aurelia (Samuel Sebastian Wesley)
MH (1935)-381.  Aurelia (Samuel Sebastian Wesley)
AMEH-375.  Aurelia (Samuel Sebastian Wesley)
MH (1966)-297.  Aurelia (Samuel Sebastian Wesley)
1229.  Weary of earth, and laden with my sin,/I look at heaven and
long to enter in
MH (1905)-284.  Langran

STOWE, HARRIET BEECHER
1230.  Abide with me, Lord, and I in Thee;/From this good hour, O
leave me never more
AMEH-268.  Morecombe (Frederick Cook Atkinson)
1231.  Knocking, knocking, who is there?/Waiting, waiting, Oh, how
fair!
MSSH-136.  Knocking, Knocking, Knocking (George Frederick
Root)
AMEH-256.  Knocking, Knocking, Knocking (George Frederick
Root)
1232.  Still, still with Thee, when purple morning breaketh,/When
the bird waketh, and the shadows flee
MH (1905)-43.  Consolation (Felix Mendelssohn-Bartholdy)
MSSH-44.  Consolation (Felix Mendelssohn-Bartholdy)
MH (1935)-40.  Consolation (Felix Mendelssohn-Bartholdy)
AMEH-13.  Consolation (Felix Mendelssohn-Bartholdy)
MH (1966)-264.  Consolation (Felix Mendelssohn-Bartholdy)

STOWELL, HUGH
    1233.  From every stormy wind that blows,/From every swelling tide
            of woes
            HMEC-684.  Retreat (Thomas Hastings)
            MH (1905)-495.  Retreat (Thomas Hastings)
            MH (1935)-317.  Retreat (Thomas Hastings)
            AMEH-373.  Retreat (Thomas Hastings)
            MH (1966)-232.  Retreat (Thomas Hastings)
    1234.  Jesus is our Shepherd,/Wiping every tear
            MSSH-155.  Deepdale (W.H. Robson)
    1235.  Lord of all power and might,/Father of love and light
            MH (1905)-206.  Fiat Lux (John Bacchus Dykes)
            MH (1935)-392.  Stowell (Isaac Hickman Meredith)

STRAPHAN, JOSEPH
    1236.  Delightful work! young souls to win,/And turn the rising
            race
            HMEC-877.  Siloam (Isaac Baker Woodbury)

STRATTON, MRS. F.K.
    1237.  O Lord, our God, almighty King,/We fain would make this
            temple ring
            MH (1905)-664.  Shortle (Charles Gourlay Goodrich)
                         Los Angeles David Stanley Smith)

STRONG, NATHAN
    1238.  Swell the anthem, raise the song;/Praises to our God belong
            HMEC-1093.  Jefferson (Hans George Naegeli, arr. Joseph
                        Perry Holbrook)
            MH (1905)-711.  Messiah (Louis Joseph Ferdinand Herold,
                        arr, George Kingsley)

STRYKER, MELANCTHON WOOLSEY
    1239.  Almighty Lord,with one accord/We offer Thee our youth
            MH (1905)-687.  Patten (Peter Christian Lutkin)
            MH (1935)-558.  Patten (Peter Christian Lutkin)

STUDDERT-KENNEDY, GEOFFREY ANKETELL
    1240.  Awake, awake to love and work,/The lark is in the sky
            MH (1935)-555.  Sheltered Dale (German traditional me-
                        lody)
            MH (1966)-190.  Morning Song (Wyeth's Repository of Sa-
                        cred Music, 1813)

STUTSMAN, GRACE M.
    1241.  In Bethlehem, 'neath star lit skies,/Alleluia, Alleluia!
            MH (1935)-103.  Waits' Carol (Grace M. Stutsman)
            MH (1966)-377.  Waits' Carol (Grace M. Stutsman)

SWAIN, JOSEPH
    1242.  How sweet, how heavenly is the sight,/When those who love
            the Lord
            HMEC-780.  Hermon (Lowell Mason)
            MH (1905)-554.  Mount Calvary (Robert Prescott Stewart)
    1243.  Thou, in whose presence my soul takes delight,/On whom in

affliction I call
HMEC-759. Meditation (Freeman Lewis)
MH (1905)-530. Meditation (Freeman Lewis)
MH (1935)-346. Beloved (Freeman Lewis)
AMEH-128. Meditation (Freeman Lewis)
MH (1966)-129. Davis (Wyeth's Repository of Sacred Music, 1813)

SWAIN, LEONARD
1244. My soul, weigh not thy life/Against thy heavenly crown
HMEC-584. Clapton (William Jones)

SYMONDS, JOHN ADDINGTON
1245. These things shall be: a loftier race/Than e'er the world
hath known shall rise
MH (1935)-512. Truro (Psalmodia Evandelica, 1789)
AMEH-217. Mozart (Johann Christian Wolfgang Amadeus Mozart)
MH (1966)-198. Truro (Psalmodia Evangelica, 1789)

TANNER, B.T.
1246. We are the children of the church,/Our mothers reared by
pray'r
AMEH-363. Our Father's Church (L.J. Coppin)

TAPPAN, WILLIAM BINGHAM
1247. There is an hour of peaceful rest,/To mourning wanderers
given
HMEC-1039. Varina (Johann Christian Heinrich Rink)
MH (1905)-609. Woodland (Nathaniel Duren Gould)
1248. 'Tis midnight; and on Olives' brow/The star is dimmed that
lately shone
HMEC-217. Olives' Brow (William Batchelder Bradbury)
MH (1905)-147. Olives' Brow (William Batchelder Bradbury)
MH (1935)-133. Olives' Brow (William Batchelder Bradbury)
AMEH-311. Olives' Brow (William Batchelder Bradbury)
MH (1966)-431. Olives' Brow (William Batchelder Bradbury)

TARRANT, WILLIAM GEORGE
1249. Long ago the lilies faded,/Which to Jesus seemed so fair
AMEH-74. Brocklesbury (Charlotte Alington Barnard)
1250. Now praise we great and famous men,/The fathers named in
story
MH (1966)-532. Ach Gott und Herr (As Hymnodus Sacer,
Leipzig, 1625)

TATE, NAHUM
1251. O God, we praise Thee, and confess/That Thou the only Lord
HMEC-120. Oxford (William Coombs)

1252.  While shepherds watched their flocks by night,/All seated
    on the ground
    HMEC-192.  Christmas (George Frederick Handel)
    MH (1905)-115.  Christmas (George Frederick Handel)
    MSSH-64.  Bethlehem (Gottfried Wilhelm Fink)
    MH (1935)-88.  Christmas (George Frederick Handel)
    AMEH-97.  Christmas (George Frederick Handel)
    MH (1966)-394.  Winchester Old (arr. George Kirbye)

TATE, NAHUM, AND NICHOLAS BRADY, eds.  "THE NEW VERSION" of Psalms
 1253.  As pants the hart for cooling streams,/When heated in the
    chase
    HMEC-550.  Church (Joseph Perry Holbrook)
    MH (1905)-316.  Simpson (Louis Spohr)
    MH (1935)-366.  Spohr (Louis Spohr)
    MH (1966)-255.  Ayrshire (Kenneth George Finlay)
 1254.  O Lord, our fathers oft have told,/In our attentive ears
    HMEC-1097.  Palestrina (Giovanni Patri Aloysius Palestrina)
    MH (1905)-700.  Westminster (James Turle)
    MH (1935)-498.  St. Anne (William Croft)
    MH (1966)-54.  Winchester Old (George Este's The Whole
        Booke of Psalmes, 1592)
 1255.  O render thanks to God above,/The fountain of eternal love
    HMEC-13.  Truro (Charles Burney)
 1256.  Through all the changing scenes of life,/In trouble and in
    joy
    MH (1935)-14.  Irish (A Collection of Hymns and Sacred
        Poems, Dublin, 1749)
    AMEH-61.  Azmon (Carl Gotthelf Glasser)
    MH (1966)-56.  Irish (A Collection of Hymns and Sacred
        Poems, Dublin, 1749)

TAYLOR, GEORGE LANSING
 1257.  Dare to do right!/Dare to be true!
    MSSH-222.  Dare To Do Right (William Batchelder Brad-
        bury)

TAYLOR, SARAH E.
 1258.  O God of light, Thy Word, a lamp unfailing,/Shines through
    the darkness of our earth;y way
    MH (1966)-371.  Welwyn (Alfred Scott-Gatty)

TAYLOR, THOMAS RAWSON
 1259.  There was a time when children sang,/The Saviour's praise
    with sacred glee
    MH (1905)-684.  Palm Sunday (Karl Pomeroy Harrington)

TAYLOR, WALTER REGINALD OXENHAM
 1260.  The bread of life, for all men broken!/He drank the cup on
    Golgatha (trans. from Timothy Tingfang Lew)
    MH (1966)-317.  Sheng En (Su Yin-Lan, arr. Bliss Wiant)

TENNYSON, ALFRED LORD
 1261.  Late, late, so late! and dark the night, and chill!/Late,
    late, so late! But we can enter still
    HMEC-375.  Too Late (Joseph Perry Holbrook)

1262.   Ring out the old, ring in the new,/Ring, happy bells, across the snow
  AMEH-270.   Waltham (John Baptiste Calkin)
1263.   Ring out, wild bells, to the wild, wild sky,/The flying cloud, the frosty light
  MH (1935)-537.   Wild Bells (Henry Lahee)
1264.   Strong Son of God, immortal!/Love, whom we, that have not seen Thy face
  MH (1905)-139.   Grostette (Henry Wellington Greatorex)
  MH (1935)-206.   Keble (John Bacchus Dykes)
  MH (1966)-146.   Keble (John Bacchus Dykes)
1265.   Sunset and evening star,/And one clear call for me!
  MH (1935)-368.   Crossing the Bar (Joseph Barnby)
1266.   Sweet and low, sweet and low,/Wind of the western sea
  AMEH-551.   Sweet and Low (Joseph Barnby)

THALHEIMER, ELSIE
  1267.   Thou art my Shepherd,/Caring in every need
    MSSH-157.   Thou Art My Shepherd (German melody)

THOMAS, ALEXCENAH
  1268.   Hark! 'Tis the Shepherd's voice, I hear/Out in the desert dark and drear
    AMEH-568.   Bring Them In (William A. Ogden)

THOMPSON, ALEXANDER RAMSAY
  1269.   O Thou, whose filmed and failing eye,/Ere yet it closed in death
    HMEC-670.   Cooling (Alonzo Judson Abbey)

THOMPSON, J.O.
  1270.   Far and near the fields are teeming/With the sheaves of ripened grain
    MSSH-251.   The Call for Reapers (J.B.O. Clemm)

THOMPSON, WILL LAMARTINE
  1271.   A sinner was wand'ring at eventide,/His tempter was watching close by at his side
    AMEH-291.   The Sinner and the Song (Will Lamartine Thompson)
  1272.   Jesus is all the world to me,/My life, my joy, my all
    AMEH-499.   Jesus Is All the World to Me (Will Lamartine Thompson)
    MH (1966)-97.   Elizabeth (Will Lamartine Thompson)
  1273.   Lead me gently home, Father,/Lead me gently home
    AMEH-505.   Lead Me Gently Home (Will Lamartine Thompson)
  1274.   Softly and tenderly Jesus is calling,/Calling for you and for me
    MSSH-134.   Softly and Tenderly (Will Lamartine Thompson)
    MH (1935)-239.   Softly and Tenderly (Will Lamartine Thompson)
    AMEH-341.   Softly and Tenderly (Will Lamartine Thompson)

THOMSON, JOHN
  1275.   Jehovah, God, Thy gracious power/On every hand we see
    HMEC-159.   Dundee (Guillaume Franc)

THOMSON, MARY ANN
    1276.  O Zion, haste, thy mission high fulfilling;/To tell to all
               the world that God is Light
               MH (1905)-654. Tidings (James Walsh)
               MSSH-245. Tidings (James Walsh)
               MH (1935)-475. Tidings (James Walsh)
               AMEH-211. Tidings (James Walsh)
               MH (1966)-299. Tidings (James Walsh)

THRELFALL, JEANNETTE
    1277.  Hosanna, loud hosanna/The little children sing
               MH (1935)-127. Ellacombe (Gesangbuch der Herzogl, Wir-
                          temburgischen Katholischen Hofka-
                          pelle, 1784)
               AMEH-404. Ellacombe (Gesangbuch der Herzogl, Wirtembur-
                          gischen Katholischen Hofkapelle, 1784)
               MH (1966)-423. Ellacombe (Gesangbuch der Herzogl, Wir-
                          temburgischen Katholischen Hofka-
                          pelle, 1784)

THRING, GODFREY
    1278.  Fierce raged the tempest o'er the deep,/Watch did Thine
               anxious servants keep
               AMEH-138. St. Aelred (John Bacchus Dykes)
    1279.  Grant us, O our heavenly Father,/Now in these our early
               days
               MSSH-137. St. Oswald (John Bacchus Dykes)
    1280.  I saw the holy city,/The New Jerusalem
               MH (1905)-626. Patmos (Henry Johnson Storer)
    1281.  Jesus came, the heavens adoring,/Came with peace from
               realms on high
               AMEH-107. Regent Square (Henry Smart)
    1282.  Saviour, blessed Saviour,/Listen while we sing
               MH (1905)-344. Godfrey (John Allison West)
               MSSH-17 (Goshen (Marchel Davis)
    1283.  The radiant morn hath pass'd away,/And spent too soon her
               golden store
               MSSH-51. Colorado (Lindsay Bartholomew Longacre)
               MH (1935)-41. Oldbridge (Robert Newton Quaile)

THRUPP, DOROTHY ANN
    1284.  Come, Christian children, come and raise/Your voice with
               one accord
               HMEC-876. Siloam (Isaac Baker Woodbury)
    1285.  Saviour, like a shepherd lead us,/Much we need Thy tender-
               est care
               HMEC-872. Saviour, Like a Shepherd (William Batchelder
                              Bradbury)
               MH (1905)-677. Bradbury (William Batchelder Bradbury)
               MSSH-179. Bradbury (William Batchelder Bradbury)
               MH (1935)-337. Bradbury (William Batchelder Bradbury)
               AMEH-178. Bradbury (William Batchelder Bradbury)
               MH (1966)-121. Bradbury (William Batchelder Bradbury)

TILLETT, WILBUR FISK

1286.  O Son of God incarnate,/O Son of man divine!
           MH (1935)-117.  Incarnation (Alfred Wooler)
           MH (1966)-85.  Far-Off Lands (arr. Charles Winfred Doug-
                         las)

TINDLEY, CHARLES A.
    1287.  Beams of heaven, as I go,/Thro' this wilderness below
           AMEH-461.  Beams of Heaven (Charles A. Tindley)
    1288.  Nothing between my soul and the Saviour,/Naught of this
               world's delusive dream
           AMEH-351.  Nothing Between (Charles A. Tindley)
    1289.  We are tossed and driven on the restless sea of time:/Som-
               ber skies and howling tempest oft succeed a bright
               sunshine
           AMEH-542.  We Are Tossed and Driven (Charles A. Tindley)
    1290.  When the storms of life are raging,/Stand by me
           AMEH-287.  Stand By Me (Charles A. Tindley)
           MH (1966)-244.  Stand By Me (Charles A. Tindley, arr.
                         Daniel L. Ridout)

TIPLADY, THOMAS
    1291.  Above the hills of time the cross is gleaming,/Fair as the
               sun when night has turned to day
           MH (1935)-145.  Londonderry (Irish traditional)

TOKE, EMMA
    1292.  Thou art gone up on high/To mansions in the sky
           HMEC-236.  Rialto (George Frederick Root)

TOPLADY, AUGUSTUS MONTAGUE
    1293.  Deathless spirit, now arise;/Soar, thou native of the
               skies!
           HMEC-1004.  Talmar (Isaac Baker Woodbury)
    1294.  If, on a quiet sea,/Toward heaven we calmly sail
           HMEC-636.  Selvin (Lowell Mason)
           MH (1905)-446.  Selvin (Lowell Mason)
           MH (1935)-321.  Selvin (Lowell Mason)
           MH (1966)-147.  Venice (William Amps)
    1295.  Jesus, the sinner's rest Thou art,/From guilt, and fear,
               and pain
           HMEC-534.  Avon (Hugh Wilson)
    1296.  Rock of ages, cleft for me,/Let me hide myself in Thee
           HMEC-415.  Toplady (Thomas Hastings)
           MH (1905)-279.  Toplady (Thomas Hastings)
           MSSH-175.  Gethsemane (Richard Redhead)
                         Toplady (Thomas Hastings)
           MH (1935)-204.  Toplady (Thomas Hastings)
           AMEH-155.  Toplady (Thomas Hastings)
           MH (1966)-120.  Toplady (Thomas Hastings)
    1297.  When languor and disease invade/This trembling house of
               clay
           HMEC-612.  Naomi (Hans George Naegeli, arr. Lowell Ma-
                         son)
    1298.  Your harps, ye trembling saints,/Down from the willows take
           HMEC-633.  Olmutz (Lowell Mason)

TORREY, BRADFORD
    1299.  Not so in haste, my heart!/Have faith in God and wait
            MH (1935)-323.  Dolomite Chant (Austrian melody)

TUCKER, FRANCIS BLAND
    1300.  All praise to Thee, for Thou, O King divine,/Didst yield
            the glory that of right was Thine
            MH (1966)-74.  Sine Nomine (Ralph Vaughan Williams)
    1301.  Alone Thou goest forth, O Lord,/In sacrifice to die (trans.
            from Peter Abelard)
            MH (1966)-427.  Bangor (William Tans'ur)
    1302.  Father, we thank Thee who hast planted/Thy holy name with-
            in our hearts
            MH (1966)-307.  Commandments (Louis Bourgeois)

TURNEY, EDWARD
    1303.  O love divine! O matchless grace!/Which in this sacred rite
            HMEC-837.  Simpson (Louis Spohr)
            AMEH-328.  Jerusalem (Charles F. Roper)

TUTTIETT, LAURENCE
    1304.  Father, let me dedicate/All this year to Thee
            MH (1935)-535.  Dedication (George Alexander MacFarren)
    1305.  Go forward, Christian soldier,/Beneath His banner true
            HMEC-568.  Webb (George James Webb)
            MH (1905)-387.  Lancashire (Henry Smart)
            MSSH-210.  Laurentius (H. Loren Clements)

TWEEDY, HENRY HALLAM
    1306.  Eternal God, whose power upholds/Both flower and flaming
            star
            MH (1935)-476.  Everyland (Lily Rendle)
            MH (1966)-476.  Halifax (George Frederick Handel)
    1307.  O gracious Father of mankind,/Our spirits' unseen friend
            MH (1935)-305.  St. Michel's (Franz Joseph Haydn)
            MH (1966)-260.  Llangloffan (Traditional Welsh melody)
    1308.  O Spirit of the living God,/Thou light and fire divine
            MH (1935)-182.  St. Leonard (Henry Bliss)
            MH (1966)-136.  Llanfyllin (Welsh melody)

TWELLS, HENRY
    1309.  At even, ere the sun was set,/The sick, O Lord, around
            Thee lay
            MH (1905)-54.  Abends (Herbert Stanley Oakeley)
            MH (1935)-48.  Abends (Herbert Stanley Oakeley)
            AMEH-137.  Angelus (George Josephi)
            MH (1966)-501.  Abends (Herbert Stanley Oakeley)

UFFORD, EDWIN S.
    1310.  Throw out the life line across the dark wave,/There is a
            brother whom some one should save

AMEH-566.   Throw Out the Life Line (Edwin S. Ufford)

UHLER, GRACE ELMA
   1311.   O gift of God, we praise Thee,/That ever Thou didst come
            MSSH-56.   Donum Dei (Latham True)

"UNKNOWN"
   1312.   Among assembled men of might,/The mighty God doth stand
            AMEH-330.   St. Agnes (John Bacchus Dykes)
   1313.   Angels we have heard on high/Sweetly singing o'er the
            plains
            MH (1966)-374.   Gloria (Traditional French carol)
   1314.   Away in a manger, no crib for a bed,/The little Lord Jesus
            laid down His sweet head
            MSSH-70.   Afton Water (Jonathan E. Spilman)
            MH (1935)-434.   Muller (Carl Muller)
            AMEH-552.   Muller (Carl Muller)
            MH (1966)-384.   Away in a Manger (James R. Murray)
   1315.   Break forth, O beauteous heavenly light,/And usher in the
            morning
            MH (1966)-373.   Ermuntre Dich (Johann Schop)
   1316.   Cast thy burden on the Lord,/Only lean upon His word
            MH (1905)-468.   St. Bees (John Bacchus Dykes)
   1317.   Come, Thou almighty King,/Help us Thy name to sing
            HMEC-6.   Italian Hymn (Felice Giardini)
            MH (1905)-2.   Italian Hymn (Felice Giardini)
            MH (1935)-2.   Italian Hymn (Felice Giardini)
            AMEH-316.   Italian Hymn (Felice Giardini)
            MH (1966)-3.   Italian Hymn (Felice Giardini)
   1318.   Come to Jesus, Come to Jesus,/Come to Jesus just now
            AMEH-292.   Come to Jesus (Unknown)
   1319.   Daughter of Zion, awake from Thy sadness;/Awake, for Thy
            foes shall oppress Thee no more
            HEMC-778.   Hanover (Johann Christian Wolfgang Amadeus
            Mozart)
   1320.   Fairest Lord Jesus!/Ruler of all nature! (trans. from the
            German)
            MH (1905)-118.   Crusader's Hymn (Richard Storrs Willis)
            MSSH-12.   Crusader's Hymn (Richard Storrs Willis)
            MH (1935)-111.   Crusader's Hymn (Richard Storrs Willis)
            AMEH-310.   Crusader's Hymn (Richard Storrs Willis)
            MH (1966)-79.   St. Elizabeth (arr. Richard Storrs Willis)
   1321.   Father Almighty, bless us with Thy blessing,/Answer in love
            Thy children's supplication
            AMEH-30.   Integer Vitae (Frederick F. Flemming)
   1322.   "Follow Me," the Master said;/We will follow Jesus
            MSSH-150.   Follow Me (German Traditional)
   1323.   God rest you, merry gentlemen,/Let nothing you dismay
            MH (1966)-378.   God Rest You Merry (Traditional English
            melody)
   1324.   Hear the temperance call,/Freeman, one and all!
            MSSH-252.   The Temperance Call (Franz Abt)
   1325.   Hear us, heav'nly Father,/Thou whose gentle care
            AMEH-549.   Hear Us (John Adcock)
   1326.   Hearken all! What holy singing/Now is sounding from the

          sky!
          MH (1935)-108.  Gloria (Old French carol)
1327.  Holy Father, send Thy blessing/On Thy children gathered
          here
          HMEC-887.  Gaylord (Joseph Perry Holbrook)
1328.  How firm a foundation, ye saints of the Lord,/Is laid for
          your faith in His excellent word!
          HMEC-679.  Portuguese Hymn (Unknown)
          MH (1905)-461.  Portuguese Hymn (Unknown)
                          Foundation (American traditional)
          MSSH-160.  Portuguese Hymn (Unknown)
          MH (1935)-315.  Adeste Fideles/Portuguese Hymn (Un-
                          known)
          AMEH-280.  Kirkman (Unknown)
          AMEH-281.  Adeste Fideles/Portuguese Hymn (Unknown)
          MH (1966)-48.  Foundation (Early American melody)
1329.  How lovely is Thy dwelling place,/O Lord of hosts, to me!
          (from the Scottish Psalter, 1650)
          MH (1935)-383.  Salzburg (Johann Michael Haydn)
          MH (1966)-295.  Salzburg (Johann Michael Haydn)
1330.  I sought the Lord, and afterward I knew/He moved my soul to
          seek Him, seeking me
          MH (1935)-316.  Peace (George Whitefield Chadwick)
          MH (1966)-96.  Wachusett (Katherine K. David)
1331.  In a lonely graveyard, many miles away,/Lies your dear old
          mother, 'neath the cold, cold clay
          AMEH-372.  In a Lonely Graveyard (W.S. Nickle)
1332.  I've seen the lightning flashing,/And heard the thunder
          roll
          AMEH-525.  Never Alone (English traditional)
1333.  Let the words of my mouth,/Let the words of my mouth
          AMEH-476.  Sentence and the Lord's Prayer (C.E. Leslie)
1334.  Let us break bread together on our knees;/Let us break
          bread together on our knees
          MH (1966)-330. Let Us Break Bread (American folk hymn)
1335.  Let us keep steadfast guard/With lighted hearts all night
          HMEC-580.  Leighton (Henry Wellington Greatorex)
1336.  Life from the dead, Almighty God,/'Tis Thine alone to give
          HMEC-899.  Return (Theodore Freelinghuysen Seward)
1337.  Life's sea oft-times is dark and dreary,/And maddening bil-
          lows loudly roar
          AMEH-487.  I Cannot Drift (James S. Hatcher)
1338.  Lord, I want to be a Christian/In my heart, in my heart
          AMEH-617.  In My Heart (Unknown)
          MH (1966)-286.  I Want To Be a Christian (American folk
                          hymn)
1339.  Lord Jesus, I love Thee, I know Thou art mine,/For Thee all
          the follies of sin I resign
          MH (1935)-234.  Gordon (Adoniram Judson Gordon)
1340.  Lord, teach me how to pray,/Teach me to love it, too
          AMEH-669.  Alice (Robert Roberts
1341.  My hope, my all, my Saviour Thou,/To Thee, lo, now my soul
          I bow!
          MH (1905)-444.  Washington (Carl Fowler Price)
1342.  My Shepherd is the Lord most high,/And all my wants shall
          be supplied

AMEH-477.  Hebron (Lowell Mason)
AMEH-478.  Mendon (German traditional)

1343.  Not heaven's wide range of hallowed space/Jehovah's presence
    can confine
    HMEC-860.  Duke Street (John Hatton)
1344.  Now cheer our hearts this eventide,/Lord Jesus Christ, and
    with us bide (trans. from Nicolaus Selnecker)
    MH (1935)-58.  Jam Lucis (Plainsong melody)
1345.  O come, Creator Spirit blesr!/Within these souls of Thine
    to rest
    HMEC-269.  Fulton (William Batchelder Bradbury)
1346.  O for a heart of calm repose,/Amid the world's loud roar
    MH (1905)-276.  Geer (Henry Wellington Greatorex)
    MH (1935)-363.  Spohr (Louis Spohr)
1347.  O God, to us show mercy,/And bless us in Thy grace
    HMEC-50.  Ellacombe (St. Gall's Collection, Switzerland)
1348.  O I know the Lord, I know the Lord,/I know the Lord's laid
    His hands on me
    AMEH-619.  I Know the Lord (Unknown)
1349.  O my soul, bless God, the Father;/All within me bless His
    name
    MH (1935)-80.  Stuttgart (Psalmodia Sacra, 1715)
    MH (1966)-65.  Stuttgart (Henry John Gauntlett)
1350.  O, speed thee, Christian, om thy way,/And to thy armor cling
    AMEH-656.  Without tune
1351.  O Thou, my Saviour, Brother, Friend,/Behold a cloud of in-
    cense rise
    AMEH-389.  Ward (arr. Lowell Mason)
1352.  Our highest joys succeed our griefs,/And peace is born of
    pain
    MH (1905)-474.  Plymouth (Alfred George Wathall)
1353.  Praise the Lord! ye heavens adore Him!/Praise Him, angels,
    in the height
    MH (1935)-11.  Hyfrydol (Rowland Hugh Prichard)
    MH (1966)-42.  Austria (Franz Joseph Haydn)
1354.  Ring out the bells for Christmas,/The happy, happy day
    MSSH-57.  Bells (John Sebastian Bach Hodges)
1355.  Send out Thy light and Thy truth, let them lead me;/O let
    them bring me to Thy holy hill
    AMEH-614.  Lux Fiat (Charles Francois Gounod)
1356.  Spring has now unwrapped the flowers,/Day is fast reviving
    MH (1966)-442.  Tempus Adest Floridum (Piae Cantiones,
        1582)
1357.  Steal away, steal away to Jesus!/Steal away, steal away home
    AMEH-616.  Steal Away! (Unknown)
1358.  Sweet is the prayer whose holy stream/In earnest pleading
    flows
    HMEC-711.  Woodstock (Deodatus Dutton, Jr.)
1359.  Swing low, sweet chariot,/Coming for to carry me home
    AMEH-618.  Swing Low (Unknown)
1360.  That solemn hour will come for me,/When, though their charms
    I own
    HMEC-975.  Ditson (Unknown)
1361.  The beautiful bright sunshine,/That smiles on all below
    MSSH-265.  Sunshine (George Edgar Oliver)

1362. The fields are all white,/And the reapers are few
      MSSH-208. Little Reapers (Myles Birket Foster)
1363. The first Nowell, the Angel did say,/Was to certain poor
      shepherds in fields as they lay
      MSSH-66. The First Nowell (English traditional)
      MH (1935)-97. The First Nowell (English traditional)
      AMEH-94. The First Nowell (English traditional)
      MH (1966)-383. The First Nowell (English traditional)
1364. The Lord bless thee and keep thee;/The Lord make His face
      shine upon thee, and be gracious unto thee
      AMEH-408. The Lord Bless Thee and Keep Thee (Lucy Rider
          Meyer)
1365. The Lord's my Shepherd, I'll not want;/He makes me down to
      lie
      MH (1935)-70. Martyrdom (Hugh Wilson)
      MH (1966)-68. Evan (William Henry Havergal, arr. Lowell
          Mason)
1366. The man that doth in secret place/Of God Most High reside
      AMEH-331. St. Agnes (John Bacchus Dykes)
1367. The man who once has found abode/Within the secret place of
      God (Variant of 1366)
      MH (1935)-74. Tallis' Canon (Thomas Tallis)
      MH (1966)-216. Tallis' Canon (Thomas Tallis)
1368. The wise may bring their learning,/The rich may bring their
      wealth
      MH (1935)-439. Ellon (George Frederick Root)
1369. There is a balm in Gilead, to make the wounded whole;/There
      is a balm in Gilead, to heal the sin-sick soul
      MH (1966)-212. Balm in Gilead (American folk hymn, arr.
          Daniel L. Ridout)
1370. Tho' clouds may hover o'er us,/There's a bright and golden
      ray
      AMEH-621. Tho' the Clouds May Hover o'er Us (Antonio J.
          Haskell)
1371. To bless the earth, God sendeth/From His abundant store
      MH (1966)-512. Far-Off Lands (arr. Charles Winfred
          Douglas)
1372. Unto the hills I lift mine eyes;/O whence shall come my aid?
      MH (1966)-57. Dunfermline (Scottish Psalter, 1615)
1373. We are climbing Jacob's ladder,/We are climbing Jacob's lad-
      der
      MH (1966)-287. Jacob's Ladder (American folk hymn)
1374. We'll praise the Lord for He is great,/And in His presence
      angels wait
      AMEH-70. Nazrey (J.T. Layton)
1375. Were you there when they crucified my Lord?/Were you there
      when they crucified my Lord?
      AMEH-405. Were You There? (Unknown)
      MH (1966)-436. Were You There? (Unknown)
1376. What wondrous love is this,/O my soul, O my soul
      MH (1966)-432. Wondrous Love (Southern Harmony, 1835)
1377. Who but Thou, almighty Spirit,/Can the heathen world re-
      claim?
      HMEC-942. Hamden (Lowell Mason)
1378. Within Thy house, O Lord, our God,/In majesty appear (first
      appeared in Hymns Adapted to the Public Worship in the

Christ Church, Princeton, New Jersey, 1828)
HMEC-65.  Marlow (John Chetham)

"UNKNOWN," and CHARLES WESLEY
1379.  Jesus Christ is risen today, Alleluia!/Our triumphant holy
day, Alleluia!
MH (1935)-155.  Llanfair (Robert Williams)
AMEH-400.  Llanfair (Robert Williams)
ME (1966)-443.  Llanfair (Robert Williams)

VAN ALSTYNE, FRANCES JANE CROSBY
1380.  All the way my Saviour leads me;/What have I to ask beside?
AMEH-183.  All the Way (Robert Lowry)
MH (1966)-205.  All the Way (Robert Lowry)
1381.  Blessed assurance, Jesus is mine!/O what a foretaste of
glory divine!
MH (1905)-548.  Blessed Assurance (Mrs. Phoebe P. Fair-
child Knapp)
MSSH-151.  Blessed Assurance (Mrs. Phoebe P. Fairchild
Knapp)
MH (1935)-238.  Blessed Assurance (Mrs. Phoebe P. Fair-
child Knapp)
AMEH-332.  Blessed Assurance (Mrs. Phoebe P. Fairchild
Knapp)
MH (1966)-224.  Blessed Assurance (Mrs. Phoebe P. Fair-
child Knapp)
1382.  Come with rejoicing, come with delight,/Nature is waking,
glad and bright
MSSH-270.  Come with Rejoicing (Mary Ann Bachelor Knapp)
1383.  Hark! there comes a whisper/Stealing on thine ear
AMEH-251.  Give Thy Heart to Me (William Howard Doane)
1384.  I am Thine, O Lord, I have heard Thy voice,/And it told Thy
love to me
MSSH-161.  I Am Thine (William Howard Doane)
MH (1935)-252.  I Am Thine (William Howard Dpane)
AMEH-267.  Crosby (William Howard Doane)
MH (1966)-159.  I Am Thine (William Howard Doane)
1385.  In a lowly manger sleeping,/Calm and still a Babe we see
AMEH-92.  Adoration (William Howard Doane)
1386.  In thy cleft, O Rock of Ages,/Hide thou me
AMEH-429.  Hide Thou Me (Robert Lowry)
1387.  Jesus is tenderly calling thee home--/Calling today, Call-
ing today
MSSH-130.  Jesus Is Calling (George Coles Stebbins)
AMEH-346.  Jesus Is Calling (George Coles Stebbins)
MH (1966)-110.  Jesis Is Calling (George Coles Stebbins)
1388.  Jesus, keep me near the cross;/There a precious fountain
MH (1935)-248.  Near the Cross (William Howard Doane)
AMEH-144.  Near the Cross (William Howard Doane)
MH (1966)-433.  Near the Cross (William Howard Doane)
1389.  March onward, march onward!/Our banner of light
MSSH-216.  March Onward (Mary Ann Bachelor Knapp)

1390.  Now just a word for Jesus,/Your dearest Friend so true
           AMEH-335.  Now Just a Word for Jesus (William Howard
                       Doane)
1391.  O come, sinner, come, there's room for thee,/Hark! 'tis mer-
           cy's call
           AMEH-273.  Mercy's Call (William Howard Doane)
1392.  Only a step to Jesus!/Then why not take it now?
           AMEH-264.  Only a Step ( William Howard Doane)
1393.  Pass me not, O gentle Saviour,/Hear my humble cry
           MH (1905)-329.  Pass Me Not (William Howard Doane)
           MSSH-138.  Pass Me Not (William Howard Doane)
           MH (1935)-231.  Pass Me Not (William Howard Doane)
           AMEH-182.  Pass Me Not (William Howard Doane)
           MH (1966)-145.  Pass Me Not (William Howard Doane)
1394.  Praise Him! praise Him! Jesus, our blessed Redeemer!/Sing,
           O Earth--His wonderful love proclaim
           MSSH-4.  Praise Him (Chester G. Allen)
           AMEH-546.  Praise Him (Chester A. Allen)
1395.  Rescue the perishing,/Care for the dying
           MH (1905)-697.  Rescue the Perishing (William Howard
                            Doane)
           MSSH-231.  Rescue the Perishing (William Howard Doane)
           MH (1935)-250.  Rescue the Perishing (William Howard
                            Doane)
           AMEH-379.  Rescue the Perishing (William Howard Doane)
           MH (1966)-175.  Rescue the Perishing (William Howard
                            Doane)
1396.  Safe in the arms of Jesus,/Safe in His gentle breast
           AMEH-181.  Arms of Jesus (William Howard Doane)
1397.  Saviour, more than life to me,/I am clinging close to Thee
           MH (1905)-490.  Every Day and Hour (William Howard Doane)
           MH (1935)-236.  Every Day and Hour (William Howard Doane)
           AMEH-369.  Every Day and Hour (William Howard Doane)
           MH (1966)-226.  Every Day and Hour (William Howard Doane)
1398.  Thou my everlasting portion,/More than friend or life to me
           MH (1905)-332.  Close to Thee (Silas Jones Vail)
           MH (1935)-235.  Close to Thee (Silas Jones Vail)
           AMEH-359.  Close to Thee (Silas Jones Vail)
           MH (1966)-176.  Close to Thee (Silas Jones Vail)
1399.  Though your sins be as scarlet,/They shall be as white as
           snow
           MSSH-123.  Though Your Sins (William Howard Doane)
           AMEH-371.  Though Your Sins (William Howard Doane)
1400.  To the work! to the Work! we are servants of God,/Let us
           follow the path that our Master hath trod
           AMEH-494.  To the Work (William Howard Doane)
1401.  When Jesus comes to reward His servants,/Wheth er it be
           noon or night
           AMEH-573.  When Jesus Comes (William Howard Doane)

VAN DEVENTER, JUDSON W.
1402.  I never can forget the day/I heard my mother kindly say
           AMEH-370.  I Never Can Forget the Day (Winfield S. Wee-
                       den)
1403.  Over the river, faces I see,/Fair as the morning, looking

for me
            AMEH-576.  Looking This Way (Judson W. Van Deventer)

VAN DYKE, HENRY
    1404.  Joyful, joyful, we adore Thee,/God of glory, Lord of love
            MH (1935)-12.  Hymn to Joy (Ludwig van Beethoven)
            AMEH-301.  Hymn to Joy (Ludwig van Beethoven)
            MH (1966)-38.  Hymn to Joy (Ludwig van Beethoven)
    1405.  No form of human framing,/No bond of outward might
            MH (1935)-421.  Alford (John Bacchus Dykes)

VOKES, MRS.  ---
    1406.  Behold, the heathen waits to know/The joy the gospel will
                bestow
            HMEC-923.  Arnheim (Samuel Holyoke)
    1407.  Soon may the last glad song arise,/Through all the millions
                of the skies)
            HMEC-917.  Migdol (Lowell Mason)
            MH (1905)-630.  Migdol (Lowell Mason)
    1408.  Sovereign of the worlds! display Thy power;/Be this Thy
                Zion's favored hour
            HMEC-918.  Migdol (Lowell Mason)
    1409.  Ye messengers of Christ!/His sovereign voice obey
            AMEH-412.  Boylston (Lowell Mason)

VON CHRISTIERSON, FRANK
    1410.  As men of old their first fruits brought/Of orchard, flock,
                and field
            MH (1966)-511.  High Popples (Samuel Walter)
    1411.  Break forth, O living light of God,/Upon the world's dark
                hour!
            MH (1966)-356.  St. Stephen (William Jones)



W., B.J.
    1412.  Here on earth where foes surround us,/While our trembling
                souls within
            HMEC-727.  Nettleton (John Wyeth)

WALFORD, WILLIAM W.
    1413.  Sweet hour of prayer, sweet hour of prayer,/That calls me
                from a world of care
            HMEC-688.  Sweet Hour of Prayer (William Batchelder
                        Bradbury)
            MH (1905)-516.  Sweet Hour of Prayer (William Batchelder
                        Bradbury)
            MH (1935)-301.  Sweet Hour of Prayer (William Batchelder
                        Bradbury)
            AMEH-260.  Sweet Hour of Prayer (William Batchelder
                        Bradbury)
            MH (1966)-275.  Sweet Hour of Prayer (William Batchelder
                        Bradbury)

WALKER, JAMES T.
    1414.  Bear the cross, ye sons of men,/With love's best ambition
          AMEH-436.  Bear the Cross (James T. Walker)

WALKER, JOHN
    1415.  Thou God of power, Thou God of love,/Whose glory fills the
          realms above
          HMEC-18 (Ariel (arr. Lowell Mason)

WALLACE, JOHN AIKMAN
    1416.  There is an eye that never sleeps/Beneath the wing of
          night
          HMEC-707.  Salome (Ludwig van Beethoven)

WALTER, HOWARD ARNOLD
    1417.  I would be true, for there are those who trust me;/I would
          be pure, for there are those who care
          MSSH-186.  Peek (Joseph Yates Peek)
          AMEH-557.  Peek (Joseph Yates Peek)
          MH (1966)-156.  Peek (Joseph Yates Peek)

WALWORTH, CLARENCE
    1418.  Holy God, we praise Thy name:/Lord of all, we bow before
          Thee (trans. from Ignaz Franz)
          MH (1966)-8.  Grosser Gott (<u>Katholisches</u> <u>Gesangbuch</u>,
                Vienna, <u>1774</u>)

WARDLAW, RALPH
    1419.  Christ, of all my hopes the ground,/Christ, the spring of
          all my joy
          HMEC-721.  Vienna (William Henry Havergal)

WARE, HENRY (THE YOUNGER)
    1420.  All nature's works His praise declare,/To whom they all be-
          long
          MH (1935)-552.  Bethlehem (Gottfried Wilhelm Fink)
          MH (1966)-343.  Bethlehem (Gottfried Wilhelm Fink)
    1421.  Happy the home when God is there,/And love fills every
          breast
          HMEC-101.  Warwick Samuel Stanley)
          MH (1935)-428.  St. Agnes (John Bacchus Dykes)
          MH (1966)-516.  St. Agnes (John Bacchus Dykes)
    1422.  Lift your glad voices in triumph on high,/For Jesus hath
          risen, and man shall not die
          HMEC-227.  Resurrection (John Edgar Gould)
          MH (1905)-159.  Epiphany (William Charles Filby)
    1423.  We rear not a temple like Judah's of old,/Whose portals
          were marble, whose vaultings were gold
          HMEC-868.  Portuguese Hymn (Unknown)
          MH (1905)-666.  Portuguese Hymn (Unknown)

WARING, ANNA LETITIA
    1424.  Father, I know that all my life/Is portioned out for me
          HMEC-675.  Waring (Louis Spohr)
          MH (1905)-465.  Waring (Louis Spohr)

1425. Go not far from me, O my Strength,/Whom all my times obey
      HMEC-676. Waring (Louis Spohr)
1426. In heavenly love abiding,/No change my heart shall fear
      HMEC-642. Endsleigh (Salvatore Ferretti)
      MH (1905)-452. Day of Rest (James William Elliott)
      MH (1935)-352. Day of Rest (James William Elliott)
      MH (1966)-230. Nyland (Traditional Finnish melody)
1427. My Saviour, on the word of truth/In earnest hope I live
      HMEC-510. Spohr (Louis Spohr)
      MH (1905)-364. Spohr (Louis Spohr)

WARNER, ANNA BARTLETT
1428. Jesus loves me! this I know,/For the Bible tells me so
      MSSH-190. Jesus Loves Me (William Batchelder Bradbury)
      AMEH-548. Jesus Loves Me (William Batchelder Bradbury)
1429. One more day's work for Jesus,/One less of life for me!
      HMEC-572. Edinburgh (Robert Lowry)
      MH (1905)-419. One More Day's Work (Robert Lowry)
1430. The world looks very beautiful/And full of joy to me
      MSSH-149. Cliftonville (Frederick Charles Maker)
1431. We would see Jesus; for the shadows lengthen/Across this
      little landscape of our life
      MH (1905)-323. Visio Domini (John Bacchus Dykes)

WARREN, WILLIAM FAIRFIELD
1432. I worship Thee, O Holy Ghost,/I love to worship Thee
      HMEC-272. Chesterfield (Thomas Haweis)
      MH (1905)-186. Cooling (Alonzo Judson Abbey)
      MH (1935)-174. Cooling (Alonzo Judson Abbey)
1433. Out on the ocean all boundless we ride,/We're homeward
      bound
      MSSH-254. Homeward Bound (Calvin Sears Harrington)

WATERBURY, JARED BELL
1434. Soldiers of the cross, arise!/Lo! your Leader from the
      skies
      HMEC-566. Caledonia (Scottish traditional)
      MH (1905)-385. Caledonia (Scottish traditional)
      MH (1935)-281. Caledonia (Scottish traditional)

WATTS, ALARIC ALEXANDER
1435. When shall we meet again,/Meet ne'er to sever?
      HMEC-807. Unity (Lowell Mason)

WATTS, ISAAC
1436. A broken heart, my God, my King,/To Thee a sacrifice I
      bring
      MH (1905)-266. Louvan (Virgil Corydon Taylor)
      AMEH-162. Hursley (Franz Joseph Haydn)
1437. Ah, how shall fallen man/Be just before his God?
      HMEC-310. Shawmut (Lowell Mason)
1438. Alas! and did my Saviour bleed?/And did my Sovereign die?
      HMEC-214. Communion (Stephen Jenks)
      MH (1905)-146. Communion (Stephen Jenks)
                  Avon (Hugh Wilson)

MH (1935)-142. Martyrdom (Hugh Wilson)
AMEH-124. Martyrdom (Hugh Wilson)
AMEH-300. Chelmsford (Amzi Chapin)
AMEH-319. At the Cross (Ralph E. Hudson)
AMEH-430. Alas, and Did My Saviour Bleed? (E.C. Deas)
MH (1966)-415. Martyrdom (Hugh Wilson)
1439. Am I a soldier of the cross,/A follower of the Lamb
HMEC-593. Arlington (Thomas Augustine Arne)
MH (1905)-393. Arlington (Thomas Augustine Arne)
MSSH-204. Arlington (Thomas Augustine Arne)
MH (1935)-284. Arlington (Thomas Augustine Arne)
AMEH-50. Arlington (Thomas Augustine Arne)
AMEH-534. Am I a Soldier (English traditional)
MH (1966)-239. Arlington (Thomas Augustine Arne)
1440. And must this body die,/This well-wrought frame decay?
HMEC-995. Capello (Lowell Mason)
AMEH-651. Without tune
1441. Awake, our souls! away, our fears!/Let every trembling
thought be gone!
MH (1905)-405. Doane (John Baptiste Calkin)
1442. Before Jehovah's awful throne,/Ye nations bow with sacred
joy
HMEC-9. Old Hundred (Guillaume Franc)
MH (1905)-6. Old Hundred (Guillaume Franc)
MH (1935)-3. Old Hundred (Genevan Psalter)
AMEH-667. Without tune
MH (1966)-27. Old 100th (Louis Bourgeois)
1443. Begin, my tongue, some heavenly theme,/And speak some bound-
less thing
MH (1905)-89. Maker (Frederick Charles Maker)
1444. Behold the glories of the Lamb/Amidst his Father's throne
MH (1905)-167. Miles' Lane (William Shrubsole)
1445. Behold the sure Foundation-stone/Which God in Zion lays
HMEC-776. St. Ann's (William Croft)
1446. Behold, what wondrous grace/The Father has bestowed
AMEH-73. State Street (Jonathan Call Woodman)
1447. Blest are the sons of peace,/Whose hearts and hopes are one
HMEC-799. Dennis (Hans George Naegeli)
1448. Broad is the road that leads to death,/And thousands walk
together there
AMEH-224. Windham (Daniel Read)
1449. Come, happy souls, approach your God/With new melodious
songs
AMEH-168. Heber (George Kingsley)
1450. Come, Holy Spirit, heavenly Dove,/With all Thy quickening
powers
HMEC-277. St. Martin's (William Tans'ur)
MH (1905)-183. St. Martin's (William Tans'ur)
Azmon (Carl Gotthelf Glaser, arr. Lowell
Mason)
MH (1935)-172. St. Martin's (William Tans'ur)
AMEH-200. Maitland (George Nelson Allen)
AMEH-203. St. Martin's (William Tans'ur)
MH (1966)-134. Grafenberg (Johann Cruger)
1451. Come, let our voices join to raise/A sacred song of solemn

praise
AMEH-388.  Ward (arr. Lowell Mason)
1452.  Come, let us join our cheerful songs/With angels round the throne
HMEC-2.  Azmon (Carl Gotthelf Glaser, arr. Lowell Mason)
MH (1905)-24.  Newbold (George Kingsley)
MSSH-6.  Nativity (Henry Laker)
AMEH-275.  Elizabethtown (George Kingsley)
1453.  Come saints, and drop a tear or two/For Him who groaned beneath your load
HMEC-234.  Grace Church (Ignace Josef Pleyel)
1454.  Come, sound His praise abroad,/And hymns of glory sing
HMEC-3.  Silver Street (Isaac Smith)
MH (1905)-3.  Silver Street (Isaac Smith)
MH (1935)-22.  Silver Street (Isaac Smith)
MH (1966)-24.  Cambridge (Ralph Harrison, arr. Samuel Sebastian Wesley)
1455.  Come ye, that love the Lord,/And let your joys be known
HMEC-41.  Waugh (Ralph Harrison)
MH (1905)-22.  St. Thomas (Aaron Williams)
MH (1935)-227.  St. Thomas (Aaron Williams)
AMEH-541.  We're Marching to Zion (Robert Lowry)
MH (1966)-5.  St. Thomas (Aaron Williams)
1456.  Eternal power, whose high abode/Becomes the grandeur of a God
HMEC-38.  Miller (Carl Philip Emmanuel Bach, arr. Edward Miller)
MH (1905)-17.  Miller (Carl Philip Emmanuel Bach, arr. Edward Miller)
1457.  Far from my thoughts, vain world, be gone!/Let my religious hours alone
HMEC-84.  Rockingham (Lowell Mason)
1458.  Father, how wide Thy glory shines,/How high Thy wonders rise!
HMEC-146.  Stephens (William Jones)
MH (1905)-79.  Beatitudo (John Bacchus Dykes)
1459.  From all that dwell below the skies,/Let the Creator's praise arise
HMEC-8.  Old Hundred (Guillaume Franc)
MH (1905)-5.  Duke Street (John Hatton)
MH (1935)-17.  Duke Street (John Hatton)
AMEH-10.  Woodworth (William Batchelder Bradbury)
AMEH-317.  Duke Street (John Hatton)
MH (1966)-14.  Duke Street (John Hatton)
1460.  Give me the wings of faith, to rise/Within the veil, and see
HMEC-1045.  Newbold (George Kingsley)
MH (1905)-606.  Newbold (George Kingsley)
MH (1935)-424.  St. Peter (Alexander Robert Reinagle)
MH (1966)-533.  Sims (William Jensen Reynolds)
1461.  "Go preach mt gospel," saith the Lord,/"Bid the whole world my grace receive. . . ."
HMEC-820.  Griswold (Unknown)
AMEH-415.  Retreat (Thomas Hastings)
1462.  God is the name my soul adores,/The almighty Three, the eternal One

HMEC-130.  Hamburg (Lowell Mason)
MH (1905)-80.  Janes (Johann Christian Wolfgang Amadeus
   Mozart)

1463.  God is the refuge of His saints,/When storms of sharp dis-
   tress
   HMEC-773.  Appleton (William Boyce)
   MH (1905)-218.  Ward (Lowell Mason)

1464.  Great God, attend while Zion sings/The joy that from Thy
   presence springs
   HMEC-69.  Gilead (Etienne Henri Mehul)
   MH (1905)-213.  Park Street (Frederick Marc Antonio Ven-
    ua)
   AMEH-40.  All Saints (William Knapp)
   MH (1966)-25.  Park Street (Frederick Marc Antonio Ven-
    ua)

1465.  Great God, how infinite art Thou!/What worthless worms are
   we!
   AMEH-59.  Dundee (Scottish Psalter, 1615)

1466.  Great is the Lord our God,/And let His praise be great
   HMEC-871.  Dundee (Guillaume Franc)

1467.  Hark! from the tombs a doleful sound;/My ears, attend the
   cry
   HMEC-972.  China (Timothy Swan)
   AMEH-666.  Without tune

1468.  He dies! the Friend of sinners dies!/Lo! Salem's daughter
   weep around
   MH (1905)-165.  Storrs (Timothy Richard Matthews)

1469.  Hear what the voice from heaven proclaims/For all the pious
   dead!
   MH (1905)-588.  Sabbata (Henry Frederic Hemi)

1470.  High in the heav'ns, Eternal God,/Thy goodness in full
   glory shines
   MH (1935)-82.  DePauw (Robert Guy McCutchan)

1471.  How beauteous are their feet/Who stand on Zion's hill
   HMEC-821.  Griswold (Unknown)
   AMEH-15.  Dennis (Hans George Naegeli)

1472.  How did my heart rejoice to hear/My friends devoutly say
   AMEH-41.  Mear (Aaron Williams)

1473.  How pleasant, how divinely fair,/O Lord of hosts, Thy dwellings are!
   MH (1905)-215.  All Saints (William Knapp)

1474.  How sad our state by nature is!/Our sin, how deep it
   stains!
   HMEC-302.  Haven (Thomas Hastings)
   MH (1905)-268.  Southwell (Herbert Stephen Irons)

1475.  How shall the young secure their hearts,/And guard their
   lives from sin?
   MH (1905)-204.  Salome (Ludwig van Beethoven)

1476.  How strong Thine arm is, mighty God,/Who would not fear Thy
   name?
   AMEH-663.  Without tune

1477.  How vain are all things here below!/How false, and yet how
   fair!
   HMEC-662.  Heber (George Kingsley)

1478.  I lift my soul to God,/My trust is in His name

AMEH-474. Gerar (Lowell Mason)
1479. I love the Lord: He heard my cries,/And pitied every groan
HMEC-621. Gould (John Edgar Gould)
AMEH-662. Without tune
1480. I sing the almighty power of God,/That made the mountain
rise
MH (1966)-37. Forest Green (arr. Ralph Vaughan Williams)
1481. I'll praise my Maker while I've breath,/And when my voice
is lost in death
HMEC-740. St. Catherine (J.G. Walton)
MH (1905)-534. Monmouth (G. Davis)
Nashville (Lowell Mason)
MH (1935)-513. Old 113th/Lucerne (Ernest MacMillan)
MH (1966)-9. Old 113th Matthaus Greiter)
1482. I'm not ashamed to own my Lord,/Or to defend His cause
HMEC-595. Arlington (Thomas Augustine Arne)
MH (1905)-441. Chesterfield (Thomas Haweis)
AMEH-6. Varina (George Frederick Root)
1483. In all my vast concerns with Thee,/In vain my soul would
try
AMEH-63. Downs (Lowell Mason)
1484. Jesus, my great High Priest,/Offered His blood and died
AMEH-141A. Claremont (William Batchelder Bradbury)
1485. Jesus shall reign were'er the sun/Does his successive jour-
ney run
HMEC-919. Migdol (Lowell Mason)
MH (1905)-631. Duke Street (John Hatton)
MSSH-242. Duke Street (John Hatton)
MH (1935)-479. Duke Street (John Hatton)
AMEH-522. Duke Street (John Hatton)
AMEH-570. Sessions (Luther Orlando Emerson)
MH (1966)-472. Duke Street (John Hatton)
1486. Jesus, Thou everlasting King,/Accept the tribute which we
bring
HMEC-12. Truro (Charles Burney)
MH (1905)-7. Truro (Charles Burney)
1487. Join all the glorious names/Of wisdom, love, and power
HMEC-243. Ortonville (Thomas Hastings)
AMEH-141. Claremont (William Batchelder Bradbury)
1488. Joy to the world! the Lord is come;/Let earth receive her
king
HMEC-183. Antioch (George Frederick Handel)
MH (1905)-107. Copenhagen (Peter Christian Lutkin)
Antioch (George Frederick Handel)
MSSH-60. Antioch (George Frederick Handel)
MH (1935)-89. Antioch (George Frederick Handel)
AMEH-90. Antioch (George Frederick Handel)
MH (1966)-392. Antioch (George Frederick Handel)
1489. Kingdoms and thrones to God belong;/Crown Him, ye nations,
in your song
HMEC-162. Hamburg (Lowell Mason)
1490. Laden with guilt and full of fears,/I fly to Thee, O Lord
AMEH-386. St. Martin's William Tans'ur)
1491. Let all on earth their voices raise,/To sing the great Je-
hovah's praise

> HMEC-17.  Ariel (arr. Lowell Mason)
> MH (1905)-9.  Ariel (arr. Lowell Mason)
> MH (1935)-19.  Ariel (arr. Lowell Mason)
> MH (1966)-39.  Old 113th (Matthaus Greiter)

1492.  Let every mortal ear attend,/And every heart rejoice
> HMEC-326.  Cambridge (John Randall)

1493.  Let every tongue Thy goodness speak,/Thou sovereign Lord of all
> HMEC-154.  Belmont (Samuel Webbe)

1494.  Lo, what a glorious sight appears/To our believing eyes
> HMEC-1035.  Harris (Louis Devereaux)
> AMEH-574.  Cambridge (John Randall)

1495.  Long have I sat beneath the sound/Of Thy salvation, Lord
> MH (1905)-281.  Siloam (Isaac Baker Woodbury)

1496.  Lord, all I am is known to Thee;/In vain my soul would try
> HMEC-123.  Bemerton (Henry Wellington Greatorex)

1497.  Lord, how secure and blest are they/Who feel the joys of pardoned sin
> HMEC-418.  Wimborne (John Whitaker)
> MH (1905)-439.  Wimborne (John Whitaker)

1498.  Lord, in the morning Thou shalt hear/My voice ascending high
> HMEC-98.  Warwick (Samuel Stanley)
> MH (1905)-41.  Warwick (Samuel Stanley)
> AMEH-44.  Warwick (Samuel Stanley)

1499.  Lord of the worlds above,/How pleasant and how fair
> HMEC-15.  Darwall (John Darwall)

1500.  Lord, Thou hast searched and seen me thro':/Thine eye commands, with piercing view
> AMEH-60.  Ward (Lowell Mason)

1501.  Lord, we are vile, conceived in sin,/And born unholy and unclean
> HMEC-305.  Louvan (Virgil Corydon Taylor)

1502.  My dear Redeemer and my Lord,/I read my duty in Thy word
> MH (1905)-140.  Kiel (Peter Christian Lutkin)

1503.  My drowsy powers, why sleep ye so?/Awake, my sluggish soul!
> HMEC-547.  Dedham (William Gardiner)

1504.  My God, how endless is Thy love!/Thy gifts are every evening new
> HMEC-104.  Hursley (Peter Ritter, arr. William Henry Monk)
> AMEH-66.  St. Polycarp ( Ignace Josef Pleyel)

1505.  My God, my Life, my Love,/To Thee, Thee, I call
> AMEH-751.  Whitefield (Edward Miller)

1506.  My God, my Portion, and my Love,/My everlasting all
> HMEC-698.  Emmons (Friedrich Burgmuller)

1507.  My God, the spring of all my joys,/The life of my delights
> HMEC-704.  Roscoe (Edward Little White)
> MH (1905)-535.  Chesterfield (Thomas Haweis)
> AMEH-649.  Without tune

1508.  My Saviour, my almighty Friend,/When I begin Thy praise
> HMEC-699.  Emmons (Friedrich Burgmuller)

1509.  My soul, repeat His praise,/Whose mercies are so great
> HMEC-172.  Magata (John Black)
> MH (1905)-94.  Ben Rhydding (Alexander Robert Reinagle)

AMEH-223.  Devizes (Isaac Tucker)
1510.  My thoughts surmount these lower skies,/And look within the veil
    AMEH-308.  Geneva (John Cole)
1511.  Not all the blood of beasts,/On Jewish altars slain
    AMEH-218.  Boylston (Lowell Mason)
1512.  Not to the terrors of the Lord,/The tempest, fire, and smoke
    HMEC-787.  Hummel (Heinrich Christopher Zeuner)
1513.  Now may the God of grace and power/Attend His people's humble cry
    HMEC-1104.  Duke Street (John Hatton)
1514.  Now to the Lord a noble song!/Awake, my soul, awake my tongue
    AMEH-72.  Duke Street (John Hatton)
1515.  O bless the Lord, my soul!/His grace to thee proclaim
    HMEC-749.  Whitefield (Edward Miller)
1516.  O for an overcoming faith,/To cheer my dying hours
    HMEC-985.  Ashwell (Lowell Mason)
1517.  O God, our help in ages past,/Our hope for years to come
    HMEC-964.  Mear (Aaron Williams)
    MH (1905)-577.  St. Anne (William Croft)
                Mear (Aaron Williams)
    MH (1935)-533.  St. Anne (William Croft)
    AMEH-165.  St. Anne (William Croft)
    AMEH-192.  Maitland (George Nelson Allen)
    MH (1966)-28.  St. Anne (William Croft)
1518.  O that I knew the secret place/Where I might find my God!
    AMEH-172.  Warwick (Samuel Stanley)
1519.  O 'tis delight without alloy,/Jesus, to hear Thy name
    AMEH-703.  Roscoe (Edward Little White)
1520.  Once more, my soul, the rising day/Salutes thy waking eyes
    HMEC-95.  Peterboro' (Ralph Harrison)
    AMEH-193.  Maitland (George Allen Nelson)
1521.  Plunged in a gulf of dark  despair,/We wretched sinners lay
    HMEC-304.  Haven (Thomas Hastings)
    MH (1905)-242.  Balerma (Robert Simpson)
    AMEH-146.  Byefield (Thomas Hastings)
1522.  Praise ye the Lord, y' immortal choirs/That fill the world above
    HMEC-153.  Tappan (George Kingsley)
    AMEH-116.  Warwick (Samuel Stanley)
1523.  Salvation! O the joyful sound!/What pleasure to our ears
    HMEC-324.  Cambridge (John Randall)
    MH (1905)-287.  Mount Calvary (Robert Prescott Stewart)
    AMEH-169.  St. Peter (Alexander Robert Reinagle)
    AMEH-220.  Cambridge (John Randall)
1524.  Shall we go on to sin,/Because Thy grace abounds?
    AMEH-670.  Without tune
1525.  Show pity, Lord, O Lord, forgive;/Let a repenting rebel live
    HMEC-391.  Windham (David Read)
    MH (1905)-270.  St. Cross (John Bacchus Dykes)
    AMEH-163.  Hirsley (Franz Joseph Haydn)
1526.  Sweet is the work, my God, my King,/To praise Thy name,

give thanks, and sing
HMEC-81. Rockingham (Lowell Mason)
MH (1905)-71. Rockingham (Lowell Mason)
1527. That awful day will surely come,/The appointed hour makes haste
HMEC-1020. Windsor (George Kirbye)
AMEH-647. Without tune
1528. The heavens declare Thy glory, Lord;/In every star Thy wisdom shines
HMEC-292. Uxbridge (Lowell Mason)
MH (1905)-202. Gilead (Etienne Henri Mahul)
MH (1966)-365. Hebron (Lowell Mason)
1529. The Lord declares His will,/And keeps the world in awe
AMEH-29. Greenwood (Joseph Emerson Sweetser)
1530. The Lord Jehovah reigns,/His throne is built on high
HMEC-142. Millennium (Traditional English)
MH (1905)-81. Millennium (Traditional English)
MSSH-16. Millennium (Traditional English)
MH (1935)-63. Millennium (Traditional English)
MH (1966)-31. Millennium (Traditional English)
1531. Thee we adore, eternal Name,/And humbly own to Thee
HMEC-965. Mear (Aaron Williams)
1532. There is a land of pure delight,/Where saints immortal reign
HMEC-1037. Varina (Johann Christian Heinrich Rink)
MH (1905)-604. Varina George Frederick Root)
MH (1935)-528. Varina (George Frederick Root)
AMEH-465. Varina (George Frederick Root)
1533. This is the day the Lord hath made,/He calls the hours His own
AMEH-37. Christmas (George Frederick Handel)
1534. Thou art my portion, O my God!/Soon as I know Thy way
AMEH-103. Arlington (Thomas Augustine Arne)
1535. Thus far the Lord hath led me on,/Thus far His power prolongs my days
HMEC-108. Hebron (Lowell Mason)
MH (1905)-51. Hebron (Lowell Mason)
1536. To God the only wise,/Our Saviour and our King
AMEH-507. Old 134th/St. Michael (from the Genevan Psalter, 1551)
1537. Unveil thy bosom, faithful tomb;/Take this new treasure to thy trust
HMEC-984. Ashwell (Lowell Mason)
MH (1905)-586. Dirge (George Frederick Handel)
1538. Welcome, sweet day of rest,/That saw the Lord arise
HMEC-85. Lisbon (Daniel Read)
MH (1905)-64. Lisbon (Daniel Read)
AMEH-33. State Street (Jonathan Call Woodman)
AMEH-228. Lisbon (Daniel Read)
1539. What equal honors shall we bring/To Thee, O Lord our God, the Lamb
AMEH-87. Missionary Chant (Heinrich Christoph Zeuner)
1540. What sinners value I resign;/Lord, 'tis enough that Thou art mine
HMEC-1042. Park Street (Frederick Marc Antoine Venua)

1541.  When I can read my title clear/To mansions in the skies
         HMEC-659.  Clinton (Jeseph Perry Holbrook)
         MH (1905)-440.  Arlington (Thomas Augustine Arne)
         AMEH-249.  I Will Trust in the Lord (E.C. Deas)
         AMEH-325.  Moore (Samuel Webbe)
         AMEH-525.  Pisgah (J.C. Lowry)
1542.  When I survey the wondrous cross/On which the Prince of
         glory died
         HMEC-211.  Eucharist (Isaac Baker Woodbury)
         MH (1905)-141.  Eucharist (Isaac Baker Woodbury)
         MSSH-86.  Eucharist (Isaac Baker Woodbury)
         MH (1935)-148.  Eucharist (Isaac Baker Woodbury)
         AMEH-104.  Hamburg (Lowell Mason)
         AMEH-457.  Eucharist (Isaac Baker Woodbury)
         MH (1966)-435.  Hamburg (Lowell Mason)
1543.  Why do we mourn for dying friends,/Or shake at death's
         alarms?
         HMEC-970.  China (Timothy Swan)
         MH (1905)-595.  Claudius (Arthur Henry Mann)
1544.  Why should the children of a King/Go mourning all their
         days?
         HMEC-424.  Evan (William Henry Havergal)
         MH (1905)-299.  Holy Trinity (Joseph Barnby)
1545.  Why should we start, and fear to die?/What timorous worms
         we mortals are!
         HMEC-976.  Bristol (Edward Little White)
         MH (1905)-681.  Pentecost (William Boyd)
1546.  With joy we meditate the grace/Of our High Priest above
         HMEC-254.  Heber (George Kingsley)
         AMEH-236.  Jerusalem (Charles F. Roper)

WELLS, MARCUS MORRIS
1547.  Holy Spirit, faithful Guide,/Ever near the Christian's
         side
         MH (1905)-193.  Holy Spirit, Faithful Guide (Marcus Mor-
                 ris Wells)
         MH (1935)-293.  Holy Spirit, Faithful Guide (Marcus Mor-
                 ris Wells)
         AMEH-202.  Guide (Marcus Morris Wells)
         MH (1966)-106.  Faithful Guide (Marcus Morris Wells)

WESLEY, CHARLES
1548.  A charge to keep I have,/A God to glorify
         HMEC-574.  Boylston (Lowell Mason)
         MH (1905)-388.  Boylston (Lowell Mason)
         MSSH-213.  Boylston (Lowell Mason)
         MH (1935)-287.  Boylston (Lowell Mason)
         AMEH-293.  St. Thomas (Unknown)
         MH (1966)-150.  Boylston (Lowell Mason)
1549.  A stranger in the world below,/I calmly sojourn here
         HMEC-1031.  Devizes (Isaac Tucker)
1550.  A thousand oracles divine/Their common beams unite
         HMEC-34.  Arlington (Thomas Augustine Arne)
         MH (1905)-75.  Azmon (Carl Gotthelf Glaser, arr. Lowell
                 Mason)

1551.  Abba, Father, hear Thy child,/Late in Jesus reconciled
          HMEC-440.  Viola (William Batchelder Bradbury)
1552.  Abraham, when severely tried,/His faith by his obedience
              showed
          HMEC-471.  Saxby (Timothy Richard Matthews)
1553.  Ah! whither should I go,/Burdened, and sick, and faint?
          HMEC-402.  Owen (Joseph Emerson Sweetser)
          MH (1905)-283.  Leominster (Arthur Seymour Sullivan)
          AMEH-167.  Dunbar (E.W. Dùnbar)
          AMEH-673.  Dunbar (E.W. Dunbar)
1554.  All praise to Him who dwells in bliss,/Who made both day
              and night
          HMEC-97.  Peterboro' (Ralph Harrison)
1555.  All praise to our redeeming Lord,/Who joins us by His grace
          HMEC-789.  Armenia (Sylvanus Billings Pond)
          MH (1905)-553.  Armenia(Sylvanus Billings Pond)
          MH (1935)-417.  Armenia (Sylvanus Billings Pond)
          MH (1966)-301.  Armenia (Sylvanus Billings Pond)
1556.  All praise to the Lamb! accepted I am,/Through faith in the
              Saviour's adorable name
          HMEC-454.  Lyons (Franz Joseph Haydn)
1557.  Am I born to die?/To lay this body down?
          HMEC-996.  Tioga (Thomas Hastings)
          MH (1905)-590.  Nearer Home (Isaac Baker Woodbury, arr.
                                  Arthur Seymour Sullivan)
          AMEH-653.  Without tune
1558.  And am I only born to die?/And must I suddenly comply
          HMEC-968.  Venetia (Traditional English)
1559.  And are we yet alive,/And see each other's face?
          HMEC-798.  Dennis (Hans George Naegeli)
          MH (1905)-560.  Dennis (Hans George Naegeli)
          MH (1935)-402.  Dennis (Hans George Naegeli)
          AMEH-295.  St. Thomas (Unknown)
          AMEH-302.  Dennis (Hans George Naegeli)
          MH (1966)-336.  Dennis (Hans George Naegeli)
1560.  And can I yet delay/My little all to give?
          HMEC-401.  Boylston (Lowell Mason)
          MH (1905)-275.  Boylston (Lowell Mason)
          AMEH-167A.  Hudson (Ralph Harrison)
          AMEH-354.  State Street (Jonathan Call Woodman)
1561.  And can it be that I should gain/An interest in the Savi-
              our's blood?
          HMEC-422.  Evanston (Joseph Perry Holbrook)
          MH (1905)-310.  Fillmore (Jeremiah Ingalls)
          MH (1935)-229.  Fillmore (Jeremiah Ingalls)
          MH (1966)-527.  Fillmore (Jeremiah Ingalls)
1562.  And let our bodies part,/To different climes repair
          HMEC-816.  Olmutz (Lowell Mason)
          MH (1905)-227.  Olmutz (Lowell Mason)
          MH (1935)-403.  Boylston (Lowell Mason)
          AMEH-303.  Boylston (Lowell Mason)
          AMEH-414.  Boylston (Lowell Mason)
1563.  And let this feeble body fail,/And let it faint or die
          HMEC-1032.  Devizes (Usaac Tucker)
          MH (1905)-607.  Rex Regnum (John Stainer)
          AMEH-466.  Varina (George Frederick Root)

1564.   And must I be to judgment brought,/And answer in that day
        HMEC-1021.   Windsor (George Kirbye)
        MH (1905)-600.   Sinai (Joseph Barnby)
        AMEH-34.   Avon (Hugh Wilson)
1565.   And wilt Thou yet be found,/And may I still draw near?
        HMEC-399.   Boylston (Lowell Mason)
1566.   Are there not in the labourer's day/Twelve hours, in which
            he safely may
        HMEC-570.   Mendelssohn (Otto Nicolai)
1567.   Arise, my soul, arise;/Shake off thy guilty fears
        HMEC-438.   Lenox (Lewis Edson)
        MH (1905)-301.   Lenox (Lewis Edson)
        MH (1935)-211.   Lenox (Lewis Edson)
        MH (1966)-122.   Lenox (Lewis Edson)
1568.   Arm of the Lord, awake, awake!/Thine own immortal strength
            put on!
        HMEC-1043.   Park Street (Frederick Marc Antonio Venua)
        MH (1905)-216.   Thanksgiving (Francis Reginald Statham)
1569.   Author of faith, eternal Word,/Whose Spirit breathes the
            active flame
        HMEC-445.   Samson (George Frederick Handel)
        MH (1905)-298.   Samson (George Frederick Handel)
        MH (1966)-139.   Mainzer (Joseph Mainzer)
1570.   Author of life divine,/Who has a table spread
        MH (1966)-315.   Author of Life (Robert J. Powell)
1571.   Author of our salvation, Thee,/With lowly, thankful hearts,
            we praise
        HMEC-851.   St. Alban (Unknown)
1572.   Author of the faith, to Thee I cry,/To Thee, who wouldst not
            have me die
        HMEC-377.   Auburndale (Olen Lester Carter)
1573.   Awake, Jerusalem, awake!/No longer in thy sins lie down
        HMEC-775.   Appleton (William Boyce)
        MH (1905)-217.   Luton (George Burder)
1574.   Away, my needless fears,/And doubts no longer mine
        HMEC-173.   Haydn (Franz Joseph Haydn)
1575.   Away, my unbelieving fear!/Fear shall in me no more have
            place
        HMEC-626.   Fillmore (Jeremiah Ingalls)
1576.   Away with our sorrow and fear,/We soon shall recover our
            home
        HMEC-1063.   Alford (John Bacchus Dykes)
1577.   Be it my only wisdom here,/To serve the Lord with filial
            fear
        HMEC-571.   Mendelssohn (Otto Nicolai)
1578.   Behold the servant of the Lord!/I wait Thy guiding hand to
            feel
        HMEC-475.   Yoakley (William Yoakley)
1579.   Being of beings, God of love,/To Thee our hearts we raise
        HMEC-508.   Manoah (Etienne Henri Mehul and Franz Joseph
                    Haydn)
1580.   Blessed be the dear uniting love,/That will not let us part
        HMEC-782.   Hermon (Lowell Mason)
        MH (1905)-228.   Faith (John Bacchus Dykes)
        MH (1935)-404.   Tiplady (John Porter)
        AMEH-431.   Coventry (Unknown)

MH (1935)-338.  Evan (William Havergal, arr. Lowell Mason)

1581. Blow ye the trumpet, blow,/The gladly solemn sound!
     HMEC-331.  Lenox (Lewis Edson)
     MH (1905)-294.  Lenox (Lewis Edson)
     MH (1935)-189.  Lenox (Lewis Edson)
     MH (1966)-100.  Lenox (Lewis Edson)
1582. Brethren in Christ, and well beloved,/To Jesus and His servants dear
     HMEC-791.  Tichorah (Lowell Mason)
1583. But can it be that I should prove/Forever faithful to Thy love
     HMEC-541.  Habakkuk (Edward Hodges)
1584. Call'd from above I rise,/And wash away my sin
     AMEH-228B.  Lisbon (Daniel Read)
1585. Captain  of Israel's host, and guide/Of all who seek the land above
     MH (1966)-46.  Eisenach (Johann Hermann Schein)
1586. Captain of our salvation, take/The souls we here present to Thee
     HMEC-825.  Valete (Arthur Seymour Sullivan)
1587. Christ, from whom all blessings flow,/Perfecting the saints below
     HMEC-806.  Onido (Ignace Josef Pleyel)
     AMEH-406.  Herndon (Henri Abraham Caesar Malan)
     MH (1966)-530.  Canterbury (Orlando Gibbons)
1588. Christ the Lord is risen today, Halelujah!/Sons of men and angels say: Halelujah! (See also 1379)
     HMEC-260.  Essex (Thomas Clark)
     MH (1905)-156.  Easter Hymn (from Lyrica Davidica, 1708)
                  Paschale Gaudium (John Stainer)
     MSSH-91.  Easter Hymn (from Lyrica Davidica, 1708)
     MH (1935)-154.  Easter Hymn (from Lyrica Davidica, 1708)
     AMEH-131.  Anglia (Henry Carey)
     MH (1966)-439.  Easter Hymn (from Lyrica Davidica, 1708)
1589. Christ, whose glory fills the skies,/Christ, the true, the only Light
     HMEC-416.  Toplady (Thomas Hastings)
     MH (1935)-32.  Ratisbon (Old German melody)
     MH (1966)-401.  Ratisbon (arr. William Henry Monk)
1590. Come, and let us sweetly join,/Christ to praise in hymns divine
     HMEC-805.  Onido (Ignace Josef Pleyel)
1591. Come, Father, Son, and Holy Ghost,/Honour the means ordained by Thee
     HMEC-831.  Ward (Lowell Mason)
     MH (1905)-229.  Ward (Lowell Mason)
1592. Come, Father, Son, and Holy Ghost,/To whom we for our children cry
     MH (1966)-344.  St. Catherine (Henri Frederick Hemy)
1593. Come, Holy Ghost, all-quickening fire,/My consecrated heart inspire
     HMEC-481.  Nashville (Lowell Mason)
1594. Come, Holy Ghost, our hearts inspire;/Let us Thine influence prove
     HMEC-279.  St. Martin's (William Tans'ur)

        MH (1905)-181.  Winchester Old (George Kirbye)
        MH (1935)-175.  Winchester Old (George Kirbye)
        MH (1966)-131.  Winchester Old (George Kirbye)
1595.  Come, Holy Spirit, raise our songs/To reach the wonders of
        that day
        HMEC-275.  Melcombe (Samuel Webbe)
1596.  Come, let us anew our journey pursue,/Roll round with the
        year
        HMEC-955.  Lucas (James Lucas)
1597.  Come, let us anew our journey pursue,/With vigor arise
        HMEC-1074.  New Year's Hymn (Samuel Webbe)
        MH (1905)-568.  Lucas (James Lucas)
        MH (1935)-536.  Lucas (James Lucas)
1598.  Come, let us ascend,/My companion and friend
        HMEC-1073.  Going Home (William McDonald)
1599.  Come, let us join our friends above/That have obtained the
        prize
        HMEC-1033.  Burlington (John Freckleton Burrowes)
        MH (1905)-611.  Holmfirth (Benjamin Gill)
        MH (1935)-422.  Dundee (Scottish Psalter, 1615)
        MH (1966)-302.  Pisgah (J.C. Lowry)
1600.  Come, let us join with one accord/In hymns around the
        throne!
        MH (1905)-63.  Chesterfield (Thomas Haweis)
        AMEH-38.  Christmas (George Frederick Handel)
1601.  Come, let us rise with Christ our Head/And seek the things
        above
        MH (1966)-457.  St. Matthew (William Croft)
1602.  Come, let us use the grace divine,/And all, with one accord
        HMEC-945.  St. Martin's (William Tans'ur)
        MH (1905)-569.  St. Martin's (William Tans'ur)
        MH (1935)-540.  St. Martin's (William Tans'ur)
        MH (1966)-507.  St. Martin's (William Tans'ur)
        MH (1966)-508.  Covenant Hymn (Thomas Canning)
1603.  Come, let us who in Christ believe,/Our common Saviour
        praise
        HMEC-28.  Andrews (John Black)
        MH (1905)-36.  Belmont (William Gardiner)
        MH (1966)-111.  Campmeeting (Early American melody)
1604.  Come, O my God, the promise seal,/This mountain, sin, remove
        HMEC-522.  Simpson (Louis Spohr)
1605.  Come, O Thou all-victorious Lord,/Thy power to us make known
        HMEC-368.  Mear (Aaron Williams)
        MH (1905)-241.  St. Peter's, Oxford (Alexander Robert
                    Reinagle)
        AMEH-176.  Mount Auburn (George Kingsley)
        AMEH-177.  Morn (Unknown)
1606.  Come, O Thou greater than our heart,/And make Thy faithful
        mercies known
        HMEC-524.  Janes (Johann Christian Wolfgang Amadeus Mo-
                zart)
1607.  Come, O Thou Traveler unknown,/Whom still I hold, but cannot
        see
        HMEC-737.  St. Catherine (J.G. Walton)
        MH (1905)-511.  St. Catherine (J.G. Walton)
        MH (1935)-311.  Candler (Scottish traditional)

MH (1966)-529.  Candler (Scottish traditional)
1608. Come, O ye sinners, to the Lord,/In Christ to paradise re-
           stored
       HMEC-351.  Wells (Israel Holdroyd)
1609. Come on, my partners in distress,/My comrades through the
           wilderness
       HMEC-657.  Ganges (S. Chandler)
       MH (1905)-432.  Habakkuk (Edward Hodges)
1610. Come, sinners, to the gospel feast;/Let every soul be Jesus'
           guest
       HMEC-364.  Hamburg (Lowell Mason)
       MH (1905)-256.  Uxbridge (Lowell Mason)
       MH (1935)-186.  Uxbridge (Lowell Mason)
       AMEH-27.  Hebron (Lowell Mason)
       MH (1966)-102.  Winchester New (arr. William Henry Haver-
           gal)
1611. Come, Thou almighty King,/Help us Thy name to sing
       HMEC-6.  Italian Hymn (Felice Giardini)
       MH (1905)-2.  Italian Hymn (Felice Giardini)
       MSSH-1.  Italian Hymn (Felice Giardini)
1612. Come, Thou everlasting Spirit,/Bring to every thankful mind
       HMEC-854.  Autumn (Francois Hippolyte Barthelemon)
1613. Come, Thou long-expected Jesus,/Born to set Thy people free
       HMEC-334.  Wilson (Felix Mendelssohn-Bartholdy)
       MH (1905)-116.  Wilson (Felix Mendelssohn-Bartholdy)
       MSSH-55.  Stuttgart (from Psalmodia Sacra)
       MH (1935)-84.  Hyfrydol (Rowland Hugh Prichard)
       AMEH-246.  Greenville (Jean Jacques Rousseau)
       MH (1966)-360.  Hyfrydol (Rowland Hugh Prichard)
1614. Come, weary sinners, come,/Groaning beneath your load
       HMEC-359.  Capello (Lowell Mason)
1615. Comfort, ye ministers of grace,/Comfort the people of your
           Lord
       HMEC-926.  Promise (Francois Hippolyte Barthelemon)
       AMEH-296.  Rest (William Batchelder Bradbury)
1616. Deepen the wound Thy people have made/In this weak, helpless
           soul
       HMEC-538.  Llandaff (Edwin Moss)
1617. Depth of mercy! can there be/Mercy still reserved for me?
       HMEC-379.  Pleyel's Hymn (Ignace Josef Pleyel)
       MH (1905)-267.  Seymour (Carl Maria von Weber)
       MH (1935)-200.  Seymour (Carl Maria von Weber)
       AMEH-175.  Zerah (Lowell Mason)
       MH (1966)-94.  Seymour (Carl Maria von Weber)
1618. Draw near, O Son of God, draw near;/Us with Thy flaming eye
           behold
       HMEC-815.  Bartholdy (Felix Mendelssohn-Bartholdy)
       AMEH-296.  Rest (William Batchelder Bradbury)
1619. Equip me for the war,/And teach my hands to fight
       HMEC-586.  Clapton (William Jones)
1620. Eternal beam of light divine,/Fountain of unexhausted love
       HMEC-623.  He Leadeth Me (William Batchelder Bradbury)
1621. Eternal Son, eternal Love,/Take to Thyself Thy mighty power
       MH (1966)-471.  Hebron (Lowell Mason)
1622. Eternal Sun if righteousness,/Display Thy beams divine
       HMEC-428.  Burlington (John Freckleton Burrowes)

1623. Ever fainting with desire,/For Thee, O Christ, I call
      HMEC-494. Peyton (Walter Bond Gilbert)
1624. Except the Lord conduct the plan,/The best concerted schemes
      are vain
      HMEC-809. Clare (Hubert Platt Main)
1625. Father, hear the blood of Jesus,/Speaking in Thine ears
      above
      HMEC-258. Diademata (Sir George Job Elvy)
1626. Father, I dare believe/Thee merciful and true
      HMEC-503. St. Thomas (George Frederick Handel)
1627. Father, I stretch my hands to Thee;/No other help I know
      HMEC-406. Parsons (Samuel Hubbard)
      MH (1905)-277. Naomi (Hans George Naegeli)
      MH (1935)-202. Naomi (Hans George Naegeli)
      AMEH-299. Chelmsford (Amzi Chapin)
      AMEH-321. I Do Believe (American traditional)
      MH (1966)-140. Naomi (Hans George Naegeli)
1628. Father in whom we live,/In whom we are, and move
      HMEC-42. Waugh (Ralph Harrison)
      MH (1966)-465. St. Bride (Samuel Howard)
1629. Father of everlasting grace,/Thy goodness and Thy truth we
      praise
      HMEC-480. Nashville (Lowell Mason)
1630. Father of Jesus Christ, my Lord,/My Saviour, and my Head
      HMEC-432. Woodland (Nathaniel Dater Gould)
      MH (1905)-297. Upham (Peter Christian Lutkin)
      MH (1935)-203. Evanston (Karl Pomeroy Harrington)
1631. Father, Son, and Holy Ghost,/One in Three, and Three in One
      HMEC-470. Durbin (William Dalrymple Maclagan)
1632. Father, to Thee my soul I lift;/My soul on Thee depends
      HMEC-124. Bemerton (Henry Wellington Greatorex)
1633. Forever here my rest shall be,/Close to Thy bleeding side
      HMEC-533. Avon (Hugh Wilson)
      MH (1905)-357. Avon (Hugh Wilson)
      MH (1935)-373. Martyrdom/Avon (Hugh Wilson)
      AMEH-373A. Martyrdom/Avon (Hugh Wilson)
1634. Forth in Thy name, O Lord, I go,/My daily labours to pursue
      HMEC-606. Federal Street (Henry Kemble Oliver)
      MH (1905)-400. Keble (John Bacchus Dykes)
      MH (1935)-290. Keble (John Bacchus Dykes)
      MH (1966)-152. Keble (John Bacchus Dykes)
1635. Fountain of life, to all below/Let Thy salvation roll
      HMEC-431. Woodland (Nathaniel Dater Gould)
1636. Full of trembling expectation,/Feeling much, and fearing
      more
      HMEC-645. Ellesdie (Johann Christian Wolfgang Amadeus
            Mozart)
1637. Gentle Jesus, meek and mild,/Look upon a little child
      MSSH-174. Simplicity (John Stainer)
      MH (1935)-444. Gentle Jesus (Martin Shaw)
1638. Give me a new. a perfect heart,/From doubt and fear, and
      sorrow free
      MH (1905)-366. Overberg (Johann Christian Heinrich Rink)
1639. Giver of concord, Prince of Peace,/Meek, lamb-like Son of
      God
      MH (1905)-563. Hampstead (Egbert F. Horner)

1640. Giver of peace and unity,/Send down Thy mild, pacific Dove
    HMEC-793. Tichorah (Lowell Mason)
1641. Glory be to God above,/God, from whom all blessings flow
    HMEC-802. Nuremberg (Johann Rudolf Ahle)
1642. Glory be to God on high,/God whose glory fills the sky
    HMEC-26. Monkland (John B. Wilkes)
1643. Glory to God, whose sovereign grace/Hath animated senseless
    stones
    HMEC-451. Darley (W.H.W. Darley)
1644. God is gone upon high,/With a triumphant noise
    HMEC-245. Christ Church (Charles Steggall)
1645. God is in this and every place;/But O, how dark and void
    HMEC-303. Haven (Thomas Hastings)
1646. God of all power, and truth, and grace,/Which shall from
    age to age endure
    HMEC-528. Janes (Johann Christian Wolfgang Amadeus Mo-
        zart)
    MH (1905)-378. Janes (Johann Christian Wolfgang Amadeus
        Mozart)
    MH (1966)-281. Von Himmel Hoch (Martin Luther)
1647. God of almighty love,/By whose sufficient grace
    HMEC-484. Mornington (Lowell Mason)
1648. God of eternal truth and grace,/Thy faithful promise seal
    HMEC-523. Simpson (Louis Spohr)
1649. God of Israel's faithful three,/Who braved a tyrant's ire
    HMEC-677. Jeshurun (Henry John Gauntlett)
1650. God of love, who hearest prayer,/Kindly for Thy people care
    HMEC-722. Vienna (William Henry Havergal)
    MH (1905)-562. Mercy (Louis Moreau Gottschalk, arr. Ed-
        win Pond Parker)
    AMEH-507. Herndon (Henri Abraham Caesar Malan)
1651. God of my life, what just return/Can sinful dust and ashes
    give?
    HMEC-458. Percy (H. Percy Smith)
1652. God of my life, whose gracious power/Through varied deaths
    my soul hath led
    AMEH-169. St. Peter (from a German chorale)
1653. God of my salvation, hear,/And help me to believe
    HMEC-386. Even Me (William Batchelder Bradbury)
1654. Gracious Redeemer, shake/This slumber from my soul!
    HMEC-555. Ozrem (Isaac Baker Woodbury)
1655. Gracious soul, to whom are given/Holy hungerings after hea-
    ven
    HMEC-487. Horton (Xavier Schnyder Wartensee)
1656. Granted is the Saviour's prayer,/Sent the gracious Comforter
    HMEC-264. Fulton (William Batchelder Bradbury)
1657. Hail, Father, Son, and Holy Ghost,/One God in Persons Three
    HMEC-121. Oxford (William Coombs)
1658. Hail the day that sees Him rise,/Ravished from our wishful
    eyes!
    HMEC-261. Essex (Thomas Clark)
    MH (1905)-162. Essex (Thomas Clark)
    AMEH-127. Ascension (William Henry Monk)
1659. Happy soul, thy days are ended,/All thy mourning days below
    HMEC-1003. Talmar (Isaac Baker Woodbury)
1660. Happy the man who finds the grace,/The blessings of God's

chosen race
> HMEC-329.  Rockingham (Lowell Mason)
> MH (1905)-372.  Hesperus (Henry Williams Baker)
> AMEH-525.  Dover (Thomas Williams)

1661.  Happy the souls to Jesus joined,/And saved by grace alone
> HMEC-765.  St. Ann's (William Croft)
> MH (1966)-535.  Ballerma (Francois Hippolyte Barthelemon)

1662.  Hark! a voice divides the sky,--/Happy are the faithful
dead!
> HMEC-1001.  Leavitt (Joseph Perry Holbrook)

1663.  Hark! how the watchmen cry!/Attend the trumpet's sound
> HMEC-582.  Laban (Lowell Mason)
> AMEH-14.  Dennis (Hans George Naegeli)

1664.  Hark! the herald angels sing,/"Glory to the newborn King
. . . ."
> HMEC-190.  Herald Angels (Felix Mendelssohn-Bartholdy)
> MH (1905)-111.  Mendelssohn (Felix Mendelssohn-Bartholdy)
> MSSH-61.  Mendelssohn (Felix Mendelssohn-Bartholdy)
> MH (1935)-86.  Mendelssohn (Felix Mendelssohn-Bartholdy)
> AMEH-85.  Herald Angels (Felix Mendelssohn-Bartholdy)
> MH (1966)-387.  Easter Hymn (Lyra Davidica, 1708)
> MH (1967)-388.  Mendelssohn (Felix Mendelssohn-Bartholdy)

1665.  He comes! He comes! the Judge severe!/The seventh trumpet
speaks Him near
> HMEC-1018.  Grace Church (Ignace Josef Pleyel)

1666.  He wills that I should holy be:/That holiness I long to feel
> HMEC-529.  Janes (Johann Christian Wolfgang Amadeus Mo-
zart)

1667.  Head of the Church triumphant,/We joyfully adore Thee
> HMEC-680.  Grasmere (Edwin Moss)

1668.  Head of the Church, whose Spirit fills/And flows through
every faithful soul
> HMEC-924.  Promise (Francois Hippolyte Barthelemon)

1669.  Hearts of stone, relent!/Break, by Jesus' cross subdued
> HMEC-339.  Rosefield (Henri Abraham Caesar Malan)

1670.  Help, Lord, to whom for help I fly,/And still my tempted
soul stand by
> HMEC-543.  Habakkuk (Edward Hodges)

1671.  Ho! every one that thirsts, draw nigh:/'Tis God invites the
fallen race
> MH (1905)-258.  St. Crispin (Sir George Job Elvy)

1672.  Holy, and true, and righteous Lord,/I wait to prove Thy gracious will
> HMEC-525.  Janes (Johann Christian Wolfgang Amadeus Mo-
zart)
> MH (1905)-377.  Sutherland (Emma Louise Ashford)

1673.  Holy as Thou, O Lord, is none;/Thy holiness is all Thine own
> AMEH-131.  Hamburg (Lowell Mason)

1674.  How can a sinner know/His sins on earth forgiven?
> HMEC-437.  Badea (German melody)
> MH (1905)-303.  Rhodes (Charles Warwick Jordan)
> MH (1935)-208.  Old 134th/St. Michael (Genevan Psalter,
1551)
> AMEH-473.  Gerar (Lowell Mason)
> MH (1966)-114.  St. Michael (William Crotch)

1675.  How do Thy mercies close me round!/Forever be Thy name

adored
HMEC-170.  St. Peter (from a German chorale)

1676.  How happy are Thy servants, Lord,/Who thus remember Thee!
MH (1966)-328.  Martyrdom (Hugh Wilson)

1677.  How happy every child of grace,/Who knows his sins forgiven!
AMEH-1030.  Devizes (Isaac Tucker)
MH (1905)-605.  Materna (Samuel Augustus Ward)
MH (1935)-522.  Abida (Early American melody)
AMEH-586.  Abida (Early American melody)
AMEH-657.  Without tune
MH (1966)-115.  Cleansing Fountain (American folk melody)

1678.  How happy, gracious Lord, are we,/Divinely drawn to follow
Thee!
HMEC-744.  Ariel (Lowell Mason)

1679.  How many pass the guilty night/In reveling and frantic
mirth!
HMEC-952.  Stella (Unknown )

1680.  I and my house will serve the Lord:/But first, obedient to
His work
HMEC-573.  Edinburgh (Robert Lowry)

1681.  I ask the gift of righteousness,/The sin-subdoing power
HMEC-535.  Avon (Hugh Wilson)

1682.  I know that my Redeemer lives,/And ever prays for me
HMEC-512.  Evan (William Henry Havergal)
MH (1905)-370.  Bradford (George Frederick Handel)
AMEH-139.  Manoah (Franz Joseph Haydn)
AMEH-140.  Bradford (George Frederick Handel)

1683.  I long to behold Him arrayed/With glory and light from
above
HMEC-1064.  Desire ("J.B.")

1684.  "I the good fight have fought,"/O when shall I declare?
HMEC-585.  Clapton (William Jones)
MH (1905)-391.  Victory (H.A. Whitehead)

1685.  I, too, forewarned by Jesus' love,/Must shortly lay my body
down
HMEC-1116.  Neumarck (George Neumarck)

1686.  I want a heart to pray,/To pray, and never cease
HMEC-506.  Hope (Henry Stephen Cutler)

1687.  I want a principle within,/Of jealous, godly fear
HMEC-511.  Spohr (Louis Spohr)
MH (1905)-320.  Spohr (Louis Spohr)
MH (1935)-299.  Gerald (Louis Spohr)
MH (1966)-279.  Gerald (Louis Spohr)
MH (1966)-280.  Euclid (Lloyd A. Pfautsch)

1688.  If death my friend and me divide,/Thou dost not, Lord, my
sorrow chide
HMEC-967.  Venetia (Traditional English)

1689.  In age and feebleness extreme,/Who shall a helpless worm redeem?
HMEC-1117.  Vale (John Duncan Buckingham)

1690.  In that sad, memorable night,/When Jesus was for us betrayed
HMEC-833.  Ward (Lowell Mason)

1691.  Infinite God, To Thee we raise/Our hearts in solemn songs of
praise
HMEC-48.  Wavertree (William Shore)
MH (1905)-10.  St. Chrysostom (Joseph Barnby)

1692. Jesus, a word, a look from Thee,/Can turn my heart and make it clean
      HMEC-307. Louvan (Virgil Corydon Taylor)
1693. Jesus, all-redeeming Lord,/Magnify Thy dying word
      HMEC-848. Innocents (William Henry Monk)
1694. Jesus, at whose supreme command,/We now approach to God
      HMEC-835. Dundee (Guillaume Franc)
      AMEH-324. Moore (Samuel Webbe)
1695. Jesus Christ is risen today, Allelulia!/Our triumphant holy day, Allelulia! (see 1379)
1696. Jesus, Friend of sinners, hear/Yet once again, I pray
      HMEC-559. Penitence (William Henry Oakley)
1697. Jesus, from whom all blessings flow,/Great Builder of Thy Church below
      HMEC-795. Linwood (Gioacchimo Rossini)
      MH (1905)-561. Louvan (Virgil Corydon Taylor)
1698. Jesus, great Shepherd of the sheep,/To Thee for help we fly
      HMEC-790. Elizabethtown (George Kingsley)
      AMEH-451. Heber (George Kingsley)
1699. Jesus hath died that I might live,/Might live to God alone
      HMEC-520. Azmon (Carl Gotthelf Glaser, arr. Lowel Mason)
1700. Jesus, in whom the Godhead's rays/Beam forth with mildest majesty
      HMEC-527. Janes (Johann Christian Wolfgang Amadeus Mozart)
1701. Jesus is our common Lord,/He our living Saviour is
      HMEC-719. Seymour (Carl Maria Von Weber)
1702. Jesus, let all Thy lovers shine,/Illustrious as the sun
      MH (1905)-321. Nativity (Henry Laher)
1703. Jesus, let Thy pitying-eye/Call back a wandering sheep
      HMEC-558. Penitence (William Henry Oakley)
      MH (1905)-491. Contrition (William Henry Oakley)
1704. Jesus, Lord, we look to Thee,/Let us in Thy name agree
      HMEC-804. Nuremburg (Johann Rudolf Ahle)
      MH (1966)-309. Savannah (Foundery Collection, 1742)
1705. Jesus, Lover of my soul,/Let me to Thy bosom fly
      HMEC-656. Refuge (Joseph Perry Holbrook)
              Martyn (Simeon Butler Marsh)
      MH (1905)-463. Hollingside (John Bacchus Dykes)
              St. Fabian (Joseph Barnby)
              Martyn (Simeon Butler Marsh)
      MSSH-167. Hollingside (John Bacchus Dykes)
              Refuge (Joseph Perry Holbrook)
              Martyn (Simeon Butler Marsh)
      MH (1935)-338. Martyn (Simeon Butler Marsh)
              Hollingside (John Bacchus Dykes)
              Aberystwyth (Joseph Parry)
      AMEH-170. Martyn (Simeon Butler Marsh)
      AMEH-195. Refuge (Joseph Perry Holbrook)
      AMEH-615. Jesus, Lover of My Soul (J.T. Layton)
      MH (1966)-125. Aberystwyth (Joseph Parry)
      MH (1966)-126. Martyn (Simeon Butler Marsh)
1706. Jesus, my Advocate above,/My Friend before the throne of Love
      HMEC-239. Ware (George Kingsley)
1707. Jesus, my Life, Thyself apply;/Thy Holy Spirit breathe

HMEC-519. Azmon (Carl Gotthelf Glaser, arr. Lowel Mason)
1708. Jesus, my Saviour, Brother, Friend,/On whom I cast my every
      care
    HMEC-686. Retreat (Thomas Hastings)
1709. Jesus, my strength, my hope,/On Thee I cast my care
    HMEC-505. Hope (Henry Stephen Cutler)
    MH (1905)-340. Chalvey (Leighton George Hayne)
                Richmond (Asa Brooks Everett)
    MH (1935)-343. Richmond (Asa Brooks Everett)
    MH (1966)-253. Ich Halte Treuliche Still (Johann Sebas-
                tian Bach)
1710. Jesus, my Truth, my Way,/My sure, unerring Light
    HMEC-483. Mornington (arr. Lowell Mason)
    MH (1905)-471. Ferguson (George Kingsley)
1711. Jesus, Redeemer of mankind,/Display Thy saving power
    HMEC-374. Faithful (Samuel Parkman Tuckerman)
1712. Jesus, the all-restoring word,/My fallen spirit's hope
    MH (1905)-331. Spring (L.C. Everett)
1713. Jesus, the Conqueror, reigns,/In glorious strength arrayed
    HMRC-251. Carlisle (Charles Lockhart)
    MH (1905)-172. Ferguson (George Kingsley)
1714. Jesus, the Life, the Truth, the Way,/In whom I now believe
    HMEC-517. Bridgman (Ludwig van Beethoven, arr. George
            Kingsley)
1715. Jesus! the name high over all,/In hell, or earth, or sky
    HMEC-822. Coronation (Oliver Holden)
    MH (1905)-222. Coronation (Oliver Holden)
    MH (1935)-400. Grafenberg (Johann Cruger)
    AMEH-5. Varina (George Frederick Root)
    AMEH-7. Grafenberg (Johann Cruger)
    MH (1966)-341. Grafenberg (Johann Cruger)
1716. Jesus, the sinner's Froend, to Thee,/Lost and undone, for
    aid I flee
    HMEC-392. Windham (Daniel Read)
    MH (1905)-271. Federal Street (Henry Kemble Oliver)
    MH (1935)-201. Federal Street (Henry Kemble Oliver)
    MH (1966)-118. Federal Street (Henry Kemble Oliver)
1717. Jesus, the truth and power divine,/Send forth these messen-
    gers of Thine
    MH (1905)-220. Truro (Charles Burney)
1718. Jesus, the word bestow,/The true immortal seed
    HMEC-289. Dover (Aaron Williams)
1719. Jesus, the word of mercy give,/And let it swiftly run
    HMEC-824. Coronation (Oliver Holden)
1720. Jesus, Thine all-victorious love/Shed in Thy heart abroad
    HMEC-518. Azmon (Carl Gotthelf Glaser, arr. Lowell Ma-
            son)
    MH (1905)-375. Azmon (Carl Gotthelf Glaser, arr. Lowell
                Mason)
    MH (1935)-371. Azmon (Carl Gotthelf Glaser, arr. Lowell
                Mason)
    MH (1966)-278. Azmon (Carl Gotthelf Glaser, arr. Lowell
                Mason)
1721. Jesus, Thou all-redeeming Lord,/Thy blessing we implore
    HMEC-32. Arlington (Thomas Augustine Arne)
    MH (1905)-263. Prescott (Peter Christian Lutkin)

1722. Jesus, Thou soul of all our joys,/For whom we now lift up
         our voice
         HMEC-19.  Ariel (arr. Lowell Mason)
1723. Jesus, Thy far-extended fame/My drooping soul exults to hear
         HMEC-398.  Rose Hill (Joseph Emerson Sweetser)
1724. Jesus, to Thee I now can fly,/On whom my help is laid
         HMEC-430.  Downs (Lowell Mason)
1725. Jesus, to Thee our hearts we lift.--/Our hearts with love to
         Thee o'erflow
         HMEC-650.  Eaton (Zerubbabel Wyvill)
1726. Jesus, united by Thy grace,/And each to each endeared
         HMEC-785.  Cornell (John Henry Cornell)
         MH (1905)-557.  Maitland (George Nelson Allen)
         MH (1935)-419.  Beatitudo (John Bacchus Dykes)
         MH (1966)-193.  St. Agnes (John Bacchus Dykes)
1727. Jesus, we look to Thee,/Thy promised presence claim
         HMEC-7.  Packington (John Black)
         MH (1935)-24.  Mornington (Garret Wellesley, Earl of Mor-
                                 nington)
         AMEH-413.  Boylston (Lowell Mason)
         MH (1966)-310.  Mornington (Garret Wellesley, Earl of
                                 Mornington)
1728. Lamb of God, for sinners slain,/To Thee I humbly pray
         HMEC-382.  Perrina (Joseph Perry Holbrook)
1729. Lamb of God, whose dying love/We now recall to mind
         HMEC-383.  Perrina (Joseph Perry Holbrook)
1730. Leader of faithful souls, and Guide/Of all that travel to
         the sky
         HMEC-648.  Admah (Lowell Mason)
         MH (1905)-459.  Magdalen (John Stainer)
1731. Let all who truly bear/The bleeding Saviour's name
         HMEC-846.  Nassau (Johann Rosenmuller)
1732. Let earth and heaven agree,/Angels and men be joined
         HMEC-332.  Lenox (Lewis Edson)
         MH (1905)-565.  Lischer (Friedrich Schneider)
1733. Let Him to whom we now belong,/His sovereign right assert
         HMEC-649.  Barby (William Tans'ur)
         MH (1905)-373.  Mount Calvary (Robert Prescott Stewart)
1734. Let not the wise their wisdom boast,/The mighty glory in
         their might
         HMEC-452.  Darley (W.H.W. Darley)
         MH (1905)-308.  Luton (George Burder)
1735. Let the world their virtue boast,/Their works of righteous-
         ness
         HMEC-385.  Even Me (William Batchelder Bradbury)
1736. Lift up your hearts to things above,/Ye followers of the
         Lamb
         HMEC-786.  Hummel (Heinrich Christopher Zeuner)
         MH (1905)-558.  Hummel (Heinrich Christopher Zeuner)
1737. Lift your eyes of faith, and see/Saints and angels joined in
         one
         HMEC-1069.  Amsterdam (James Nares)
1738. Lift your heads, ye friends of Jesus,/Partners in His pa-
         tience here
         HMEC-1014.  Novello (Vincent Novello)
1739. Light of life, seraphic fire,/Love divine, thyself impart

HMEC-489.  Onido (Ignace Josef Pleyel)

1740. Light of those whose dreary dwelling/Borders on the shades
         of death
         HMEC-943.  Faben (John Henry Wilcox)
         MH (1905)-638.  Faben (John Henry Wilcox)
                         Light of the World (Ferdinand Heinrich
                         Himmel)

1741. Lo! He comes, with clouds descending,/Once for favored sin-
         ners slain
         HMEC-1013.  Novello (Vincent Novello)
         MH (1905)-601.  Novello (Samuel Webbe)
         MH (2966)-364.  Bryn Calfaria (William Oliver)

1742. Lo! I come with joy to do/The Master's blessed will
         HMEC-609.  St. Catherine (Henri Frederick Hemy)

1743. Lo! on a narrow neck of land,/'Twixt two unbounded seas, I
         stand
         MH (1905)-579.  Meribah (Lowell Mason)

1744. Lord, and is Thine anger gone,/And art Thou pacified?
         HMEC-455.  Rockport (Isaac Baker Woodbury)

1745. Lord, fill me with a humble fear;/My utter helplessness re-
         veal
         HMEC-497.  Woodworth (William Batchelder Bradbury)

1746. Lord, I believe a rest remains/To all Thy people known
         HMEC-513.  Evan (William Henry Havergal)
         MH (1905)-356.  Evan (William Henry Havergal)

1747. Lord, I believe Thy every word,/Thy every promise true
         HMEC-668.  Maitland (George Nelson Allen)

1748. Lord, I despair myself to heal;/I see my sin, but cannot
         feel
         HMEC-397.  Rose Hill (Joseph Emerson Sweetser)

1749. Lord, if at Thy command/The word of life we sow
         HMEC-817.  Olmutz (Lowell Mason)
         MH (1905)-648.  Swabia (William Henry Havergal)

1750. Lord, in the strength of grace,/With a glad heart and free
         HMEC-473.  Marshall (George Jarvis Greer)
         MH (1905)-352.  Greenwood (Joseph Emerson Sweetser)
         MH (1935)-217.  Greenwood (Joseph Emerson Sweetser)
         MH (1966)-182.  Franconia (Johann Balthasar Koenig)

1751. Lord of earth, and air, and sea,/Supreme in power and grace
         HMEC-1109.  Penitence (William Henry Oakley)

1752. Lord of the harvest, hear/Thy needy servants' cry
         HMEC-818.  Olmutz (Lowell Mason)
         MH (1966)-339.  St. Bride (Samuel Howard)

1753. Lord of the wide, extensive main,/Whose power the wind, the
         sea, controls
         HMEC-1112.  Gratitude (Thomas Hastings)

1754. Lord, whom winds and seas obey,/Guide us through the watery
         way
         HMEC-1115.  Theodora (George Frederick Handel)
         MH (1905)-103.  Nuremberg (Johann Rudolf Ahle)

1755. Love divine, all love excelling,/Joy of heaven, to earth
         come down!
         HMEC-491.  Love Divine (John Zundel)
         MH (1905)-355.  Weston (John Edward Roe)
                         Love Divine (John Zundel)
         MSSH-193.  Love Divine (John Zundel)

MH (1935)-372.  Love Divine (John Zundel)
AMEH-229.  Beecher (John Zundel)
AMEH-230.  Madrid (Benjamin Carr)
MH (1966)-283.  Beecher (John Zundel)

1756. Lovers of pleasure more than God,/For you He suffered pain
HMEC-357.  Mear (Aaron Williams)

1757. Loving Jesus, gentle Lamb,/In Thy gracious hands I am
MH (1905)-374.  Vienna (Justin Heinrich Knecht)

1758. May I throughout this day of Thine/Be in Thy Spirit, Lord
AMEH-39.  Christmas (George Frederick Handel)

1759. My God, I am Thine; what a comfort divine,/What a blessing
to know that my Jesus is mine!
HMEC-757.  Kelbrook (John Riley)

1760. My God, I know, I feel Thee mine,/And will not quit my calm
HMEC-536.  Llandaff (Edwin Moss)

1761. My God, my God, to Thee I cry;/Thee only would I know
HMEC-425.  Evan (William Henry Havergal)
AMEH-364.  Azmon (Carl Gotthelf Glaser, arr. Lowell Ma-
son)

1762. My soul and all its powers/Thine, wholly, Thine, shall be
HMEC-472.  Warsaw (Thomas Clark)

1763. O come and dwell in me,/Spirit of power within
HMEC-502.  St. Thomas (George Frederick Handel)
MH (1905)-362.  Carlisle (Charles Lockhart)
MH (1935)-377.  Old 134th/St. Michael's (Genevan Psalter,
1551)
MH (1966)-277.  St. Michael's (Genevan Psalter, 1551)

1764. O for a heart to praise my God,/A heart from sin set free
HMEC-521.  Simpson (Louis Spohr)
MH (1905)-354.  Simpson (Louis Spohr)
Arlington (Thomas Augustine Arne)
MH (1935)-370.  Belmont (William Gardiner's Sacred Melo-
dies, 1812)
AMEH-365.  Azmon (Carl Gotthelf Glaser, arr. Lowell Ma-
son)
MH (1966)-282.  Irish (arr. John Friedrich Lampe)

1765. O for a thousand seraph tongues/To bless th' incarnate Word!
AMEH-222.  Devizes (Isaac Tucker)

1766. O for a thousand tongues, to sing/My great Redeemer's praise
HMEC-1.  Azmon (Carl Gotthelf Glaser, arr. Lowell Mason)
MH (1905)-2.  Azmon (Carl Gotthelf Glaser, arr. Lowell
Mason)
MSSH-5.  Azmon (Carl Gotthelf Glaser, arr. Lowell Mason)
MH (1935)-162.  Azmon (Carl Gotthelf Glaser, arr. Lowell
Mason)
AMEH-1.  Azmon (Carl Gotthelf Glaser, arr. Lowell Mason)
MH (1966)-1.  Azmon (Carl Gotthelf Glaser, arr. Lowell
Mason)

1767. O for that tenderness of heart/Which bows before the Lord
HMEC-410.  Bemerton (Henry Wellington Greatorex)
MH (1905)-278.  Dalehurst (Arthur Cottman)

1768. O glorious hope of perfect love!/It lifts me up to things
above
HMEC-542.  Habakkuk (Edward Hodges)
MH (1905)-365.  Meribah (Lowell Mason)

1769. O God, most merciful and true,/Thy nature to my soul impart

HMEC-531.  Janes (Johann Christian Wolfgang Amadeus Mozart)
　　　MH (1905)-401.  Sebastian (Samuel Sebastian Wesley)
1770.  O God, Thy faithfulness I plead,/My present help in time of need
　　　HMEC-544.  Habakkuk (Edward Hodges)
1771.  O happy are they,/Who the Saviour obey
　　　HMEC-442.  Rapture (R.D. Humphreys)
　　　MH (1905)-311.  City Road (John Jones)
　　　MH (1935)-356.  Rapture (R.D. Humphreys)
　　　MH (1966)-227.  True Happiness (Southern Harmony, 1835)
1772.  O Jesus, at Thy feet we wait,/Till Thou shalt bid us rise
　　　HMEC-514.  Evan (William Henry Havergal)
　　　AMEH-366.  Azmon (Carl Gotthelf Glaser, arr. Lowell Mason)
1773.  O Jesus, full of grace,/To Thee I make my moan
　　　HMEC-557.  Ozrem (Isaac Baker Woodbury)
1774.  O Jesus, full of truth and grace,/O all-atoning Lamb of God
　　　HMEC-526.  Janes (Johann Christian Wolfgang Amadeus Mozart)
1775.  O joyful sound of gospel grace!/Christ shall in me appear
　　　HMEC-515.  Bridgman (Ludwig van Beethoven, arr. George Kingsley)
　　　MH (1905)-371.  Laud (John Bacchus Dykes)
1776.  O Lamb of God, for sinners slain,/I plead with Thee, my suit to gain
　　　HMEC-378.  Auburndale (Olen Lester Carter)
1777.  O Love divine, how sweet thou art!/What shall I find my willing heart
　　　HMEC-540.  Habakkuk (Edward Hodges)
　　　MH (1905)-368.  Habakkuk (Edward Hodges)
　　　MH (1935)-218.  Ariel (Lowell Mason)
　　　MH (1966)-285.  Allgutiger, Mein Preisgesang (Georg Peter Weimar)
1778.  O love divine, what hast thou done!/The incarnate God hath died for me!
　　　HMEC-220.  Selena (Isaac Baker Woodbury)
　　　MH (1905)-153.  Selena (Isaac Baker Woodbury)
　　　MH (1935)-137.  Selena (Isaac Baker Woodbury)
　　　MH (1966)-420.  Selena (Isaac Baker Woodbury)
1779.  O Love, Thy sovereign aid impart,/And guard the gift Thyself hast given
　　　HMEC-462.  Sessions (Luther Orlando Emerson)
1780.  O that I could my Lord receive,/Who did the world redeem
　　　HMEC-407.  Parsons (Samuel Hubbard)
1781.  O that I could repent!/O that I could believe!
　　　HMEC-311.  Shawmut (Lowell Mason)
　　　MH (1905)-264.  Gerar (Lowell Mason)
1782.  O that I could repent,/With all my idols part
　　　HMEC-404.  Owen (Joseph Emerson Sweetser)
　　　MH (1905)-265.  Shawmut (Lowell Mason)
1783.  O that my load of sin were gone!/O that I could at least submit
　　　HMEC-495.  Woodworth (William Batchelder Bradbury)
　　　MH (1905)-381.  Hamburg (Lowell Mason)
1784.  O that Thou wouldst the heavens rend,/In majesty come down

HMEC-413.  Grigg (Joseph Grigg)
1785.  O the depth of love divine,/Th' unfathomable grace!
    MH (1966)-332.  Barnabas (French Psalter, 1561)
1786.  O Thou eternal Victim, slain/A sacrifice for guilty man
    HMEC-250.  Coronation (Oliver Holden)
1787.  O Thou, our Saviour, Brother, Friend,/Behold a cloud of in-
        cense rise
    HMEC-46.  Malvern (Lowell Mason)
1788.  O Thou who camest from above,/The pure celestial fire to im-
        part
    HMEC-562.  Galilee (Richard Langdon)
    MH (1905)-313.  Angelus (Georg Josephi)
    MH (1935)-344.  Eisenach (Johann Hermann Schein)
    MH (1966)-172.  Eisenach (Johann Hermann Schein)
1789.  O Thou who hast our sorrows borne,/Help us to look on Thee,
        and mourn
    HMEC-381.  Pleyel's Hymn (Ignace Josef Pleyel)
1790.  O Thou, who when we did complain,/Didst all our griefs re-
        move
    HMEC-157.  Dundee (Guillaume Franc)
1791.  O Thou, whom all Thy saints adore,/We now with all Thy saints
        agree
    HMEC-37.  Ward (arr. Lowell Mason)
    MH (1905)-13.  Holy Hill (William Henry Pontius)
1792.  O what a mighty change/Shall Jesus sufferers know
    HMEC-1057.  Haverhill (Lowell Mason)
1793.  O what delight is this,/Which now in Christ we know
    HMEC-842.  Prayer (Leonard Marshall)
1794.  O what shall I do my Saviour to praise,/So faithful and true,
        so plenteous in grace
    HMEC-453.  Houghton (William Gardiner)
1795.  O when shall we sweetly remove,/O when shall we enter our
        rest
    HMEC-1065.  Desire ("J.B.")
1796.  O wondrous power of faithful prayer!/What tongue can tell the
        almighty grace?
    HMEC-735.  St. Catherine (J.G. Walton)
1797.  Oft I in my heart have said,--/Who shall ascend on high
    HMEC-443.  Ra½ture (R.D. Humphreys)
1798.  Our Lord is risen from the dead;/Our Jesus is gone up on
        high
    HMEC-237.  Rialto (George Frederick Root)
    MH (1905)-158.  Jordan (Joseph Barnby)
1799.  Pass a few swiftly fleeting years,/And all that now in bo-
        dies live
    HMEC-963.  Seasons (Ignace Josef Pleyel)
1800.  Peace, doibting heart! my God's I am;/Who formed me man for-
        bids my fear
    HMEC-651.  Eaton (Zerubbabel Wyvill)
1801.  Praise the Lord who reigns above,/And keeps His court below
    MH (1966)-15.  Amsterdam (Foundery Collection, 1742)
1802.  Pray, without ceasing pray,/Your Captain gives the word
    HMEC-589.  Benjamin (Franz Joseph Haydn)
1803.  Prisoners of hope, lift up your heads,/The day of liberty
        draws near
    HMEC-479.  St. Matthias (William Henry Monk)

1804. Rejoice and sing, the Lord is King!/Your Lord and King adore
  AMEH-277. Elizabethtown (George Kingsley)
1805. Rejoice, the Lord is King!/Your Lord and King adore
  HMEC-244. Christ Church (Charles Steggall)
  MH (1905)-178. Christ Church (Charles Steggall)
  MSSH-104. Darwall (John Darwall)
  MH (1935)-171. Darwall (John Darwall)
  MH (1966)-483. Darwall (John Darwall)
1806. Saviour of all, to Thee we bow,/And own Thee faithful to Thy
  word
  HMEC-794. Linwood (Gioacchimo Rossini)
1807. Saviour of the sin-sick soul,/Give me faith to make me whole
  HMEC-486. Horton (Xavier Schnyder Wartensee)
  AMEH-428. Pleyel's Hymn (Ignace Josef Pleyel)
1808. Saviour, on me the grace bestow,/That, with Thy children, I
  may know
  HMEC-545. Habakkuk (Edward Hodges)
1809. See how great a flame aspires,/Kindled by a spark of grace!
  HMEC-936. Watchman (Lowell Mason)
  MH (1905)-643. Messiah (Louis Ferdinand Herold, arr.
    George Kingsley)
  MH (1935)-500. Culford (Edward John Hopkins)
  MH (1966)-464. Arfon/Major (Welsh hymn melody)
1810. See, Jesus, Thy disciples see,/The promised blessing give
  HMEC-30. Andrews (John Black)
1811. See the Lord, thy Keeper, stand/Omnipotently near
  HMEC-746. Bromley (Unknown)
1812. Servant of all, to toil for man/Thou didst not, Lord, refuse
  MH (1966)-186. Shaddick (Bates G. Burt)
1813. Servant of God, well done!/Thy glorious warfare's past
  HMEC-991. Owen (Joseph Emerson Sweetser)
  MH (1905)-593. Victory (H.A. Whitehead)
  MH (1935)-518. Mornington (Garret Wellesley, Earl of
    Mornington)
  MH (1966)-288. Diademata (George Job Elvey)
1814. Shepherd divine, our wants relieve/In this our evil day
  HMEC-715. Woodstock (Deodatus Dutton, Jr.)
1815. Shepherds of souls, with pitying eye/The thousands of our
  Israel see
  HMEC-927. Appleton (William Boyce)
1816. Shrinking from the cold hand of death,/I soon shall gather
  up my feet
  HMEC-961. Seasons (Ignace Josef Pleyel)
1817. Sing to the great Jehovah's praise;/All praise to Him belongs
  HMEC-946. St. Martin's (William Tans'ur)
  MH (1905)-575. Gould (John Edgar Gould)
  MH (1935)-538. Evangelist (Felix Mendelssohn-Bartholdy)
  MH (1966)-510. Lobt Gott, Ihr Christen (Nicholaus Her-
    mann)
1818. Sinners, obey the gospel word;/Haste to the supper of my
  Lord
  HMEC-350. Wells (Israel Holdroyd)
  AMEH-28. Hebron (Lowell Mason)
1819. Sinners, turn; why will ye die?/God, your Maker, asks you
  why
  HMEC-347. Hollingside (John Bacchus Dykes)

       MH (1905)-247.  Hollingside (John Bacchus Dykes)
       MH (1935)-191.  Hollingside (John Bacchus Dykes)
       AMEH-251.  Pleyel's Hymn (Ignace Josef Pleyel)
       MH (1966)-112.  Arfon (Welsh hymn melody)

1820.  Soldiers of Christ arise,/And put your armour on
       HMEC-587.  Benjamin (Franz Joseph Haydn)
       MH (1905)-382.  Diademata (George Job Elvey)
       MSSH-209.  Silver Street (Isaac Smith)
       MH (1935)-282.  Diademata (George Job Elvey)
       AMEH-306.  Diademata (George Job Elvey)
       MH (1966)-250.  Diademata (George Job Elvey)

1821.  Soldiers of Christ, lay hold/On faith's victorious shield
       HMEC-588.  Benjamin (Franz Josef Haydn)

1822.  Son of the carpenter, receive/This humble work of mine
       HMEC-592.  Winchester Old (Thomas Este's Whole Booke of
              Psalmes)

1823.  Spirit of faith, come down,/Reveal the things of God
       HMEC-435.  Morris (John Black)
       MH (1905)-191.  Bealoth (Lowell Mason)
       MH (1935)-183.  Bealoth (Lowell Mason)
       MH (1966)-137.  Bealoth (Lowell Mason)

1824.  Stand the omnipotent decree!/Jehovah's will be done!
       HMEC-1025.  Falkirk (Thomas Augustine Arne)
       MH (1905)-598.  Falkirk (Thomas Augustine Arne)

1825.  Stay, Thou insulted Spirit, stay,/Thou I have done Thee such
       despite
       HMEC-390.  Windham (Daniel Read)
       MH (1905)-269.  Uxbridge (Lowell Mason)

1826.  Still for Thy loving-kindness, Lord,/I in Thy temple wait
       AMEH-171.  Warwick (Samuel Stanley)

1827.  Still out of the deepest abyss/Of trouble, I mournfully cry
       HMEC-681.  Grasmere (Edwin Moss)

1828.  Talk with us, Lord, Thyself reveal,/While here o'er earth we
       rove
       HMEC-712.  Woodstock (Deodatus Dutton, Jr.)
       MH (1905)-499.  Soho (Joseph Barnby)
       MH (1935)-309.  Soho (Joseph Barnby)
       AMEH-327.  Manoah (Giaochimo Antonio Rossini)
       MH (1966)-262.  Grafenberg (Johann Cruger)

1829.  The great archangel's trump shall sound,/While twice ten
       thousand thunders roar
       HMEC-1019.  Grace Church (Ignace Josef Pleyel)

1830.  The heavenly treasure now we have/In a vile house of clay
       HMEC-1046.  Newbold (George Kingsley)

1831.  The Lord of earth and sky,/The God of ages, praise
       HMEC-953.  Zebulon (Lowell Mason)

1832.  The praying spirit breathe,/The watching power impart
       HMEC-753.  Supplication (Joseph Barnby)

1833.  The saints who die of Christ possessed,/Enter into immediate
       rest
       HMEC-983.  Ashwell (Lowell Mason)

1834.  The sun of righteousness on me/Hath risen with healing in
       His wings
       HMEC-739.  St. Catherine (J.G. Walton)

1835.  The thing my God doth hate/That I no more may do
       HMEC-482 (Mornington (arr. Lowell Mason)

1836.  Thou God of glorious majesty,/To Thee, against myself, to
          Thee
          HMEC-966.  Meribah (Lowell Mason)
1837.  Thou God of truth and love,/We seek Thy perfect way
          HMEC-801.  St. Ebbe (Richard Redhead)
1838.  Thou great mysterious God unknown,/Whose love hath gently
          led me on
          HMEC-439.  Lenox (Lowell Mason)
          MH (1905)-318.  Ariel (Lowell Mason)
1839.  Thou hidden source of calm repose,/Thou all-sufficient love
          divine
          HMEC-736.  St. Catherine (J.G. Walton)
          MH (1905)-466.  Pater Omnium (Henry James Ernest Holmes)
          MH (1935)-339.  St. Petersburg (Dimitri Stepanovich Bort-
                          niansky)
          AMEH-497.  St. Petersburg (Dimitri Stepanovich Bortnian-
                     sky)
          MH (1966)-89.  St. Petersburg (Dimitri Stepanovich Bort-
                         niansky)
1840.  Thou Judge of quick and dead,/Before whose bar severe
          HMEC-1024.  Reynoldstone (Timothy Richard Matthews)
1841.  Thou seest my feebleness;/Jesus, be Thou my power
          HMEC-556.  Ozrem (Isaac Baker Woodbury)
1842.  Thou Shepherd of Israel, and mine,/The joy and desire of my
          heart
          HMEC-748.  Contrast (Lewis Edson)
1843.  Thou Son of God, whose flaming eyes/Our inmost thoughts per-
          ceive
          HMEC-372.  Faithful (Samuel Parkman Tuckerman)
          MH (1905)-245.  Jazer (Augustus Edmonds Tozer)
1844.  Thou very-present Aid/In suffering and distress
          HMEC-178.  Dennis (Hans George Naegeli)
1845.  Thy ceaseless, unexhausted love,/Unmerited and free
          HMEC-317.  St. Bernard (London Tune Book, 1875)
1846.  Thy presence, Lord, the place shall fill;/My heart shall be
          Thy throne
          HMEC-537.  Llandaff (Edwin Moss)
          AMEH-432.  Coventry (Unknown)
1847.  'Tis finished! the Me-siah dies,--Cut off for sins, but not
          His own
          HMEC-210.  German (Ludwig von Beethoven)
          MH (1966)-429.  Winchester New (arr. from the German by
                          William Havergal)
1848.  To God your every want/In instant prayer display
          MH (1905)-512.  Shirland (Samuel Stanley)
1849.  To the haven of Thy breast,/O Son of man, I fly
          HMEC-678.  Jeshurun (Henry John Gauntlett)
1850.  To the hills I lift mine eyes,/The everlasting hills
          HMEC-745.  Bromley (Unknown)
1851.  Try us, O God, and search the ground/Of every sinful heart
          HMEC-784.  Cornell (John Henry Cornell)
          MH (1905)-555.  Beatitudo (John Bacchus Dykes)
          AMEH-646.  Arlington (Thomas Augustine Arne)
1852.  Unchangeable, almighty Lord,/Our souls upon Thy truth we
          stay
          HMEC-792.  Tichorah (Lowell Mason)

1853.  Urge on your rapid course,/Ye blood-besprinkled bands
       HMEC-583.  Laban (Lowell Mason)
1854.  Vain, delusive world, adieu,/With all of creature good!
       HMEC-456.  Rockport (Isaac Baker Woodbury)
1855.  We have no outward righteousness,/No merits or good works to
       plead
       HMEC-446.  Samson (George Frederick Handel)
1856.  We know, by faith we know,/If this vile house of clay
       HMEC-1056.  Haverhill (Lowell Mason)
1857.  Weary souls, that wonder wide/From the central point of
       bliss
       HMEC-337.  Rosefield (Henri Abraham Caesar Malan)
       MH (1905)-262.  Rosefield (Henri Abraham Caesar Malan)
1858.  Weep not for a brother deceased,/Our loss is his infinite
       gain
       HMEC-1011.  Vernon (from the German)
       MH (1905)-594.  St. Cyprian (John Goss)
1859.  What could your Redeemer do,/More than He hath done for you?
       HMEC-348.  Hollingside (John Bacchus Dykes)
1860.  What is our calling's glorious hope,/But inward holiness?
       HMEC-539.  Llandaff (Edwin Moss)
       MH (1905)-358.  Llandaff (Edwin Moss)
1861.  What! never speak one evil word,/Or rash, or idle, or unkind
       HMEC-532.  Janes (Johann Christian Wolfgang Amadeus Mo-
       zart)
1862.  What shall I do, my God, to love?/My loving God to praise
       HMEC-433.  Woodland (Nathaniel Dater Gould)
       MH (1966)-130.  Richmond (Thomas Haweis)
1863.  What shall I render to my God/For all His mercy's store?
       MH (1966)-196.  Armenia (Sylvanus Billings Pond)
1864.  When, gracious Lord, when shall it be/That I shall find my
       all in Thee?
       HMEC-395.  Woodworth (William Batchelder Bradbury)
1865.  When, my Saviour, shall I be/Perfectly resigned to Thee?
       AMEH-427.  Pleyel's Hymn (Ignace Josef Pleyel)
1866.  When quiet in my house I sit,/Thy book be my companion still
       HMEC-291.  Dover (Aaron Williams)
1867.  When shall Thy love constrain,/And force me to Thy breast?
       HMEC-400.  Boylston (Lowell Mason)
1868.  Where shall my wondering soul begin?/How shall I all to hea-
       ven aspire?
       MH (1966)-528.  Fillmore (Jeremiah Ingalls)
1869.  Wherefore should I make my moan,/Now the darling child is
       dead?
       HMEC-1006.  Our Father (Edward Little White)
1870.  Wherewith, O Lord, shall I draw near,/And bow myself before
       Thy face?
       HMEC-389.  Ashwell (Lowell Mason)
       MH (1905)-244.  Rivaulx (John Bacchus Dykes)
1871.  Which of the monarchs of the earth/Can boast a guard like
       ours
       HMEC-155.  Belmont (Samuel Webbe)
1872.  While we walk with God in light,/God our hearts doth still
       unite
       HMEC-803.  Nuremberg (Johann Rudolf Ahle)
1873.  Who are those arrayed in white,/Brighter than the noonday

        sun
      HMEC-1066.  Beulah (Elam Ives, Jr.)
      MH (1905)-619.  Leyden (Louis Spohr, arr. Samuel Sebas-
           tian Wesley)
1874.  Who in the Lord confide,/And feel His sprinkled blood
      HMEC-772.  Amantus (William Augustus Muhlenberg)
1875.  Wisdom ascribe, and might, and praises,/To God, who leng-
         thens out our days
      HMEC-951.  Stella (Unknown)
1876.  With glorious clouds encompassed round,/Whom angels dimly
         see
      HMEC-216.  Communion (Stephen Jenks)
      MH (1905)-327.  Holy Trinity (Joseph Barnby)
1877.  Would Jesus have the sinner die?/Why hangs He then on yon-
         der tree?
      HMEC-221.  Selena (Isaac Baker Woodbury)
1878.  Ye faithful souls who Jesus know,/If risen indeed with Him
         ye are
      HMEC-600.  Bishop (Joseph Perry Holbrook)
1879.  Ye ransomed sinners, hear,/The prisoners of the Lord
      HMEC-493.  Peyton (Walter Bond Gilbert)
1880.  Ye servants of God, your Master proclaim,/And publish abroad
         His wonderful Name
      HMEC-51.  Lyons (Franz Joseph Haydn)
      MH (1905)-11.  Hanover (William Croft)
      MH (1935)-169.  Hanover (William Croft)
      MH (1966)-409.  Hanover (William Croft)
1881.  Ye virgin souls, arise,/With all the dead, awake
      HMEC-954.  Zebulon (Lowell Mason)
1882.  Yield to me now, for I am weak,/But confident in self-des-
         pair
      HMEC-738.  St. Catherine (J.G. Walton)
1883.  Young men and maidens, raise/Your tuneful voices high
      HMEC-16.  Darwall (John Darwall)

WESLEY, ERNEST G.W.
1884.  God's words to thee are spoken:/"Go forth, the fields to
         reap"
      MSSH-250.  Missionary Call (John Henry Gower)
1885.  Jesus, take this heart of mine;/Cleanse from sin and make it
         Thine
      MSSH-148.  Take This Heart (Joseph W. Lermer)

WESLEY, JOHN
1886.  Come, Saviour Jesus from above,/Assist me with Thy heavenly
         Grace (trans. from Antoinette Bourignon)
      HMEC-457.  Percy (H. Percy Smith)
      MH (1905)-379.  Bartholdy (Felix Mendelssohn-Bartholdy)
1887.  Commit thou all thy griefs/And ways unto His hands (trans.
         from Paul Gerhardt)
      HMEC-672.  Schumann (Robert Schumann)
      MH (1905)-435.  Schumann (Robert Schumann)
1888.  Eternal depth of love divine,/In Jesus, God with us, dis-
         played (trans. from Nicholaus von Zinzendorf)
      HMEC-128.  All Saints (William Knapp)
1889.  Extended on a cursed tree,/Covered with dust, and sweat, and

blood (trans. Paul Gerhardt)
     HMEC-212.  Eucharist (Isaac Baker Woodbury)
     AMEH-397.  Essex (Thomas Clark)
1890.  Father of all, whose powerful voice/Called forth this uni-
          versal frame!
     HMEC-139.  Creation (Franz Joseph Haydn)
1891.  Give to the winds thy fears;/Hope, and be undismayed (trans.
          from Paul Gerhardt)
     HMEC-673.  Schumann (Robert Schumann)
     MH (1905)-437.  St. George (Henry John Gauntlett)
     AMEH-484.  Norwood (Swiss melody)
     MH (1966)-51.  St. Bride (Samuel Howard)
1892.  High on His everlasting throne,/The King of saints His work
          surveys (trans. from Augustus Gottlieb Spangenberg)
     HMEC-811.  Migdol (Lowell Mason)
     MH (1905)-221.  St. Vincent (John Uglow)
     AMEH-411.  Duke Street (John Hatton)
1893.  Ho! every one that thirsts draw nigh:/'Tis God invites the
          fallen race
     HMEC-362.  Hamburg (Lowell Mason)
1894.  Holy Lamb, who Thee receive,/Who in Thee begin to live
          (trans. from Anna Schindler Dober)
     HMEC-490.  Onido (Ignace Josef Pleyel)
1895.  How happy is the pilgrim's lot,/How free from every anxious
          thought
     HMEC-1078.  Leoni (Myer Leoni)
     MH (1905)-624.  Habakkuk (Edward Hodges)
1896.  I thank Thee, uncreated Sun,/That Thy bright beams on me
          hath shined (trans. from Johann Angelus Scheffler)
     HMEC-478.  St. Matthias (William Henry Monk)
     MH (1905)-367.  Silesius (Arthur Henry Mann)
1897.  I thirst, Thou wounded Lamb of God,/To wash me in Thy clean-
          sing blood (trans. from Nicholaus von Zinzendorf)
     HMEC-461.  Sessions (Luther Orlando Emerson)
     MH (1905)-335.  Beloit (Carl Gottlieb Rissiger)
1898.  Into Thy gracious hands I fall,/And with the arms of faith
          embrace (trans from Wolfgang Christopher Dessler)
     HMEC-448.  Rockingham (Lowell Mason)
     MH (1905)-305.  Calm (John Bacchus Dykes)
1899.  Jesus, Thy blood and righteousness/My beauty are, my glo-
          rious dress (trans. from Nicholaus von Zinzendorf)
     HMEC-238.  Ware (George Kingsley)
     MH (1905)-148.  Malvern (Lowell Mason)
     MH (1935)-205.  Ombersley (William Henry Gladstone)
     MH (1966)-127.  Herr Jesu Christ, Mein Leiben's Licht
                       (As Hymnodus Sacer, Leipzig, 1625)
1900.  Jesus, Thy boundless love to me/No thought can reach, no
          tongue declare (trans. from Paul Gerhardt)
     HMEC-476.  Yoakley (William Yoakley)
     MH (1905)-333.  Yoakley (William Yoakley)
     MH (1935)-222.  Yoakley (William Yoakley)
     MH (1966)-259.  St. Catherine (Henri Frederick Hemy)
1901.  Lo! God is here! let us adore,/And own how dreadful is this
          place (trans. from Gerhard Tersteegen)
     HMEC-47.  Wavertree (William Shore)
1902.  My soul before Thee prostrate lies;/To Thee, her Source, my

spirit flies (trans. from Christian Friedrich Richter)
HMEC-394. Woodworth (William Batchelder Bradbury)
MH (1905)-273. Elven (Felix Mendelssohn-Bartholdy, arr.
William Dressler)

1903. Now I have found the ground wherein/Sure my soul's anchor
may remain (trans. from Johann Andreas Rothe)
HMEC-420. Wimborne (John Whitaker)
MH (1905)-302. St. Chrysostom (Joseph Barnby)

1904. O God, of good the unfathomed sea!/Who would not give his
heart to Thee? (trans. from Johann Angelus Scheffler)
HMEC-119. Nashville (Lowell Mason)

1905. O God, Thou bottomless abyss!/Thee to perfection who can
know? (trans. from Ernest Lange)
HMEC-126. All Saints (William Knapp)

1906. O God, what offering shall I give/To Thee, the Lord of
earth and skies? (trans. from Joachim Lange)
HMEC-474. Yoakley (William Yoakley)

1907. O Sun of righteousness, arise/With healing in Thy wing
HMEC-441. Bemmerton (Henry Wellington Greatorex)

1908. O Thou, to whose all-searching sight/The darkness shineth
as the light
HMEC-496. Woodworth (William Batchelder Bradbury)
MH (1905)-359. Bera (John Edgar Gould)
MH (1935)-360. Bera (John Edgar Gould)
MH (1966)-213. Rockingham/Mason (Lowell Mason)

1909. O Thou who all things canst control;/Chase this dread slumber from my soul (trans. from Sigmund Christian Gmelin)
HMEC-560. Warren (Virgil Corydon Taylor)

1910. Saviour of men, Thy searching eye/Doth all mine inmost
thoughts descry (trans. from Johann Joseph Winkler)
HMEC-814. Bartholdy (Felix Mendelssohn-Bartholdy)

1911. Shall I, for fear of feeble man,/The Spirit's course in me
restrain (trans. from Johann Joseph Winkler)
HMEC-813. Bartholdy (Felix Mendelssohn-Bartholdy)
MH (1905)-225. Hamburg (Lowell Mason)

1912. Thine, Lord, is wisdom, Thine alone;/Justice and truth before Thee stand (trans. from Ernest Lange)
HMEC-127. All Saints (William Knapp)

1913. Thou hidden love of God, whose height,/Whose depths unfa-
thomed, no man knows (trans. from Gerhard Tersteegen)
HMEC-477. St. Matthias (William Henry Monk)
MH (1905)-345. St. Chrysostom (Joseph Barnby)
MH (1935)-375. New 113th (William Hayes)
MH (1966)-531. Vater Unser (Geistliche Lieder, Leipzig,
1539)

1914. Thou Lamb of God, Thou Prince of peace,/For Thee my thirsty
soul doth pine (trans. from Christian Friedrich Richter)
HMEC-631. Zephyr (William Batchelder Bradbury)

1915. Though waves and storms go o'er my head,/Though strength,
and health, and friends be gone (trans. from Johann
Andreas Rothe)
HMEC-649. Admah (Lowell Mason)

1916. We lift our hearts to Thee,/O Day-Star from on high!
HMEC-111. Kentucky (Jeremiah Ingalls)
MH (1905)-45. Mornington (Garret Colley Wellesley, Earl

of Mornington)
MH (1935)-36.  Mornington (Garret Colley Wellesley, Earl
of Mornington)
MH (1966)-492.  St. Thomas (Aaron Williams)
1917.  Ye simple souls that stray/Far from the path of peace
HMEC-356.  Olney (Lowell Mason)

WESLEY, SAMUEL THE ELDER
1918.  Behold the Saviour of mankind/Nailed to the shameful tree
HMEC-215.  Communion (Stephen Jenks)
MH (1905)-242.  Avon (Hugh Wilson)
MH (1935)-136.  Dundee (Christopher Tye)
AMEH-399.  Dundee (Christopher Tye)
MH (1966)-428.  Windsor (William Damon's Booke of Musicke,
1591)
1919.  The Sun of Righteousness appear,/To set in blood no more
AMEH-101.  Arlington (Thomas Augustine Arne)
1920.  What shall I render to my God/For all His mercy's store?
HMEC-467.  Barby (William Tans'ur)

WESLEY, SAMUEL THE YOUNGER
1921.  The Lord of Sabbath, let us praise,/In concert with the
blest
HMEC-75.  Merton (Henry Kemble Oliver)
1922.  The morning flowers display their sweets,/And gay their sil-
ken leaves unfold
HMEC-977.  Bristol (Edward Little White)

WEST, ROBERT ATHOW
1923.  Come, let us tune our lóftiest song,/And raise to Christ
our joyful strain
HMEC-66.  Duke Street (John Hatton)
MH (1905)-21.  Duke Street (John Hatton)
MH (1935)-21.  Duke Street (John Hatton)
MH (1966)-23.  Duke Street (John Hatton)

WHITE, HENRY KIRKE
1924.  Christians, brethren, ere we part,/Every voice and every
heart
HMEC-22.  Pleyel's Hymn (Ignace Josef Pleyel)
1925.  Oft in danger, oft in woe,/Onward, Christians, onward go
(alt. by Frances Sara Fuller-Maitland, Edward Henry
Bickersteth, and William John Hall)
MH (1905)-412.  Eighmey (William Henry Portius)
MSSH-217.  University College (Henry John Gauntlett)
1926.  The Lord our God is clothed with might,/The winds obey His
will
HMEC-151.  Tappan (George Kingsley)
MH (1905)-99.  Tappan (George Kingsley)
MH (1935)-61.  Tappan (George Kingsley)
MH (1966)-32.  Detroit (Kentucky Harmony Supplement,
1820)
1927.  Through sorrow's night, and danger's path,/Amid the deepen-
ing gloom
HMEC-973.  Ditson (Unknown)
1928.  When, marshaled on the mighty plain,/The glittering host be-

stud the sky
> HMEC-187.  Missionary Chant (Heinrich Christopher Zeuner)
> MH (1905)-124.  Crimea (Thoro Harris)

WHITFIELD, FREDERICK
1929.  There is a name I love to hear;/I love to sing its worth
> AMEH-86.  Evan (William Henry Havergal)

WHITING, WILLIAM
1930.  Eternal Father! strong to save,/Whose arm hath bound the
restless wave
> HMEC-1108.  St. Petersburg (Dimitri Stepanovich Bortni-
ansky)
> MSSH-273.  Melita (John Bacchus Dykes)
> MH (1935)-553.  Melita (John Bacchus Dykes)
> MH (1966)-538.  Melita (John Bacchus Dykes)

WHITTIER, JOHN GREENLEAF
1931.  All as God wills, who wisely heeds/To give or to withhold
> MH (1935)-340.  Stracathro (Charles Hutcheson)
1932.  All things are Thine; no gift have we,/Lord of all gifts,
to offer Thee
> MH (1966)-347.  Herr Jesu Christ, Dich Zu (Pensum Sacrum,
Gorlitz, 1648)
1933.  Dear Lord and Father of mankind,/Forgive our feverish ways
> MH (1905)-543.  Elton (Frederick Charles Maker)
> MH (1935)-342.  Rest/Elton (Frederick Charles Maker)
> AMEH-356.  Whittier (Frederick Charles Maker)
> MH (1966)-235.  Rest (Frederick Charles Maker)
1934.  I bow my forehead in the dust,/I veil mine eyes for shame
> MH (1905)-472.  St. Leonard (Henry Hiles)
1935.  I know not what the future hath/Or marvel or surprise
> MH (1935)-517.  Cooling (Alonzo Judson Abbey)
> MH (1966)-290.  Cooling (Alonzo Judson Abbey)
1936.  Immortal Love, forever full,/Forever flowing free
> MH (1966)-157.  Ayrshire (Kenneth George Finlay)
> MH (1966)-158.  Serenity (William Vincent Wallace)
1937.  It may not be our lot to wield/The sickle in the ripened
field
> HMEC-602.  Illinois (Jonathan Spilman)
> MH (1905)-398.  Abends (Herbert Stanley Oakeley)
> MH (1935)-291.  Abends (Herbert Stanley Oakeley)
1938.  O brother man, fold to thy heart thy brother!/Where pity
dwells, the peace of God is there
> MH (1935)-466.  Ilona (Joseph W. Lerman)
> MH (1966)-199.  Welwyn (Alfred Scott-Gatty)
1939.  O Love! O Life! Our faith and sight/Thy presence maketh one
> MH (1905)-479.  Transfiguration (Peter Christian Lutkin)
1940.  Our thought of Thee is glad with hope,/Dear country of our
love and prayer
> MH (1905)-712.  Olivarius (Peter Christian Lutkin)
> MH (1935)-506.  Beloit (Carl Gottlieb Reissiger)
1941.  We may not climb the heavenly steeps/To bring the Lord
Christ down
> HMEC-197.  Noel (Lowell Mason)
> MH (1905)-128.  Serenity (William Vincent Wallace)

MSSH-80.  Serenity (William Vincent Wallace)
MH (1935)-120.  Serenity (William Vincent Wallace)
AMEH-121.  Serenity (William Vincent Wallace)
1942.  When on my day of life the night is falling,/And, in the
wind from unsunned spaces blown
MH (1905)-589.  Diadema (Joseph Barnby)
MH (1925)-519.  Journey's End (William Ketcham Anderson)

WHITTLE, DANIEL W.
1943.  "There shall be showers of blessing":/This is the promise
of love
AMEH-488.  There Shall Be Showers of Blessing (James Mc
Granahan)
1944.  While we pray and while we plead,/While you see your soul's
deep need
AMEH-343.  Why Not Now (Charles C. Chase)

WIANT, BLISS
1945.  Ne'er forget God's daily care;/Health and food and clothes
to wear (trans. from Chao Tzu-Ch'en)
MH (1966)-519.  Wiant (Chinese Melody, arr. Bliss Wiant)
1946.  Rise to greet the sun,/Reddening in the sky (trans. from
Chao Tzu-Ch'en)
MH (1966)-490.  Le P'ing (Chinese melody)

WIGNER, JOHN MURCH
1947.  Come to the Saviour now,/He gently calleth thee
HMEC-190.  Invitation (Frederick Charles Maker)

WILBERFORCE, ERNEST ROLAND
1948.  Lord, for tomorrow and its needs/I do not pray
MH (1905)-510.  Vincent (Horatio Richmond Palmer)

WILE, FRANCES WHITMARSH
1949.  All beautiful the march of days,/As seasons come and go
MH (1966)-33.  Forest Green (arr. Ralph Vaughan Williams)

WILKS, MATTHEW
1950.  Why should we boast of time to come,/Though but a single
day?
HMEC-366.  Mear (Aaron Williams)

WILLIAMS, BENJAMIN
1951.  Heavenly Father, sovereign Lord,/Be Thy glorious name adored!
HMEC-20.  Pleyel's Hymn (Ignace Josef Pleyel)

WILLIAMS, HELEN MARIA
1952.  While Thee I seek, protecting Power,/Be my vain wishes stil-
led
HMEC-616.  Caddo (William Batchelder Bradbury)
MH (1905)-517.  Simpson (Louis Spohr)

WILLIAMS, THEODORE CHICKERING
1953.  Hast thou heard it, O my brother,/Hast thou heard the trumpet sound?

AMEH-380.  Panoply of Light (Leonard Parker)

WILLIAMS, WILLIAM
    1954.  Guide me, O Thou great Jehovah,/Pilgrim through this barren
            land
            HMEC-171.  Zion (Thomas Hastings)
            MH (1905)-91.  Zion (Thomas Hastings)
            MSSH-195.  Caersalem (Richard Edwards)
                  Zion (Thomas Hastings)
            MH (1935)-301.  Cwm Rhondda (John Hughes)
            AMEH-77.  Cwm Rhondda (John Hughes)
                  Zion (Thomas Hastings)
            MH (1966)-271.  Cwm Rhondda (John Hughes)
    1955.  O'er the gloomy hills of darkness,/Cheered by no celestial
            ray
            HMEC-940.  Hamden (Lowell Mason)

WILLIS, LOVE MARIA WHITCOMB
    1956.  Father, hear the prayer we offer;/Not for ease that prayer
            shall be
            AMEH-381.  Carter (Edmund S. Carter)

WILLIS, NATHANIEL PARKER
    1957.  The perfect world, by Adam trod,/Was the first temple, built
            by God
            HMEC-863.  Hursley (Peter Ritter, arr. William Henry
                  Monk)
            MH (1905)-660.  Duke Street (John Hatton)

WILLS, WHITFIELD GLANVILLE
    1958.  In our work and in our play,/Jesus, ever with us stay
            MH (1935)-448.  Rosslyn (English traditional)

WILSON, LUCY
    1959.  O Lord, Thy heavenly grace impart,/And fix my frail, incon-
            stant heart (trans. from Jean Frederic Oberlin)
            HMEC-685.  Retreat (Thomas Hastings)

WINCHESTER, CALEB THOMAS
    1960.  The Lord our God above is strong;/His hands build not for
            one brief day
            HMEC-866.  Mendon (German traditional)
            MH (1905)-686.  Camp (Peter Christian Lutkin)
            MH (1935)-561.  Truro (Psalmodia Evangelica, 1789)
            MH (1966)-346.  Truro (Psalmodia Evangelica, 1789)

WINKWORTH, CATHERINE
    1961.  All my heart this night rejoices,/As I hear, far and near
            (trans. from Paul Gerhardt)
            MSSH-62.  Bonn (Johann Georg Ebeling)
            MH (1935)-91.  Stella (Horatio William Parker)
            MH (1966)-379.  Warum Sollt Ich Senn Gramen (Johann
                  Georg Ebeling)
    1962.  Blessed Jesus, at Thy Word/We are gathered all to hear Thee
            (trans. from Tobias Clausnitzer)
            MH (1935)-310.  Liebster, Jesu, Wir Sind Heir (Johann

Rudolph Ahle)
MH (1966)-357.  Liebster, Jesu, Wir Sind Hier (Johann
Rudolph Ahle)
1963.  Christ, the Lord, is risen again,/Christ hath broken every
chain (trans. from Michael Weisse)
HMEC-259.  Essex (Thomas Clark)
AMEH-396.  Essex (Thomas Clark)
1964.  Deck thyself, my soul, with gladness,/Leave the gloomy
haunts of sadness (trans. from Johann Franck)
MH (1966)-318.  Schmucke Diche (Johann Cruger)
1965.  Faith is a living power from heaven/That grasps the promise
God hath given (trans. from Petrus Herbert)
MH (1905)-286.  Confidence (W. Moore)
1966.  Fear not, O little flock, the foe/Who madly seeks your over-
throw (trans. from Jacob Fabricus)
HMEC-569.  Mendelssohn (Otto Nicolai)
MH (1905)-445.  Ravendale (Walter Stokes)
1967.  Here I can firmly rest;/I dare to boast of this (trans. from
Paul Gerhardt)
HMEC-436.  Shirland (Samuel Stanley)
1968.  I am baptized into Thy name,/O Father, Son, and Holy Ghost
(trans. from Johann Jakob Rambach)
HMEC-826.  Valete (Arthur Seymour Sullivan)
1969.  If thou but suffer God to guide thee,/And hope in Him thro'
all thy ways (trans. from Georg Neumark)
MH (1935)-272.  Bremen/Neumark (Georg Neumark)
MH (1966)-210.  Wer Nur Den Lieben Gott (George Neumark)
1970.  Jesus, priceless treasure,/Source of purest pleasure (trans.
from Johann Franck)
MH (1966)-220.  Jesu, Meine Freude (Johann Cruger)
1971.  Leave God to order all thy ways,/And hope in Him whate'er
betide (trans. from George Neumark)
MH (1905)-476.  Bremen (Georg Neumark)
1972.  Lift up your heads, ye mighty gates!/Behold, the King of
glory waits (trans. from George Weissel)
HMEC-14.  Truro (Charles Burney)
MH (1935)-126.  Truro (Charles Burney)
MH (1966)-363.  Truro (Charles Burney)
1973.  Lord Jesus Christ, my Life, my Light,/My strength by day,
my trust by night (trans. from Martin Behm)
HMEC-694.  Rolland (William Batchelder Bradbury)
1974.  Now God be with us, for the night is closing;/The light and
darkness are of His disposing (trans. from Petrus Herbert)
MH (1905)-58.  Nightfall (Joseph Barnby)
MH (1935)-49.  Nightfall (Joseph Barnby)
1975.  Now thank we all our God/With heart and hands and voices
(trans. from Martin Rinkart)
MH (1905)-30.  Nun Danket (Johann Cruger)
MSSH-13.  Nun Danket (Johann Cruger)
MH (1935)-7.  Nun Danket (Johann Cruger)
MH (1966)-49.  Nun Danket (Johann Cruger)
1976.  O Morning Star, how fair and bright!/Thou beamest forth in
truth and light! (trans. from Philipp Nicolai)
MH (1966)-399.  Wie Schon Leuchtet Der Morgenstern (Phi-
lipp Nicolai)

1977. Out of the depths I cry to Thee;/Lord, hear me, I implore
        Thee (trans. from Martin Luther)
        MH (1966)-526. Aus Tiefer Not (Martin Luther)
1978. Praise to the Lord, the Almighty, the King of creation;/O
        my soul, praise Him, for He is thy health and salva-
        tion (trans. from Joachim Neander)
        MSSH-25. Lobe den Herren (Peter Sohren)
        MH (1935)-60. Lobe den Herren (Peter Sohren)
        MH (1966)-55. Lobe den Herren (Peter Sohren)
1979. Since Jesus is my friend,/And I to Him belong (trans. from
        Paul Gerhardt)
        AMEH-479. Greenwood (Joseph Emerson Sweetser)
1980. Tender Shepherd, Thou hast stilled/Now Thy little lamb's
        brief weeping (trans. from Johann Wilhelm Meinhold)
        HMEC-1007. The Long Home (Sir Arthur Seymour Sullivan)
1981. The precious seed of weeping/To-day we sow once more (trans.
        from Carl Johann Philipp Spitta)
        HMEC-1010. Requiem (Thomas Hastings)
1982. To God on high be thanks and praise/For mercy ceasing never
        MH (1905)-93. Decius (Nickolaus Decius)
1983. Wake, awake, for night is flying;/The watchmen on the hei-
        ghts are crying (trans. from Philipp Nicolai)
        MH (1966)-366. Wachet Auf (Philipp Nicolai)
1984. We all believe in one true God,/Father, Son, and Holy Ghost
        (trans. from Tobias Clausnitzer)
        HMEC-118. Trinity (Johann Adam Miller)
        MH (1966)-463. Ratisbon (arr. William Henry Monk)
1985. We praise Thee, Lord, with earliest morning ray;/We praise
        Thee with the glowing light of day (trans. from Johann
        Franck)
        AMEH-43. Benediction (Edward John Hopkins)
1986. Welcome, Thou Victor in strife,/Now welcome from the cave!
        (trans. from Benjamin Schmolke)
        HMEC-228. Tamar (Isaac Baker Woodbury)
1987. Well for him who all things losing,/E'en himself doth count
        as naught (trans. from Gottfried Arnold)
        HMEC-492. Love Divine (John Zundel)
1988. Whate'er my God ordains is right;/His will is ever just
        (trans. from Samuel Rodigast)
        MH (1905)-487. Rodigast (Walter Bond Gilbert)

WITTER, WILL ELLSWORTH
  1989. While Jesus whispers to you,/Come, sinner, come!
        AMEH-253. Come, Sinner, Come! (Horatio Richmond Palmer)

WOLCOTT, SAMUEL
  1990. Christ for the world we sing;/The world to Christ we bring
        MH (1905)-635. Fiat Lux (John   Bacchus Dykes)
        MSSH-247. Fiat Lux (John Bacchus Dykes)
        MH (1935)-481. Kirby Bedon (Edward Bunnett)
        AMEH-212. Italian Hymn (Felice de Giardini)
        MH (1966)-292. Italian Hymn (Felice de Giardini)

WOODHULL, ALFRED ALEXANDER
  1991. Great God of nations, now to Thee/Our hymn of gratitude we
        raise

HMEC-1100.  Mendon (German traditional)
MH (1905)-706.  Grostette (Henry Wellington Greatorex)
MH (1935)-509.  Mendon (Samuel Dyer)

WORDSWORTH, CHRISTOPHER
1992.  Alleluia! alleluia!/Hearts to heaven and voices raise
     MH (1935)-153.  Longden (Van Denman Thompson)
1993.  Father of all, from land and sea/The nations sing, "Thine,
     Lord, are we. . . ."
     MH (1905)-566.  Radiant Morn (Charles Francois Gounod)
1994.  Hark! the sound of holy voices,/Chanting at the chrystal sea
     MH (1905)-613.  Carlton (Joseph Barnby)
1995.  Holy, holy, holy Lord,/God of hosts, eternal King
     HMEC-144.  Dix (William Henry Monk)
     MH (1905)-77.  St. Athanasius (Edward John Hopkins)
1996.  O day of rest and gladness,/O day of joy and light
     HMEC-72.  Mendebras (arr. Lowell Mason)
     MH (1905)-68.  Mendebras (arr. Lowell Mason)
     MSSH-38.  Mendebras (arr. Lowell Mason)
     MH (1935)-396.  Mendebras (arr. Lowell Mason)
     MH (1966)-488.  Mendebras (arr. Lowell Mason)
1997.  O Lord of heaven and earth and sea,/To Thee all praise and
     glory be!
     MH (1905)-692.  Almsgiving (John Bacchus Dykes)
     MH (1935)-541.  Oldbridge (Robert Newton Quaile)
     MH (1966)-523.  Oldbridge (Robert Newton Quaile)
1998.  The day is gently sinking to a close,/Fainter and yet more
     faint the sunlight glows
     MH (1905)-61.  Nachtlied (Henry Smart)

WORK, JOHN W.
1999.  Go, tell it on the mountain,/Over the hills and everywhere
     (adaptation of an American folk hymn)
     MH (1966)-404.  Go Tell It on the Mountain (American
             folk hymn, arr. John W. Work)

WRANGHAM, WILLIAM
2000.  Eternal God, celestial King,/Exalted by Thy gracious name
     HMEC-70.  Gilead (Etienne Henri Mehul)
2001.  To Thee, my righteous King and Lord,/My grateful soul I'll
     raise
     AMEH-672.  Without tune

WREFORD, JOHN REYNELL
2002.  Lord, while for all mankind we pray,/Of every clime and
     coast
     HMEC-1098.  Pelestrina (Giavanni Petri Aloysius Palestri-
          na)
     MH (1905)-701.  Manoah (Franz Joseph Haydn)
     MH (1935)-499.  Manoah (Franz Joseph Haydn)
     MH (1966)-551.  Harlech (Traditional Welsh melody)

YATES, JOHN H.
2003.  Encamped along the hills of light,/Ye Christian soldiers

rise
        MSSH-212.  Faith Is the Victory (Ira David Sankey)

YOUNG, ANDREW
    2004.  There is a happy land,/Far, far away
            MSSH-260.  Happy Land (Hindu Air)

YOUNG, JOHN F.
    2005.  Silent night! holy night!/All is calm, all is bright
            MH (1905)-123.  Silent Night (Franz Gruber)
            MSSH-58.  Silent Night (Franz Gruber)
            MH (1935)-106.  Stille Nacht (Franz Gruber)
            AMEH-93.  Stille Nacht (Franz Gruber)
            MH (1966)-393.  Stille Nacht (Franz Gruber)

Note:  Hymns #2006 to 2021 are to be found in the "Addenda to the Hymns"
       on p. 317.

# 2

# THE HYMNODISTS

ABELARD, PETER (1079-1142). French. Destined for a career in the military, he instead studied philosophy and theology; condemned for heresy by the Council of Soissons (1121) and by the Council of Sens (1140). His hymns discovered early in the nineteenth century at the Royal Library at Brussels and published in 1849.

ADAMS, JESSIE (1863-1954). British. Society of Friends. Taught in an adult school at Frimley, England.

ADAMS, JOHN GREENLEAF (1810-1887). American. Universalist. Co-edited Hymns for Christian Devotion (1846); edited The Gospel Psalmist (1861).

ADAMS, SARAH FLOWER (1805-1848). British. Unitarian. Publications include Vivia Perpetua (1841) and The Flock at the Fountain (1845).

ADDISON, JOSEPH (1672-1719). British. Church of England. The noted essayist, poet, and dramatist during the reign of Queen Anne; known particularly for his contributions to Tatler and Spectator--his hymns appearing in the latter periodical.

ADEBESIN, BIODUN (b. 1928). Nigerian.

ADKINS, LEON M. (b. 1896).

ALEXANDER, CECIL FRANCES (1818-1895). Irish. Church of Ireland. Publications include Narrative Hymns for Village Schools (1853), Hymns for Little Children (1848), Hymns Descriptive and Devotional (1858).

ALEXANDER, JAMES WADDELL (1804-1859). American. Presbyterian. Minister and Professor of Ecclesiastical History and Church Government at Princeton Theological Seminary.

ALFORD, HENRY (1810-1871). British. Church of England. Edited The Greek Testament, as well as Psalms and Hymns (1844) and The Year of Praise (1867).

ALINGTON, CYRIL ARGENTINE (1872-1955). British. Church of England. Headmaster of Shrewsbury (1908-1916) and Eton (1916-1933); Dean of Durham (1933-1951).

ALLEN, JAMES (1734-1804). British. Church of England, Inghamite, Sandemanian. Published Christian Songs.

ALLEN, JONATHAN (1816-1878). Scottish. Church of Scotland (Presbyterian). Published Hymns of the Christian Life (1861).

ALLEN, WILLIS BOYD.  His hymn "In the Same Country" ("The great world was weary and turned from the light") written specifically for the 1911 edition of The Methodist Sunday School Hymnal.

AMIS, LEWIS  R.  (1856-1904).  American.  Methodist.

AMBROSIUS (ST. AMBROSE) OF MILAN (340-397).  Roman Catholic.  Known as the "Father of Church Song"; introduced the practice of antiphonal chanting and concluded Gregory's task of systematizing the music of the Church.  There exists approximately ninety-two "Ambrosian" hymns, but only slighty over twelve can be assigned to him with confidence.

ANATOLIUS (fl. 6th century A.D.).  Greek.  Author of over one hundred short hymns.

ANDERSON, MARIA FRANCES HILL (b. 1819).  American (born in Paris, France).  Baptist.  Minor novelist and poet.

ANDREW OF JERUSALEM (660-732).  Archbishop of Crete.  Author of homilies and canons, the best of the homilies concerning Tutus, Bishop of Crete.  One of the earliest composers of canons.

ANSTICE, JOSEPH (1808-1836).  British.  Church of England.  Professor of Classical Literature, King's College, London.  His collection of Hymns appeared (posthumously) in 1836.

ARKWRIGHT, JOHN STANHOPE (b. 1872).

ARLOTT, LESLIE THOMAS JOHN (b. 1914).  British.  Police detective, producer with the B.B.C., cricket correspondent, poet.

ARMITAGE, ELLA SOPHIA BULLEY (1841-1931).  British.  Congregational.  Educator, archaeologist, antiquarian writer, poet.

ARNOLD, GOTTFRIED (1666-1714).  German.  Professor of History at Geissen; historiographer to the King of Prussia; involved in the "New Angel Brotherhood" of Jakob Bohme; pastor and inspector at Werben; pastor of Perleberg.  A poet of quality and some prominence; his hymns contain strong elements of mysticism and focus upon the marriage of the soul to God.

AUBER, HARRIET (1773-1862).  British.  Church of England.  Authored a psalm collection entitled The Spirit of the Psalms (1829).

BABCOCK, MALTBIE DAVENPORT (1858-1901).  American.  Presbyterian.  Pastor of churches at Lockport, New York; Baltimore; the Brick Presbyterian Church, New York City.

BACON, LEONARD (1802-1881).  American.  Congregational.  Pastor of the Centre Church, New Haven, Connecticut (1825-1866); Professor of Theology, Yale Divinity School (1866-1871).  Edited Hymns and Sacred Songs for the Monthly Concert (1823).

BAKER, SIR HENRY WILLIAMS (1821-1877). British. Church of England. Vicar of Monkland, Herefordshire (1851-1877); chaired the committee for the promotion and preparation of Hymns Ancient and Modern (1861, 1868, 1874, 1875); edited Hymns for the London Mission (1874) and Hymns for Mission Services (1876-1877).

BAKER, THEODORE (1851-1934). American. Published A Dictionary of Musical Terms and a Biographical Dictionary of Musicians (1900, 1905).

BAKEWELL, JOHN (1721-1819). British. Wesleyan Methodist. Head of the Greenwich Royal Park Academy and an itinerant preacher for the Wesleyans.

BALLANTINE, WILLIAM G. (1848-1937). American.

BANKS, GEORGE LINNAEUS (1821-1881). British. Newspaper editor and writer of verse.

BARBAULD, ANNA LAETITIA AIKEN (1743-1825). British. Independent. Authored Hymns in Prose for Children (1781). Married to the Rev. Rochmont Barbauld, a Dissenter, minister, and head of a boarding school at Palgrave, Suffolk.

BARBER, MARY ANN SERRETT (1801-1864).

BARING-GOULD, SABINE (1834-1924). British. Church of England. Rector of Lew Trenchard, Devonshire. Novelist, poet, folklorist, and antiquarian.

BARRATT, ALFRED. British. Methodist.

BARTON, BERNARD (1784-1849). British. Society of Friends. Shopkeeper, merchant, banker. Known as the "Quaker Poet"; published a dozen volumes of poetry, including Devotional Verses Founded on Select Texts of Scripture (1826).

BATEMAN, CHRISTIAN HENRY (1813-1889). British. Moravian, Congregational, Church of England. Curate of St. John's Penymynydd, Hawarden. Edited Sacred Melodies for Sabbath Schools and Families (1843) and The Children's Hymnal and Christian Year (1872).

BATES, KATHARINE LEE (1859-1929). No church affiliation. Poet, prose writer and literary critic, Professor of English at Wellesley College.

BATHURST, WILLIAM HILEY (1796-1877). British. Church of England. Scholar, poet, classicist. Published Psalms and Hymns for Public and Private Use (1831).

BAX, CLIFFORD (1886-1962). British. Artist, dramatist, poet, and writer of short fiction.

BAXTER, LYDIA (1809-1874). American. Baptist. Poet and hymnodist who wrote for Sunday school and evangelistic services.

BAXTER, RICHARD (1615-1691). British. A member of the Church of England who became a Dissenting minister in 1673; tried in violation of the Act of Uniformity (1685). A major essayist of the Commonwealth period.

BAYLY, ALBERT FREDERICK (1901-1984). British. Congregational. Poet and publisher of collections of contemporary hymns between 1935 and 1977.

BEACH, CURTIS (b. 1914). American. His hymn, "O How Glorious, Full of wonder appeared first in the Pilgrim Hymnal (1958).

BEDDOME, BENJAMIN (1717-1795). British. Baptist. Minister at Burton-on-the-Water, Gloucestershire (1740-1795). Prolific hymn writer; 830 of his hymns published by Rev. Robert Hall in 1817 under the title Hymns Adapted to Public Worship and Private Devotion.

BEHM, MARTIN (1557-1622). Austrian. Chief pastor of Lauban, Silesia (1586-1622). Author of approximately 480 hymns.

BEN JUDAH, DANIEL. Hebrew writer of the fourteenth century, best known for his composition of the Yigdal (Doxology), which rehearses, in metrical form, the thirteen articles of the Hebrew Creed.

BENNARD, GEORGE (1873-1958). American. His popular "The Old Rugged Cross" dates from 1913.

BENNETT, SANFORD FILMORE (1836-1898). American. Primarily a practicing physician; composed (to fit the music of Joseph Philbrick Webster) a number of popular gospel hymns and songs.

BENSON, LOUIS FITZGERALD (1855-1930). American. Presbyterian. After serving as minister of the Church of the Redeemer at Germantown, Pennsylvania, he resigned to edit a number of hymnals for the Presbyterian Church and to produce his own Hymns, Original and Traditional (1925). A prominent hymnologist, he authored The English Hymn: Its Development and Use in Public Worship (1915; rpt. 1962) and essays (based on a series of lectures) under the title of The Hymnody of the Christian Church (1927).

BERNARD OF CLAIRVAUX (1091-1153). French. A major contributor to Latin hymnody. Definitive editions of his poetry and prose did not appear until the early eighteenth century, beginning 1719.

BERNARD OF CLUNY-MORLAIX (fl. mid-twelfth century). English-French. Author of a three-part poem of some 3000 lines entitled De Contemptu Mundi, from which passages and fragments have been translated to serve as congregational hymns.

BETHAM-EDWARDS, MATILDA BARBARA (1836-1919). British. Church of England. Primarily a writer of stories and poems for children.

BETHUNE, GEORGE WASHINGTON (1805-1862). American. Reformed Dutch. Scholar and eminent theologian. Most of his hymns may be found in his Lays of Love and Faith (1847).

BICKERSTETH, EDWARD HENRY (1825-1906). British. Church of England.

Dean of Gloucester and Bishop of Exeter (1885-1900). Edited Psalms and Hymns (1958) and The Hymnal Companion to the Book of Common Prayer (1870, 1876).

BLACKIE, JOHN STUART (1809-1895). Scottish. Church of Scotland. Professor Latin, Marischal College, Aberdeen (1841-1850); Professor of Greek, University of Edinburgh (appointed 1850).

BLACKLOCK, THOMAS (1721-1791). Church of Scotland. An early literary friend of Robert Burns who commanded some attention as a minor poet.

BLAISDELL, JAMES ARNOLD (1867-1957). American. Methodist.

BLANCHARD, FERDINAND Q. His "O Child of lowly manger birth" dates from 1906.

BLISS, PHILIP PAUL (1838-1876). American. Methodist, Congregational. Composed Sunday school melodies for George Frederick Root, then joined with the Chicago evangelist Major D.W. Whittle. Published, with Ira David Sankey, Gospel Hymns and Sacred Songs (1874) and a number of volumes under the general title Gospel Songs (1875-1876).

BOBERG, CARL (1859-1940). Swedish.

BODE, JOHN ERNEST (1816-1874). British. Church of England. Rector of Westwell, Oxfordshire, and of Castle Camps, Cambridgeshire. Published Hymns from the Gospel of the Day for Each Sunday and Festivals of Our Lord (1860).

BOEHM, ANTHONY WILHELM (1673-1722).

BONAR, HORATIUS (1808-1889). Scottish. Church of Scotland, Free Church of Scotland. Moderator of the General Assembly of the Free Church of Scotland. Published Songs for the Wilderness (1843, 1844), The Bible Hymn Book (1845), Hymns Original and Selected (1846), Hymns of Faith and Hope (1857, 1861), Hymns of the Nativity (1879).

BONAR, JANE CATHERINE LUNDIE (1821-1844). Scottish. Free Church of Scotland. Wife of the Rev. Dr. Horatius Bonar. Her hymns appeared in her husband's Songs for the Wilderness (1843, 1844) and his Bible Hymn Book (1845).

BONAVAENTURA ((1221-1274). Professor of Theology at Paris (1245); elec-General of the Franciscan Order (1256); Bishop of Alba (1273). Only slight contributions to Latin hymnody.

BORTHWICK, JANE LAURIE (1813-1897). Scottish. Church of Scotland. Published, with her sister, Mrs. Sarah Findlater, four series of hymns under the title Hymns from the Land of Luther (1854, 1855, 1858, 1862).

BOTTOME, FRANCIS (1823-1894). British, American. Methodist Episcopal. Compiled Gospel Hymns (1872), Centenary Singer (1869), Round Lake (1872).

BOURIGNON, ANTOINETTE (1616-1680). French. A mystic and religious re-
former; wrote and preached throughout France, Holland, England, and
Scotland. Her collected works, some nineteen volumes, appeared in
Amsterdam in 1686.

BOURNE, WILLIAM ST. HILL (1846-1929). British. Church of England.
Curate of Holy Trinity, Derby; Curate of St. Paul's, St. Leonard's-
on-Sea; Vicar of All Saints, Haggerstone; Rector of Finchley. Poet
and hymnodist; published A Supplementary Hymnal (1898)

BOWIE, WALTER RUSSELL (1882-1969). American. Episcopal. Rector of
Emmanuel Church, Greenwood, Virginia (1908-1911); Rector of St.
Paul's Church, Richmond, Virginia (1911-1923); Rector of Grace
Church, New York (1923-1939). Professor of Practical Theology,
Union Theological Seminary, New York. Member of the committee that
prepared the American Revised Standard Version (RSV) of the Bible.

BOWLY, MARY PETERS (1813-1856). British. Church of England. Author of
a multi-volume history of the world. Published Hymns Intended To
Help the Communion of Saints (1847).

BOWRING, SIR JOHN (1792-1872). British. Unitarian. Edited The Westminster Review; served in Parliament; consul at Canton, governor of
Hong Kong, chief superintendent of trade with China. His published
works extend to thirty-six volumes.

BRACE, SETH COLLINS (b. 1811). American. Presbyterian, Congregational.
Essentially a writer of temperance hymns; his pieces published under the signature of "C."

BRACKENBURY, ROBERT CARR (1752-1811). British. Methodist. Served as
an itinerant preacher for the Wesleyan Methodists. Published Select Hymns, in Two Parts (1795) and Sacred Poetry, or Hymns on the
Principal Histories of the Old and New Testaments and on All the
Parables (1800).

BREWER, LEIGH RICHMOND (1839-1916).

BRIDGES, MATTHEW (1800-1894). British. Church of England, Roman Catholic. A significant British poet, he also published a collection
entitled Hymns of the Heart (1847).

BRIDGES, ROBERT SEYMOUR (1844-1930). British. Church of England. Physician, poet, Poet Laureate of England (1913-1930). Editor of the
Yattendon Hymnal (1899, rev. 1920)--one of the most highly literary
collections of modern hymnody in English.

BRIGGS, GEORGE WALLACE (1875-1959). British. Church of England. Canon
on Leicester and Worcester. Published Prayers and Hymns for Use in
Schools (1927) and Songs of Faith (1945). One of the founders of
the Hymn Society of Great Britain and Ireland.

BROMEHEAD, JOSEPH (1748-1826). British. Church of England. Curate of
Eckington, Derbyshire (1771-1826). Author of poems and of psalm
paraphrases.

BROOKE, STOPFORD AUGUSTUS (1832-1916).  British.  Church of England.
    Chaplain to the British Embassy to Berlin (1862-1865); Chaplain to
    Queen Victoria (1867); Dean of Bedford Chapel.  Published Christian
    Hymns (1881).

BROOKS, CHARLES TIMOTHY (1813-1883).  American.  Unitarian.  Pastor at
    Newport, Rhode Island (1837-1871).

BROOKS, PHILLIPS (1835-1893).  American.  Episcopal.  Rector of the
    Church of the Advent, Philadelphia; Rector of Holy Trinity, Phila-
    delphia; Rector of Trinity Church, Boston; Bishop of Massachusetts
    (1891-1893).  One of the significant preachers in the United States
    during the second half of the nineteenth century.

BROWN, PHOEBE HINSDALE (1783-1861).  American.  Congregational.  One of
    the truly superior religious poets of nineteenth-century America,
    although she did not read or write until she became eighteen, and
    her formal schooling extended for only three months.

BROWNE, SIMON (1686-1732).  British.  Independent.  Pastor of the Inde-
    pendent Chapel in the Old Jewry, London (1716-1732).  Published
    Hymns and Spiritual Songs, in Three Books, Designed as a Supplement
    to Dr. Watts (1720).

BROWNING, ELIZABETH BARRETT (1809-1861).  British.  Independent.  Wife
    of the poet Robert Browning and perhaps the leading female poet of
    the Victorian Age.  Those of her "hymns" in congregational use have
    been adapted from her secular poetry.

BROWNLIE, JOHN (1859-1925).  Scottish.  Free Church of Scotland.  Minis-
    ter of the Free Church, Portpatrick, Wigtownshire (1890-1925).  Pub-
    lished Hymns and Hymn Writers of the Church Hymnary (1899); Hymns
    of Our Pilgrimage Zionward; Hymns of the Pilgrim Life; Hymns of the
    Early Church; Hymns from the East and West; Hymns of the Greek
    Church (Series 1-4).

BRYANT, WILLIAM CULLEN (1794-1878).  American.  Congregational.  Lawyer,
    journalist, essayist, translator, and the eariest of the noted New
    England poets of the nineteenth century.  He published privately,
    in 1869, Hymns by W.C. Bryant.

BUCK, CARLTON C. (b. 1907).  American.  His "O Lord, may church and
    home combine" appeared, initially, in Thirteen New Marriage and
    Family Life Hymns (New York: Hymn Society of America, 1961).

BUCKOLL, HENRY JAMES (1803-1871).  British.  Church of England.  Rector
    of Siddington, Gloucester; assistant master of Rugby School.  Edi-
    ted the first hymn Collection for Rugby School, as well as a Collec-
    tion of Hymns for the Rugby Parish Church (1839) and the Collection
    of Hymns for the Rugby School Chapel (1850).  Also published a
    volume of Hymns Translated from the German (1842).

BUDRY, EDMUND L. (1854-1932).

BULFINCH, STEPHEN GREENLEAF (1809-1870).  American.  Unitarian.  Held se-
    veral pastorates throughout the eastern United States, the last at

East Cambridge, Massachusetts (1865-1870). His hymns focus upon the theme of Christ's miracles.

BULLOCK, WILLIAM (1798-1874). Canadian. Church of England. Served as a missionary for the Society for the Propagation of the Gospel (SPG) for thirty-two years. Dean of Nova Scotia. Published Songs of the Church (1854).

BUNTING, WILLIAM MACLARDIE (1805-1866). British. Wesleyan Methodist. Circuit minister (1824-1849). Published in excess of fifty congregational hymns.

BUNYAN, JOHN (1628-1688). British. Baptist. Those of his hymns that have been (and still remain) in congregational use come from his classic prose work, Pilgrim's Progress (1678-1679).

BURDER, GEORGE (1752-1832). British. Calvinist Methodist, Congregational. A founder of the Religious Tract Society, the London Missionary Society, the British and Foreign Bible Society. Editor of The Evangelical Magazine. Published a Collection of Hymns from Various Authors (1784).

BURDSALL, RICHARD (1735-1824). British. Wesleyan Methodist. He appended his only hymn to his Memoirs, published at York (n.d.).

BURGESS, GEORGE (1809-1866). American. Episcopal. Bishop of Maine (1847-1866). Published The Book of Psalms Translated into English Verse (1839), The American Metrical Psalter (1864), and a collection of his Poems (1868).

BURKE, CHRISTIAN (1857-1944).

BURLEIGH, WILLIAM HENRY (1812-1871). American. Unitarian. Publisher of religious periodicals and active in the temperance movement. His hymns became more popular in England than in the United States.

BURNS, JAMES DRUMMOND (1823-1864). Scottish. Free Church of Scotland. Minister of the Presbyterian Church at Funchal, Madeira (1848-1855) and of the Hampstead Presbyterian Church, London (1855-1864). Contributed the article on "Hymns" to the eighth edition of the Encyclopaedia Britannica.

BURROWES, ELISABETH (b. 1885). Her hymn "God of the ages, by whose hand" appeared initially in Twelve New World Order Hymns (New York: Hymn Society of America, 1958).

BURTON, HENRY (1840-1930). American, British. Methodist Episcopal, Wesleyan Methodist. Served churches in Lancashire and in London.

BURTON, JOHN (1773-1822). British. Baptist. One of the compilers of The Nottingham Sunday School Union Hymn Book (1812).

BYRNE, MARY ELIZABETH (1880-1931). Irish. Roman Catholic. A research worker in Irish studies for the Board of Intermediate Education; historian and specialist on Irish culture.

BYROM, JOHN (1692-1763).  British.  Church of England.  Poet, scribe, a
    teacher of shorthand systems (one of which he invented).  Elected
    to the Royal Society in 1724.

CAMERON, WILLIAM (1751-1811).  Scottish.  Church of Scotland.  Minister
    of Kirknewton (1786-1811).  One of the principal revisers of the
    Scottish  Translations and Paraphrases of 1745-1751; contributed to
    the Translations and Paraphrases of 1781.

CAMPBELL, JANE MONTGOMERY (1817-1878).  British.  Church of England.
    Taught singing to the children of her father's parish (St. James's,
    Paddington) and contributed hymnodic translations to various hymn
    collections.

CAMPBELL, MARGARET MALCOLM, LADY COCKBURN (d. 1841).  British.  Plymouth
    Brethren.  Her hymns were printed in lithograph from the original
    manuscripts and circulated privately.

CAMPBELL, ROBERT ( 1814-1868).  Scottish.  Episcopal Church of Scotland,
    Roman Catholic.  Lawyer and advocate of education for children of
    the poor.  Translator of Latin hymns and the author of Hymns and
    Anthems for the Use of the Holy Services of the Church, within the
    United Diocese of St. Andrews, Dunkeld, and Dunblane (Edinburgh,
    1850).

CANITZ, FRIEDRICH RUDOLPH LUDWIG, FREIHERR VON (1654-1699).  German.
    Gentleman of the Bedchamber to the Elector Friedrich Wilhelm (1677-
    1680); chief magistrate of Zossen and Trebbin (1680); counselor of
    the Court and Legation (1681).  His hymns published posthumously
    and anonymously, and first edited in 1700.

CARLYLE, JOSEPH DACRE (1758-1804).  British.  Church of England.  Pro-
    fessor of Arabic, University of Cambridge; vicar of Newcastle-upon-
    Tyne.

CARNEY, JULIA A. FLETCHER (b. 1823).  American.  Unitarian.  Teacher in
    the Boston, Massachusetts, primary schools held in the vestry of
    the Hollis Street Church.

CARTER, R. KELSO (1849-1926).

CARY, PHOEBE (1824-1871).  American.  Universalist.  With her sister,
    Alice, she wrote a number of popular congregational hymns; a close
    friend of the poet John Greenleaf Whittier.  The sisters' Poems
    appeared in 1849.

CASWELL, EDWARD (1814-1878).  British.  Church of England, Roman Catho-
    lic.  Perpetual curate of Stratford-sub-Castle, Wiltshire (1840-
    1847); a member of the Oratory of St. Philip Neri at Edgbaston.
    Translated the ancient Latin hymns in the Roman Breviaries.

CAWOOD, JOHN (1775-1852).  British.  Church of England.  Curate of Rib-
    besford and Dowles; perpetual curate of St. Anne's Chapel of Ease,
    Worcestershire.

CENNICK, JOHN (1718-1755). British. Church of England, Methodist, Moravian. Published four major hymn collections between 1741 and 1754.

CHADWICK, JOHN WHITE (1840-1904). American. Unitarian. Minister of the Second Unitarian Church, Brooklyn, New York (1864-1904).

CHANDLER, JOHN (1806-1876). British. Church of England. Vicar of Witley, Galdaming, Surrey (1837-1876). A talented translator, he published Hymns for the Primitive Church (1837) and Hymns of the Church (1841).

CHARLES, ELIZABETH RUNDLE (1828-1896). British. Church of England. Composed original hymns and translations from the Latin and the German. Published The Voice of Christian Life in Song; or, Hymns and Hymn Writers of Many Lands and Ages (1858).

CHATFIELD, ALAN WILLIAM (1808-1896). British. Church of England. Vicar of Stotfold, Bedfordshire (1833-1847); Vicar of Much Marcle, Herefordshire (1847-1896). Published Songs and Hymns of the Earliest Christian Poets, Bishops and Others, Translated into English Verse (1876).

CHESTERTON, GILBERT KEITH (1874-1936). British. Roman Catholic. One of the major essayists and writers of fiction of the so-called "Transition" period in British literature (1880-1920).

CHORLEY, HENRY FOTHERGILL (1808-1872). British. Journalist, essayist, art critic, and a staff writer (1830-1869) for The Athenaeum.

CLARK, ALEXANDER (1835-1879). American. Methodist Episcopal. A minister of the American Methodist Episcopal Church and the editor of the Pittsburgh (Pennsylvania) Methodist Recorder.

CLARKE, JAMES FREEMAN (1810-1888). Unitarian, Church of the Disciples. Minister at Louisville, Kentucky (1833-1840); minister of the Church of the Disciples, Boston, Massachusetts (1841-1888). Published the Hymn Book for the Church of the Disciples (1844), which he enlarged in 1852.

CLAUDIUS, MATTHIAS (1740-1815). German. Lutheran. Poet, journalist, an acquaintance of Goethe. Although a writer of religious poetry, he intended none of those pieces as congregational hymns.

CLAUSNITZER, TOBIAS (1619-1684). German. Appointed (1644) chaplain to a Swedish regiment; first pastor at Weiden (1649-1684).

CLEMENS, TITUS FLAVIUS (ST. CLEMENT OF ALEXANDRIA) (c. 170-c. 220). Embraced Christianity at Alexandria; master of the Catechetical School, Alexandria (c. 190-203). His hymns come from two poems attached to a long didactic work entitled The Tutor.

CLEPHANE, ELIZABETH CECELIA DOUGLAS (1830-1869). Scottish. Free Church of Scotland. Her hymns appeared after her death in Rev. William Arnot's The Family Treasury (1872-1874).

CODNER, MRS. ELIZABETH (b. 1835).  Actually ELIZABETH CONDER.

COGHILL, ANNA LOUISA WALKER (1836-1907).  British, Canadian.  Her most
     noted hymn, "Work, for the night is coming," appeared anonymously
     in a Canadian newspaper.

COKE, REV. THOMAS (1747-1814).  One of the two bishops (along with Fran-
     cis Asbury) whom John Wesley ordained to serve the Methodist Church
     in the American colonies.  However, the hymn "My hope, my all, my
     Saviour Thou" cannot, with certainty, be ascribed to him--as was
     done so in the American edition of Wesley's A Pocket Hymn Book;
     thus, that piece may well be  anonymous or at least of unknown ori-
     gin and authorship.

COLLYER, ROBERT (b. 1823).  British, American.  Methodist, Unitarian.
     Pastor of the Declaration of Unity Church, Chicago (1859-1879), and
     of the Church of the Messiah, New York (from 1879).

COLLYER, WILLIAM BENGO (1782-1854).  British.  Congregational.  Pastor
     of churches at Salters' Hall (1814-1826) and at Peckham (1801-1853).
     Compiled Hymns. . .Designed as a Supplement to Dr. Watts's Psalms
     and Hymns (1812).

CONDER, MRS. ELIZABETH (b. 1835).  Both the editors of HMEC and MH
     (1905) have inaccurately cast the spelling of this name as CODNER.
     The correct spelling appears only in AMEH.

CONDER, EUSTACE ROGERS (1820-1892).  British.  Congregational.  Son of
     Josiah Conder (see below).  Pastor of the Congregational Church at
     Poole, Dorset, and minister of the East Parade Chapel, Leeds.

CONDER, JOSIAH (1789-1855).  British.  Congregational.  Edited The Cong-
     regational Hymn Book (1836) and a revision of Isaac Watts's Psalms
     and Hymns (1851).  One of the prominent hymn writers of the first
     half of the nineteenth century.

COOK, JOSEPH SIMPSON (1859-1933).  British.

COOMBS, CHARLES WHITNEY (b. 1859).  American.  Organist of the Ameri-
     can Church at Dresden (1887-1891), at the Church of the Holy Com-
     munion, New York (1892-1908), and at St. Luke's, New York (begin-
     ning 1908).

COOPER, JOHN (b. 1818).

COPELAND, BENJAMIN (b. 1855).

COPENHAVER, LAURA SCHERER (1868-1940).  American.  United Lutheran
     Church.  Professor of English Literature at Marion (Virginia) Col-
     lege.

COSIN, JOHN (1594-1672).  British.  Church of England.  Chaplain to the
     Bishop of Durham, Prebendary of Durham, Archdeacon of the East
     Riding of Yorkshire, Chancellor of the University of Cambridge,
     Dean of Peterborough, Bishop of Durham.  Compiled a Collection of
     Private Devotions (1627) and participated in the revision of The

Book of Common Prayer (1662)

COSTER, GEORGE THOMAS (1835-1912). British. Congregational. Held pastorates at Barnstaple, Hull, South Norwood, and Whitby. Published
Poems and Hymns (1882) and edited Temperance Melodies and Religious Hymns (1869).

COTTERILL, JANE BOAK (1790-1825). British. Church of England.

COTTERILL, THOMAS (1779-1823). British. Church of England. Curate of
Tutbury (1803-1808); Incumbent of Lane End, Staffordshire (1808-
1817); Perpetual Curate of St. Paul's, Sheffield (1817-1823). Compiled a Selection of Psalms and Hymns (1810; 9th ed., 1820).

COWPER, FRANCES MARIA MADAN (1727-1797). British. Church of England.

COWPER, WILLIAM (1731-1800). British. Church of England. A major poet of the eighteenth century who joined with the Rev. John Newton
(see below) in producing the 1779 collection that became known as
the Olney Hymns. To the late eighteenth century, Cowper represented the poet of the new religious revival (as exemplified by Wesleyan Methodism), as John Milton (see below) had stood as the poet
of a sterner Puritanism in the preceding century.

COX, CHRISTOPHER CHRISTIAN (1816-1882). American. Protestant Episcopal. Practiced medicine in Baltimore; became Brigade Surgeon, U.S.
Army (1861-1864).

COX, FRANCES ELIZABETH (1812-1897). British. Church of England. One
of the most successful translators of German hymns: Sacred Hymns
from the German (1841), Hymns from the German (1864).

COXE, ARTHUR CLEVELAND (1818-1896). American. Episcopal. Rector of
St. John's Church, Hartford, Connecticut (1842-1851); rector of
Grace Church, Baltimore (1854-1863); rector of Calvary Church, New
York (1863-1865); Bishop of Western New York (1865-1896). A mem-
ber of the editorial committee for the Episcopal Hymnal of 1872.

CRABBE, GEORGE (1754-1832). British. Church of England. Curate of Al-
dborough and Stathorn; incumbent of Evershot, Mirston, and Trow-
bridge. A significant figure in the history of British poetry of
the late eighteenth century prior to the poetic achievements of
Wordsworth and Coleridge.

CREWDSON, JANE FOX (1809-1863). British. More than a dozen of her
hymns, especially those written for children, have remained in common congregational use.

CROLY, GEORGE (1780-1860). Irish. Church of Ireland. Published, in
1854, his Psalms and Hymns for Public Worship.

CROSBY, FANNY. See below under VAN ALSTYNE, FRANCES JANE CROSBY.

CROSS, ADA CAMBRIDGE (b. 1844). British. Church of England. Published Hymns on the Holy Communion (1866) and Hymns on the Litany
(1865).

CROSS, ALLEN EASTMAN (b. 1864). American. Congregational. Held pas-
torates at Cliftondale, Massachusetts (1892-1896), Springfield,
Massachusetts (1896-1901); Old South Church, Boston (1901-1912),
Milford, Massachusetts (1916-1925).

CROSWELL, WILLIAM (1805-1851). American. Protestant Episcopal. Rec-
tor of Christ Church, Boston (1829-1840); rector of St. Peter's
Church, Auburn, New York (1840-1844); rector of the Church of the
Advent, Boston (1844-1851).

CRUM, J.M.C. (1872-1958).

CUMMINS, JAMES JOHN (1795--1867). Irish, English. Church of England.
Published Poetical Meditations and Hymns (1839) and Hymns, Meditations, and Other Poems (1849).

CUNINGGIM, MAUDE MERRIMON (1874-1965).

CUNNINGHAM, REV. JOHN WILLIAM (1780-1861). British. Church of England.
Curate of Ripley, Surrey (1802-1803); vicar of Harrow (1811-1861).

CUSHING, WILLIAM ORCUTT (b. 1823). American. Author of hymns for Sunday schools that appeared in Ira David Sankey's Sacred Songs and
Solos (London, 1873).

CUTTER, WILLIAM (1801-1867). American. Congregational. Engaged in
business in Portland, Maine, and Brooklyn, New York.


DAVIES, SAMUEL (1723-1761). American. Presbyterian. President of New
Jersey Presbyterian College at Princeton, succeeding Jonathan Edwards.

DAVIS, OZORA STEARNS (1866-1931). American. Congregational. Minister
of Congregational churches at Springfield, Vermont; Newtonville,
Massachusetts; New Britain, Connecticut. President of Chicago Theological Seminary (1909-1920).

DAVIS, WILLIAM T. (b. 1822). American. Lawyer. His hymn, "To Thee, O
God, whose guiding hand" (1870), celebrates the 250th anniversary
of the landing of the Pilgrims at Plymouth, Massachusetts.

DEARMER, PERCY (1867-1936). British. Church of England. Curate of
St. Anne's, Lambeth; curate of St. John's, London; curate of Berkeley Chapel, Mayfair; curate of St. Mark's, London; vicar of St.
Mary the Virgin, Primrose Hill (1901-1915); Professor of Ecclesiastical Art, King's College, London. Secretary of the committee that
prepared The English Hymnal and one of the compilers of The Oxford
Book of Carols (1928).

DECK, JAMES GEORGE (1802-1884). British. Plymouth Brethren. In 1852,
he settled in New Zealand. Published--at Melbourne, Australia, in
1876--Hymns and Sacred Poems.

DEEMS, REV. CHARLES FORCE, D.D. (1819-1893).

DENHAM, DAVID (1791=1848). British. Baptist. Pastor of the Baptist
Church at Horsell Common, London (1810-1816); pastor at Plymouth
(1816-1826), at Margate (1826-1834); pastor of the Baptist Church
in Unicorn Yard, Tooley Street, Southwark (1834-1837). In 1837,
he published The Saints' Melody, a New Selection of Hymns.

DENNY, SIR EDWARD (1796-1889). British. Plymouth Brethren. Published
A Selection of Hymns (1839) and Hymns and Poems (1848; 3rd. ed.,
1870).

DESSLER, WOLFGANG CHRISTOPH (1660-1722). German. Amanuensis and translator for Erasmus Finx at Nurnberg. Corrector of the School of
the Holy Ghost, Nurnberg (1705-1720). The majority of his more
than one hundred hymns appeared in his volume of meditations, Got-
tgcheiligter Christen Nutzlich Ergetzende Seelenlust (1692).

DEXTER, HENRY MARTYN (1821-1890). American. Congregational. Pastor
at Manchester, New Hampshire; pastor at New Haven, Connecticut;
pastor of the Berkeley Street Congregational Church, Boston. Edited, in 1867, The Congregationalist.

DICKINSON, CHARLES ALBERT (1849-1906). American. Congregational. His
most popular hymns were written for youth and Sunday school services.

DICKSON, DAVID (1583-1663). Scottish. Church of Scotland. Presbyterian minister and Professor of Divinity at Glasgow (1640) and at
the University of Edinburgh (1650).

DIX, WILLIAM CHATTERTON (1837-1898). British. Church of England. A
large and significant contributor to Hymns Ancient and Modern, he
published his own Hymns of Love and Joy (1861), Altar Songs (1867),
Vision of All Saints (1871), Seekers of a City (1878). Served as
manager of a marine insurance company in Glasgow.

DOANE, GEORGE WASHINGTON (1799-1859). American. Episcopal. Assistant
minister of Trinity Church, New York (1821-1824); Professor of Bel-
les-Lettres , Trinity College, Hartford, Connecticut (1824-1828);
rector of Trinity Church, Boston (1828-1832); Bishop of New Jersey
(1832-1859). Edited, in 1832, the first American edition of John
Keble's Christian Year (for Keble, see below).

DOANE, WILLIAM CROSWELL (1832-1913). American. Episcopal. Son of Rev.
George Washington Doane (see above). Rector of churches at Burlington, Vermont; Hartford, Connecticut; Albany, New York. Bishop
of Albany (1869-1913).

DOBELL, JOHN (1757-1840). British. Published A New Selection of Seven
Hundred Evangelical Hymns (1806).

DOBER, ANNA SCHINDLER (1713-1739). German. Moravian Brethren. Joined
Anna Nitschmann in forming the "Jungfrauenbund" of the unmarried
sisters at Herrnhut (1730). Married (1737) L.J. Dober, then the
General Elder of the Moravian Church. Her hymns focus upon personal devotion and trust.

DODDRIDGE, PHILIP (1702-1751). British. Independent. Ministered to congregations at Kibworth (1723-1725) and Market Harborough (1725-1729); served the Castle Hill Meeting at Northampton from 1729 to 1751--when, in the final stage of consumptive illness, he left England for Lisbon. His hymns were published after his death, in 1755, by his friend, Rev. Job Orton; over seventy-five of those remain in common congregational use in England and America.

DRAPER, WILLIAM HENRY (1855-1933). British. Church of England. Curate of St. Mary's, Shrewsbury; vicar of Alfreton; vicar of the Abbey Church, Shrewsbury; rector of Adel, Leeds; rural dean of Shrewsbury; vicar of Axbridge (1930-1933). Published Hymns for Holy Week, The Victoria Book of Hymns (1897); edited collections of hymns by Thomas Campion (1919) and by Orlando Gibbons (1925).

DRYDEN, JOHN (1631-1700). British. Church of England, Roman Catholic. The major literary figure of the Restoration period. Poet Laureate of England (1670-1700). His significant contributions to hymnody focus upon translations of Latin hymns; see George Rapall Noyes and George Reuben Potter (eds.), Hymns Attributed to John Dryden (Berkeley: University of California Press, 1937).

DUFFIELD, GEORGE, JR. (1818-1888). American. Presbyterian. Held pastorates at Brooklyn, New York (1840-1847); Bloomfield, New Jersey (1847-1852); Philadelphia ((1852-1861); Adrian, Michigan (1861-1865); Galesburg, Illinois (1865-1869); Saginaw, Michigan (1869-1885).

DUNCAN, MARY LUNDIE (1814-1840). Scottish. Church of Scotland. She wrote hymns for her own children between July and December 1839; those appeared in 1841 and then in 1842 as Rhymes for My Children.

DUNN, ROBINSON PORTER (1825-1867). American. Baptist. Taught at Brown University.

DWIGHT, JOHN SULLIVAN (1812-1893). American. Unitarian. Abandoned the ministry for the Brook Farm Community near West Roxbury, Massachusetts. Helped to found the influential Harvard Medical Association (1837); became one of the first members of the Transcendental Club; taught music and Latin at Brook Farm; edited Dwight's Journal of Music (1852-1881); established a professorship of music at Harvard.

DWIGHT, TIMOTHY (1752-1817). American. Congregational. Tutor at Yale College (1771-1777) and then chaplain in the U.S. Army. Held pastorates at Fairfield, Connecticut, where he also taught at the local academy. President of Yale College (1795-1817). Edited a major nineteenth-century edition of Isaac Watts' Psalms of David Imitated and has been recognized as the most significant contributor to early American hymnody.

DYER, SIDNEY (1814-1898). American. Baptist. Missionary to the Choctaw Indians; pastor at Indianapolis (1852-1859) and Secretary to the Baptist Publication Society.

EASTBURN, JAMES WALLACE (1797-1819). American. Episcopal. Rector at
    Accomac, Virginia (1818-1819).

ECKING, SAMUEL (1757-1785). British. Baptist. Contributed hymns to
    The Gospel Magazine (1778-1779)--the principal voice of opposi-
    tion to Wesleyan Methodism in eighteenth-century England.

EDGAR, MARY S. (b. 1889).

EDMESTON, JAMES (1791-1867). British. Church of England. Churchwarden
    of St. Barnabas's Church, Homerton. Wrote over 2000 hymns, most
    of which he published in his Sacred Lyrics (1820-1822), Cottage
    Minstrel (1821), Hymns for Sunday Schools (1821), Missionary Hymns
    (1822), Original Hymns (1833), Hymns for the Chamber of Sickness
    (1844), Closet Hymns and Poems (1844), Hymns for the Young (1846),
    Sacred Poetry (1847).

ELA, DAVID HOUGH (b. 1831). American. Methodist Episcopal. An ordai-
    ned minister of the Methodist Episcopal Church.

ELLERTON, JOHN (1823-1893). British. Church of England. Curate at
    Easebourne, Sussex (1850); curate of Brighton and lecturer of St.
    Peter's, Brighton (1850-1852); vicar of Crew Green (1860-1872);
    rector of Hinstock (1872-1876), Barnes (1876-1886), White Roding
    (1886-1892). Nominated to a prebendal stall in St. Alban's Cathe-
    dral Church. Chief compiler and editor of Hymns for Schools (1859),
    Church Hymns, The Children's Hymn Book; a joint-compiler of the
    1875 edition of Hymns Ancient and Modern and advisor to The Hymnal
    Companion to the Book of Common Prayer. His own Hymns, Original
    and Translated appeared in 1888.

ELLIOTT, CHARLOTTE (1789-1871). British. Church of England. Author
    of 150 hymns, most of which are characterized by their tenderness,
    simplicity of language, piety, and almost perfect rhythm. She pub-
    lished Hymns for a Week (1839), The Invalid's Hymn Book (1834-1841).

ELLIOTT, EBENEEZER (1781-1849). British. Unitarian. A Sheffield iron-
    trader whose hymns appeared primarily in Sheffield newspapers.
    Known popularly as the "Corn Law Rhymer" for his bitter condemna-
    tion (in his Corn-Law Rhymes, 1828) of the bread tax, to which he
    attributed all national misfortunes.

ELLIOTT, EMILY ELIZABETH STEELE (1836-1897). British. Church of Eng-
    land. Edited The Church Missionary Juvenile Instructor, in which
    the majority of her hymns appeared.

ESLING, CATHERINE WATTERMAN (1812-1897). American. Protestant Episco-
    pal.

EVANS, CARA B. Canadian.

EVANS, JONATHAN (1748-1809). British. Congregational. Preached at
    Foleshill, near Coventry (1782-1795) and ministered to a congrega-
    tion there between 1795 and 1809.

EVANS, WILLIAM EDWIN (1851-1915).  American.  Methodist Episcopal
    Church, South.  Caplain at Randolph Macon College, Ashland, Virgi-
    nia.

EVEREST, CHARLES WILLIAM (1814-1877).  American.  Episcopal.  Rector of
    the Episcopal Church, Hampden, Connecticut (1842-1873).


FABER, FREDERICK WILLIAM (1814-1863).  British.  Church of England, Ro-
    man Catholic.  Rector of Elton, Huntingdonshire (1843-1846).  Pub-
    lished Hymns for the School at St. Wilfrid's, Staffordshire (1849);
    Catholic Hymns for Singing and Reading (1849); Oratory Hymns
    (1854).  Established, in London, the Priests of the Congregation
    of St. Philip Neri.

FABRICUS, JACOB (1593-1654).  Chaplain to King Gustavus Adolphus II of
    Sweden.

FARRAR, FREDERIC WILLIAM (1831-1903).  British.  Church of England.  As-
    sistant master at Harrow School (1854-1871); headmaster of Marlbo-
    rough College (1871-1876).  Canon of Westminster Abbey and rector
    of St. Margaret's, Westminster (1876-1883); archdeacon of Westmin-
    ster (1883-1903).

FARRINGTON, HARRY WEBB (1880-1930).  Bahamian, American.  Methodist.

FAWCETT, JOHN (1740-1817).  British.  Methodist, Baptist.  Minister at
    Wainsgate, Yorkshire (1765-1777); minister at Hebden Bridge, York-
    shire (1777-1817).  Published Hymns Adapted to the Circumstances
    of Public Worship and Private Devotion (1782).

FEATHERSTONE, WILLIAM R. (1842-1878).

FINDLATER, SARA LAURIE BORTHWICK (1823-1907).  Scottish.  Free Church
    of Scotland.  Published with her sister, Jane Laurie Borthwick (see
    above), Hymns from the Land of Luther (1854-1862).

FLOWERDEW, ALICE (1759-1830).  British.  Baptist.  Published Poems on
    Moral and Religious Subjects (1803).

FORD, DAVID EVERARD (1797-1875).  British.  Congregational.  Pastor of
    the Congregational Church at Lymington (1821-1841); traveling sec-
    retary to the Congregational Union (1841-1843); pastor of Green-
    gate Chapel, Salford, Manchester (1843-1875).  Published Hymns Chi-
    efly of the Parables of Christ (1828).

FORTUNATUS, VENANTIUS HONORIUS CLEMENTIANUS (530-609).  Converted to
    Christianity at Aquileia.  Spent the time 565-609 in Gaul.  Or-
    dained and subsequently appointed Bishop of Poitiers (597-609).
    Wrote a volume of hymns for all of the festivals of the Christian
    year--of which between nine and ten have survived to remain in com-
    mon congregational use.

FOSDICK, HARRY EMERSON (1878-1969).  American.  Baptist, Presbyterian.
    Lecturer in homiletics (1908-1915) and professor of practical the-

ology (1915-1946) at Union Theological Seminary, New York. Associ-minister of the First Presbyterian Church, New York; minister at Park Avenue Baptist Church, New York; minister of the Riverside Church, New York (1930-1946).

FOX, WILLIAM JOHNSON (1786-1864). British. Independent, Unitarian. Minister of the Parliament Court Chapel, London (1817-1824); minister of the chapel at South Place, Finsbury (1825-1852). Owned The Monthly Review (1831-1836). Member of Parliament for Oldham (1847-1863). Published Hymns and Anthems (1841, enlarged in 1873).

FRANCIS, BENJAMIN (1734-1799). Welsh. Baptist. Minister at Sodbury (1755-1757) and then at Horsley, Gloucestershire (1757-1799). Excelled as a writer of Welsh hymns.

FRANCIS OF ASSISI (1182-1226). Italian (full name Francesco di Pietro di Bernardone). The founder of the Franciscan Order.

FRANCIS XAVIER (1506-1552). Spanish. The missionary saint of the Roman Catholic Church. Became one of the first nine ofgnatius Loyola's Jesuit comverts.

FRANCK, JOHANN (1618-1677). German. A practicing lawyer; holder of several public offices in Guben, Brandenburg (1648-1677). His hymns appear to be high personal and indivdual in tone--as represented by "Jesus, meine Freude."

FRANZ, IGNAZ (1719-1790).

FRAZIER, PHILIP (1827-1903). British. Unitarian. Minister of the Unity Church, Islington.

FRECKLETON, REV. THOMAS WESLEY (b. 1827).

FROTHINGHAM, OCTAVIUS BROOKS (1822-1895). American. Congregational. Minister of the North Church, Salem, Massachusetts (1847-1855); the Independent Liberal Church, Jersey City, New Jersey (1855-1859); the Third Congregational Unitarian Society, New York (1859-1879).

FULLER-MAITLAND, FRANCES SARA (1809-1877). British. Fourth daughter of Ebenezer Fuller-Maitland; married (1834) John Colquhoun. Contributed anaonymous pieces to her mother's Hymns for Private Devotion (1827).

GABRIEL, CHARLES HUTCHISON (1856-1932). American. One of the most prolific of American gospel hymnodists; associated (1912-1932) with the publishing firm established by Homer Alvan Rodeheaver. Edited a wide variety of gospel hymn collections for congregation, choir, ensambles, and Sunday schools.

GAMBOLD, JOHN (1711-1771). British. Church of England, Moravian (United Brethren). Vicar of Stanton Harcourt, Oxfordshire (1739-1742); became a Moravian bishop in 1754.

GANSE, HERVEY DODDRIDGE (1822-1891).  American.  Reformed Dutch, Presbyterian.  Reformed Dutch pastor at Freehold, New Jersey (1843-
1856), and at the Northwest Reformed Dutch Church, New York (1856-
1876).  Pastor of the First Presbyterian Church, St. Louis (1876-
1891).

GATES, ELLEN HUNTINGTON (1835-1920).  American.  Author of numerous
hymns that became popular in American mission and Sunday school
collections.

GERHARDT, PAULUS (1607-1676).  German.  In Berlin, a tutor in the house
of the advocate Andreas Barthold; Lutheran Probst at Mittenwalde
(1651-1657); third diaconus of St. Nicholaus Church, Berlin (1657-
1666); archidiaconus at Lubben-on-the-Spree (1669-1676).  Ranks
next to Luther as the most gifted and popular hymnodist of the Lutheran Church.  Translations of forty-five of his hymns remain in
common congregational use in England and North America.

GIBBONS, THOMAS (1720-1785).  British.  Independent.  Minister of the
Independent Church at Hab-rdasher's Hall, London (1743-1785).  Tutor at the Dissenting Academy at Mile End, London (1754).  M.A.
from College of New Jersey (1760); D.D. from the University of
Aberdeen (1764).  Published hymnal collections in 1769, 1784.  Also
known for his definitive edition of the life and works of Isaac
Watts.

GILDER, RICHARD  WATSON (1844-1909).  American.  Methodist.  Editor of
The Century Magazine (formerly Scribner's Monthly).  Authored five
volumes of poems.

GILL, THOMAS HORNBLOWER (1819-1906).  British.  Unitarian.  In 1869, he
published The Golden Chain of Praise: Hymns by Thomas H. Gill.Ter-
med "a more intellectual Charles Wesley," he remains a prime example of a truly original congregational hymnodist.

GILLMAN, FREDERICK JOHN (1866-1949).

GILMAN, SAMUEL (1791-1858).  American.  Unitarian.  Pastor of Unitarian
congregations at Charleston, South Carolina (1819-1858).

GILMORE, JOSEPH HENRY (1834-1918).  American.  Baptist.  Teacher, preacher, editor, professor of English literature at the University of
Rochester (1868-1918).

GLADDEN, WASHINGTON (1836-1918).  American.  Congregational.  Held various pastorates in Massachusetts and New York; minister of the
First Congregational Church, Columbus, Ohio (1882-1918).

GMELIN, SIGMUND CHRISTIAN (1679-1707).  German.  Assistant pastor at
Herrenberg (1705-1706); associated himself with the Separatists,
denouncing the Church as too worldly.

GOADBY, FREDERICK WILLIAM (1840-1880).  British.  Baptist.  Pastor of
the Baptist Church at Bluntisham, Huntingtonshire (1868-1876), and
at Watford (1876-1880).

GONELLA, PETER (fl. 12th century A.D.).  A Franciscan of Tortona.

GORDON, GEORGE ANGIER (1853-1929).  Scottish, American.  Congregational.
    Minister of Old South Church, Boston (1886-1929).

GOUGH, BENJAMIN (1805-1877).  British.  Methodist.  A London merchant.
    Published Lyra Sabbatica (1865), Hymns of Prayer and Praise (1875),
    Protestant Hymns and Songs (1878).

GOULD, HANNAH FLAGG (1789-1865).  American.  Her hymns were published,
    principally, between 1832 and 1841.

GRANT, SIR ROBERT (1779-1838).  British.  Church of England.  Director
    of the East India Company.  Lawyer and parliamentarian.  Judge Ad-
    vocate General (1832) and Governor of Bombay (1834).  His Sacred
    Poems (1839, 1844, 1868) were published by his brother.

GREG, SAMUEL (1804-1877).  British.  A millowner at Ballington, near
    Macclesfield.

GREGORY I (c. 540-604).  Italian.  Roman Catholic.  Retired, in 575, as
    a Benedictine monk; appointed as one of seven Cardinal Deacons in
    577; resided in Constantinople (576-582); elevated to the Papacy
    in 590; sent St. Augustine to Britain in 596.  Contributed signi-
    ficantly to the liturgy and music of the Church.  Responsible for
    what has come to be known as the Gregorian Tone (or Chant).  The
    Benedictine editors of Gregory's works credit him with the compo-
    sition of at least eight Latin hymn texts.

GRIGG, JOSEPH (1728-1768).  British.  Presbyterian.  Assistant minister
    to the Rev. Thomas Bures at the Presbyterian Church, Silver Street,
    London (1743-1747).  Published over forty miscellaneous volumes;
    a collection of his Hymns appeared in 1806.

GROBEL, KENDRICK (1908-1965).

GUITERMAN, ARTHUR (b. 1871).

GURNEY, DOROTHY FRANCES BLOOMFIELD (1858-1932).  British.  Church of
    England.  Daughter of the Rev. Frederick George Bloomfield, Rector
    of St. Andrew's, Undershaft (London).

GURNEY, JOHN HAMPDEN (1802-1862).  British.  Church of England.  Curate
    of Lutterworth (1827-1844); rector of St. Mary's, Marylebone; pre-
    bendary of St. Paul's Cathedral.  Published Church Psalmody (1853),
    A Collection of Hymns for Public Worship (1838), Psalms and Hymns
    (1851).

GUYON, MADAME JEANNE MARIE BOUVIERES DE LA MOTHE (1648-1717).  French.
    The leader of the French Quietist movement, who spent considerable
    time in prisons as the result of her evangelical work.  She died
    in full communion with the Roman Catholic Church.  Her works, both
    poetry and prose, entend to forty volumes; more than a dozen tran-
    slations of her hymns can still be found in American hymnals.

HALL, CHRISTOPHER NEWMAN (1862-1902).  British.  Congregational.  Minister of Albion Church, Hull (1842-1854); minister of Surrey Chapel and of Christ Church, Westminster (1854-1902).  Chairman of the Congregational Union of England and Wales (1876).  Published Hymns Composed at Bolton Abbey (1858) and the Christ Church Hymnal (1876).

HALL, ELVINA MABLE (1818-1889).  American.  Methodist Episcopal.

HALL, WILLIAM JOHN (1793-1861).  British.  Church of England.  Held appointments as Minor Canon in St. Paul's Cathedral, London (1826); Priest Ordinary of the Chapel Royal, St. James's (1829); vicar of Tottenham, Middlesex (1851).  Edited Psalms and Hymns Adapted to the Services of the Church of England (London, 1836)--commonly known as the Mitre Hymn-book.

HAMILTON, MARY C.D. (b. 1915).

HAMMOND, WILLIAM (1719-1783).  British.  Calvinist Methodist, Moravian Brethren.  Published Psalms, Hymns, and Spiritual Songs (1745).

HANKEY, CATHARINE (1834-1911).  British.  Anglican Evangelical (Clapham Sect).  Published The Old, Old Story (1866), The Old, Old Story and Other Verses (1879).

HARBAUGH, HENRY (1817-1867).  American.  German Reformed.  Pastor at Lewisburgh, Lancaster, and Lebanon--all in Pennsylvania.  Professor of Theology at Marshall College, Mercersburg, Pennsylvania (1864-1867).  Edited The Guardian and The Mercersburg Review.  Published Hymns and Chants for Sunday Schools (1861).

HARKNESS, GEORGIA (1891-1974).  American.  Methodist.  Public school teacher and college instructor in applied theology; professor of applied theology, Pacific School of Theology, Berkeley, California (1950-1961).  Author of 37 books and several published essays.  Named as one of the ten most influential American Methodists.

HARLOW, SAMUEL RALPH (b. 1885).  American.  Congregational.  An ordained minister and professor of religion and social ethics at Smith College.

HARMER, SAMUEL YOUNG (b. 1809).  American.  Society of Friends, Methodist Episcopal.  Sunday school teacher and superintendent.  Admitted to the ministry in 1847.

HARRELL, J. COSTIN (b. 1885).

HART, JOSEPH (1712-1768).  British.  Moravian, Calvinist Nonconformist.  Preached regularly at the Jewin Street Independent Chapel, London.  Published Hymns Composed on Various Subjects (1759), with a Supplement (1762) and an Appendix (1765) to that volume.

HASKELL, ANTONIO L.  American.  His hymn, "Be still, and let the spirit speak," bears a copyright date of 1936.

HASTINGS, HORACE LORENZO (1831-1899). American. A practicing evangelist; founder and editor of the monthly paper, The Christian. Published Social Hymns (1865), Songs of Pilgrimage: A Hymnal for the Churches of Christ (1880, 1886).

HASTINGS, THOMAS (1784-1782). American. Presbyterian. Directed several church choirs in New York City and published over fifty books of music, a number of them with Lowell Mason (see below, in Section C) and William Batchelder Bradbury (see below, in Section C). Edited Spiritual Songs for Social Worship (1831-1832), The Mother's Hymn Book (1834, 1850), The Christian Psalmist (1836), Church Melodies (1858), Devotional Hymns (1850).

HATCH, EDWIN (1835-1889). British. Church of England. Ministered to an East London parish. Professor of classics at Trinity College, Toronto (1859-1867); vice principal of St. Mary's Hall, Oxford (1867-1880); Bampton and Grinfield Lecturer, Oxford (1880-1883); rector of Purleigh, Essex (1883-1884); University Reader in Ecclesiastical History, Oxford (1884-1888); Hibbert Lecturer, Oxford (1888-1889).

HATFIELD, EDWIN FRANCIS (1807-1883). American. Presbyterian. Pastor of the Second Presbyterian Church, St. Louis (1832-1835); of the Seventh Presbyterian Church, New York (1835-1856); of the North Presbyterian Church, New York (1856-1863). Published Freedom's Lyre; or, Psalms, Hymns, and Sacred Songs, for the Slave and His Friends (1840); The Church Hymn Book (1872); Chapel Hymns (1873).

HAVERGAL, FRANCES RIDLEY (1836-1879). British. Church of England. Skilled in French, German, Italian, Latin, Hebrew, Greek. Her hymns were often printed as single, unbound leaflets; more than fifty of them remain in congregational use.

HAWEIS, HUGH REGINALD (1838-1901). British.

HAWEIS, THOMAS (1732-1820). British. Church of England, Methodist (Countess of Huntingdon's Connexion). Assistant preacher at the Lock Hospital, London; rector of All Saints, Aldwinkle, Northamptonshire. Chaplain to Selina Shirley, Countess of Huntingdon (see below), and officiated at her chapel at Bath. Published Carmina Christo, or, Hymns of the Saviour (1792).

HAWKS, ANNIE SHERWOOD (1835-1918). American. Baptist. A contributor to the evangelical Sunday school hymn books published during the mid and late nineteenth century.

HAY, JOHN (1838-1905). American. Presbyterian. Private secretary to President Abraham Lincoln; ambassador to England; First Assistant Secretary of State (1879-1881); Secretary of State during the administrations of McKinley and Theodore Roosevelt (1898-1905).

HEARN, MARIANNE FARNINGHAM (1834-1909). British. Baptist. A staff writer for The Christian World and editor of The Sunday School Times. Published Lays and Lyrics of the Blessed Life (1861), Morning and Evening Hymns for the Week (1870), Songs of Sunshine (1878).

HEATH, GEORGE (1750-1822). British. Presbyterian. Pastor of the Presbyterian Church, Honiton, Devonshire (1770-1822).

HEBER, REGINALD (1783-1826). British. Church of England. Rector of Hodnot, Shropshire (1807-1812); prebendary of St. Asaph (1812-1822); Bishop of Calcutta (1822-1826). His Hymns Written and Adapted to the Weekly Church Service of the Year appeared posthumously in 1827.

HEDGE, FREDERICK HENRY (1805-1890). American. Unitarian. Minister of churches at Arlington, Massachusetts (1829-1835); Bangor, Maine (1835-1850); Providence, Rhode Island (1850-1856); Brookline, Massachusetts (1856-1872). Professor of ecclesiastical history (1857) and of German literature (1872-1882) at Harvard. Co-edited Hymns for the Church (1865) and edited The Christian Examiner.

HEGINBOTHAM, OTTIWELL (1744-1768). British. Independent. Minister of a Nonconformist congregation at Sudbury, Suffolk (1765-1768).

HEMANS, FELICIA DOROTHEA BROWNE (1793-1835). British. Church of England. A prolific poet, she published Hymns for Childhood (1827); Scenes and Hymns of Life (1834)--this last volume dedicated to William Wordsworth. More than twenty of her hymns remain in common congregational use.

HENLEY, JOHN (1800-1842). British. Methodist. A successful circuit minister for the Wesleyan Methodists.

HERBERT, GEORGE (1593-1633). British. Church of England. Prebend of Leighton Ecclesia, Huntingtonshire (1626-1629); rector of Bemerton, Wiltshire (1630-1633). A major poet of the first half of the seventeenth century. His hymns originate from a 1697 collection entitled Select Hymns Taken Out of Mr. Herbert's Temple and Turned into the Common Metre; in 1740, John and Charles Wesley adapted forty of those pieces and inserted them into their Hymns and Poems.

HERBERT, PETRUS (d. 1571). German. Moravian Brethren. Ordained priest of the Brehtren's Unity in 1562; one of the deputies sent to Vienna to present the revised form of the Brethren's Confession of Faith to the Emperor Maximilian II (1564). A principal compiler of the Brethren's German Hymn Book (1566), to which he contributed approximately ninety hymns; the 1639 edition identifies 104 hymns as his.

HERRMANN, JOHANN GOTTFRIED (1707-1791). German. Pastor at Altzessnitz, Saxony; diaconus at Ranis (1731-1734); diaconus at Pegau, near Leipzig (1734-1738); superintendent at Plauen (1738-1746); chief Court preacher at Dresden (1746-1791).

HERMANN, NICOLAUS (d. 1561). German. Master in the Latin School at Joachimsthal, Bohemia; cantor, organist, and choirmaster there. His hymns primarily intended for the boys and girls of school age, rather than for the church service.

HERVEY, JAMES (1714-1758). British. Church of England. A student of John Wesley at Lincoln College, Oxford. Curate of Dummer (1737); curate of Bideford (1738-1742); rector of Weston-Favell and Collingtree, Peterborough (1752-1758). His hymns originate from his Meditations among the Tombs (1746) and Contemplations on the Night (1746).

HERZOG, JOHN F. (1647-1699).

HEWITT, ELIZA E. (1851-1920).

HICKSON, WILLIAM EDWARD (1803-1870). British. A London bootmaker who retired from his business in 1840. Published The Singing Master (1836).

HIGGINSON, THOMAS WENTWORTH (1823-1911). American. Unitarian. Minister at Newburyport, Massachusetts (1847-1850) and at Worcester, Massachusetts (1852-1858). An abolitionist and a colonel of a Union regiment comprised of former slaves from South Carolina.

HILLHOUSE, AUGUSTUS LUCAS (1792-1859). American. Conducted a school in Paris, France.

HINE, STUART K. (b. 1899).

HODDER, EDWIN (1837-1904). British. Member of the English civil service; spent five years (1856-1861) in New Zealand. Published The New Sunday School Hymn Book (1863, 1868).

HODGES, GEORGE SAMUEL (1827-1899). British. Church of England. Vicar of Stubbings, Maidenhead. His hymns generally originated from The Country Palatine and Other Poems, Sacred and Secular (1876).

HOFFMAN, ELISHA ALBRIGHT (1839-1929). American. Contributor to a number of hymn collections published by Dwight Lyman Moody and Ira David Sankey. His hymns popular within the Salvation Army movement.

HOLDEN, OLIVER (1765-1844). American. Baptist. Carpenter, real estate agent, state legislator, music store owner, choir director. One of the editors of The Massachusetts Compiler (1795)--the most progressive work on psalmody prior to 1800. Published The Union Harmony (1793). Composed the tune "Coronation" (1793)--the earliest American hymn tune still in common congregational use.

HOLLAND, HENRY SCOTT (1847-1918). British. Church of England. Canon of St. Paul's, London (1884-1918). Professor of Divinity, Oxford (1910-1918). Co-edited The English Hymnal and The New Cathedral Psalter. One of the founders of the Christian Social Union.

HOLLAND, JOSIAH GILBERT (1819-1881). American. Unitarian. On the staff of the Springfield (Massachusetts) Republican and later editor of Scribner's Magazine.

HOLMES, JOHN HAYNES (1879-1964). American. Unitarian. Minister of the Third Religious Society, Dorcester, Massachusetts (1904-1907); minister of the Church of the Messiah, New York, beginning 1907.

HOLMES, OLIVER WENDELL (1809-1894). American. Unitarian. Distinguished physician and professor of anatomy and physiology at Dartmouth College (1838-1847); Chair of Anatomy, Harvard College (1847-1882). A major American essayist and a poet of more than adequate quality.

HOOD, EDWIN PAXTON (1820-1885). British. Independent. Minister at Nibley, Gloucestershire (1852-1857); minister to a number of congregations in London, Brighton, Manchester. Edited Our Hymn Book (1862, 1868, 1873, 1879) and The Children's Choir (1870).

HOPKINS, JOHN HENRY, JR. (1820-1891). American. Episcopal. Rector of Christ Church, Williamsport, Pennsylvania (1850-1891). Published Carols, Hymns, and Songs (1862, 1882).

HOPKINS, JOSIAH (1786-1862). American. Congregational, Presbyterian. Pastor of the Congregational Church, New Haven, Vermont (1809-1830) and of the First Presbyterian Church, Auburn, New York (1830-1848). Edited Conference Hymns (1846).

HOPPER, EDWARD (1816-1888). American. Presbyterian. Pastor of churches at Greenville and Sag Harbor, New York, and of the Church of the Sea and Land (Sailors' Mission), New York.

HOPPS, JOHN PAGE (1834-1912). British. Baptist, Unitarian. Ministered at Hugglesgate and Ibstock, Leicestershire (1856-1858); joined George Dawson at the Church of the Saviour, Birmingham (1858-1860). Ministered to Unitarian congregations at Sheffield, Dukinfield, and Glasgow (1860-1876); the Great Meeting at Leicester (1876-1892); a congregation that met at Little Portland Street Chapel and then at University Hall, London (1905-1909). Edited Hymns for Public Worship in the Home (1858); Hymns of Faith and Progress (1865); Hymns for Public Worship (1873); Hymns, Chants, and Anthems (1877); The Children's Hymn Book (1879); The Young People's Book of Hymns (1881); Hymns for Special Services.

HORNE, CHARLES SYLVESTER (1865-1914). British. Congregational. Minister at Whitefield's Chapel, Tottenham Court Road, London; chairman of the Congregational Union (1909); Member of Parliament for Ipswich (1910); President of the National Brotherhood Council (1913).

HOSMER, FREDERICL LUCIAN (1840-1829). American. Unitarian. Ministered to congregations at Northboro, Massachusetts; Quincy, Illinois; Cleveland and St. Louis; Berkeley, California. Lecturer in hymnody at Harvard (1908). Edited with W.C. Gannett and J.V. Blake Unity Hymns and Carols (1880, 1911) and The Thought of God in Hymns and Poems (1885, 1894).

HOSS, ELIJAH EMBREE (b. 1849). American. Methodist Episcopal. Professor of Divinity at Vanderbilt University; President of Emory and Henry College; editor of the Nashville Christian Advocate (1885-1890). Bishop of the American Methodist Church, South.

HOUSMAN, LAURENCE (1865-1959). British. Brother of the poet A.E. Housman. In addition to his fiction and drama, he composed a number of "religious" poems. During the various stages of his artistic development, he was attracted to Roman Catholicism and to the Society of Friends; he rejected the former, but never formally became a member of the latter.

HOW, WILLIAM WALSHAM (1823-1897).British.  Church of England.  Curate of St. George's. Kidderminster (1846), and of Holy Cross, Shrewsbury (1848).  Rector of Whittingham, Diocese of St. Asaph (1851-1853); rural dean of St. Asaph (1853-1860); honorary canon of the Cathedral of St. Asaph (appointed 1860).  Rector of St. Andrew's, Undershaft, London (1879-1888); Suffragan Bishop for East London, Bishop of Bedford, Bishop of Wakefield.  Published, with Rev. Thomas Baker Morrell, Psalms and Hymns (1854); joint editor of Church Hymns (1871).  He published his own Poems and Hymns in 1886.

HOWE, JULIA WARD (1819-1910).  American.  Unitarian.  Poet, philanthropist, social reformer, and advocate of women's suffrage and international peace.  Her hymns originate from three volumes of her verse: Passion Flowers (1854), Words for the Hour (1856), Later Lyrics (1866).

HOYLE, R. BIRCH (1875-1939).

HUNTER, JOHN (1848-1917).  Scottish.  Church of Scotland, Congregational.  Minister of Salem Chapel, York (1871-1882); minister of Wycliffe Chapel, Hull (1882-1887); minister of Trinity Church, Glasgow (1887-1901).  Held pastorates at King's Weigh House Church, London (1901-1904); Trinity Church, Glasgow (1904-1913).  Conducted services at Aeolian Hall, London (1913-1917).  Published Hymns of Faith and Life (1896).

HUNTER, WILLIAM (1811-1877).  Irish, American.  Methodist Episcopal.  Editor of The Conference Journal and The Christian Advocate.  Professor of Hebrew at Allegheny College (Pennsylvania); minister of the Methodist Episcopal Church, Alliance, Ohio.  Edited Minstrel of Zion (1845), Select Melodies (1851), Songs of Devotion (1859).

HUNTINGTON, DE WITT C. (1830-1912).  American.  Methodist.  Preacher, teacher, and poet who settled, eventually, in Lincoln, Nebraska.

HUNTINGTON, FREDERICK DAN (1819-1904).  American.  Unitarian, Episcopal.  Held pastorates at Boston (1842-1855).  Professor of Christian morals and University Preacher at Harvard (1855-1859).  Rector at Boston, then Bishop of Central New York (1869-1904).  An editor of the Unitarian Hymns for the Church of Christ (1853) and co-editor of Hymns of Holy Refreshment.

HUTTON, JAMES (1715-1795).  British.  Moravian.  Bookseller and cousin to Sir Isaac Newton.  An intimate of both John and Charles Wesley before he joined the Moravian Church.  He published George Whitefield's journals.

HYDE, ANN BEADLEY (1799-1872).  American.  Congregational.  Her five hymns remain in common congregational use as adaptations from her "religious" poems.

HYDE, WILLIAM DE WITT (1858-1917).  American.  Congregational.  President of Bowdoin College, Maine (1885-1917).


INGEMANN, BERNHARDT SEVERIN (1789-1862).  Danish.  Professor of Danish
    Language and Literature, Academy of Soro, Zealand, Denmark (1822-
    1862).  A poet of some reputation; his published works reached, in
    the collected edition of 1851, thirty-four volumes.  Seven of his
    hymns have been translated into English for congregational use.

IRONS, WILLIAM JOSIAH (1812-1883).  British.  Church of England.  Cur-
    ate of St. Mary Newington (1835-1837); incumbent of St. Peter's,
    Walworth (1837); vicar of Barkway; incumbent of Brompton; rector
    of St. Mary Woolnoth.  Bampton Lecturer and prebendary of St.
    Paul's Cathedral.  Edited Metrical Psalter (1857); Appendix to the
    Brompton Metrical Psalter (1861); Hymns for Use in the Church
    (1866); Psalms and Hymns for the Church (1873, 1875, 1883).  Best
    known for his tranlation of the Dies Irae.


JACOBI, JOHN CHRISTIAN (1670-1750).  German, British.  Keeper of the
    Royal German Chapel, St. James Palace, London (1708-1750).  Pub-
    lished A Collection of Divine Hymns (1720), Psalmodia Germanica
    (1722).

JENKINS, TUDOR.  His hymn, "When mother love makes all things bright,"
    appeared, initially, in 1895.

JERVIS, THOMAS (1748-1833).  British.  Presbyterian.  Classical and ma-
    thematical tutor at the Exeter Academy (1770-1772); tutor to the
    sons of the Earl of Shelburne at Bowood--where the physicist Jo-
    seph Priestley served as librarian (1772-1783).  Minister at St.
    Thomas, Southwark (1783-1796); minister at the Princes' Street
    Chapel, Westminster (1796-1808); minister at Mill Creek Chapel,
    Leeds (1808-1818).

JOHN OF DAMASCUS (c. 696-c. 780).  The next-to-the-last of the Fathers
    of the Greek Church; certainly the most significant poet of that
    denomination.  An ordained priest of the church of Jerusalem.
    Remembered prominently for his canons and great festivals, as well
    as providing Greek hymnody with strong doctrinal influence.

JOHNS, JOHN (1801-1847).1801-1847).  British.  Presbyterian.  Minister
    of the Presbyterian Chapel at Crediton (1820-1836); minister to
    the poor at Liverpool (1836-1847).  His hymns have been extracted
    directly from several of his poetry collections.

JOHNSON, ERASTUS (1826-1909).

JOHNSON, SAMUEL (1822-1882).  American.  Independent.  Pastor of the
    Free Church, Lynn, Massachusetts (1853-1870).  Joint editor of A
    Book of Hymns (1846), Supplement to A Book of Hymns (1848), Hymns
    of the Spirit (1864).

JONES, EDITH.  American.  Her hymn, "Father who art alone," appeared initially in a volume entitled The Home Hymn Book (1885).

JONES, EDMUND (1722-1765).  British.  Baptist.  Associated as a preacher and pastor of the Baptist congregation at Exeter (1742-1765).  Published Sacred Poems (1760).

JOSEPH THE HYMNOGRAPHER (d. 883 A.D.).  Italian.  Erroneously referred to by a number of hymnal editors as "Joseph of the Stadium."  A monk at Thessalonica, a resident of Constantinople, a slave on Crete.  Established a monastery on Crete in connection with the Church of St. John Chrysostom.  Appointed keeper of the sacred vessels in the Great Church at Constantinople.  The most prolific of the Greek hymn writers, having written at least two hundren canons.

"JOSEPH OF THE STADIUM."  See above under Joseph the Hymnographer.

JUDKIN, THOMAS JAMES (1788-1871).  British.  Church of England.  Minister of Somers Chapel, St. Pancreas, London (1828-1871).  Published Church and Home Psalmody (1831), Church and Home Melodies (1834).

JUDSON, ADONIRAM (1788-1850).  American.  Baptist.  Missionary to India and Burma.  Translated the Bible into various Burmese dialects.

JULIAN, JOHN (1839-1919).  British.  Church of England.  Vicar of Wincobank.  Editor of The Dictionary of Hymnology (1892, 1907)--certainly one of the most signifigant pieces of scholarly contribution to the study of world hymnody (although by now terribly outdated).

KEBLE, JOHN (1792-1866).  British.  Church of England.  Fellow of Oriel College, Oxford (1811-1823).  Curate of East Leach and Burthorpe (1816-1825); curate of Hursley (1825-1826); curate of Southrop (1826-1836); curate of Hursley (1836-1866).  Appointed Professor of Poetry at Oxford in 1831.  Published Metrical Versions of the Psalms (1839); The Christian Year (1827); The Psalter, or Psalms of David (1839); The Child's Christian Year (1841); Lyra Innocentium (1846); Lays of the Sanctuary (1859); The Salisbury Hymn Book (1857).

KELLY, THOMAS (1769-1854).  Irish.  Church of Ireland (Episcopal), Independent.  Banned from preaching in Established Church pulpits by Archbishop Fowler, afterwhich he left the Church.  Wrote approximately 765 hymns; published A Collection of Psalms and Hymns (1802), Hymns on Various Subjects of Scriptures (1804), Hymns (1815).

KEMPTHORNE, JOHN (1775-1838).  British.  Church of England.  Vicar of Northleach, Gloucestershire (1816-1827); vicar of Wedmore, Somersetshire (1827); rector of St. Michael's and chaplain of St. Mary de Grace, Gloucester (1827-1838); prebendary of Lichfield Cathedral (1826-1838).  Published Select Portions of Psalms (1810); Psalms, Hymns, and Anthems (1831).

KEN, THOMAS (1637-1711).  British.  Church of England.  Rector of Little Easton (1663-1666); Fellow of Winchester (1666-1667); rector of Brighstone (1667-1669); rector of Woodhay and prebendary of Winchester (1669-1679); chaplain to the Princess Mary at the Hague (1679-

1680); prebendary of Winchester (1680-1685); Bishop of Bath and Wells (1685-1691). Imprisoned in the Tower of London (1688) and deprived of his See (1691). The majority of his hymns were published after his death.

KENNEDY, BENJAMIN HALL (1804-1889). British. Church of England. Headmaster of Shrewsbury School (1836-1866); Regis Professor of Greek, Cambridge, and Canon of Ely (1867-1889). Published The Psalter (1860) and Hymnologia Christiana (1863).

KENNEDY, GERALD H. (b. 1907).

KERR, HUGH THOMSON (1872-1950).

KETHE, WILLIAM (d. c. 1593). British. Church of England. Rector of Childe Okeford, Dorset (1569); chaplain of the forces under the Earl of Warwick (1563, 1569). Twenty-five of his Psalm paraphrases appeared in the Anglo-Genevan Psalter of 1561.

KEY, FRANCIS SCOTT (1779-1843). American. Practiced law in Washington, D.C., and served as a United States Attorney there. His collected Poems appeared in 1857, while his other publication of note bears the title The Power of Literature and Its Connection with Religion (1834).

KIDDER, MARY ANN PEPPER (1820-1905). American. Methodist Episcopal. Lived in New York City from 1859 until her death.

KILLINGHALL, JOHN (d. 1740). British. Congregational. Pastor at Beccles, Suffolk (1697) and at the Congregational Church, Southwark (1702-1740).

KIMBALL, HARRIET McEWAN (1837-1905). American. Roman Catholic. Published her collection of Hymns in 1866.

KING, JOHN (1789-1858). British. Church of England. Curate of Wellington, Shropshire; incumbent of Christ Church, Hull.

KINGSLEY, CHARLES (1819-1875). British. Church of England. Rector of Eversley (1844-1875), canon of Chester (1869-1873), canon of Westminster (1873-1875). A major essayist and novelist of the nineteenth century. In addition to a number of "pleasant" songs and ballads, he wrote Prose Idylls (1873).

KIPLING, RUDYARD (1865-1936). British. Essayist, novelist, journalist, short fiction writer, and the unofficial "Laureate of the British Empire." His congregational hymns have been extracted from his general collections of poetry.

KIRKPATRICK, WILLIAM JAMES. See below, in Section C).

KNOWLES, JAMES DAVIS ((1798-1838). American. Baptist. Pastor of the Second Baptist Church, Boston (1825) and Professor of Divinity at Newton Theological Institute (1832).

LANIER, SIDNEY (1842-1881).  American.  Presbyterain, Independent.  A
    flute player and a major poet of post-Civil War America.  His hymns
    have been extracted from the collected Poems, published in 1884 by
    his widow; new editions of those poems appeared in 1891 and 1916.

LANGE, ERNST (1650-1727).  German.  Jurist and parliamentarian in Dan-
    zig and Warsaw.  Allied with the Mennonites and Pietists.  He wrote
    slightly over sixty hymns, most of which concerned the theme of
    thanksgiving for preservation during times of sickness; those date
    c. 1711.

LANGE, JOACHIM (1670-1744).  German.  Rector of the school at Coslin,
    in Pomerania (1696-1698); rector of the Friedrichswerder Gymnasium
    at Berlin (1698-1699); pastor of the Friedrichswerder church, Ber-
    lin (1699-1709); professor of theology at Halle (1709-1744).  Best
    known for his commentaries on the New and Old Testaments, as well
    as for his theological tracts.

LARCOM, LUCY (1826-1893).  American.  Factory worker, teacher, and poet.
    Published (among her other volumes) At the Beautiful Gate, and
    Other Songs of Faith (1892).  She has been remembered for her work
    with the Massachusetts abolitionist movement; her simple poetry on
    the themes of nature and children; her autobiographical A New Eng-
    land Childhood (1889), which provides a vivid description of life
    in the mills and homes of Lowell, Massachusetts.

LATHBURY, MARY ARTEMISIA (1841-1918).  American.  Methodist.  Associa-
    ted with the Chatauqua Assembly, Lake Chautauqua, New York; a wri-
    ter and editor for the Methodist Sunday School Union.

LAUFER, CALVIN WEISS (1874-1938).  American.  Presbyterian.  Held pas-
    torates at Long Island City, New York (1900-1905); West Hoboken,
    New Jersey (1905-1914); associated with various Presbyterian edu-
    cational and editorial boards (1914-1938).  Associate editor of
    the 1933 Presbyterian Hymnal and its supplemental Handbook (1935).

LAURENTI, LAURENTIUS (1660-1722).  German.  Cantor and director of the
    music at the cathedral church at Bremen (1684-1722).  One of the
    major hymnodists of the Pietistic movement; his hymns focus on the
    Gospels for Sundays and Festivals as they direct themselves to
    Christian life in general; thirty-four of them appeared in print
    between 1704 and 1714.

LEESON, JANE ELIZABETH (1807-1882).  British.  Catholic Apostolic, Ro-
    man Catholic.  Published Infant Hymnings (1842), Paraphrases and
    Hymns(1853).  Principally known as a children's hymnodist.

LELAND, JOHN (1754-1841).  American.  Baptist.  Preached in Virginia
    (1776-1790) and in Massachusetts (1790-1841).

LEW, TIMOTHY TINGFANG (1892-1947).

LEWIS, HOWELL ELVET (1860-1953).  Welsh.  Congregational.  Held pasto-
    rates at Buckley,Hull, Llanelly, Canonbury, and at the Welsh Taber-

nacle, King's Cross, London. Received the bardic crown at the National Eisteddfod of Wales (1888) and held the chair as Arch-Druid (1924-1927). Created a Campanion of Honour in 1948. His _Hymns of Hope and Unity_ appeared in 1947.

LITTLEDALE, RICHARD FREDERICK (1833-1890). Irish. Church of England. Curate of St. Matthew's, Thorpe Hamlet, Norwich (1856-1857); curate of St. Mary the Virgin, Soho, London (1857-1861); retired from Church duties in 1861. Published _Carols for Christmas and Other Seasons_ (1863), _The People's Hymnal_ (1867).

LITTLEFIELD, MILTON SMITH (1864-1934). American. Presbyterian.

LITTLEWOOD, WILLIAM EDENSOR (1831-1886). British. Church of England. Vicar of St. James, Bath (1872-1881).

LLOYD, WILLIAM FREEMAN (1791-1853). British. Church of England. Taught Sunday school at Oxford and London; appointed a secretary of the Sunday School Union (1810); associated with the Religious Tract Society (1876). Founded _The Sunday School Teacher's Magazine_, _The Child's Companion_, _The Weekly Visitor_. Published his _Thoughts in Rhyme_ in 1853.

LOGAN, JOHN (1748-1798). Scottish. Church of Scotland. Minister of South Leith (1770-1782). His name became embroiled in a controversy with Michael Bruce, a fellow student, concerning the preparation and publication of _Translations and Paraphrases of the Church of Scotland_. The debate over authorship of a number of hymns attributed to both Logan and Bruce continues.

LONGFELLOW, SAMUEL (1819-1892). American. Unitarian. Brother of the noted poet Henry Wadsworth Longfellow. Minister of the Second Unitarian Church, Brooklyn, New York (1853-1860); minister of the Unitarian Church, Germantown, Pennsylvania (1877-1883). Co-editor of _A Book of Hymns_ (1846, 1848), _Hymns of the Spirit_ (1864).

LONGSTAFF, WILLIAM D. (1822-1894).

LOWELL, JAMES RUSSELL (1819-1891). American. Unitarian. Lawyer; succeeded, in 1855, Henry Wadsworth Longfellow as Professor of Modern Languages and Literature at Harvard; U.S. minister to Spain (1877-1880) and then to Great Britain (1880-1885). Editor of _The Atlantic Monthly_ (1857-1862) and of _The North American Review_ (1863-1872). Those hymns remaining in common congregational use have been adapted from his poems.

LOWRY, ROBERT (1826-1899). American. Baptist. Held pulpits at West Chester, Pennsylvania; New York, New York; Hanson Place Baptist Church, Brooklyn, New York. Professor of Rhetoric at Lewisburg (Pennsylvania) University (1876). Pastor of the Second Baptist Church, Plainfield, New Jersey (1876-1899). Edited or co-edited popular Sunday school hymn books for the publishing firm of Biglow and Main, New York. More of a composer of gospel music than a writer of hymn texts--as witnessed by his muscial compositions to accompany his own verse.

LUKE, JEMIMA THOMPSON (1813-1906). British. Congregational. The wife of a Congregational minister, she performed considerable work for the education and welfare of the poor.

LUTHER, MARTIN (1483-1546). German. Dr. Julian (Dictionary of Hymnology, 1:703-704) lists nine of the principal hymn books that Luther edited, as well as lists and classifies thirty-eight of Luther's hymns that remain on common gongregational use. Julian also lables Luther the leader of the Reformation and the first evangelical hymnist. "To Luther belongs the extraordinary merit of having given to the German people in their own tongue the Bible, the Catechism, and the hymn-book, so that God might speak directly to them in His word, and that they might directly answer Him in their songs" (Julian, Dictionary of Hymnology, 1:414). See also under Section C below.

LYNCH, THOMAS TOKE (1818-1871). British. Independent. Minister of a small congregation at Highgate (1847-1849), and then of another at Mortimore Street, London (1849-1856). Forced to retire because of illness (1856-1859), he resumed his ministry in Gower Street, London (1860-1862), and then moved to Mornington Church, Hampstead Road (1862-1871). His hymns appeared in The Rivulet (1855, 1856, 1868).

LYON, P.H.B. (b. 1893). British. His hymn, "O God, before whose altar," appeared initially in Hymns Ancient and Modern.

LYTE, HENRY FRANCIS (1793-1847). Irish. Church of England. Curate of Wexford (1815-1817), of Marazion (1817-1819), of Lymington (1819-1823); perpetual curate of Lower Bixham, Devon (1823-1847). His hymns derive from various collections of his poems, published between 1833 and 1845. He edited The Poems of Henry Vaughan (1846).

MACDUFF, JOHN ROBERT (1818-1895). Scottish. Church of Scotland. Parish minister of Kettins, Forfarshire (1842-1849); of St. Madoes, Perthshire (1849-1855); of Sandyford, Glasgow (1855-1871). A member of the hymnal committee of the Church of Scotland and the author of thirty-one congregational hymns.

MACE, FRANCES LAUGHTON (b. 1836). American. A life-long resident of Maine; married a lawyer, Benjamin H. Mace, of Bangor, Maine.

MACKAY, MARGARET (1802-1887). Scottish. Church of Scotland. Married to a lieutenant-colonel of light infantry. Her Thoughts Redeemed, or, Lays of Leisure Hours (1852) contains seventy-two original hymns and poems.

MACKAY, WILLIAM PATON (1839-1885). Scottish. Church of Scotland. Practiced medicine and then became a minister of the Prospect Street Presbyterian Church, Hull (1868-1885).

MACKELLAR, THOMAS (1812-1899). American. Presbyterian. Employed as a printer by Harper Brothers, New York (1826-1833), then as a proofreader for Johnson and Smith, Philadelphia. In 1860, he became a partner in the firm of Mackellar, Smiths, and Jordan, typefounders of Philadelphia. Published his Hymns and a Few Metrical Psalms in 1883, and his collected Hymns and Poems came forth in 1900.

MACLEOD, NORMAN (1812-1872). Scottish. Established Church of Scotland. Parish minister of Loudoun, Ayrshire (1838-1843); of Dalkeith (1843 to 1851); of the Barony, Glasgow (1851-1872). Moderator of the General Assembly of the Established Church of Scotland (1869), and served on the Assembly's hymnal committee from 1854 to 1855.

MALAN, HENRI ABRAHAM CAESAR (1787-1864). French. National Church of Geneva (Unitarian). Deprived of his status as a minister of the National Church of Geneva in 1823. Engaged in extended tours of evangelistic conversion in France, Switzerland, Belgium, England, Scotland (1823-1864). Originator of the modern hymn movement in the French Reformed Church, one that focused sharply upon an analysis of Christian experience. Published a number of tracts and pamphlets on the arguments between the National and Evangelical Churches and the Church of Rome. He wrote the music to accompany his hymnodic compositions.

MANN, NEWTON (1836-1926). American. Unitarian. Served pastorates at Kenosha, Wisconsin; Troy, New York; Rochester, New York; Omaha, Nebraska.

MANT, RICHARD (1776-1848). British. Church of England. Vicar of Coggeshall, Essex (1810-1813); domestic chaplain to the Archbishop of Canterbury (1813-1816); rector of St. Botolph, Bishopsgate, London (1816-1818); rector of East Horsley (1818-1820); Bishop of Killaloe (1820), Down and Connor (1823), Dromore (1842). Published nine books, among them The Book of Psalms, in an English Metrical Version (1824), Ancient Hymns from the Roman Breviary (1837, 1871).

MARCH, DANIEL (1816-1909). American. Presbyterian, Congregational.

MARCUM, J.R. His hymn, "Thou hast been our Guide this day," dates 1917.

MARCY, ELIZABETH EUNICE (b. 1822). American. Methodist Episcopal. Her husband, Oliver Marcy, served as professor of natural history at Northwestern University, Evanston, Illinois.

MARLATT, EARL BOWMAN (b. 1892). American. Methodist. Professor of Philosophy at Boston University; Dean of the School of Theology, Boston University. An associate editor of The American Student Hymnal (1928).

MARRIOTT, JOHN (1780-1825). British. Church of England. Private tutor to the Duke of Buccleuch; rector of Church Lawford, Warwickshire. Curate of St. James's, Exeter; of St. Lawrence, Exeter; of Broadclyst, near Exeter. An intimate friend of Sir Walter Scott (see below), who dedicated to him the introduction of one of the cantos in Marmion (1808). His hymns were never published until after his death.

MARSDEN, JOSHUA (1777-1837). British. Methodist. A Wesleyan Methodist missionary to Nova Scotia, and then to Bermuda.

MARTIN, CIVILLA D. (1869-1948).

MASEFIELD, JOHN (1878-1967). British. Poet Laureate of England (1930-1967). Produced poetry steadily from 1902 through 1952.

MASON, MARY JANE (b. 1822). American.

MASON, JOHN (1645-1694). British. Church of England. Curate of Isham; vicar of Stantonbury, Buckinghamshire (1688-1673); rector of Water-Stratford (1673-1694). Published Spiritual Songs (1683). Among the first to practice hymn singing as distinct from congregational reliance upon the metrical psalter.

MASON, WILLIAM. His hymn, "Again returns the day of holy rest," dates from 1796. Born 1725, died 1797. British. Church of England. Rector of Aston and praecentor of York Minster.

MASSIE, RICHARD (1800-1887). British. Church of England. Published Martin Luther's Spiritual Songs (1854), Lyrica Domestica (1860, 1864).

MASTERMAN, JOHN HOWARD BERTRAM (1867-1933). British. Church of England. Vicar of St. Aubyn's, Devonport; principal of Midland Clergy College, Birmingham; warden of Queen's College, Birmingham; Professor of History, University of Birmingham; Hulsean Lecturer, Cambridge; vicar, canon, and sub-dean of St. Michael's, Coventry; rector of St. Mary-le-Bow, Cheapside, London; rector of Stoke Damarel; Suffragen Bishop of Plymouth (1923-1933).

MATHESON, GEORGE (1842-1906). Scottish. Church of Scotland. Minister of the parish of Innellan, Argylshire (1868-2886); served at St. Bernard's Parish Church, Edinburgh (1886-1906). Blind from the age of eighteen, a serious scholar and scientific theologian, author of Sacred Songs (1890, 1904).

MAUDE, MARY FOWLER HOOPER (1819-1887). British. Church of England. Her hymns appeared in her Twelve Letters on Confirmation (1848) and in Memorials of Past Years (1852).

MAXWELL, MARY HAMLIN (1814-1853). American. Methodist. Published a volume of Original Poems in 1849.

McCHEYNE, ROBERT MANNING (1813-1843). Scottish. Established Church of Scotland. Minister of St. Peter's Established Church, Dundee (1836-1843); went to Palestine as a member of the Mission of Enquiry to the Jews from the Church of Scotland. Published Songs of Zion in 1843.

McCOMB, WILLIAM (b. 1793). Irish. A Belfast bookseller who published several volumes of verse between 1816 and 1864.

McDONALD, WILLIAM (1820-1910). American. Baptist.

McGREGOR, ERNEST FRANK (b. 1879). His hymn, Lift high the trumpet song today!" dates from 1932.

McWHOOD, LEONARD BEECHER (b. 1879). His hymn, "All people of the Earth" (entitled "The Kingdom of God") dates from 1933.

MEDLEY, SAMUEL (1738-1799). British. Baptist. Served with the Royal Navy, after which he opened a school in London. Pastor of the Baptist Church, Watford (1767-1772), and then of a congregation at Byron Street, Liverpool (1772-1799). Published his Hymns in 1785 and again in 1794.

MEINHOLD, JOHANN WILHELM (1797-1851). German. Rector of the town academy at Usedom (1820-1821); pastor of Coserow (1821-1828); pastor of Crummin (1828-1844); pastor at Rehwinkel (1844-1850). In addition to his hymns, he wrote an historical romance, Maria Schweidler die Bernsteinhexe (1843).

MERRICK, JAMES (1720-1169). British. Church of England. Received Holy Orders, but his health would not permit him to undertake parish work. Published his Poems (1763), The Psalms of David (1765, 1766).

MERRILL, WILLIAM PIERSON (1867-1954). American. Presbyterian. Held pastorates at Philadelphia; the Sixth Presbyterian Church, Chicago; Brick Presbyterian Church, New York (1911-1938).

MIDLANE, ALBERT (1825-1909). British. Businessman and Sunday school teacher at Newport, Isle of Wright. More than 700 of his hymns appeared in Gospel Echoes (1865), The Bright Blue Sky Hymn Book (1904), Hymns for Children (1907).

MILLER, EMILY HUNTINGTON (1833-1913). American. Dean of Women at Northwestern University, Evanston, Illinois (1891-1898); author of short stories and poems. A joint editor of The Little Corporal (published in Chicago), in which a number of her hymns appeared.

MILLIGAN, JAMES LEWIS (1876-1961).

MILMAN, HENRY HART (1791-1868). British. Church of England. Poetry professor at Oxford (1821-1831). Canon of Westminster and rector of St. Margaret's; dean of St. Paul's (1849-1868). Poet, playwright, historian, and theologian. His thirteen hymns appeared in print in 1827--in Bishop Reginald Heber's (see above) collection of Hymns--and again in his own Selection of Psalms and Hymns (1837).

MILTON, JOHN (1608-1674). British. Church of England, "Puritan." The influence of this most significant poet and prose writer of the mid and late seventeenth century upon English hymnody has been limited, essentially, to nineteen versions of various Psalm passages.

MOMENT, JOHN JAMES (1875-1959). His hymn, "Men and children everywhere," dates from 1941.

MONOD, THEODORE (1836-1921). American. Presbyterian. Born in Paris, France; entered the ministry of the French Reformed Church in 1860.

MONSELL, JOHN SAMUEL BEWLEY (1811-1875). Irish. Church of Ireland. The chaplain to Bishop Richard Mant (see above); chancellor of the diocese of Connor; rector of Ramoan; vicar of Egham, Worcester; rec-

tor of St. Nicholas, Guildford.  Published his Hymns (1837); Spiritual Songs (1857); Hymns of Love and Praise (1863, 1866); The Parish Hymnal (1873).

MONTGOMERY, JAMES (1771-1854).  Scottish.  Moravian.  Edited The Sheffield Iris (1794-1825).  Received a Royal pension in 1833.  Published a dozen poetical volumes, including Songs of Zion (1822), The
Christian Psalmist (1825), The Christian Poet (1825), Original
Hymns (1853).  The total of his hymns exceeds 400.

MOORE, THOMAS (1779-1852).  Irish.  Roman Catholic.  Lawyer, government
official, poet, and musician.  Became the national lyricist of Ireland and a significant literary figure of the Romantic Age.  His
hymns derive from his Sacred Songs (1816).

MORE, HENRY (1614-1687).  British.  Church of England.  Spent his life
as a scholar and tutor.  His Divine Dialogues, with Divine Hymns
appeared in 1668.  He received Holy Orders, but refused all preferments, including two bishoprics.

MORRIS, GEORGE PERKINS (1802-1864).  American.  Edited The New York Mirror magazine and The Home Journal.  Published at least four volumes
of poetry; he is best remembered for his poem, "Woodman! Spare That
Tree" (1830).

MORRISON, JOHN (1749-1798).  Scottish.  Church of Scotland.  Parish
minister of Canisbay, Caithness (1780-1798).  A member of the committee to review and revise (1775) the Scottish Translations and
Paraphrases of 1745.

MOTE, EDWARD (1797-1874).  British.  Baptist.  Pastor at Horsham, Sussex
(1848-1874).  Published Hymns of Praise (1836).

MOULE, HANDLEY CARR GLYN (1841-1920).  British.  Church of England.  Curate of Fordington, Dorset (1867-1873); dean of Trinity College,
Cambridge (1874-1877); curate of Fordington (1877-1880); principal
of Ridley Hall, Cambridge (1880-1899); select preacher at Cambridge
(1880-1881, 1887); Norrisian Professor of Divinity at Cambridge
(1899-1901); Bishop of Durham (1901-1920).  His hymns may be found
in Poems on the Acts of the Apostles (1869) and appended to On Union
with Christ (1835) and On Spiritual Life (1887).

MOULTRIE, GERARD (1829-1885).  British.  Church of England.  Third master and chaplain at Shrewsbury School; chaplain to the Dowager Mar-
chioness of Londonderry (1855-1859); curate of Brightwaltham (1859)
and of Brinfield, Berkshire (1860); chaplain to the Donative of Bar-
row Gurney, Bristol (1864-1869); vicar of Southleigh (1869-1873);
warden of St. James's College, Southleigh (1873-1885).  Published
Hymns and Lyrics (1867).

MUHLENBERG, WILLIAM AUGUST (1796-1877).  American.  Episcopal.  Assistant rector of St. James's, Lancaster, Pennsylvania (1823-1843);
rector of the Church of the Holy Communion, New York (1843-1848);
rector of several churches in New York City.  Published Church Poetry (1823), The People's Psalter (1858), and a collection of his
original Poems (1859).

MULHOLLAND, ROSA.  Her hymn, "Give me, O Lord, a heart of grace," dates from 1886.

MURRAY, ROBERT (1832-1909).  Canadian.  Presbyterian.  An ordained minister of thr Presbyterian Church in Canada.


NEALE, JOHN MASON (1818-1866).  British.  Church of England.  Incumbent of Crowley, Sussex (1843); spent a year at Madeira (Portuguese archipelago) recouperating from a lung disease.  Warden of Sackville College, East Grimstead (1846-1866).  Devoted twenty years (1846-1866) to the study of hymnody and liturgy.  Certainly the major hymnodist, hymn translator, and hymnal editor of the nineteenth century.

NEANDER, JOACHIM (1650-1680).  German.  German Reformed Church.  Became turot to the sons of wealthy merchants at Frankfurt-am-Main (1671-1673); rector of the Latin school at Dusseldorf (1674-1679); unordained assistant at St. Martin's Church, Bremen (1679-1680).  The first important hymn writer of the German Reformed Church since the Reformation, especially in terms of expressing jubilance and praise and thanksgiving; he also wrote the melodies to approximately nineteen of those pieces.  See also below in Section C.

NEEDHAM, JOHN (d. 1786).  British.  Baptist.  Co-pastor of the Baptist meeting-house in the Pithay, Bristol (1750-1752), then of another such house of worship in Callowhill Street (1752-1786).  Published Hymns Devotional and Moral (1768).

NELSON, DAVID (1793-1844).  American.  Presbyterian.  Surgeon during the War of 1812; resigned his practice in 1823 to become a minister; founded manual labor colleges at Greenfields and Quincy--both in Illinois.

NEUMARCK, GEORGE.  See below in Section C.

NEVIN, EDWIN HENRY (1814-1889).  American.  Presbyterian.  Congregational, Reformed Church.  Held numerous pastorates in Philadelphia and throughout eastern Pennsylvania.

NEWHALL, CHARLES STEDMAN (b. 1842).  His hymn, "O Jesus, Master, when to-day" (entitled "The Kingdom of God") dates from 1914.

NEWMAN, JOHN HENRY (1801-1890).  British.  Church of England, Roman Catholic.  Curate of St. Clements Church (1824-1826); tutor of Oriel College, Oxford (1826-1828); vicar of St. Mary's, Oxford, 1828-1843.  Converted to the Roman Catholic Church in 1845; ordained priest of that denomination in 1847.  Father Superior to the Oratory of St. Philip Neri, Birmingham (1848-1854); rector of the Roman Catholic University, Dublin (1854-1858); superior of the Edgbaston Oratory, Birmingham (1858-1890).  Appointed Cardinal by Pope Leo XII in 1879.

NEWTON, JOHN (1725-1807).  British.  Church of England.  Spent twelve years at sea, another six as commander of a slave ship out of Africa.  Came under the influence of  George Whitefield and the Wesleys before taking Holy Orders and being ordained (1764) to the curacy of Olney, Buckinghamshire; there he met the poet William Cowper (see above) and they issued the noted Olney Hymns (1779). Served as rector of St. Mary Woolnoth, London (1780-1807), where he became involved with the parliamentarian William Wilberforce and the London committee to abolish the slave trade from Africa.

NICHOL, HENRY ERNEST (1862-1928). British. Church of England. Published a number of Sunday school hymns under the pseudonym of "Colin Sterne."

NICOLAI, PHILIPP ((1556-1608). German. Lutheran. Lutheran preacher at Herdecke (1583-1586); diaconus at Niederwildungen (1586-1587); pastor at Niederwildungen (1587-1588); chief pastor at Altwildungen and court preacher to the Countess Margaretha of Waldeck(1588-1596); pastor at Unna (1596-1599); chief pastor of St. Katherine's Church, Hamburg (1601-1608). His published works tend to be principally polemical; only four of his hymns found their way into print.

NOEL, BAPTISTE WRIOTHESLEY (1791-1873). British. Church of England, Baptist. Incumbent of St. John's Episcopal Chapel, Bedford Row, London; chaplain to the Queen. Pastor of St. John's Street Chapel, Bedford Row (1848-1868). Published A Selection of Psalms and Hymns (1832) and Hymns about Jesus (n.d.).

NOEL, CAROLINE MARIA (1817-1877). Scottish. Church of England. Published The Name of Jesus and Other Verses for the Sick and Lonely (1861, 1870, 1878). The niece of Baptiste Wriothesley Noel (see immediately above).

NOEL, GERARD THOMAS (1782-1851). Scottish. Church of England. Curate of Radwell, Hertfordshire; vicar of Rainham and Romsey; canon of Winchester Cathedral. Compiled A Selection of Psalms and Hymns (1810, 1820).

NORTH, FRANK MASON (1850-1835). American. Methodist Episcopal. Held pastorates in New York and Connecticut (1873-1892); a founder and secretary (1892-1912) of the New York City Extension and Missionary Society; a founder and secretary of the Methodist Board of Foreign Missions (1912-1935). Also President of the Federal Council of the Churches of Christ in America (1912-1916).

OAKELEY, FREDERICK (1802-1880). British. Church of England, Roman Catholic. Prebendary of Lichfield Cathedral (1832-1837); preacher at Whitehall (1837-1839); minister of Margaret Chapel, Margaret Street, London (1839-1845). Became canon of the Pro-Cathedral in the Roman ecclesiastical district of Westminster. Published Lyra Liturgica (1865).

OAKEY, EMILY SULLIVAN (1829-1883). American. A native of Albany, New York; taught languages and literature at the Albany Female Academy.

OBERLIN, REV. JEAN FREDERIC (1740-1826).

OLIVERS, THOMAS (1725-1799). British. Methodist. Served as one of
    John Wesley's itinerant preachers in Cornwall (1753-1799) and for a
    time co-edited (with Wesley) The Arminian Magazine.

OLSON, ERNEST WILLIAM (1870-1958).

ONDERDONK, HENRY USTICK (1789-1858). American. Episcopal. Rector of
    St. Anne's Church, Brooklyn, New York; assistant bishop of Phila-
    delphia (1827-1836); Bishop of Philadelphia (1836-1844, 1856-1858).
    A member of the committee that compiled the American Prayer Book
    Collection (1826).

OPIE, AMELIA ALDERSON (1769-1853). British. Unitarian, Society of
    Friends. A writer of short fiction and poetry. Married to John
    Opie, the painter; intimate with Sydney Smith (one of the founders
    of the Edinburgh Review), Richard Brinsley Sheridan, and Madame de
    Stael.

OWENS, PRISCILLA JANE (1829-1907). American. Presbyterian. A resident
    of Baltimore; a public school and Sunday school teacher.

OXENHAM, JOHN (1852-1941). British. Congregational. Businessman, poet,
    minor novelist. A deacon of the Ealing Congregational Church.


PAGE, KATE STEARNS (1873-1963).

PALGRAVE, FRANCIS TURNER (1824-1897). British. Church of England.
    Served in the Education Department of the Privy Council (1846-1884);
    Professor of Poetry at Oxford (1885-1897). Published his Hymns in
    1867 (further editions in 1868 and 1870). A major nineteenth-cen-
    tury literary anthologist and "bowdlerizer."

PALMER, HORATIO RICHMOND (1834-1907). American. An organist at age
    seventeen; director of Rushford Academy of Music, New York (1857-
    1861). Settled in Chicago and established the journal Concordia
    (1866). Returned to New York (1874) and headed (1884) the Church
    Choral Union, a society dedicated to the improvement of church mu-
    sic. Became dean of the School of Music at Chautauqua (1887). Pub-
    lished The Song Queen, The Song King, The Song Herald; wrote a The-
    ory of Music and A Manual for Teachers.

PALMER, RAY (1808-1887). American. Congregational. Pastor of the Cen-
    tral Congregational Church, Bath, Maine (1835-1850); a pastor of
    the First Congregational Church, Albany, New York (1850-1865). Cor-
    responding Secretary of the American Congregational Union (1865-
    1878); retired to Newark, New Jersey (2878-1887). Published Hymns
    and Sacred Pieces (1865), Hymns of My Holy Hours (1868).

PARK, JOHN EDGAR (1879-1956). Irish-American. Congregational. Minis-
    ter of the First Congregational Church, West Newton, Massachusetts.
    President of Wheaton (Massachusetts) College (1928-1956).

PARK, ROSWELL (1807-1869). American. Protestant Episcopal. Served in the U.S. Army; appointed Professor of Chemistry, University of Pennsylvania. President of Racine College (1858-1863); principal of a school in Chicago (1863-1869). Published several volumes of poetry. A graduate of the U.S. Military Academy (1846); ordained as a minister of the Protestant Episcopal Church (1843); served churches in Pomfret, Connecticut (1843-1852).

PARKER, EDWIN POND (1836-1925). American. Congregational. Minister of the Second Church of Christ, Hartfird, Connecticut (1860-1910). Editor in chief of The Book of Praise (1874) and editor of The Christian Hymnal (1877). Appointed (1906) chaplain of the senate of the State of Connecticut.

PARKER, WILLIAM HENRY (1845-1929). British. Baptist. Head of an insurance company and active in Sunday school work.

PARKIN, CHARLES (b. 1894). American.

PEABODY, WILLIAM BOURNE OLIVER (1799-1847). American. Unitarian. Pastor of the Unitarian congregation at Springfield, Massachusetts (1820-1847). Edited The Springfield Collection of Hymns for Sacred Worship (1835).

PENNEFATHER, WILLIAM (1816-1873). Irish. Established Church of Ireland. Curate of Ballymacugh, Kilmore (1841-1844); vicar of Mellifont, Drogheda (1844-1848); held incumbencies at Trinity Church, Walton, Aylesbury (1848-1852); at Christ Church, Barnet (1852-1864); at St. Jude's, Mildmay Park (1864-1873). Published Hymns Original and Selected (1872) and Original Hymns (1873).

PENNEWELL, ALMER T. (b. 1876).

PERRONET, EDWARD (1726-1792). British. Methodist. Ministered to one of the Calvinist Methodist chapels sponsored by the Countess of Huntingdon (see below, this section) in Watling Street, Canterbury; then served as pastor to a small Congregational church in Canterbury. Published Select Passages of the Old and New Testament Versified (1756); A Small Collection of Hymns (1782); Occasional Verses, Moral and Sacred (1785).

PHELPS, SYLVANUS DRYDEN (1816-1895). American. Baptist. Pastor of the First Baptist Church, New Haven, Connecticut (1846-1882). His hymns appeared in poetry collections published between 1842 and 1867.

PHILLIPS, HARRIET CECELIA (1806-1884). American. Methodist Episcopal. An active worker in various Sunday schools throughout New York City.

PIERPONT, FOLIOTT SANDFORD (1835-1917). British. Church of England. Classical master at Somersetshire College. Authored the "Hymns for the Canonical Hours" in The Hymnal Noted (1852, 1854).

PIERPONT, JOHN (1785-1866). American. Unitarian. Practiced law and business; pastor of the Unitarian Church, Hollis Street, Boston (1819-1840); pastor of the Unitarian Church, Troy, New York (1845-1849); pastor of the Unitarian Church at Medford, Massachusetts (1849-1859). U.S. Army chaplain (1862-1864) and a clerk in the U.S.

Treasury Department (1864-1866). Published Poems and Hymns (1840-1854).

PIERSON, ARTHUR TAPPAN (1837-1911). American. Presbyterian. Held pastorates at Binghampton and Waterford, New York; at Fort Street, Detroit; at the Bethany Presbyterain Church, Philadelphia.

PIGGOTT, WILLIAM CHARTER (1872-1943). British. Congregational. Held pastorates at Grenville Place, London; at Bunyan Meeting, Bedford; at Whitefield's Chapel, Tottenham Court Road, London; at Streatham. Chairman of the Congregational Union during 1931-1932.

PLUMPTRE, EDWARD HAYES (1821-1891). British. Church of England. Assistant preacher at Lincoln's Inn; select preacher at Oxford; professor of pastoral theology, King's College, London; Dean of Queen's College, Oxford; prebendary in St. Paul's Cathedral, London; Professor of Exegesis of the New Testament in King's College, London; Boyle Lecturer; Grinfield Lecturer on the Septuagint, Oxford; examiner in the theological schools, Oxford; member of the Old Testament company for the revision of the Authorized Version of the Holy Scriptures. Rector of Pluckley (1869-1873); vicar of Bickley, Kent (1873-1881); Dean of Wells (1881-1891).

POLLARD, ADELAIDE ADDISON (1862-1934).

POLLOCK, THOMAS BENSON (1836-1896). British. Church of England. Curate of St. Luke's, Leek, Staffordshire; curate of St. Alban's, Birmingham (1865-1896). Published Metrical Litanies (1870).

POPE, ALEXANDER (1688-1744). British. Roman Catholic. Although certainly the most significant poet of the first half of the eighteenth century, Pope wrote no hymns intended for congregational purposes; those that do appear in common use have been extracted from larger poetic pieces essentially philosophic in nature.

POTT, FRANCIS (1832-1909). British. Church of England. Curate of Bishopsworth, Gloucestershire (1856-1858); curate of Ardingly, Berkshire (1858-1861); curate of Ticehurst, Sussex (1861-1866); rector of Norhill, Ely (1866-1891). Published Hymns Fitted to the Order of Common Prayer (1861) and The Free Rhythm Psalter (1898). A member of the original committee for Hymns Ancient and Modern (1861).

POTTER, THOMAS JOSEPH (1827-1873). British. Roman Catholic. Chair of Pulpit Eloquence and English Literature at the Foreign Missionary College, All Hallows, Dublin. Translated the Vesper hymns in The Catholic Psalmist; published Legends, Lyrics, and Hymns (1862).

PRENTISS, ELIZABETH PAYSON (1818-1878). American. Presbyterian. Published her Religious Poems in 1873.

PROCTER, ADELAIDE ANNE (1825-1864). British. Roman Catholic. Her hymns have been derived, essentially, from Legends and Lyrics (1858, 1862).

PRID, WILLIAM (fl. 1585-1593). British.

PRUDENTIUS, MARCUS AURELIUS CLEMENS (348-c.413). Spanish. The most pro-

minent and most prolific author of sacred Latin poetry--particular-
ly during the beginnings of that genre.  Retired, at age fifty-se-
ven, into poverty and privacy, during which time he began to com-
pose his sacred verse.  His liturgical hymns have been compiled
from two of his earlier works--Liber Cathemerinon and Liber Peris-
tephanon.

PRYNNE, GEORGE RUNDLE (1818-1903).  British.  Church of England.  Vicar
of St. Peter's, Plymouth (1848-1903).  Published The Dying Soldier's
Visions, and Other Poems (1881) and The Hymnal Suited for the Services of the Church (1858).

PYPER, MARY (1795-1870).  British.  Daughter of a common British soldier;
earned her meagre living as a needlewoman.  Published Select Pieces
(1847).

RAFFLES, THOMAS (1788-1863).  British.  Congregational.  Held pastorates
at Hammersmith (1809-1812) and at the Great George Street Congregational Church, Liverpool (1812-1861).  Helped to found the Lancashire Independent College.  Published a Supplement to the Psalms
and Hymns (1853)  of Isaac Watts (see below, this section), as well
as his own volume of Hymns, which appeared in 1868.

RAMBACH, JOHANN JAKOB (1693-1735).  German.  Appointed an adjunct of
the Theological College at Halle (1723); extraordinary professor of
theology at Halle (1726); ordinary professor and preacher at the
Schulkirche, Halle (1727); superintendent and first professor of
theology and director of the Paedagogium at Giessen (1731-1735).
His hymns, extremely lyrical in quality, tend toward the didactic
and the scriptural; they number approximately 180, of which between
fifteen and twenty have gained popular congregational acceptance.

RANKIN, JEREMIAH EAVES (1828-1904).  American.  Congregational.  Held
pastorates at New York, St. Albans, Charlestown, Washington, D.C.
Edited The Gospel Temperance Hymnal (1878) and Gospel Bells.  President of Howard University, Washington, D.C.

RAWNSLEY, HARDWICKE DRUMMOND (1850-1920).  British.  Church of England.
Curate of St. Barnabas, Bristol (1875-1877); vicar of Low Wray, Lancashire (1878-1883); vicar of Crosthwaite (1883-1920); rural dean
of Keswick (1883); honorary canon of Carlisle (1893); a chaplain to
the King.

RAWSON, GEORGE (1807-1899).  British.  Congregational.  A practicing solicitor in Leeds.  Assisted in the compilation of Psalms and Hymns
and Passages of Scripture for Christian Worship (1853) and the Baptist Psalms and Hymns (1858).  Published his own Hymns, Verses, and
Chants (1876) and Songs of Spiritual Thought (1885).

RAYMOND, ROSSITER WORTHINGTON (1840-1918).  American.  Congregational.  A
resident of Brooklyn, New York, and a consulting mining engineer.
Edited The Journal of Mining; also wrote poetry and short stories
for children.

REED, ANDREW (1781-1862). British. Congregational. Pastor of the New
Road Chapel, St. George's-in-the-East, and Wycliffe Chapel (London).
Founded the London Orphan Asylum for Fatherless Children, the Asylum for Idiots, the Infant Orphan Asylum, the Hospital for Incura-
bles. Published a Hymn Book (1817, 1825, 1842).

REED, E.M.G. (1885-1933).

REED, ELIZABETH HOLMES (1794-1867). British. Congregational. Wife of
the Rev. Andrew Reed (see immediately above). Wrote approximately
twenty hymns that she contributed to her husband's collections.

REES, BRYN AUSTIN (b. 1911).

RHABANUS, MAURUS (c. 776-856). German. Archbishop of Mainz. Versions
of his poetry have been adapted to congregational hymnody and have
derived from his Poemata, Carmina, and a prose piece entitled De
Universo.

RICE, CAROLINE LAURA (b. 1819). American. Wife of the Rev. William
Rice of Springfield, Massachusetts.

RICHARDSON, CHARLOTTE SMITH (1775-1825). British. Born and died at
York. Published Poems Written on Different Subjects (1806), from
which her hymns have been extracted.

RICHTER, CHRISTIAN FRIEDRICH (1676-1711). German. Inspector of the
Paedagogium at Halle (1698; engaged in chemical experiments and
developed a number of compounds that came to be known as the "Halle
Medicines." An important Pietist hymn writer whose verse develops
the notion of spiritual union with Christ as the Bridegroom of the
soul.

RILEY, JOHN ATHELSTANE LAURIE (1858-1945). British. Church of England.
A member of the House of Laymen of the Province of Canterbury. One
of the compilers of The English Hymnal (1906).

RINGWALDT, BARTHOLOMAUS (1532-c. 1599/1600). German. Pastor of Lang-
feld, near Sonnenburg, Brandenburg (1566-1599). A staunch Lutheran
and a poet whose lines captured his strong sense of popular commit-
ment and nationalism.

RINKART, MARTIN (1586-1649). German. A foundation scholar and chorister of the St. Thomas's School, Leipzig (1601); a student in theology at the University of Leipzig (1602). Master in the gymnasium
at Eisleben and cantor of St. Nicholas Church (1610); diaconus of
St. Anne's Church, in the Neustadt of Eisleben (1611-1613); pastor
at Erdeborn and Lyttichendorf (1613-1617); archidiaconus at Eilen-
burg ((1617-1649). Wrote, in addition to hymns, longer poetic pieces and a number of comic dramas.

ROBBINS, HOWARD CHANDLER (1876-1952). American.

ROBERT II, KING OF FRANCE (c. 970-1031). King from 988 to 1031. Devoted considerable time to the society of monks, whom he assisted in
the services of the Church and on pious pilgrimages. Approximately

five hymns and hymn sequences have been ascribed to him.

ROBERTS, DANIEL CRANE (1841-1907). American. Episcopal. Rector of St. Thomas Church, Brandon, Vermont; rector of St. Paul's Church, Concord, New Hampshire.

ROBERTS, THOMAS (b. 1804).

ROBINSON, GEORGE (b. 1842).

ROBINSON, RICHARD HAYES (1842-1892). British. Church of England. Curate of St. Paul's, Penge; incumbent of the Octagon Chapel, Bath; incumbent of St. German's Blackheath (1884-1892).

ROBINSON, ROBERT (1735-1790). British. Methodist, Baptist. Ministered to an Independent congregation at Norwich (1758-1759) and to a Baptist congregation at Cambridge (1759-1790). A noted Nonconformist theologian and church historian.

RODIGAST, SAMUEL (1649-1708). German. Adjunct of the philosophical faculty, University of Jena (1668); conrector of the Greyfriars Gymnasium at Berlin (1698-1708).

ROOT, GEORGE FREDERICK (1820-1895). American. Principally a composer of popular music and gospel hymn tunes. Published music in Chicago; popularized the teaching of music in the American public school system.

ROSCOE, JANE (1798-1853). British. Unitarian. The second daughter of William Roscoe of Liverpool (see immediately below). Published two volumes of Poems in 1820 and 1843.

ROSCOE, WILLIAM (1753-1831). British. Unitarian. Published prose tracts against the slave trade, served in Parliament (1807), wrote significant histories and biographies of Renaissance figures (Lorenzo de Medici, Pope Leo X), founded the Liverpool Athenaeum in 1789, Helped to prepare A Selection of Psalms and Hymns (1818) for the Renshaw Street Unitarian Chapel, Liverpool.

ROSSETTI, CHRISTINA GEORGINA (1830-1894). British. Church of England. A major nineteenth-century poet; her hymns have been extracted and altered from her poetry. Technically a member of the Church of England, she evidenced strong inclinations toward the Roman Catholic Church; she struck a compromise that allowed her to believe and practice Catholic Christianity within the Anglican Communion.

ROTHE, JOHANN ANDREAS (1688-1758). German. Licensed at Gorlitz, in Silesia, as a general preacher (1712); tutor in the family of Herr von Schweinitz, at Leube (1718); pastor at Berthelsdorf (1722-1739), where the Moravian community of Herrnhut formed part of his parish. After breaking with Zinzendorf's Moravians, he accepted a pastorate at Hermsdorf; assistant, then chief pastor, at Thommendorf, near Bunzlau (1739-1742, 1742-1758). Composed approximately forty hymns for congregational use.

ROUS, FRANCIS (1579-1659). British. Lawyer and parliamentarian. Pro-

vost of Eton College.  His authorized Psalter appeared in 1641,
1643, 1646.

ROWLAND, MAY (1870-1959).

RUMBAUGH, VIDA (b. 1927).

RUSSELL, ARTHUR TOZER (1806-1874).  British.  Church of England.  Curate
   of Great Gransden, Huntingtonshire (1829-1830); vicar of Caxton
   (1830-1852); vicar of Whaddon, Cambridgeshire (1852-1866); rector
   of St. Thomas's, Toxteth Park, Liverpool (1866-1867); vicar of
   Wrockwardine Wood, Shropshire (1867-1874); rector of Southwick,
   Brighton (1874).  Published Hymns for Public Worship (1848), Psalms
   and Hymns (1851); composed approximately 140 hymns for worship.

RYDEN, ERNEST EDWIN (b. 1886).

RYLAND, JOHN (1753-1825).  British.  Baptist.  Co-pastor, with his father, at Northampton (1781-1794).  President of the Baptist College
   and pastor of the Baptist church at Broadmead, Bristol (1794-1825).
   A founder of the Baptist Missionary Society.  His Hymns and Verses
   appeared in 1862.

RYLE, BISHOP JOHN C. (fl. 1850-1875).  British.  Church of England. Edi-
   The Additional Hymn Book (1875).

SAMMIS, JOHN H. (1846-1919).

SARGENT, LUCIUS MANLIUS (1786-1867).

SCHEFFLER, JOHANN ANGELUS SILESIUS (1624-1677).  German.  Lutheran, Roman Catholic.  Graduated M.D. and Ph.D. from Padua (1648).  Private
   physician to Duke Sylvius Nimrod of Wurttemberg-Oels (1649-1652);
   appointed by Emperor Ferdinand III to the titular position of Imperial Court Physician; entered the Order of St. Francis (1661);
   ordained a priest of the Roman Catholic Church (1661); appointed
   Raff and Hofmarschall to Sebastian von Rostock, Prince Bishop of
   Breslau; retired to the monastery at Breslau (1671-1677).

SCHLEGEL, CATHARINA AMALIA DOROTHEA  (b. 1697).  Attached to the minor
   ducal court at Cothen.  Of the approximately twenty hymns ascribed
   to her, only one--"Stille mein Wille, dein Jesus hilft siegen" ("Be
   still, my soul!--the Lord is on thy side")--has achieved the status
   of popular English congregational song.

SCHMOLCK, BENJAMIN (1672-1737).  German.  Lutheran.  Ordained his father's assistant at Brauchitzchdorf, Silesia (1701); diaconus of the
   Friedenskirche at Schweidnitz in Silesia (1702).  A popular preacher
   and certainly the most popular hymnodist of his day.

SCHUTZ, JOHANN JAKOB (1640-1690).  German.  A practicing lawyer in
   Frankfurt.  His hymns have come from his Christliche Lebensregeln
   (1677) and Christliches Gedenckbuchlein zu Beforderung eines an-

_fangenden_ _neuen_ _Lebens_ (1675).

SCHWEDLER, JOHANN CHRISTOPH (1672-1730). German. Assistant minister at Niederwiese, near Greifenberg (1698)--later to become diaconus in 1698 and pastor in 1701.

SCOTT, CLARA H. (1841-1897).

SCOTT, ELIZABETH (1708-1776). American. Independent. At one time married to Elisha Williams, rector of Yale College. Manuscript volumes of her hymns were originally deposited with the Yale College library.

SCOTT, ROBERT B.Y. (b. 1899).

SCOTT, THOMAS (1705-1775). British. Presbyterian. Brother of Elizabeth Scott (see above). Early ministries at Wortwell and Harleston, Norfolk; then moved to Lowestoft. Co-pastor (1734-1740) and pastor (1740-1774) of the Presbyterian congregation at St.Nicholas Street Chapel, Ipswich. His _Lyric_ _Poems_, _Devotional_ _and_ _Moral_, appeared in 1773.

SCOTT, SIR WALTER (1771-1832). Scottish. Church of Scotland. This major novelist of the Romantic period did not write hymns as such; those in common congregational use have come from pieces of poetry included in his fiction. Recipient of the first baronetcy created (31 March 1820) by King George IV.

SCRIVEN, JOSEPH (1820-1886). Irish, Canadian. His hymn, "What a Friend we have in Jesus," was composed either on the occasion of his mother's death or after the accidental drowning of his intended bride on the eve of their wedding day.

SEAGRAVE, ROBERT (1693-1759). British. Church of England. Sunday evening lecturer at Loriner's Hall, London (1739-1750). Preached for a time at George Whitefield's Chapel in London. Published _Hymns_ _for_ _Christian_ _Worship_ (1742, 1748).

SEARS, EDMUND HAMILTON (1810-1876). American. Unitarian. Pastor of the First Church, Wayland, Massachusetts (1838), and of the Unitarian Church at Lancaster, Massachusetts (1839-1847). Returned to Wayland (1847), then settled at Weston, Massachusetts (1865-1876). Published _Sermons_ _and_ _Songs_ _of_ _the_ _Christian_ _Life_ (1875) and co-edited _The_ _Monthly_ _Religious_ _Magazine_.

SELNECKER, NICOLAUS (1532-1592). German. Second court preacher at Dresden and tutor to Prince Alexander (1557-1565); Professor of Theology at Jena (1565); Professor of Theology at Leipzig and pastor of St. Thomas's Church, Leipzig (1568-1570); court preacher and general superintendent at Wolfenbuttel (1570-1572); pastor of St. Thomas Church, Leipzig (1574-1589), where he built the noted Motett Choir (which Bach afterward conducted). A prominent ecclesiastical figure of the sixteenth century and the author of over two hundred volumes of prose and poetry.

SEYMOUR, AARON CROSSLY HOBART (1789-1870). Irish. Church of Ireland.

A noted essayist and biographer--particularly biographies of Se-
line Shirley, Countess of Huntingdon (see below this section) and
George Whitefield.

SHACKFORD, JOHN W. (b. 1878). American. His "O Thou who art the Shepherd" appeared, initially, in Seven New Social Welfare Hymns (New
York: Hymn Society of America, 1961).

SHEPHERD, ANNE HOULDITCH (1809-1857). British. Church of England. Minor novelist. Published a collection of her Hymns for juveniles
(1847, 1855).

SHEPHERD, THOMAS (1665-1739). British. Church of England, Independent.
Held preferments in Huntingdonshire and Buckinghamshire. Pastor
of the Castle Hill Meeting House, Nottingham (1694-1700); ministered to an Independent congregation at Bocking, near Braintree, Essex (1700-1739).

SHERWIN, WILLIAM FISK (1826-1888). American. Baptist. Studied music
in Boston under Lowell Mason; became a teacher of vocal music in
Massachusetts and New York. Became associated with Robert Lowry
(see above, this section) in the preparation of the Sunday school
music series, Bright Jewels.

SHILLITO, EDWARD (1872-1948). British. Congregational. Ministered at
Albion, Tunbridge Wells (1889-1901); at Clifton Road, Brighton
(1901-1906); at Harlesdon, London (1906-1909); at Brockhurst Hill,
E-sex (1918-1920). Served as editorial secretary of the London
Missionary Society (1920-1932).

SHIRLEY, SELINA HASTINGS, COUNTESS OF HUNTONGDON (1707-1791). British.
Methodist. A member of the first Methodist society in Fetter Lane,
London; the first Methodist Conference occurred in her home. With
George Whitefield, she formed the Calvinist connexion of British
Methodism; sponsored Trevecca College, South Wales, and built more
than fifty chapels for her connexion. Published her own Collection
of Hymns (1764, 1765, 1770, 1774, 1778, 1780).

SHRUBSOLE, WILLIAM, JR. (1759-1829). British. Church of England, Congregational. Clerk at the Bank of England; secretary of the Committee of the Treasury. A communicant at St. Anne's, Blackfriars;
then joined (1809) the Hoxton Academy Chapel. Active in the London Missionary Society, the Bible Society, the Religious Tract Society. Contributed hymns to various religious periodicals between
1775 and 1813.

SHURTLEFF, ERNEST WARBURTON (1862-1917). American. Congregational.
Held pastorates at Venture, California (1887-1891); at Plymouth,
Massachusetts (1891-1898); at the First Church, Minneapolis, Min-
nesota (1898-1905). Organized the American Church, Frankfurt a/M,
Germany (1905). Worked among American students in Paris, France
(1905-1917).

SHUTTLEWORTH, HENRY CARY (1850-1900). British. Church of England.
Chaplain of Christ Church, Oxford; monor canon of St. Paul's; rector of St. Nicholas, Cole Abbey, London (1883-1900). Professor of

pastoral and liturgical theology, lecturer of ecclesiastical history and English literature, and lecturer in the New Testament--all
at King's College, London.  Published Hymns for Private Use (1896)
and an Appendix to Church Hymns.

SIGOURNEY, LYDIA HUNTLEY (1791-1865).  American.  Presbyterian.  Published Moral Pieces in Prose and Verse (1815).  Pioneered higher education for women.

SIENA, BIANCO DA (d. 1434).  Roman Catholic.  Entered the Order of Jesu-
ates (1367).  Spent most of his life in Venice.  His hymns were
not published until 1851, when an edition appeared at Lucca under
the title Laudi Spirituali del Bianco da Siena, containing ninety-
two pieces; four of those have been translated into English and
have gained entrance into congregational hymnody.

SILL, EDWARD ROWLAND (1841-1887).  American.  Unitarian.  Professor of
English literature, University of California (1874-1882).  Published several volumes of poems, including The Hermitage (1867) and Ve-
nus of Milo (1883).  Spent his last years in Ohio, where, under the
pseudonym of "Andrew Hedbrooke," he contributed essays and poems to
a number of magazines.

SIMPSON, WILLIAM JAMES SPARROW (1860-1952).  British.  Church of England.
Chaplain to St. Mary's Hospital, Great Ilford (1904).

SLADE, MARY B.C. (1826-1882).

SMALL, JAMES GRINDLEY (1817-1888).  Scottish.  Free Church of Scotland.
Minister of the Free Church at Bervie, near Montrose (1847).  Published Hymns for Youthful Voices (1859), Psalms and Sacred Songs
(1866).

SMITH, SIR JAMES EDWARD, M.D. (1759-1828).  British.  Unitarian.  Bota-
nist and physician; preseident of the Linnaean Society (1788-1828);
knighted in 1814.  Belonged to a congregation meeting at the Octagon Chapel, Norwich.

SMITH, SAMUEL FRANCIS (1808-1895).  American.  Baptist.  Minister of the
Baptist Church, Waterville, Maine (1834-1842); minister of the
First Baptist Church, Newton Centre, Massachusetts (1842-1854); Secretary of the Baptist Missionary Union (1854-1869).  Co-editor,
with Rev. Baron Stow, of The Psalmist (1843); published Lyric Gems
(1854), Rock of Ages (1870).

SMITH, WALTER CHALMERS (1824-1908).  Scottish.  Free Church of Scotland.
Held pastorates at Chadwell Street, Islington, London; at Orwell
Free Church, Milnathort; at the Free Church, Glasgow; at the Free
High Schurch, Edinburgh (1876-1894).  Moderator of the Free Church
of Scotland (1893).  Published Hymns of Christ (1876, 1886).

SMYTHE, REV. EDWARD. (fl. 1793).  British.  Published, at Manchester
in 1793, a Collection of Hymns, in which he introduced a version
of the hymn "Lord, dismiss us with Thy blessing"--a piece in which
the question of authorship remains in doubt.

SPANGENBERG, AUGUSTUS GOTTLIEB (1704-1792). German. Lutheran, Moravian. Adjunct of the theological faculty and superintendent of the orphanage schools at Halle (1732-1733); received into the Moravian community at Herrnhut (1733); served the Moravians in Georgia and Pennsylvania (1735-1739); appointed a member of the Unity's Direction and made director of the organization's financial affairs in London; founded (1742) the first English Moravian settlement at Smith House, Yorkshire. Consecrated Moravian Bishop for North America (1744); spent the period 1744-1762 principally in Pennsylvania; succeeded Count Nicholaus von Zinzendorf (see below, this section) as the senior member of the Unity's Direction (1762).

SPITTA, CARL JOHANN PHILIPP (1801-1859). German. A tutor in the family of Judge Jochmus, at Lune (1824-1828); assistant pastor at Sudwalde (1828-1830); assistant chaplain to the garrison and to the prison at Hameln (1830-1837); pastor at Wechold (1837-1847); Lutheran superintendent at Wittingen (1847), at Peine (1853), at Burgdof (1859). His hymns appeared principally in three collections: Christliche Monatsschrift zur Hauslichen Erbauung fur alle Stande (1826), Psalter und Harfe. Eine Sammlung Christlicher Lieder zur Hauslichen Erbauung (1833), and a second series of Psalter und Harfe (1843).

STAMMERS, JOSEPH (1801-1885). British. London solicitor and barrister for the Northern Circuit.

STANLEY, ARTHUR PENRHYN (1815-1881). British. Church of England. College tutor, University College, Oxford (1840-1852). Select preacher for Oxford University (1845-1846); secretary to the Oxford commissioners (1850-1852). Canon of Canterbury (1851-1855). Regius Professor of Ecclesiastical History, Oxford, and canon at Christ Church (1855-1863). Dean of Westminster (1863-1881). Lord Rector of the University of St. Andrews (1875-1881). An eminent essayist, literary critic, historian, and biographer.

STEAD, LOUISA M.R. (c. 1850-1917).

STEELE, ANNE (1716-1778). British. Baptist. Published Poems on Subjects Chiefly Devotional (1760). Her hymns were not available for congregational use until 1769; approximately seventy-five of them remain popular in Britain and America.

STEELE, HARRIET BINNEY (b. 1826).

STENNETT, JOSEPH (1663-1713). British. Baptist. Preached to the Baptist Sabbatarian congregation at Devonshire Square, London (1689-1713). The earliest English Baptist hymn writer. Published Hymns in Commemoration of the. . .Holy Supper (1697, 1703); Hymns Composed for. . .Baptism (1712, 1722).

STENNETT, SAMUEL (1727-1795). British. Baptist. Grandson of Joseph Stennett (see immediately above). Assistant (1748-1758) at the Baptist Church, Little Wild Street, Lincoln's Inn Fields, London; pastor there from 1758 to 1795. Contributed thirty-eight hymns to Rippon's Collection of 1787.

"STERNE, COLIN." See above, this section, under NICHOL, HENRY ERNEST.

STERNHOLD, THOMAS (d. 1549). British. Church of England. Groom of the Robes to King Henry VIII. Published nineteen psalm versions under the title Certayne Psalmes, Chose out of the Psalmes of David; a second edition appeared, posthumously, in the year of his death (1549).

STOCKER, JOHN (fl. 1776-1777). Sometime resident of Honiton, Devonshire. Contributed nine hymns to The Gospel Magazine between 1776 and 1777.

STOCKING, JAY THOMAS (1870-1936). American. Congregational. Minister of several Congregational churches and moderator of the Congregational Council (1934).

STOCKTON, JOHN HART 1813-1877).

STONE, LLOYD (b. 1912).

STONE, SAMUEL JOHN (1839-1900). British. Church of England. Curate of Windsor (1862-1870); curate of St. Paul's, Haggerston (1870-1890); rector of All-Hallows-on-the-Wall, London (1890-1900). Published Hymns (1896) and served on the committee that compiled Hymns Ancient and Modern (1861).

STOWE, HARRIET BEECHER (1812-1896). American. Congregational. In addition to her classic work, Uncle Tom's Cabin (1852), she also published Religious Poems (1867).

STOWELL, HUGH (1799-1865). British. Church of England. Held curacies at Shepscombe, Gloucestershire, and at Holy Trinity, Huddersfield; curate in charge of St. Stephen's, Salford, and rector of Christ Church, Salford (1831-1845). Honorary canon of Chester Cathedral (1845-1851); Bishop of Manchester and rural dean of Eccles (1851-1865). Published A Selection of Psalms and Hymns (1831; 12th edition 1864).

STRAPHAN, JOSEPH (b. 1757).

STRONG, NATHAN (1748-1816). American. Congregational. Pastor of the First Congregational Church, Hartford, Connecticut (1774-1816). Founded The Connecticut Evangelical Magazine (1800); one of the founders of the Connecticut Home Missionary Society (1801). The principal editor of The Hartford Selection (1799).

STRYKER, MELANCTHON WOOLSEY (1851-1929). American. Presbyterian. Held pastorates at Auburn, New York; at Ithaca, New York; at Holyoke, Massachusetts. President of Hamilton (New York) College (1892-1917). Edited Christian Chorals (1885), New Alleluia (1880-1886), Church Song (1889), College Hymnal (1897, 1904). Joint editor of The Church Praise Book (1882). Published his own Hymns and Other Verses (1883) and Song of Mirriam and Other Hymns and Verses (1883).

STUDDERT-KENNEDY, GEOFFREY ANKETELL (1883-1929). British. His hymn, "Awake, awake to love and work," extracted from his volume entitled The Unutterable Beauty.

STUTSMAN, GRACE M. (b. 1886).

SWAIN, JOSEPH (1761-1796). British. Baptist. A converted engraver's apprentice who became minister of a Baptist congregation in East Street, Walworth (1791-1796). Published Walworth Hymns (1792),with a Supplement in 1794.

SWAIN, LEONARD (1821-1869). American. Congregational. Minister at Nashua, New Hampshire; at New Haven, Connecticut; at Central Church, Providence, Rhose Island (1852-1869).

SYMONDS, JOHN ADDINGTON (1840-1893). British. Church of England. Historian, essayist, poet--his hymns having been extracted from his verse. Suffered from ill-health and thus spent much of his life in Italy; excelled as a translator, particularly versions from the classical Greek poets and the sonnets of Michaelangelo and Campanella (1878). Certainly a major literary figure of the late Victorain Age.

SYNESIUS OF CYRENE (c. 375-430). Philosopher and statesman. Bishop of Ptolemais (410-430). The hymns that have come into common congregational use in Britain and America have been extracted from his odes.

TANNER, REV. B.T. Tanner's "We are the children of the church" dates from 1882.

TAPPAN, WILLIAM BINGHAM (1794-1849). American. Congregational. Superintendent of the American Sunday School Union (1822-1840). Published no less than ten volumes of religious and moral verse.

TARRANT, WILLIAM GEORGE (1853-1928). British. Unitarian. Minister of the Wandsworth Unitarian Christian Church (1883-1927). Editor of The Inquirer (1888-1897). One of the editors of The Essex Hall Hymnal (1890) and of its revision in 1902.

TATE, NAHUM (1652-1715). Irish. Church of England. Poet Laureate of England (1690-1715); historiographer royal (1702-1715). Poet and major Restoration dramatist. Published, with Nicholas Brady, the so-called "New Version" (1696)of the Psalms, the successor to the "Old Version" of Sternhold and Hopkins.

TAYLOR, SARAH ELLEN (1883-1954). Her hymn, "O God of light, Thy Word a lamp unfailing," appeared initially in Ten New Bible Hymns (New York: Hymn Society of America, 1952).

TAYLOR, THOMAS RAWSON (1807-1835). British. Congregational. Minister of the Howard Street Chapel, Sheffield (July 1830-January 1831). Classical tutor at Airedale College, Sheffield.

TAYLOR, WALTER REGINALD OXENHAM (1889-1973). British. Church of England. Served with the Church Missionary Society to the Missionary Diocese of West China (1924-1929); posted to Hangchow (1930-1950). Vicar of St. Margaret's Underriver (1950-1960).

TENNYSON, ALFRED LORD (1809-1892). British. Church of England. Poet
    Laureate of England (1850-1892); raised to the peerage in 1884.
    Passages from his poetry have been extracted and adapted as congre-
    gational hymns; those pieces tend to echo the poet's idea of reli-
    gion as an expression of personal feelings to support the idea of
    Christianity as the most beautiful and ethically potent means by
    which to express all that is higher than the self.

TERSTEEGEN, GERHARD (1697-1769). German. Reformed Church. A religious
    teacher among the so-called "Stillen im Lande"--attenders at mystic
    prayer meetings. Originally in business as a weaver (1717-1728).
    The majority of his hymns come from Geistliches Blumen-Gartlein--
    first edition in 1729, the eighth in 1778.

THEODULPH OF ORLEANS (d. 821). Italian. Brought to France by Charles
    the Great in 781; Bishop of Orleans (785); Abbot of Fleury (785);
    imprisoned at Angers from 818 until his death.

THOMAS OF CELANO (d. 1255). Italian. Went from Celano to Assisi, where
    he joined the Order of St. Francis; custos of the convents of Co-
    logne, Worms, and Mentz; sole custos of the Rhine districts (until
    c. 1230). In addition to his hymns, he wrote a life of St. Fran-
    cis.

THOMPSON, ALEXANDER RAMSAY (1812-1895). American. Reformed Dutch. Pas-
    tor of the Reformed Church at East Brooklyn, New York; at St.Paul's
    Reformed Protestant Dutch Church, New York; of the North Reformed
    Church, Brooklyn (1874). A joint editor of the Reformed Dutch se-
    lection of Hymns of the Church (1869) and Hymns of Prayer and Pra-
    ise (1871).

THOMPSON, WILL LAMARTINE (1847-1909). American.

THOMSON, JOHN (1782-1818). British. A physician of Leeds. Contributed
    three hymns to Robert Aspland's Psalms and Hymns for Unitarian Wor-
    ship (1810).

THOMSON, MARY ANN FAULKNER (1834-1923). British, American. Protestant
    Episcopal. Married to John Thomson, librarian of the Free Library
    of Philadelphia. Wrote in excess of forty-five congregational
    hymns.

THRELFALL, JEANNETTE (1821-1880). British. Church of England. A life-
    long invalid. Her hymns have been extracted from a volume of her
    published poems (1856, 1873).

THRING, GODFREY (1823-1903). British. Church of England. Curate of
    Stratfield-syae (1850-1853); rector of Alford-with-Hornblotton,
    Somerset (1858-1867); rural dean (1867-1876) and then prebend of
    East Harptree (1876-1893). Published Hymns Congregational and Oth-
    ers (1866); Hymns and Verses (1866); Hymns and Sacred Lyrics (1874);
    A Church of England Hymn Book (1880, 1882). Composed in excess of
    seventy-five hymns for congregational use.

THRUPP, DOROTHY ANN (1779-1847). British. Church of England. Edited
    Hymns for the Young (1830, 1836).

TILLETT, WILLIAM FISK (1854-1936). American. Methodist. Chaplain of Vanderbilt University; later professor and Dean of the theological faculty and Vice Chancellor of the University.

TINDLEY, CHARLES A. (1856-1933). American.

TIPLADY, THOMAS (b. 1882).

TISSERAND, JEAN (d. 1494).

TOKE, EMMA LESLIE (1812-1872). Irish. Church of Ireland. Contributed hymns to the Society for the Propagation of Christian Knowledge and to various Sunday school hymnals. Her fa ther, John Leslie, served as Bishop of Kilmore; in 1837 she wed the Rev. Nicholas Toke, Godington Park, Ashford, Kent.

TOPLADY, AUGUSTUS MONTAGUE (1740-1778). British. Church of England. Vicar of Broadhembury (1762-1775); minister of the Chapel of the French Calvinists, Leicester Fields, London (1775-1778). Published Psalms and Hymns (1776); Hymns and Sacred Poems. Edited The Gospel Magazine (1771-1776), which served as a forum for his attacks upon John Wesley and the Methodists.

TORREY, BRADFORD (1843-1912).

TUCKER, FRANCIS BLAND (1895-1984). American. Protestant Episcopal. Rector of Grammer Parish, Brunswick County, Virginia (1920-1925); rector of St. John's, Georgetown, Washington, D.C. (1925-1945);rector of Old Christ Church, Savannah, Georgia--John Wesley's church during his mission to the Georgia colony (1735-1736). Member of the Committee to revise (c. 1940) the Hymnal of the Protestant Episcopal Church.

TURNEY, EDWARD (1817-1872). American. Baptist. Pastor at Hartford, Connecticut; at Granville, Ohio (1842-1847); Professor of Biblical Criticism, Madison University (New York, 1850); Professor of Biblical Literature, Fairmount Theological Seminary, Cincinnati, Ohio (1853-1858). Published Baptismal Hymns (1862); Memorial Poems and Hymns (1864).

TUTTIETT, LAURENCE (1825-1897). British. Church of England. Vicar of Lea Marston, Warwickshire (1854-1870); incumbent of the Episcopal Church of St. Andrews, Scotland (1870-1880); prebendary of St. Ninian's Cathedral, Perth (1880-1897). Published Hymns for Churchmen (1854); Hymns for the Children of the Church (1862).

TWEEDY, HENRY HALLAM (1868-1953). American. Congregational. Pastor of the Plymouth Congregational Church, Utica, New York (1898-1902); pastor of the South Congregational Church, Bridgeport, Connecticut (1902-1909). Professor of Practical Divinity and Theology, Yale University Divinity School (1909-1937). Published The Minister and His Hymnal and edited Christian Worship and Praise (1939).

TWELLS, HENRY (1823-1900). British. Church of England. Curate of Great Berkhamsted (1849-1851); sub-vicar of Stratford-on-Avon from 1851 to 1854; master of St. Andrews House School, Mells, Somerset

(1854-1856); headmaster of Godolphin School, Hammersmith (1856-1870); rector of Baldock, Hertfordshire (1870); rector of Waltham-on-the-Wolds (1871-1873); select preacher at Cambridge (1873-1874); honorary canon of Peterborough Cathedral (1884); priest-in-charge of St. Augustine, Bournemouth (1890-1900). Assisted in the preparation of Hymns Ancient and Modern (1861) and served on the committee for the Appendix of 1889. His own Hymns and Other Stray Verses appeared in 1901.

TZU-CH'EN, CHAO (b. 1888). Chinese.


UHLER, GRACE ELMA. American. Methodist. Her "O gift of God, we praise Thee" dates from 1911.


VAN ALSTYNE, FRANCES JANE CROSBY (1820-1915). American. Methodist Episcopal. Blind from infancy. A teacher at the New York City Institution for the Blind (1847-1858). Married Alexander Van Alstyne, a blind musician, in 1858. Author of over six thousand hymn texts, she spent her later life in Bridgeport, Connecticut.

VAN DYKE, HENRY (1852-1933). American. Presbyterian. Pastor of the United Congregational Church, Newport, Rhode Island (1879-1883); pastor of the Brick Presbyterian Church, New York (1883-1900). Professor of English literature at Princeton University (1900-1923), where he held a chair especially endowed for him by alumni and named for Dean James Ormsbee Mirray (1827-1899)--the individual who had preceded Van Dyke as pastor of the Brick Presbyterian Church and as Professor of English at Princeton. Appointed by Woodrow Wilson as Minister to the Netherlands and Luxembourg (1913-1917). Author of the popular Christmas story, The Other Wise Man. Chairman of the committee for the composition of The Book of Common Worship of the Presbyterian Church (1906) and of the committee to revise that volume in 1932.

VICTORINUS, SANTOLIUS (1630-1697). French. One of the regular canons of St. Victor, at Paris. Distinguished as a writer of Latin poetry; his pieces appeared in the Clunic Breviary (1686) and the Paris Breviaries of 1680 and 1736. His Hymni Sacri et Novi appeared in Paris in 1689, with an enlarged edition published in 1698.

VOKES, MRS. (fl. 1797-1812). British. According to Julian, in his Dictionary of Hymnology (2:1226-1227), hymns by a "Mrs. Vokes" appeared in A Selection of Missionary and Devotional Hymns (1797), in a New Selection of Seven Hundred Evangelical Hymns (1806), in A Collection of Psalms and Hymns (1812).

VON CHRISTIERSON, FRANK (b. 1900). American. His "Break forth, O living light of God" appeared initially in Ten New Bible Hymns (New York: Hymn Society of America, 1952); another piece, "As men of old their first fruits brought," was published in Ten New Stewardship

_Hymns_ (New York: Hymn Society of America, 1961).

WALFORD, WILLIAM (1772-1850). British. A blind preacher, who wrote his noted "Sweet hour of prayer" in 1849.

WALKER, JOHN (1769-1833). Irish. Church of England, Independent ("Walkerite"). Initially a fellow of Trinity College, Dublin, and a clergyman of the Established Church; ex½elled from the University of Dublin in 1800, after which he originated his own "Church of God." Principally noted and remembered for his various editions of Livy's works.

WALLACE, JOHN AIKMAN (1802-1870). Scottish. Free Church of Scotland. Minister of the Free Church of Scotland at Hawick.

WALTER, HOWARD ARNOLD (1884-1918). American. Congregational. Teacher at missionary schools in Japan; secretary to the Y.M.C.A. in India.

WALWORTH, CLARENCE ALPHONSUS (1820-1900). American. Roman Catholic. Rector of St. Mary's, Albany, New York (1864-1900). One of the founders of the Order of the Paulists in the United States.

WARDLAW, RALPH (1779-1853). Scottish. Congregational. Minister of Albion Church, Glasgow. Professor of Divinity in the Congregational Theological Hall, Glasgow. Published A Selection of Hymns for Public Worship (1803).

WARE, HENRY THE YOUNGER (1794-1843). American. Unitarian. Assistant master at Exeter Academy, Exeter, New Hampshire (1812-1814). Pastor of the Second Church of Boston (1817-1829). Professor of Pulpit Eloquence and Pastoral Care, Cambridge Theological School (1829-1842). Edited The Christian Disciple (1813-1824).

WARING, ANNA LETITIA (1823-1910). Welsh. Church of England. Published Hymns and Meditations (1850, 1854, 1863), followed by Additional Hymns (1858).

WARNER, ANNA BARTLETT (1820-1915). American. Episcopal. Novelist; editor of Hymns of the Church Militant (1858) and Wayfaring Hymns, Original and Translated (1869).

WARREN, WILLIAM FAIRFIELD (1833-1929). American. Methodist. Professor of Systematic Theology at the Methodist Episcopal Mission Institute at Bremen, Germany (1861-1866). Appointed President of Boston University in 1873.

WATERBURY, JARED BELL (1799-1876). American. Congregational. Pastor at the Congregational Church, Hudson, New York; pastor at Bowdoin Street Congregational Church, Boston.

WATTS, ALARIC ALEXANDER (1797-1864). British. Editor of The Leeds Intelligencer, The Manchester Courier, The United Service Gazette. His hymns appeared in his Poetical Sketches (1822, 1824).

WATTS, ISAAC (1674-1748). British. Independent. Pastor of the Independent congregation at Mark Lane, London (1702-1712). Received the Doctor of Divinity degree from the University of Edinburgh in 1728. Wrote in excess of six hundred hymns and Psalm paraphrases, contained principally in Hymns and Spiritual Songs (1707), Divine and Moral Songs for the Use of Children (1715), The Psalms of David Imitated (1719). The originator of English congregational song as we have come to recognize and appreciate that form.

WEISSE, MICHAEL (c. 1480-1534). German. Roman Catholic, Bohemian Brethren. For some time a monk at Breslau; became a German preacher to the Bohemian Brethren at Landskron (Bohemia) and Fulnek (Moravia). Edited the first German hymn book of the Bohemian Brethren, Ein Neu Gesengbuchlen (1531).

WEISSEL, GEORG (1590-1635). German. Rector of the school at Friedland, near Domnau (1614-1617); pastor of the Altrossgart church at Konigsburg (1623-1635). One of the most important of the earlier hymn writers of Prussia; authored approximately twenty congregational hymns, principally in celebration of the Christian year.

WESLEY, CHARLES (1707-1788). British. Church of England. The youngest son and eighteenth child of Susanna and Samuel Wesley (see below, this section). Secretary to General James Oglethorpe in Savannah, Georgia (1735-1736). Active itinerancy in behalf of the Methodist societies from 1739 to 1756. Failing health forced him to take up residence in London and to supervise the work of the Methodist societies there. Authored upward of 8900 hymns--of which approximately three hundred have found their way into English congregational use. With his brother John (see immediately below), he published in excess of fifty separate volumes of hymnody.

WESLEY, JOHN (1703-1791). British. Church of England. Elected fellow of Lincoln College, Oxford (1726); assistant rector to his father at Epworth and Wroote, in Lincolnshire (1726-1727, 1727-1729); fellow of Lincoln College, Oxford (1729-1735). Parish priest of Savannah, Georgia (1735-1738). Active leadership of British Methodism from 1739 to 1791. Author of original hymns; translator of hymns from the German, Latin, and Greek; editor of hymn books for the Methodist societies.

WESLEY, SAMUEL THE ELDER (1662-1735). British. Church of England. Father of John, Charles, and Samuel Wesley (see this section). Held curacies in and near London, and also served as a chaplain in the Royal Navy. Vicar of South Ormsby, Lincolnshire, and chaplain to the Marquis of Normanby (1693-1697). Rector of Epworth and Wroot, Lincolnshire (1697-1735). In addition to to his hymns, he deserves some attention as a minor writer of religious and occasional verse, as will as a minor Biblical translator.

WESLEY, SAMUEL THE YOUNGER (1691-1739). British. Church of England. The eldest child of Susanna and Samuel Wesley (see immediately above); the brother of John and Charles Wesley (see above, this section). Usher at Westminster School; headmaster of the Free School at Tiverton (1732-1739). Published A Collection of Poems (1736), from which his hymns have been extracted and adapted to public worship.

WEST, ROBERT ATHOW (1802-1865). British, American. Methodist Episcopal. Official reporter of the General Conference of the Methodist Episcopal Church (1844). Edited Hymns for the Use of the Methodist Episcopal Church (1849).

WHITE, HENRY KIRKE (1785-1806). British. Church of England. Studied law with a Nottingham firm; independently pursued Latin, Greek, the modern languages, music, and drawing. Entered St. John's College, Cambridge (1804), to prepare for Holy Orders; died there two years later after having fallen ill from excessive study and attacks of consumption. Published Clifton Grove, and Other Poems (1803). Attracted the attention of Robert Southey and the praise of Lord Byron, but little survives of his literary labors except the hymns.

WHITFIELD, FREDERICK (1829-1904). British. Church of England. Curate of Otley; vicar of Kirby-Ravensworth; senior curate of Greenwich; vicar of St. John's, Bexley; preferred curate of St. Mary's, Hastings. His hymns appeared in his own Sacred Poems and Prose (1861, 1864).

WHITING, WILLIAM (1825-1878). British. Church of England. Master of the Winchester College Choristers' School and author of Rural Thoughts (1851).

WHITTIER, JOHN GREENLEAF (1807-1892). American. Society of Friends. At least fifty hymns of this major American poet may be found in modern and contemporary British and American hymnals; most of those pieces constitute adaptations from longer poems. His Quaker background led him from farming to poetry, from abolitionism to pacifism.

WHITTLE, DANIEL W. American. Held the rank of major in the United States Army. Published his hymns under the pseudonym of "El Nathan."

WIANT, BLISS (b. 1895). American.

WIGNER, JOHN MURCH (b. 1844). British. Baptist. Connected with the India Home Civil Service. Contributed hymns to the Baptist Psalms and Hymns for School and Home (1880, 1882).

WILBERFORCE, REV. ERNEST ROLAND (b. 1840).

WILE, FRANCES WHITMARSH (1875-1939). American.

WILLIAMS, BENJAMIN (1725-1795). British. Presbyterian. Ministered to a Presbyterian congregation at Salisbury. Published a volume of Sermons (1770); edited The Salisbury Hymn Book (1778), The Book of Psalms as Translated, Paraphrased or Imitated by Some of the Most Eminent English Poets (1781).

WILLIAMS, HELEN MARIA (1762-1827). British. Published her Poems in two volumes (1786, 1791). Resided in Paris during the French Revolution and engaged in political prose writings there--which had a negative effect upon her personal and literary reputation. Afterward she moved to Amsterdam. Her hymns have been especially popular among Unitarian congregations in England and America.

WILLIAMS, THEODORE CHICKERING (1855-1915). American. Unitarian. Minister of All Souls' Church, New York (1883-1896). Headmaster of Hackley School, Tarrytown, New York, from its founding in 1899 until 1905.

WILLIAMS, WILLIAM (1717-1791). Welsh. Established Church of Engalnd. Curate of Llanwrtyd and Llanddewi-Abergwesyn. Composed over eight hundred hymns in Welsh and over one hundred others in English. He spent the least thirty-five years of his life as an itinerant preacher, principally for the Welsh Calvinistic Methodist Connexion led by the Rev. Howell Harris--a rival of John Wesley. Published Alleluia (1745-1747), his first book of Welsh hymns, printed in six parts at Bristol.

WILLIS, LOVE MARIA WHITCOMB (1824-1908). American. Married to an upstate New York physician; contributed hymns to popular periodicals.

WILLIS, NATHANIEL PARKER (1807-1867). American. Unitarian. Wrote for The American Monthly magazine and then The New York Mirror. Attached to the American legation at the French court (1831-1837). An editor of The Corsair and the author of Sacred Poems (1843).

WILLS, WHITFIELD GLANVILLE (1841-1891). British. Published Hymns for Occasional Use (1881).

WILSON, LUCY ATKINS (1802-1863). British. Church of England. The wife of the Rev. Daniel Wilson, vicar of Islington. Author of The Memoirs of John Frederic Oberlin (1829).

WINCHESTER, CALEB THOMAS (1847-1920). American. Methodist. Professor of Rhetoric and English Literature at Wesleyan University, Middletown, Connecticut. Participated in the compiliations of the Methodist hymnals of 1889 and 1905; published The Life of John Wesley (1906); respected literary scholar and literary historian.

WINKLER, REV. JOHANN JOSEPH (1670-1722).

WINKWORTH, CATHERINE (1827-1878). British. Church of England. Resided near Manchester, then Clifton (Bristol). Published Lyrica Germanica (1855, 1858); The Choral Book for England (1863). Assumed an active roll in the Clifton Association for the Higher Education of Women. Certainly one of the foremost translators of hymn texts during the mid-nineteenth century.

WITTER, WILL ELLSWORTH (b. 1854). American. Baptist.

WOLCOTT, SAMUEL (1813-1886). American. Congregational. A missionary in Syria (1840-1842). Pastor of Congregational churches at Belchestown, Massachusetts; at Providence, Rhode Island; at Chicago and Cleveland. Secretary of the Ohio Home Missionary Society. Author of more than two hundred congregational hymns.

WOODHULL, ALFRED ALEXANDER (1810-1836). American. Presbyterian. Practiced medicine at Princeton, New Jersey.

WORDSWORTH, CHRISTOPHER (1807-1885). British. Church of England. Headmaster of Harrow School (1836-1844). Canon of Westminster (1844-1848); Hulsean lecturer at Cambridge (1848-1849). Vicar of Stanford-in-the-Vale cum Goosey, Berkshire ((1850-1869). Bishop of Lincoln (1869-1885). Nephew of the poet and Poet Laureate, William Wordsworth. Published upward of a dozen volumes of prose and verse, including The Holy Year (1862)--a work that contains over fifty of his hymns.

WORK, JOHN W. (b. 1901). American. His "Go, tell it on the mountain" dates from 1940.

WRANGHAM, WILLIAM (d. 1832). British, Methodist. A tradesman in the town of Louth, Lincolnshire. Published New Methodist Version of the Psalms (1829).

WRERFORD, JOHN REYNELL (1800-1881). British. Unitarian. Co-pastor of the New Meeting, Birmingham (1826-1831). Opened a school at Edgbaston in 1831.

YIN-LAN, SU (1915-1937). Chinese.

YOUNG, JOHN F. (1820-1885).

ZINZENDORF, NICOLAUS LUDWIG VON (1700-1760). German. Moravian. The leader of the German Moravians at Herrnhut, as well as that denomination's most prolific hymn writer. He edited collections of Moravian hymnody, published between 1725 and 1760.

# THE HYMN-TUNE
# COMPOSERS
# AND ARRANGERS

ABBEY, ALONZO JUDSON (1825-1887).

ABT, FRANZ (1819-1885). German. Court conductor at Bernburg, Zurich, and Brunswick. Visited America in 1872. Gained a reputation as a writer of popular songs; wrote seven secular cantatas and numerous choruses.

ADCOCK, JOHN (1838-1919).

AHLE, JOHANN RUDOLF (1625-1673). German. Educated at Gottingen and Erfurt. Appointed (1646) cantor at St. Andreas's Church; director of the music school at Erfurt. Appointed organist of St. Blasius's Church, Muhlhausen, in 1649. Cultivated the simple style of the chorale, avoiding polyphonic counterpoint.

ALLEN, CHESTER G. (1838-1878).

ALLEN, GEORGE NELSON (1812-1877). American. A pupil of Lowell Mason (see below, this section) and a graduate (1838) of the Oberlin Conservatory; instructor in music at Oberlin (1838-1841); Professor of Sacred Music at Oberlin (1841-1864). Organized the Oberlin College chorus and orchestra, preparing the way for the noted Oberlin Conservatory of Music (founded 1865). Compiled his own collection, The Social and Sabbath Hymn Book (1849).

AMBROSE, ROBERT (1824-1908). American. Resident of Hamilton, New York, where he taught piano in the public schools and at the Collegiate Institute.

AMPS, WILLIAM (1824-1910). British. Conductor of the Cambridge University Musical Society. Organist of King's College, Cambridge (1855-1876).

ANDERSON, WILLIAM KETCHAM (b. 1888). American. His hymn tune, "Journey's End," dates from 1935.

ARNE, THOMAS AUGUSTUS (1710-1778). British. Became composer to Drury Lane Theatre in 1738, then composer to all of the principal London theatres. Considered the major composer of the eighteenth century, particularly noted for his songs. Also composed oratorios--airs from which have been adapted as hymn tunes.

ASHFORD, EMMA LOUISE (b. 1850).

ATKINSON, FREDERICK COOK (1841-1897).

AVISON, CHARLES (1710-1770). British. Organist of the Church of St. Nicholas, Newcastle-upon-Tyne (1736-1770). Published An Essay on Musical Expression (1752); edited, with John Garth, a version of Benedetto Marcello's Psalms, Adapted to English (1757).

BACH, CARL PHILIPP EMMANUEL (1714-1788). German. Son of Johann Sebastian Bach (see immediately below). Studied law and philosophy at Leipzig and Frankfurt; conducted a singing society at Frankfurt (1737-1738); chamber musician and claveanist to Frederick the Great (1746-1757); church music director at Hamburg (1757-1788). One of the principal virtuosos of the age; the founder of the so-called "modern school" of piano playing.

BACH, JOHANN SEBASTIAN (1685-1750). German. Cantor of the Thomas Shule at Leipzig (1723-1750); director of the music in the two principal churches at Leipzig. Considered "the father of modern music." His oratorios, church cantatas, and organ music rely heavily upon the old German chorales.

BAKER, SIR HENRY WILLIAMS. See in Section B above.

BARING-GOULD, SABINE. See in Section B above.

BAMBRIDGE, WILLIAM SAMUEL (1842-1923).

BARNARD, CHARLOTTE ALINGTON (1830-1869). British. Known by the pseudonymn of "Claribel." A composer of popular songs and ballads be-1858 and 1869. Published Thoughts, Verses, and Songs.

BARNBY, JOSEPH (1838-1896). British. Chorister at York Minster; organist at St. Andrew's, Wells Street, London (1863-1871); organist at St. Anne's, Soho, and at Eton. Conducted the first performance in an English church of J.S. Bach's St. Matthew Passion--at Westminster Abbey on Maundy Thursday, 1871. Conductor of the Royal Albert Hall Choral Society. Musical editor of The Hymnary (1872).

BARTHELEMON, FRANCOIS HIPPOLYTE (1741-1808). French. Composer and violinist. First visited England in 1765; eventually settled and died there. Composed for the theatre and public gardens, but produced church music only on rare occasions.

BARTLETT, MARIO LUMMIS (1847-1919). American. Studied at Oberlin College. Conducted choral societies in Meadville, Pennsylvania, and at Newark, New Jersey; taught public school at Newark and New York City. Appointed to the head of the Department of Music at Drake University in 1889.

BASSFORD, WILLIAM KIPP (1839-1902). American. Studied piano under Samuel Jackson. Eventually settled in New York as an organist and music teacher. He last served as organist of Calvary Church, East Orange, New Jersey.

BAUM, JOHN WESLEY (b. 1862).

BEETHOVEN, LUDWIG VAN (1770-1827). German. Spent his early years in
Bonn and Cologne; resided in Vienna from 1792 until his death. The
"Ode to Joy" hymn tune comes from the choral finale of the Symphony
No. 9 (the words from Schiller's "Hymn to Joy"). Composed two mas-
ses, one oratorio, one cantata.

BENNARD, GEORGE. See in Section B above.

BERGGREEN, ANTON (or ANDREAS) PETER (1801-1880). Danish. Composer of
operas and cantatas; best known for his national songs and his compositions for the church. Published a collection of psalm tunes in
1853. Organist to the Church of the Trinity, Copenhagen (1838-
1880); professor of voice at the Metropolitan School, Copenhagen
(1843-1880). Appointed, in 1859, inspector of the Danish public
singing schools.

BISHOP, HENRY ROWLEY (1786-1855). British. Composer and conductor at
Covent Garden, London (1810-1811); musical director at Vauxhall,
London (1825-1830); professor of music at Edinburgh (1841-1843);
professor of music at Oxford (1848-1855). One of the original members of the Philharmonic Society, founded in 1813.

BLACK, REV. JOHN (1817-1871).

BLANCHARD, WILLIAM GODWIN (b. 1905). American.

BLISS, PHILIP PAUL. See in Section B above.

BLUMENTHAL, JACOB (1829-1908). German, British. Born in Hamburg; came
to London in 1848; died at Chelsea. A composer of songs that gained popularity throughout England. A pianist to Queen Victoria and
a fashionable teacher of piano.

BOND, HUGH (d. 1792). British. Lay vicar of Exeter Cathedral (1762-
1792) and organist of the Church of St. Mary the Arches, Exeter.
Published Twelve Hymns and Four Anthems for Four Voices.

BOOTH, JOSIAH (1852-1930). British. Organist at the Wesley Chapel at
Bambury; student at the Royal Academy of Music; organist at Park
Chapel, Crouch End, London. Edited the music for the chants and
anthems for The Congregational Church Hymnal (1887); principal musical adviser for The Congregational Hymnary (1916).

BORTNIANSKY, DIMITRI STEPANOVICH (1751-1825). Russian. Studied harpsichord and organ under Baldassare Galuppi (1706-1785) at Venice and
at St. Petersburg. Director of the Imperial Choir at St. Petersburg, where he exercised significant influence upon Russian church
music.

BOST, PAUL AMI ISAAC (1790-1874).

BOURGEOIS, LOUIS (1510-1561). French. A parisian musician noted for
his direction of music at Geneva between 1541 and 1557; rearranged
and composed melodies for the Genevan Psalter, which owes its musical excellence to him. Issued, for private use, two books of
settings of those psalms in four parts (1547).

BOYCE, WILLIAM (1710-1779). British. Chorister of St. Paul's, London; composer and one of the organists of the Chapel Royal; composed oratorios, odes, and church music pieces. When his hearing failed, he devoted his energies to collecting and editing older English church music. His Cathedral Music collection appeared between 1760 and 1778.

BOYD, WILLIAM (1847-1928). British. Educated at Hurstpierpont; choral scholar of Worcester College, Oxford. Took Holy Orders in 1877. Vicar of All Saints, Norfolk Square, London, from 1893.

BRADBURY, WILLIAM BATCHELDER (1816-1868). American. Student of Sumner Hill and Lowell Mason (see below, this section). Taught singing classes at Machias, Maine, and St. John's, New Brunswick. Organist at the Baptist Tabernacle, New York City; organist at the Baptist Church, Brooklyn, New York; Organized, at New York, singing classes for children, juvenile music festivals, classes, and conventions. Published The Young Choir (1841), The Jubilee (1858), Fresh Laurels; wrote two Sunday school cantatas--Daniel (1853) and Esther (1856).

BRAHAMS, JOHANNES (1833-1897). German, Austrian. Conductor to the Prince of Lippe-Detmold; retired for study at Hamburg (1858-1862); conductor of the Singakademie, Vienna (1863-1864). Ignored a Mus. Doc. degree from Cambridge (1877); accepted at Doc. Phil. degree from Breslau (1881); Knight of the Prussian Order of Merit (1886). An acknowledged master of every form of music composition (except opera).

BRIDGE, JOHN FREDERICK (1844-1924). British. Chorister at Rochester Cathedral; organist at Westminster Abbey, from 1882. Succeeded Sir Joseph Barnby (see above, this section) as conductor of the Royal Albert Hall Choral Society. Gresham Professor of Music (appointed 1890); Professor of Music, London University (appointed in 1902).

BROWNE, MARY ANNE (1822-1844).

BUCKINGHAM, JOHN DUNCAN (b. 1855).

BULLINGER, ETHELBERT WILLIAM (1837-1913).

BUNNETT, EDWARD (1835-1923). British. Norwich city organist, St. Andrew's Hall, from 1880; assistant organist, Norwich Cathedral; organist of St. Peter's Moncroft, Norwich (from 1908). His Magnificat and Nunc Dimittis in F (1867) became the most popular pieces of church music in the smaller parishes throughout England.

BURDER, GEORGE. See in Section B above).

BURDETT, GEORGE ALBERT (b. 1856). American. Graduated from Harvard in 1881; studied music in Boston; studied further in Hanover and Berlin; settled in Boston as church organist, principally at the New Old South Church. Organist; choir director; composer of church music, songs, piano pieces.

BURGMULLER, FRIEDRICH (1806-1874).  German.  Elder brother of the composer Norbert Burgmuller (1810-1836).  Wrote mainly pianoforte pieces
intended primarily for children.

BURNAP, UZZIAH CHRISTOPHER (1834=1900).

BURNEY, CHARLES (1726-1814).  British.  One of the most noted pre-nine-
teenth-century musical historians, and certainly an eminent figure
of his day.  Studied with his brother, James, at Shrewsbury, then
with Thomas Augustus Arne (see above, this section) in London.  Organist of St. Dionis-Backchurch, Fenchurch Street, London (1749-
1751); organist of Lyn-Reg is, Norfolk (1751-1760).  Returned to
London in 1760; Bachelor and then Doctor of Music, Oxford (1769);
elected a Fellow of the Royal Society in 1773.  Published his celebrated History of Music (1767-1789).  Appointed organist of Chelsea
College in 1783.

BURROWES, JOHN FRECKLETON (1787-1852).  British.  Composer and organist;
a pupil of Wilbur Horsley; an original member of the Philharmonic
Society.  For nearly forty years he held the post of organist at
St. James' Church, Picadilly, London.

BURT, BATES G. (1878-1948).

CALDBECK, GEORGE THOMAS (1852-1912).  British.  Studied music at Islington Training College; later taught music in Ireland.

CALDICOTT, ALFRED JAMES (1842-1897).  British.  Organist at St. Stephen's
Church, Worcester; corporation organist of Worcester; appointed professor of music at the Royal Music College of London (1883); conductor at the Albert Palace (1885-1897).

CALDWELL, WILLIAM (b. 1830).

CALKIN, JOHN BAPTISTE (1827-1905).  British.  Pianist, organist, composer.  Professor of Music at the Guildhall School of Music, London.

CALLCOTT, WILLIAM HUTCHINS (1807-1882).  British.  Younger son of the
coted songwriter, John Wall Callcott (1766-1821).  Attained distinc-
tion as an organist, pianist, composer, and arranger.

CAMP, HARVEY CLARK (b. 1849).

CAMP, JOHN SPENCER (1858-1946).  American.  Organist at the Park Congregational Church, Hartford, Connecticut (1882-1906); at the First
Congregational Church, Hartford, Connecticut (1906-1918).  Conductor
of the Hartford Philharmonic Orchestra (1902-1911).  A founder of
the American Guild of Organists (1896); president of the Connecticut
Music Teachers' Association (1898); treasurer of the Austin Organ
Company, Hartford.

CANNING, THOMAS (b. 1911).

CAREY, HENRY (1692-1743). British. A prolific writer of burlesques, farces, ballad operas, vivacious songs and poems; particularly remembered for one song, "Sally in our alley." Only incidentally did he write music for the church. The authorship of "God Save the King" (or the National Anthem) has been attributed to him, but without strong foundation.

CARR, BENJAMIN (1768-1831). American. Established music shops in New York and Philadelphia; printed the first edition of "Yankee Doodle" and the initial imprint of "Hail Columbia." Singer, actor, organist, arranger, pianist, concert manager, composer. Editor of The Musical Journal.

CARTER, EDMUND SARDINSON (b. 1845).

CARTER, OLEN LESTER (b. 1853).

CARTER, R. KELSO (1849-1926).

CHANDLER, S. (fl. 1790). Supposed author of the hymn tune "Ganges," which accompanies Charles Wesley's "Come on, my partners in distress" and Sir Robert Grant's "Thy mercy heard my infant prayer," in HMEC-657, 658.

CHADWICK, GEORGE WHITEFIELD (1854-1931). American. Head of the Music Department, Olivet (Michigan) College (1876); organist at Boston and teacher of harmony, composition, and instrumentation at the New England Conservatory (1880-1897); director of the New England Conservatory (1897-1931). Conductor of the Worcester Music Festival (1897-1902).

CHALLINOR, FREDERIC ARTHUR (1866-1952).

CHAPIN, AMZI (1768-1835). American.

CHASE, CHARLES CLINTON (1843-1918). American. A pupil of George Frederick Root (see in Section B, above). Compiler of evangelistic church music books--among them Church Anthems, The Harvest of Song, Case's Chorus Collection.

CHETHAM, JOHN (1700-1763). British. Schoolmaster and curate at Skipton (1725-1737). Edited A Book of Psalmody, All Set in Four Parts, published in 1718--a work that remained popular for over a century and a half.

CHOPE, RICHARD ROBERT (1830-1907). British. Curate of Stapleton (1856-1858); curate of Sherborne, Dorset (1858-1859); curate of Upton Scudamore (1859-1861); curate of Brompton (1861-1907). Published The Congregational Hymn and Tune Book (1857, enlarged 1862); The Canticles, Psalter. . .of the Prayer Book, Noted and Pointed (1862), Carols for Use in Church during Christmas and Epiphany (1875), Carols for Easter and Other Tides (1887). Trained the chorus of the Warmisnter district for the first choral festival in Salisbury Cathedral (1859). One of the originators of The Choir and Musical Record; the proprietor and assistant editor of the Literary Churchman.

CLARK, THOMAS (1775-1859). British. A cobbler by trade; a musician by talent. A leader of psalmody in the Wesleyan Church, Canterbury; led psalmody at a Unitarian congregation that worshiped in a dilapidated monestary of the Blackfriars. A prolific composer of hymn tunes, publishing in excess of twenty sets of them. Reharmonized the second edition of The Union Tune Book (1842) for the Sunday School Union.

CLARKE, JEREMIAH (1670-1707). British. A chorister of the Chapel Royal under Dr. John Blow (1649-1708); organist of Winchester College (1692-1695); organist of St. Paul's (1695-1705); vicar choral of St. Paul's (1705-1707); joint organist, with William Croft (see below, this section), of the Chapel Royal (1704-1707). Undoubtedly officiated at Father Smith's Great Organ at the opening of St. Paul's Cathedral, 2 December 1697. Wrote anthems, psalm tunes, operatic music, songs; John Gay adapted one of his pieces for The Beggar's Opera.

CLARKE, JOHN (1770-1836). British. Organist of the parish church of Ludlow (1789-1793); master of the choristers at St. Patrick's Cathedral and Christ Church, Dublin (1793-1794); organist of Armagh Cathedral (1794-1797); organist and master of the choristers of Trinity and St. John's Colleges, Cambridge (1799-1820); organist and minister of the choristers of Hereford Cathedral (1820-1832); professor of music, University of Cambridge (1821-1832).

COLE, I.P. The editors of HMEC assign the hymn tune entitled, simply, "Melody," to I.P. Cole; it accompanies Anne Steele's "Father of mercies, in Thy word" (299), Harriet Auber's "Bright was the guiding star that led" (300), and John Cawood's "Almighty God, Thy word is cast" (301).

COLE, JOHN (1774-1855). American. Born in Tewksbury, England; came to America in 1785 and settled in Baltimore. Musician, music publisher, composer. Leader of a regimental band known as "The Independent Blues" that played during the War of 1812. Published Episcopalian Harmony (1800, 1811), A Collection of Anthems (n.d.), A Collection of Psalm Tunes (1803), The Beauties of Psalmody (1805, 1827), The Divine Harmonist (1808), Ecclesiastical Harmony (1810), Minstrel Songs (1812), Devotional Harmony (1814), Songs of Zion (1818), Seraph (1821, 1827), Sacred Melodies (1828), Union Harmony (1829), Laudate Dominum (1842, 1847).

COLES, GEORGE (1792-1858). American. Born in Stewkley, England; died in New York City. Editor of The New York Christian Advocate and The Sunday School Advocate.

CONKEY, ITHMAR (1815-1867). American. A noted bass singer with the choir of Calvary Church, New York City.

CONVERSE, CHARLES CROZAT (1832-1918). American. Studied music in Germany; graduated from the Albany Law School (1861). Practiced law in Erie, Pennsylvania; a partner in the Burdette Organ Company. Composed hymn tunes, symphonies, oratorios. Often wrote under the name of "Karl Reden."

COOKE, WILLIAM HENRY (1820-1912).

COOMBS, WILLIAM (fl. 1770). Assigned, by the editors of HMEC, authorship of the hymn tune "Oxford," which accompanied Nahum Tate's "O
God, we praise Thee, and confess" (120), Charles Wesley's "Hail,
Father, Son, and Holy Ghost" (121), and Amelia Opie's "There seems
a voice in every gale" (122).

COPES, V.EARLE (b. 1921).

CORBEIL, PIERRE DE (d. 1222). French. Consecrated Bishop of Cambrai
in 1199; became Archbishop of Sens in 1200.

CORNELL, JOHN HENRY (1828-1894). American. Organist at St. John's
Chapel, New York (1848-1868); organist at St. Paul's Chapel, Trinity Parish, New York (1868-1877); organist at the Brick Presbyterian Church, New York (1877-1882). A trained composer of church
music. Published A Manual of Roman Chant (1871), The Introit
Psalms (1871), The Congregational Tune Book (1875).

COSTER, ARTHUR VENNELL (1864-1931).

COTTMAN, ARTHUR (1842-1879).

CROFT, WILLIAM (1678-1879). British. Organist of St. Anne's, Soho,
and gentleman extraordinary of the Chapel Royal (1700); joint organist, with Jeremiah Clarke (see above, this section), of the Chapel Royal (1704); organist of the Chapel Royal (1707); organist of
Westminster Abbey and composer to the Chapel Royal (1708). Began
by writing songs for the theatre, sonatas, and odes; then concen-
trated upon sacred music and became one of the most significant
contributors to English sacred music. Provided the earliest exam-
ples of the English psalm tune, as distinguished from the Genevan
version. Published Divine Harmony and Musica Sacra.

CROSS, MOSES SMITH (1854-1911).

CROTCH, WILLIAM (1775-1847). British. A child prodigy: began to play
the organ at two years of age; composed an oratorio, The Captivity of Judah, at age fourteen. Organist of Christ Church, Oxford
(1790); Professor of Music at Oxford (1797), at age twenty-two.
The first principal of the Royal Academy of Music, London (1823-
1832). Wrote anthems and chants; his oratorio, Palestine, suppo-
sedly his most notable music schievement.

CRUGER, JOHANN (1598-1662). German. Tutor, at Berlin, in the family
of Colonel Christoph von Blumenthal (1615-1620). Cantor of the
Cathedral Church of St. Nicholas, Berlin (1622-1662), where he
founded its celebrated choir. Composed chorales; published motets,
concertos, and a collection of magnificats. The chorales appeared
in his Praxis Pietatis Melica (1644).

CUTHBERT, ELIZABETH HOWARD (1800-1857).

CUTLER, HENRY STEPHEN (1825-1902). American. Organist at the Church
of the Advent, Boston (1852-1858); organist at Trinity Church, New

York (1858-1865); organist at churches in New York, Brooklyn, Providence, Philadelphia, and Troy (New York). Received the Mus. D. degree from Columbia University in 1864.

CUTTS, PETER (b. 1937).

DANKS, HART PEASE (1834-1903). American. A church singer dating from about 1850, principally in Chicago, where he also engaged in the composition of hymn tunes and popular songs. In addition, he composed anthems and at least one operetta.

DARLEY, W.H.W. (1801-1872). American. Edited, with J.H.C. Stanbridge, a tune book entitled Cantus Ecclesiae (Philadelphia, 1844).

DARWALL, JOHN (1731-1789). British. First curate, and then (1769-1789) vicar, of Walsall, Staffordshire. Wrote hymns and poetical pieces; an enthusiastic amateur musician. Composed a tune for each of the 150 metrical psalms, written in two parts only--treble and bass. Published two volumes of pianoforte sonatas, A Christmas Hymn and Tune, A Charity Hymn and Tune, and A Hymn.

DAVIES, HENRY WALFORD (1869-1941). British. Assistant organist at St. George's, Windsor (1885-1890); teacher of counterpoint, Royal College of Music (1895); conductor, London Church Association (1901-1913); conductor, London Bach Choir (1903-1907); organist of the Temple Church (1890-1919); Professor of Music, University College of Wales, Aberystwyth (1919-1941); Gresham Professor of Music (1924); organist of St. George's, Windsor, and master of the music to the King (1927); Master of the King's Music (1934); co-editor of The Church Anthem Book (1933); edited The Fellowship Song Book, Fifty-Two Hymn Tunes, Hymns of the Kingdom, A Student's Hymnal. Authored Music and Christian Worship.

DAVIS, G. (1770-1816).

DAVIS, MICHAEL (fl. 1848).

DEARLE, EDWARD (1806-1891).

DECIUS, NICOLAUS (1490-1541). German. Probst of the cloister at Steterburg (1519-1522); master in the St. Katherine and Egidien School at Brunswick (1522-1523); evangelical preacher at Stettin (1523-1535); pastor of St. Nicholas's, Stettin (1535-1541). Composed and adapted melodies to his own hymn compositions.

DICKINSON, CHARLES JOHN (1822-1883).

DOANE, WILLIAM HOWARD (1832-1915). American. Principally a manufacturer of woodworking machinery. From 1862, he emerged as one of the more prominent writers of gospel hymns. Denison University conferred upon him the degree of Mus. D. in 1875.

DOUGLAS, CHARLES WINFRED (1867-1944). American. Assistant organist at

St. Paul's Cathedral, Syracuse, New York (1889-1891); organist at Zion and St. Timothy's Churches, New York (1892-1893); minor canon and assistant organist, St. John's Cathedral, Denver, Colorado (1894-1897); canon preceptor at St. Paul's Cathedral, Fon du Lac, Wisconsin (1907-1910); instructor in plain-chant, General Theological Seminary, New York (1914-1916); appointed director of music for the Sisterhood of St. Mary (1907). Published Plain-Song (1909), Recent Contributions to the Philosophy of Music (1911), The History and Work of the Schola Cantorum (1913); edited the music for the Protestant Episcopal Hymnal (1919); edited Songs for the Church (1921), A Capella Choruses from the Russian Liturgy, and--with Kurt Schindler--Old Spanish Motets.

DOWNES, LEWIS THOMAS (1827-1907).

DRESE, ADAM (1620-1701). German. Kapelmeister to Duke Wilhelm IV of Weimar; secretary to Duke Bernhard (1662-1672); town mayor of Jena (appointed 1672). His hymns originally sung at Pietist meetings. The position of musical director at Arnstadt proved his final appointment.

DRESSLER, WILLIAM (b. 1826).

DUCKWORTH, FRANCIS (1862-1941).

DUNHAM, HENRY MORTON (1853-1929). American. Teacher of organ, New England Conservatory, from 1878; also taught music at Boston University; music director, Lasell Seminary, Auburndale, New York. Organist of the Porter Congregational Church, Brockton, Massachusetts (1873-1883); organist of the Ruggles Street Baptist Church, Boston (1883-1896); organist of the Shawmut Congregational Church (1896-1906); organist of the Harvard Congregational Church, Brookline, Massachusetts (1906-1911).

D'URHAN, CRETIEN (1790-1845). French. Violinist and composer. A pupil of Jean Francois LeSueur (1760-1837). Joined the Paris Opera orchestra in 1816, and became its leader in 1831.

DUTTON, DEODATUS, JR. (1808-1832). American. Edited, with Elam Ives, Jr. (see below, this section), a Hartford collection, American Psalmody (1829, 1830).

DYER, SAMUEL (1785-1835). American. Edited New Selection of Sacred Music (Baltimore, 1817), Selection of Anethems (Baltimore, 1817), Philadelphia Selection of Sacred Music (1828).

DYKES, JOHN BACCHUS (1823-1876). British. Took Holy Orders in 1847; curate of Malton, Yorkshire (1847-1849); minor canon and precentor of Durham Cathedral (1849-1862); vicar of St. Oswald, Durham (1862-1876). Conductor of the Cambridge University Musical Society; M.A. Cambridge; Doctor of Music, University of Durham; active in the compilation of Hymns Ancient and Modern (1861). Wrote approximately three hundred hymn tunes.

EBELING, JOHANN GEORG (1637-1676).  German.  Succeeded (1662) Johann
    Cruger (see above, this section) as cantor of St. Nicholaus Church,
    Berlin, and as associate director of music at the College of St.
    Charles (Carolinen Gymnasium), Stettin.  Published Archaeologiae
    Orphicae, sive antiquitates Musicae (1675); Pauli Gerhardi Geist-
    liche Andachten, bestenhend in 120 Liedern mit 6 Singstimmen, 2
    violinen und general-bass (1666-1667).

EDSON, LEWIS (1748-1820).  American.  Assisted Lewis and Thaddeus Sey-
    mour in the publication of The New York Selection of Sacred Music
    (New York, 1809, 1816).

EDWARDS, RICHARD (1797-1862).

ELLIOTT, JAMES WILLIAM (1833-1915).  British.  Organist of Leamington
    Chapel and to the Earl of Wilton at Heaton Hall; organist to the
    Parish Church, Banbury, as well as at the following: St. Mary Bol-
    ton's, Brompton; All Saints' Church, St. John's Wood; St. Mark's,
    Hamilton Terrace--where he served for thirty-six years.  Active in
    the preparation of the musical edition of Church Hymns (1874).

ELLOR, JAMES (1819-1899).

ELVEY, GEORGE JOB (1816-1893).  British.  Chorister of Canterbury Cathe-
    dral under the noted organist Highmore Skeats.  Organist of St.
    George's Chapel, Windsor (1835-1882); conducted the Windsor and Ea-
    ton Choral Society, as well as the Glee and Madrigal Society.  En-
    gaged, principally, in the composition of anthems for thr Church.

EMERSON, LUTHER ORLANDO (1820-1915).  American.  Active as a composer,
    from about 1840, at Salem, Boston, and Greenfield (Massachusetts).
    Published various tune books between 1853 and 1915--the most noted
    being his Romberg Collection (Boston, 1853).

ETT, KASPAR (1788-1847).  German.  Court musician and composer.

EVERETT, ASA BROOKS (1828-1875).  American.  A Virginian who studied mu-
    sic in Boston and Leipzig; organized--with his brother, L.C. Eve-
    rett (see immediately below, this section)--a system of normal in-
    struction at Richmond, Virginia.

EVERETT, L.C. (1818-1867).  American.  Elder brother of Asa Brooks Eve-
    rett (see immediately above, this section).  Studied in Boston and,
    with his brother, organized a system of normal instruction at Rich-
    mond, Virginia, which existed as a "rival" to that institution be-
    gun in Boston and New York by Lowell Mason (see below, this sec-
    tion).

EWING, ALEXANDER (1830-1895).  British.  Entered the British Army after
    completing formal studies for the law.  Married, in 1867, the popu-
    lar writer, Juliana H. Gatty.

EXCELL, EDWIN OTHELLO (1851-1921).  American.  Composer, writer, and
    publisher of gospel and Sunday school songs and song books.

FERRETTI, SALVATORE (1817-1874). Italian. Lived, for a time, in England, where he edited a journal entitled L'Eco di Savonarola; published Inni e Salmi ad uso dei Cristiani d'Italia (London, 1850). Afterward returned to Florence, where he established a Protestant orphanage.

FILBY, WILLIAM CHARLES (b. 1836).

FINK, GOTTFRIED WILHELM (1783-1846). German. Theologian and music critic. Editor of the Allegemeine Musikalische Zeitung (1827-1841). Professor of Music at the University of Leipzig (1842).

FINLAY, KENNETH GEORGE (1882-1974). Scottish. A member of the Institute of Naval Architecture and an amateur musician. Contributed tunes to The Missionary Hymn Book; taught singing at Irvine, Ayrshire; composed two cantatas: The Saviour's Birth (1928), Before the Dawn (1938).

FISCHER, WILLIAM GUSTAVUS (1835-1912). American. A Philadelphia bookbinder, music teacher, and choral director. Taught music at Gerard College; spent thirty years as a piano dealer (1868-1898).

FLEMMING, FRIEDRICH FERDINAND (1778-1813). German. Studied medicine at Wittenberg (1796-1800); further medical studies at Jena, Vienna, and Trieste; practiced medicine in Berlin. Composed a number of songs for male voices and a setting of the Horatian ode, "Integer vitae."

FLETCHER, DOUGLAS (b. 1884).

FLOTOW, FRIEDERICH VON (1812-1883). German. Composer of light and popular operas; wrote for the theatres of Paris and Hamburg; composed ballets and comic operas. Appointed Indendent of the Court Theatre at Schwerin (1856-1863). Resided at Paris (1863-1868) and then in Vienna. Elected (1864) a corresponding member of the Institut de France.

FOSTER, MYLES BIRKET (1851-1922). British. Organist at St. James's Church, Marylebone, and at St. George's, Campden Hill; organist at the Foundling Hospital, London (1880-1892), and also at Her Majesty's Theatre; choirmaster of St. Alban's, Holborn. Author of The History of the Philharmonic Society (London, 1913).

FRANC, GUILLAUME (1505-1570). French. Fled to Geneva to avoid persecution from the Reformation (1541). Master of the children and a singer at St. Peter's, Geneva. Left Geneva in 1545 and joined the choir of the Cathedral of Lausanne (1545-1570). Connected with the Psalter published at Geneva for the reformed churches (1542, 1562); edited a psalter published at Lausanne in 1565.

GABRIEL, CHARLES HUTCHISON (1856-1932). American. Writer and publisher of songs and tunes for Sunday schools and evangelistic societies. Associated with Homer Alvin Rodeheaver's publishing firm (1912-1932).

GARDINER, WILLIAM (1770-1853). British. A stocking manufacturer whose travels provided opportunities to meet numerous musicians. Published songs and duets of his own composition. Edited Sacred Melodies (1815), which attempted to replace extant Psalm versions.

GARRETT, GEORGE MURSELL (1834-1897). British. A student of Samuel Sebastian Wesley (see below, this section). Became organist of St. Madras Cathedral (1857-1897); then appointed organist of St. John's College, Cambridge, and of Cambridge University.

GAUNTLETT, HENRY JOHN (1805-1876). British. Studied law, but turned to music in 1844, embarking upon a career as organist and composer. Organist at St. Cleve's, Southwark; at Christ Church, in Newgate Street, London; at Union Chapel, Islington; at St. Bartholomew the Less, Smithfield. Published The Gregorian Hymnal (1844), The Church Hymn and Tune Book (1844-1851), National Psalmody (1876), and a dozen additional hymnals. Chosen by Felix Mendelssohn to play the organ part in Elijah at its production in Birmingham on 26 August 1846.

GAY, ANNABETH McCLELLAND (b. 1925). American.

GEIBEL, ADAM (1855-1933). German, American. Studied in Philadelphia; became an active organist, conductor, and publisher. Although blind, he performed and conducted regularly, and wrote a number of sacred cantatas.

GEORGE, GRAHAM (b. 1912).

GESIUS, BARTHOLOMAUS (1555-1621). German. Proflific writer and cantor at Frankfurt. Edited ten collections of hymns.

GIARDINI, FELICE (1716-1796). Italian. Trained as a chorister in Milan Cathedral. In 1750, he made his first appearance in England as a violinist; became leader of the Italian opera at London--then advanced to impressario there. Later went to Milan and then to Moscow, where he died.

GIBBONS, ORLANDO (1583-1625). British. A member of the choir of King's College, Cambridge (1596); organist of the Chapel Royal, London (1604); King's musician for the virginals (1619); organist at Westminster Abbey (1623). A major polyphonic writer of his day. Composed the tunes for George Wither's Hymns and Songs for the Church (1623).

GILBERT, WALTER BOND (1829-1910). British. A founder of the Royal College of Organists. Organist at Trinity Chapel, New York (1869-1899); spent his retirement in England. Edited The Parish Church Manual (1854), The Canticle (1856), The Church Chorister (1872),

The Psalter (1882).

GILL, BENJAMIN (b. 1843).

GLADSTONE, WILLIAM HENRY (1840-1891). The son of the Rt. Hon. William
Ewart Gladstone, Prime Minister. Member of the House of Commons;
a Greek and Latin scholar; a musician and music historian interes-
ted in Anglican Church music; an accomplished organist.

GLASER, CARL GOTTHELF (1784-1829). German. Music director, music dealer, composer and writer.

GODFREY, NATHANIEL S. (1817-1883).

GOODRICH, CHARLES GOURLAY (b. 1869).

GORDON, ADONIRAM JUDSON (1836-1899). American. Entered the Baptist
ministry after his graduation from Brown University (1860); pastor
of the Clarendon Street Baptist Church, Boston (1869-1899). Published The Vestry Hymn and Tune Book (1872); one of the editors of
The Service of Song (1871).

GOSS, JOHN (1800-1880). British. Trained as one of the children of
the Chapel Royal. Organist of St. Paul's (1838); a composer of the
Chapel Royal (1856); knighted in 1872. Edited Parochial Psalmody
(1826), Chants Ancient and Modern (1841); music editor of the Church
Psalter and Hymn Book (1856).

GOTTSCHALK, LOUIS MOREAU (1829-1869). American. Son of an English father and a French mother. Noted pianist, composer, and conductor.

GOULD, JOHN EDGAR (1822-1875). American. Wrote music for Edward L.
White's Modern Harp (Boston, 1846) and Harmonia Sacra (Boston,
1851).

GOULD, NATHANIEL DUREN (1781-1864). American. An active teacher in the
Boston singing schools who claimed to have taught 50,000 pupils between 1800 and 1843. Wrote a History of Church Music in America
(1853); edited Social Harmony (1822), National Church Harmony
(1830), Sacred Minstrel (1840).

GOUNOD, CHARLES FRANCOIS (1818-1893). French. Studied church music at
Rome (1839); conducted his own Requiem at Vienna in 1842; precentor
and organist of the Missions Estrangers, Paris; studied theology
with the intent of taking Holy Orders. Lived in London (1870-1876)
and there founded Gounod's Choir.

GOWER, JOHN HENRY (1855-1922).

GRAPE, JOHN T. (b. 1833).

GREATOREX, HENRY WELLINGTON (1811-1858). American. Actually an English
organist who settled first in Hartford, Connecticut, and then in
New York City. Edited A Collection of Psalm and Hymn Tunes,Chants,
Anthems, and Sentences (Boston, 1851).

GREER, REV. GEORGE JARVIS (b. 1821).

GREITER, MATTHAUS (1490-1552).   Ghrman.   Originally a monk and choir-
    singer in Strassburg Minster; embraced Lutheranism in 1524.   Compo-
    sed psalm-lieder and voice settings.

GREY, FRANCIS RICHARD (1813-1890).   British.   Composed the hymn tune,
    "St. Aidan."

GRIGG, JOSEPH (1815-1852).

GRUBER, FRANZ (1787-1863).   Austrian.   A member of the Roman Catholic
    Church, he served, from 1818, as schoolmaster and organist at Arns-
    dorf, near Oberndorf.   There, Joseph Mohr, who wrote the words to
    "Stille Nacht," was priest.

HAMILTON, CLARENCE GRANT (b. 1865).   American.   Teacher and organist at
    Providence, Rhode Island (1889-1904); professor at Wellesley Col-
    lege and organist of the Wellesley, Massachusetts, Congregational
    Church (from 1904).   From 1913, director of a summer music school
    at Boothbay Harbor, Maine.   Composer of choral music and author of
    texts on music pedagogy.

HANDEL, GEORGE FREDERICK (1685-1759).   German.   Chapelmaster to the Elec-
    tor of Hanover (later King George I of England).   First visited
    England in 1710; returned in 1713 and remained until his death.
    Chapelmaster to the Duke of Chandos, in whose employ he composed
    te deums and anthems, in addition (in 1720) to his first oratorio,
    Esther.   Blindness occurred in 1753.

HARDING, JAMES P. (1860-1911).

HARPER, EARL ENYEART (b . 1895).

HARRINGTON, CALVIN SEARS (1826-1886).

HARRINGTON, CLAUDE WALLACE (1861-1897).

HARRINGTON, KARL POMEROY (1861-1953).

HARRIS, THORO   (b. 1874).

HARRISON, RALPH (1748-1810).   British.   Assistant minister of the Pres-
    byterian Chapel, Shrewsbury (1769-1771); minister of Cross Street
    Chapel, Manchester (1771-1810).   Compiled Sacred Harmony (1784; 2nd
    edition 1791) and a collection of psalm tunes for the Manchester
    district.

HASSLER, HANS LEO (1564-1612).   German.   In 1585, he was given a home in
    the house of the Fuggers, the merchant "princes" and art patrons
    of Augsburg; musical director of Augsburg in 1600; organist of the
    Frauenkirche, Nurnberg (1601-1607).   Entered the service of the
    Elector of Saxony (1608), where he served until his death.

HASTINGS, THOMAS (1787-1872). American. Worked as a compiler, composer, and author in the field of psalmody--first in Utica, New York (1823-1832), then in New York City (1832-1872). Recognized for having developed singing and musical instruction in New York state. Published Musica Sacra (Utica, 1816), Musical Reader (Utica, 1817, 1819), Spiritual Songs for Social Worship (Utica, 1831), Union Minstrel (Philadelphia, 1834), Sacred Lyre (New York, 1840), The Psalmodist (New York, 1844), Psalmista (New York, 1851), Church Melodies (New York, 1859). Served as Lowell Mason's (see below, this section) special coadjutor in the movement for improving church music.

HATTON, JOHN (d. 1793). British. Resided in St. Helen's, in the township of Windle, in a street whose name he gave to the one hymn tune for which he has been remembered--"Duke Street."

HAVERGAL, FRANCES RIDLEY. See above, Section B.

HAVERGAL, WILLIAM HENRY (1793-1870). British. Ordained in 1816; served two churches in Gloucestershire; rector of Astley, near Bewdley (1829). Reprinted Ravenscroft's Psalter (1844) and then published his own Old Church Psalmody (1847). Rector of St. Nicholas, Worcester (1842-1860) and honorary canon of Worcester Cathedral (1845); rector of Shareshill, near Wolverhampton (1860-1867). Published A History of the Old Hundredth Psalm Tune, with Specimens (1854), A Hundred Psalm and Hymn Tunes (1859), and a collection of songs, rounds, and carols entitled Fireside Music.

HAWEIS, THOMAS. See above, Section B.

HAYDN, FRANZ JOSEPH (1732-1809). Austrian. Chapelmaster to Prince Anton Paul Esterhazy for thirty years. Visited England in 1791 and again in 1794. A deeply religious person; every one of his scores prefaced by "In nomine Domini," and concluded with "Laus Deo."

HAYDN, JOHANN MICHAEL (1737-1806). Austrian. Younger brother of Franz Joseph Haydn (see immediately above). Kapelmeister at Grosswardein to the bishop, Count Firmian; kapelmeister at Salzburg to Archbishop Sigismund (1762). Organist to the churches of the Holy Trinity and St. Peter, Salzburg.

HAYES, WILLIAM (1706-1777). British. Chorister of Gloucester Cathedral and organist at Worcester Cathedral (1731-1734); organist at Magdalen College, Oxford. Professor of Music at Oxford (1742-1777).

HAYNE, LEIGHTON GEORGE (1836-1883). British. Appointed (1863) Coryphaeus (conductor of the chorus) at Oxford University and public examiner in the School of Music there. Organist of Eton College (1868-1871); rector of Mistley and vicar of Bradfield, Essex (1871 to 1881). Co-editor of The Merton Tune Book.

HEWS, GEORGE (1806-1873). American. Tenor soloist, teacher, organist, and piano maker in Boston; a prominent member of the Handel and Haydn Society, Boston.

HEINS, FRANCIS DONALDSON (1878-1949).

HEMY, HENRI FREDERICH (1818-1901).

HERBST, MARTIN (1654-1681). German. Rector of the Gymnasium at Eisleben and pastor of the Church of St. Andreas, Eisleben. Died at
Eisleben as the result of plague.

HERMANN, NICHOLAUS (1485-1561). German. Came to Joachimsthal in 1518
to teach at the Latin school there; became organist and choirmaster of the Lutheran church at Joachimsthal; wrote hymns for the
children there. Published Die Sonntags-Evangelia uber das ganz
Jar (1560), containing 101 hymns, and Die Historien von der Sint-
flut (1562), containing an addition seventy-five hymns.

HEROLD, LOUIS JOSEPH FERDINAND (1791-1833). French. Eminent composer
of opera, the major pieces written between 1815 and 1832.

HERVEY, FREDERICK ALFRED JOHN (1846-1910). British. Rector of Sandrin-
gham (1878-1907), canon of Norwich (1897), and domestic chaplain
to the King (1901).

HEWLETT, WILLIAM HENRY (1873-1940).

HILES, HENRY (1826-1904). British. Organist at Shrewsbury; at Bury
(1846); at Bishopwearmouth (1847); at St. Michael's, Wood Street
(1859); at the Blind Asylum, Manchester (1859); at Bowden (1861);
at St. Paul's, Manchester (1863-1867). Lecturer in harmony and
composition at Owens College (1976-1879); lecturer at the Victoria
University (1879). Conductor of several musical societies in Lancashire and Yorkshire; editor and proprietor of The Quarterly Musical Review (1885-1888). Professor at the Manchester College of
Music (1893-1904).

HILLER, JOHANN ADAM (1728-1804). German. Flutist and teacher; tutor
to the son of Count Bruhl (1754-1758); conducted the Leipzig Ge-
wandhaus concerts; founded (1771) a singing school; cantor and director of the Thomasschule (1789-1801); founded the Singspiel,
from which German comic opera developed.

HIMMEL, FRIEDRICH HEINRICH (1765-1814). German. Studied theology at
Halle, but evenetually educated by Frederick William II as a musician. Kapellmeister at Berlin, from 1795.

HODGES, EDWARD (1796-1867). British. Organist of Clifton Church and
the churches of St. James (1819) and St. Nicholas (1821), both in
Bristol. Engaged in organ building and in organ remodeling. In
1838, he left England for America; appointed organist of the cathedral of Toronto (1838) and then (1839) director of music for Trinity Parish, New York City. Published An Essay on the Cultivation of
Church Music (1841). Returned to England in 1863.

HODGES, JOHN SEBASTIAN BACH (1830-1915). British, American. Son of Edward Hodges (see immediately above). Came to New York in 1845;
graduated from Columbia University (1850) and the General Theological Seminary (1854). Assistant at Trinity Church, Pittsburgh,Penn-
sylvania (1854-1856); taught at Nashotah Theological Seminary of
Wisconsin (1856-1859); rector of Grace Church, Newark, New Jersey

(1860), and of St. Paul's, Baltimore (1870-1906). Compiled The Book of Common Praise (1868) and served as an editor of the Episcopal Hymnal. Founded, in Baltimore, the earliest choir school in the United States.

HOFFMAN, ELISHA ALBRIGHT (1839-1929). American. Best known for the hymn "Are you washed in the blood of the Lamb" (1878), a piece adopted and popularized by the Salvation Army.

HOLBROOK, JOHN PARRY (1822-1888).

HOLDEN, OLIVER (1765-1844). American. A carpenter who turned to the teaching of music and the compiling of hymn tunes, as well as the selling of books. Compiled American Harmony (1792), Union Harmony (1793), Charlestown Collection (1803), Plain Psalmody (1800).

HOLDROYD, ISRAEL (fl. 1733-1753). Wrote and published under the pseudonym of "Philo Musicae." Published Chants and Anthems (1733) and The Spiritual Man's Companion. . .A Set of Psalm Tunes (1752).

HOLMES, HENRY JAMES ERNEST (1852-1938).

HOLST, GUSTAV THEODORE (1874-1934). British. Entered the Royal College of Music in 1893; first trombone with the Carl Rosa Opera Company; organist of the Royal Opera, Covent Garden; music director at Morley College; music master at St. Paul's Girls' School; taught composition at Reading College (1919-1923); known principally for his long list of compositions. Visited the United States in 1923; appointed Cramb Lecturer at the University of Glasgow (1925).

HOLYOKE, SAMUEL ADAMS (1762-1820). American. Studied at Dartmouth College and became a teacher of psalmody at Salem, Massachusetts (beginning 1805); led an instrumental club at Salem and also (1808-1809) presented choral concerts there. Published Harmonia Americana (Boston, 1791), Massachusetts Compiler (Boston, 1795), Columbian Repository (Exeter, 1800, 1802), Christian Harmonist (Salem, 1804).

HOPKINS, EDWARD JOHN (1818-1901). British. Trained as a child of the Chapel Royal; played services at Westminster Abbey before he had reached age sixteen; organist of Mitcham Parish Church (1834); organist at St. Peter's, Islington; organist at St. Luke's, Berwick Street; organist of the Temple Church (1843-1898). Edited The Temple Choral Service Book and hymnals for various Protestant denominations.

HOPKINS, JOSIAH (1786-1862). American. Pastor of a Congregational church at New Haven, Vermont (1809-1830); pastor of the First Presbyterian Church, Auburn, New York (1830-1848). Editor of Conference Hymns (Auburn, New York, 1846); contributed hymns and tunes to The Christian Lyre (New York, 1830).

HORNER, EGBERT F. (fl. 1864-1928).

HORSLEY, WILLIAM (1774-1858). British. Organist of Ely Chapel, Holborn (1794-1802); organist of the Asylum for Female Orphans (1802-1812); organist of the Charterhouse school (1838-1858). One of the founders of the Philharmonic Society.

HOWARD, SAMUEL (1710-1782). British. A child of the Chapel Royal. Organist of St. Bride's and St. Clement's Danes, both London. Wrote for the stage, as well as composed church music.

HOYT, WILLIAM STEVENSON (b. 1844). British. Organist of All Saints Church, Margaret Street, London (1868-1907); writer of church music.

HUDSON, RALPH E. (1843-1901).

HUGHES, JOHN (1873-1932). Welsh. Employed in the traffic department of the Great Western Railway; a member of the Salem Baptist Church, where he served as deacon and precentor.

HULLAH, JOHN PYKE (1812-1884). British. Pursued vocal instruction in Paris, where he also wrote for the stage. Professor of vocal music at King's College, London (1844-1874); organist of the Charterhouse school (1858).

HUMPHREYS, R.D. (b. c. 1826).

HUSBAND, EDWARD (1843-1908). Received Holy Orders in 1866; curate of Atherstone and Folkstone (1866-1874); vicar of St. Michael and All Angels, Folkstone (1874). Compiled and published The Mission Hymnal (1874) and its Supplement (41 hymns, 35 original hymn tunes).

HUSBAND, JOHN J. (1760-1825).

HUTCHESON, CHARLES (1792-1860).

INGALLS, JEREMIAH (1764-1828). American. Published Christian Harmony (1805).

IRONS, ROBERT STEPHEN (1834-1905). British. Chorister of Canterbury Cathedral. Organist and precentor of St. Columbia's College, Rathfarnham; organist and master of the choristers, Southwell Minster; assistant organist, Chester Cathedral; organist of St. Andrew's, Nottingham; organist and accompanist to the Sacred Harmonic Society, Nottingham.

IVES, ELAM, JR. (1802-1864). American. Edited, with Deodatus Dutton, Jr. (see above, this section), American Harmony (Hartford, 1829, 1830).

JACKSON, ROBERT (1842-1914).

JEFFERY, JOHN ALBERT (1854-1929).

JEFFERYS, CHARLES (1807-1865).

JENKS, STEPHEN (1772-1856). American. Resident of Connecticut and
    Ohio. Published the New England Harmonist (New Haven, 1800), Roy-
    al Harmony of Zion (1810), Zion's Harp (New York, 1824).

JONES, CHARLES (fl. 1913). American.

JONES, DARIUS ELIOT (1815-1881). American. Compiler of two noted hym-
    nals for American Congregationalists: Temple Melodies (1851) and
    Songs of the New Life (1869).

JONES, JOHN (1728-1796). British. Organist of the Middle Temple (1749-
    1753), of the Charterhouse (1753-1755), and of St. Paul's Cathe-
    dral (from 1755).

JONES, WILLIAM (1726-1800). British. Educated at Charterhouse and Uni-
    versity College, Oxford; vicar of Bethersden, Kent (1764); rector
    of Pluckley, Kent; rector of Paston, Northamptonshire; perpetual
    curate of Nayland, Suffolk; rector of Hollingbourne, Kent (1798-
    1800). Published A Treatise on the Art of Music (1784), Ten Church
    Pieces for the Organ, with Four Anthems in Score (1789).

JORDAN, CHARLES WARWICK (b. 1840).

JOSEPHI, GEORG (fl. c. 1650). German. A musician in the service of
    the Bishop of Breslau; wrote the music for the hymn collection en-
    titled Heilige Seelenlust odor geistliche Hirtenlieder der in ih-
    ren Jezu verliebten Psyche (1657).

JUDE, WILLIAM HERBERT (1851-1922).

KINGSLEY, GEORGE (1811-1884). American. Published Harp of David (New
    York, 1830), Sacred Choir (1839), Sacred Harmonist, and Templi Car-
    mina (Northampton, Massachusetts, 1853).

KIRBYE, GEORGE (c. 1565-1634). British. Composer of motets and madri-
    gals; contributed to Thomas Este's Psalter of 1592. His Bright
    Phoebus, a madrigal in six parts, appeared in Thomas Morley's col-
    lection of English madrigals, The Triumphs of Oriana (1601, 1603).

KIRKPATRICK, WILLIAM JAMES (1838-1921). American. Studied music while
    learning to be a carpenter. Joined the Methodist Episcopal Church
    and later assisted A.S. Jenks in collecting camp-meeting songs for
    the latter's Devotional Melodies (1858). Compiled some eighty-
    seven books of gospel songs, more than half of them in association
    with John R. Sweny (see below, this section).

KNAPP, MARY ANN BACHELOR (1839-1908). American.

KNAPP, PHOEBE FAIRCHILD (1839-1908). American. Possibly the same as
    Mary Ann Bachelor Knapp (see immediately above and Julian's Dic-
    tionary, 2: 1566, 1609).

KNAPP, WILLIAM (1698-1768).  British.  Organist at Wareham and Poole.
Published New Psalms and Anthems in four parts. . .and an Introduc-
tion to Psalmody after a plain and familiar manner (1738) and New
Church Melody; a sett of Anthems, Psalms, and Hymns, in four parts,
with an Introduction wrote by Charles I. during his captivity in
Carisbrooke Castle (1753).

KNECHT, JUSTIN HEINRICH (1752-1817).  German.  A rival of Abbe Georg Josef Vigler as organist; a theorist, conductor, composer.  Musik-di-
rektor and professor of literature at Biberach; an editor of the
Vollstandige Sammlung (Stuttgart, 1799).

KOCHER, CONRAD (1786-1872).  German.  Studied in St. Petersburg; composed and performed in Germany and Italy; organist of the Stiftskir-
che, Stuttgart (1827-1865); founded a school of sacred song (Gesang-
vereins Liederkranz) that spread throughout Wurtemberg.  Published
a large collection of chorales under the title Zionsharfe (1854-
1855); wrote an oratorio, Der Tod Abels, and several operas and sonatas.

KOENIG, JOHANN BALTHASAR (1691-1758).  German.  Director of the music
in several churches in Frankfurt am Main; editor of the most comprehensive choral book of the eighteenth century, Harmonischer Lieder Schatz, oder Allgemeines Evangelisches Choralbuch (1738), containing 1,940 tunes--including those for the French Protestant versions of psalms.

KOSCHAT, THOMAS (1845-1914).  Austrian.  Studied science at Vienna; joined the concert opera chorus, then became leader of that group; later joined the Vienna Cathedral choir (1874) and the Hofkapelle
(1878).  Began, in 1871, to publish original poems in the Carinthi-
an dialect, which he set to music for male quartets.  Founded, in
1875, the Karnthner Quintette.

KREMSLER, EDWARD (1838-1914).  Austrian.  Chorusmaster (1869-1914) of the
Vienna Mannergesangverein.  Composed the noted Altniederlandische
Volkslieder.


LAHEE, HENRY (1826-1912).  British.  Studied under Sterndale Bennett,
Sir John Goss, and Cipriani Potter; organist of Holy Trinity Church
in Brompton(1847-1874); after 1874 removed to Croydon.  Compiled
One Hundred Hymn Tunes.

LAMPE, JOHN FRIEDRICH (1703-1751).  German, British.  Came to England in
1725 as a bassoon player at the opera.  A close friend of Charles
Wesley (see above, Section B), whose hymns Lampe set to music for
the former's Hymns on the Great Festivals (1746).

LANE, SPENCER (1843-1903).

LANGDON, RICHARD (fl. 1775).  British.  Compiled Divine Harmony (1774).

LANGRAN, JAMES (1835-1909).  British.  Pupil of John Baptiste Calkin (see above, this section). Organist of St. Paul's Church, Tottenham (1870-1909).

LAUFER, CALVIN WEISS. See above, in Section B.

LEACH, ROWLAND (b. 1885).

LEMARE, EDWIN HENRY (1865-1929). British. Fellow of the Royal College of Organists (1884); organist at Carnegie Hall, Pittsburgh, Pennsylvania (1902-1904); returned to London in 1905. Toured the world as a concert organist; city organist of San Francisco (1917).

LERMAN, JOSEPH W. (1865-1935).

LEWIS, FREEMAN (1780-1859). American. Published Beauties of Harmony (1813, 1816).

LINDEMANN, JOHANN (c. 1550-c. 1632). German. Cantor at Gotha from 1572 to 1631; wrote sacred songs and published (1598) a collection of New Year and Christmas songs by various authors under the title Amorum Filii Dei Decades Duae: Das ist Zwantzig liebliche und gantz ammutige lateinische und deutsche newe Jharss oder Weyhenachten Gesenglein.

LLOYD, JOHN AMBROSE (1815-1874). British. Founder of the Welsh choral union of Liverpool; an adjudicator at the National Eisteddfodau. Published two collections of hymn tunes--Casgliad o Donau (1843), Aberth Moliant (1873); wrote a cantata, The Prayer of Habakkuk,published in Wales.

LLOYD, WILLIAM (1786-1852).

LOCKHART, CHARLES (1745-1815). British. Blind from infancy, he became a noted musician and trainer of children's choirs. Organist of the Lock Hospital, London; at St. Catherine Cree, London; at St. Mary's Church, Lambeth; at Orange Street Chapel; at the Lock Hospital, for a second term of appointment. Began publishing tunes in 1791 on separate sheets; published A Set of Hymns, Tunes, and Anthems for Three Voices (1810).

LONGACRE, LINDSAY BARTHOLOMEW (b. 1870).

LORENZ, EDMUND SIMON (b. 1854-1920). American. Graduated from Otterbein (Ohio) College and Yale Divinity School; pastor at Dayton, Ohio (1885-1887); president of Lebanon Valley College, Annville, Pennsylvania (1887-1888); in 1890 founded--at Dayton, Ohio--The Lorenz Publishing Company, a firm devoted to church music (principally for the United Brethren) for various denominations; branches of the firm opened in New York (1902) and Chicago (1914). Lorenz published, in 1909, a manual on Practical Church Music.

LOVELACE, AUSTIN C. (b. 1919). American.

LOWRY, ROBERT. See in Section B. above.

LUCAS, JAMES (b. 1762).

LUTHER, MARTIN (1483-1546). German. In concerning himself with church music, Luther issued, in 1523, Formula Missae and a new order for the German mass. Authored approximately thirteen choral tunes, the most noted being "Ein feste Burg is unser Gott" and "Jesaia den Propheten das gescha"; he would play the tunes on the flute while his assistants--particularly Konrad Rupff and Cantor Johann Walther who worked most closely with him--wrote them in manuscript.

LUTKIN, PETER CHRISTIAN (1858-1931). Amwrican. Teacher, conductor, and composer; theory teacher at the American Conservatory, Chicago (1888-1891); taught at the school of music, Northwestern University (1891-1898); conducted the annual Chicago North Shore Festivals. Organist at St. Clement's, Chicago (1891-1897). A founder and the dean of the School of Music at Northwestern University.

LVOV, ALEXIS FEDOROVITCH (1799-1871). Russian. Trained for the army; adjutant to Czar Nicholas I; left the army to succeed his father as head of the Imperial Choir at Petrograd; wrote the Russian national anthem, "God Save the Czar," in 1833--the piece inserted by Tchaikovsky into his 1812 Overture.

LYON, MEYER (d. 1797). British. Chorister at the Great Synagogue, London; cantor at the Jewish Synogogue at Kingston, Jamaica, where he died. Composed small pieces for the Jewish ritual.

MacFARREN, SIR GEORGE ALEXANDER (1813-1887). British. Became a professor at the Royal Academy of Music (1834); principal there in 1875; Professor of Music at Cambridge University; a gradual failure of his sight led to total blindness.

MacLAGLAN, WILLIAM DALRYMPLE (1826-1910). Scottish. Served in the curacies of St. Saviour's (Paddington) and St. Stephen's (Marylebone); curate of Enfield; rector of Newington; vicar of Kensington; prebendary of Reculverland in St. Paul's Cathedral; Bishop of Lichfield (1878-1891); Archbishop of York (1891-1908). Crowned Queen Alexandria at the coronation of Edward VII (1901).

MacMILLAN, ERNEST CAMPBELL (1893-1973). Canadian. Conductor, organist, composer. Concert organist from the age of ten; Fellow of the Royal College of Organists (1906); studied at Edinburgh and at Paris. Principal, Toronto Conservatory of Music (1926-1942); dean of music at Toronto University (1927-1952); conductor of the Toronto Symphony Orchestra (1931-1956). Composed choral works and arranged Canadian folk songs. The first Canadian knighted (1935) for services to music.

MAIN, HUBERT PLATT (1839-1926). American. Performed clerical and editorial work in New York City; in 1867, entered the employ of the Bradbury Music Company; continued with its successors, Biglow and Main.

MAINZER, JOSEPH (1801-1851). German, British. Ordained priest and then Abbe; singing master to the seminary at Treves; came to England in

1841--first to Edinburgh, then on to Manchester. Started (July 1842) Mainzer's Musical Times.

MAKER, FREDERICK CHARLES (1844-1927).

MALAN, HENRI ABRAHAM CAESAR. See in Section B above.

MANN, ARTHUR HENRY (1850-1929). British. Trained as a chorister at Norwich Cathedral. Organist at St. Peter's, Wolverhampton' at Teltenhall Parish Church; at Beverly Minster; at King's College, Cambridge. Organist to the University of Cambridge and music master of the Leys School, Cambridge. Edited Thomas Tallis's (see below, in this section) motet for forty voices; musical editor of The Church of England Hymnal.

MARSH, SIMEON BUTLER (1798-1875).

MARSHALL, LEONARD (b. 1809; fl. 1849-1855). American. Published The Antiquarian (1849) and The Harpsichord, or Union Collection of Tunes (1852).

MARTIN, GEORGE WILLIAM (1828-1881). British. Professor of Music at the Normal College for Army Schoolmasters; music master at St. John's Training College, Battersea (1845-1853); organist of Christ Church, Battersea (1849).

MARTIN, W. STILLMAN (1862-1935).

MASON, HARRY SILVERTONE (1881-1964).

MASON, LOWELL (1792-1872). American. Bank clerk at Savannah, Georgia, where he also conducted a Presbyterian choir and compiled his first collection of hymn tunes--Sacred Melodies (1822). Organist at Lyman Beecher's church, Boston; founded (1832) the Boston Academy of Music. Published The Sabbath Hymn and Tune Book (1859) and The Hallelujah.

MATTHEWS, TIMOTHY RICHARD (1826-1910). British. Educated at Bedford Grammar School and at Caius College, Cambridge. Ordained in 1853; rector of North Coates, West Grimsby (1869-1908). Edited The North Coates Supplemental Tune Book and The Village Organist.

McCUTCHAN, ROBERT GUY (1877-1958). American. Organized the Music Department at Baker University, Kansas ((1904-1910); directed the choir at the American Church, Berlin (1911); dean of the School of Music, DePauw University (Indiana) from 1911. Adopted the pseudonym of "John Porter."

McDONALD, REV. WILLIAM. See in Section B above.

McGRANAHAN, JAMES (1840-1907). Assisted Ira David Sankey (see below, in this section) in the later editions of Gospel Hymns (1891-1894). A "pioneer" in employing men's choirs in his evangelical meetings.

McINTOSH, RIGDON McCOY (1836-1899).

McWHOOD, LEONARD BEECHER (b. 1870). American. Taught at Columbia University, Vassar College, Drew Theological Seminary, National Park Seminary, Dartmouth College.

MEHUL, ETIENNE HENRI (1763-1817). French. Tirty pieces for the operatic stage between 1790 and 1807; one of the significant contributors to French opera; also composed cantatas and masses.

MENDELSSOHN-BARTHOLDY, FELIX (1809-1847). German. In 1819, his setting of Psalm 19 sung by the Berlin Singakademie; made ten visits to England. His great masses of composition include two oratorios--St. Paul and Elijah--as well as a number of pieces adapted by others as hymn tunes.

MEREDITH, ISAAC HICKMAN (b. 1872).

MERRICK, GEORGE PURNELL (b. 1840). British.

MESSITER, ARTHUR HENRY (1834-1916). British, American. Organist of Trinity Church, New York City (1866-1897); historian of the music at Trinity Church (1907).

MEYER, JOHANN DAVID (fl. c. 1692). German. A town councilor at Ulm; published Geistliche Seelenfreund, oder Davidische Hauss-Capell at Ulm (1692); the piece contains 111 melodies--fifty-four of them being of his own composition.

MILLER, EDWARD (1731-1807). British. Played the German flute in Handel's orchestra; organist of Doncaster Parish Church (1756-1807). Edited The Psalms of David, with Tunes (1790); Psalms and Hymns set to Music (1801); Sacred Music. . .an Appendix to Dr. Watts's Psalms and Hymns (1802).

MILLER, WILLIAM (1801-1878).

MONK, WILLIAM HENRY (1823-1889). British. Organist of Eton Chapel, Pimlico; of St. George's Chapel, Albermarle Street, London; of Portman Chapel, Marylebone; of St. Matthias, Stoke Newington. Director of the choir and organist of King's College, London, and (1874-1889) professor of music there. Professor in the National Training School for Music and in Bedford College (1876). The forst music editor of Hymns Ancient and Modern; edited Hymns of the Church, The Holy Year, Fifty-Two Simple Chants; The Scottish Hymnal and A Book of Anthems were edited for the Church of Scotland.

MOSS, EDWIN (b. 1838).

MOZART, CHRISTIAN WOLFGANG AMADEUS (1756-1791). Austrian. In addition to his long religious pieces, a number of hymn tunes bear Mozart's name--and those, principally, have come from adaptations of and extracts from the longer works. For instance, hymn-tune names associated with Mozart include Agnus dei, Ariel, Ave verum corpus, Cava, Dona nobis pacem, Easton, Ellesdie, Folsom, Home, Jubilee, O Gottes Lamm, Pa jorden ar allting foranderligt, Sonata, Stars of glory.

MUHLENBERG, WILLIAM AUGUSTUS. See in Section B above.

MULLER, CARL FREDERICK (1892-1982).

MURRAY, JAMES R. (1841-1905).

NAEGELI, JOHANN HANS GEORG (1773-1836). German. Began a music publishing business in 1792; started the periodical Repertoire des clave-
cinistes (1803); composed vocal pieces for the Church; a developer
in the field of music education; revived male choir singing (Lie-
dertafel).

NARES, JAMES (1715-1783). British. A chorister of the Chapel Royal; a
deputy organist of St. George's Chapel, Windsor; organist of York
Minster (1734-1756); organist and composer of the Chapel Royal
(1756) and master of the children there (1756-1780).

NEANDER, JOACHIM (1650-1680). German. Headmaster of the Reformed Grammar School at Dusseldorf (1674); preacher at St. Martin's, Bremen
(1679-1680). Wrote over sixty hymns and tunes published under the
title Alpha und Omega, Joachimii Neander Glaubund Liebes-ubung and
dated 1680.

NEUKOMM, SIGISMUND RITTER (1778-1858). Austrian. Chorister at Salzburg
Cathedral (1788-1793); studied music with Joseph Haydn. Kapellmeister and director of the Emperor's German theatre at St. Petersburg
(1806); resided in France and Luxemburg, as well as in Portugal;
lived in France and England between 1838 and 1858.

NEUMARCK, GEORGE (1621-1681). German. Secretary and librarian to the
ducal court at Weimar. His principal work entitled Musik alisch-
poetischer Lustwald (1657), a collection of sacred and secular song
pieces. Best known for his tune, "War nur den lieben Gott lasst
walten."

NICHOL, HENRY ERNEST. See in Section B above.

NICOLAI, OTTO (1810-1849). German. Organist of the embassy chapel at
Rome; theatre conductor at Rome and Vienna; conducted the opera and
cathedral choir at Berlin (1847-1849).

NICOLAI, PHILIPP (1556-1608). German. Ordained in 1576 at Mengering-
hausen, Waldeck; resigned his office in 1586; ministered to a secret Lutheran congregation in the Catholic stronghold of Cologne;
held pastorates at Niederwildungen and Altwildungen; court preacher
to the dowager countess of Waldeck; chief pastor of St. Katherine,
Hamburg (1601-1608). Published Freuden-Spiegel des ewigen Lebens
(Frankfurt, 1599).

NOVELLO, VINCENT (1781-1861). British. A chorister at the Sardinian
Chapel, Duke Street, Lincoln's Inn Fields (london); organist of the
Portuguese Chapel, South Street, Grosvenor Square (1797-1822); pianist to the Italian Opera Company at the Pantheon (1812); an original member of the Philharmonic Society; organist of the Roman Catholic Chapel, Moorfields, London; a founder of the Classical Har-

monists and Choral Harmonists Societies; left England in 1849 and
spent the remainder of his years at Nice.  Published A Collection
of Sacred Music (2 vols., 1811); The Psalmist; The Congregational
and Chorister's Psalm and Hymn Book; edited five volumes of Italian church music of the seventeenth century under the title The
Fitzwilliam Music (1825).  Founded the publishing house of Novello
and Company (1811); helped to prepare the way for the Bach revival
in England.

OAKELEY, HERBERT STANLEY (1830-1903).  British.  Professor of Music at
   the University of Edinburgh (1865-1891).  Composed a dozen anthems
   and a number of hymn tunes.

OAKLEY, WILLIAM HENRY (1809-1881).

O'KANE, TULLIUS CLINTON (1830-1912).  American.  His hymns and hymn tunes appeared, principally, in Ira David Sankey's (see below, this
   section) collections of Sacred Songs and Solos (1878-1881).

OLDBERG, ARNE (b. 1874).  American.  Head of the Piano Department (beginning 1899) at Northwestern (Illinois) University.

OLIVER, HENRY KEMBLE (1800-1885).  American.  Taught music at Salem and
   Lawrence, Massachusetts; founded choral societies in both of those
   cities.  Author of essays upon the manufacture and employment of
   mathematical instruments.  Published The National Lyre (with Samuel Parkman Tuckerman--see below, this section); A Collection of
   Church Music (1860); Original Hymn Tunes (1875).

OLIVERS, THOMAS.  See above in Section B.

OWEN, WILLIAM (1814-1893).

PAISIELLO, GIOVANNI (1740-1816).  Italian.  Composed a number of masses
   before turning his attention almost completely to opera.

PALESTRINA, GIOVANNI PETRI ALOYSIUS (1525-1594).  Italian.  One of the
   most revered names in liturgical music and the finest and foremost
   composer of the Roman Catholic Church.  Became magister capellae
   at the Vatican in 1551; founded the Italian School of Polyphonists.

PALMER, HORATIO RICHMOND.  See in Section B above.

PALMER, W. ST. CLAIR (b. 1865).

PARKER, EDWIN POND (1836-1925).

PARKER, HORATIO WILLIAM (1863-1919).  American.  Taught music in St.
   Paul's School and in St. Mary's  School--both at Garden City, Long

Island; taught counterpoint in the National Conservator of Music, New York; director of music and organist at Trinity Church, Boston; his most noteworthy piece, Hora Novissima, was first performed on 3 May 1893. Appointed Professor of Music at Yale in 1894, and served there until his death.

PARKER, JAMES CUTLER DUNN (1828-1916). American. Organist at Trinity Church, Boston (1864-1891); organist of the Handel and Haydn Society, Boston; teacher of piano, organ, and harmony at the New England Conservatory and at Boston University.

PARRY, JOSEPH (1841-1903). Welsh. Emigrated to America in 1854, but returned to England in 1869. Professor of Music at University College, Aberystwyth (1874-1888); lecturer in music, University College of South Wales, Cardiff (1888). Edited the collection of old Welsh songs known as Cambrian Minstrelsie.

PEACE, ALBERT LISTER (1844-1912). British. Organist of Halmfirth Parish Church, Yorkshire (1853)--at age nine. Organist at the following churches: Dewsbury Parish Church; St. Thomas's, Huddersfield; Brunswick Street Chapel, Huddersfield; Providence Place Chapel and Checkleton's Trinity Congregational Church--both in Glasgow; the University of Glasgow; St. John's Episcopal Church, Hilhead Parish Church, St. Andrew's Hall--all in Glasgow. Organist at Glasgow Cathedral (1879-1897); organist at St. George's Hall, Liverpool, from 1897 to 1912.

PEEK, JOSEPH YATES (1843-1911).

PEERY, ROB ROY (b. 1900). American.

PERKINS, EMILY SWAN (b. 1866). American.

PERKINS, THEODORE EDSON (1831-1912). American.

PFAUTSCH, LLOYD A. (b. 1921).

PHILLIPS, PHILIP (1834-1895). American. A leader of singing schools in Ohio from c. 1853; a music dealer and publisher in Cincinnati (1860-1867); moved to New York in 1867 and published popular sacred song books; sang in and conducted song services in various parts of the world.

PLEYEL, IGNACE JOSEPH (1757-1831). Austrian. A pupil of Haydn who later became Kapellmeister at Strassbourg. Traveled in England and throughout Europe as a conductor and composer. Settled in Paris and there founded the firm of Pleyel and Wolff.

POND, SYLVANUS BILLINGS (1792-1871). American. A piano manufacturer in Albany, New York, who began his business prior to 1820. Moved to New York in 1832 and joined the instrument firm of Firth and Hall; in 1863, he helped to begin the business of William A. Pond and Company. Compiled United States Psalmody (New York, 1841).

PONTIUS, WILLIAM HENRY (b. 1850).

"PORTER, JOHN." See above, this section, under McCutchan, Robert Guy.

POWELL, ROBERT J. (b. 1932). American.

PRAETORIUS, MICHAEL (1571-1621). German. Kapellmeister at Luneburg; prior of the monastery of Ringelheim, Goslar. Published Musae Sionae (1609) and Syntagma Musicum (1614, 1619).

PRICE, CARL FOWLER (b. 1881). American.

PRICHARD, ROWLAND HUGH (1811-1887). Welsh. In 1880, he moved from his native Bala to Holywell Mill, there to become a loom-tender's assistant. Composed the noted tune "Hyfrydol"; published (1844) a collection of tunes entitled Cyfaill y Cantorion ("The Singer's True Friend").

PURDAY, CHARLES HENRY (1799-1885). British. Composer, writer, lecturer on subjects pertaining to music; also a reputable vocalist. Active in bringing about changes in the copyright acts. Conductor of psalmody for the Scottish Church, Crown Street, Covent Garden. Best known for his tune to Newman's "Lead,kindly light."

QUAILE, ROBERT NEWTON (1867-?).

RANDALL, JOHN (1715-1799). British. A chorister of the Chapel Royal; organist of King's College, Cambridge (1743); Professor of Music, Cambridge University (1755); organist of Trinity College, Cambridge (from 1756). Published A Collection of Psalm Tunes, Some of Which Are New, and Others, by Permission of the Authors, with Six Chants and Te Deums, calculated for the use of Congregations in General (1794).

READ, DANIEL (1757-1836). American. A combmaker and ivory worker who, from 1785, produced pieces and collections of psalmody. Published American Singing Book (New Haven, 1785; editions to 1793); The Musical Magazine (New Haven, 1786-1787), Introduction to Psalmody (New Haven, 1790); Columbian Harmonist (New Haven, 1793-1810); American Musical Miscellany (Northampton, 1798); The New Haven Collection (Dedham, 1818).

REDHEAD, RICHARD (1820-1894). British. Organist of Margaret Chapel, Margaret Street, Cavendish Square, London (1835-1864); organist of St. Mary Magdalene, Paddington (1864-1894); edited, with Canon Frederick Oakeley, the first Gregorian psalter, Laudes Diurnae. Composed tunes for Church Music; Hymns for Holy Seasons; The Celebrant's Office Book; The Parish Tune Book; The Book of Common Prayer, with Ritual Song; Ancient Hymns, Melodies, and Other Church Tunes; The Cathedral and Church Choir Book.

REDNER, LEWIS HENRY (1831-1908).

REED, EDITH MARGARET GELLIBRAND (1885-1935). British. Assistant editor of Pan Pipes (1922-1930) and editor of Music and Youth (1923-1926).

A contributor to the Kingsway Carol Book, Sunday School Praise, and The School Assembly.

REINAGLE, ALEXANDER ROBERT (1799-1877). British. Organist of St. Peter's-in-the-East, Oxford (1822-1853). Composed the well known hymn tune, "St. Peter."

REISSIGER, CARL GOTTLIEB (1798-1859). German. Singer and opera composer. Succeeded, in 1827, von Weber as conductor of the German opera at Dresden. In addition to his operas, he composed masses, liturgical music, and an oratorio, David.

RENDLE, LILY (1875-?).

REYNOLDS, WILLIAM JENSEN (b. 1920). American.

RICHARDSON, JOHN (1816-1879).

RIDOUT, DANIEL (b. 1898). American.

RIGHINI, V INCENZO (1756-1812). Italian. Opera singer and composer. Singing master to Princess Elisabeth of Wurtemberg; conductor of the Italian opera at Vienna. Director of the Italian opera of Berlin (1793); composed a Te Deum, a Requiem, a Missa Solemnis, and several cantatas.

RILEY, JOHN (?-?). British. A native and resident of Mytholmroyd, in Yorkshire.

RIMBAULT, EDWARD FRANCIS (1816-1876). British. Organist at the Swiss church, Soho; at St. Peter's, Vere Street, London; at St. John's Wood Presbyterian Church, London; at St. Giles-in-the-Fields, London. Edited The Cathedral Service of Thomas Tallis (see below, in this section) and the Order of Daily Service, as well as Thomas Este's The Whole Booke of Psalmes and Marbecke's Book of Common Prayer Noted.

RINCK, JOHANN CHRISTIAN HEINRICH (1770-1846). German. Organist and a composer of organ music. Organist at Giessen (1790-1805); organist at Darmstadt and professor at the college there (1805-1813); court organist (1813) and chamber musician (1817) to the Grand Duke Ludwig. Composed for the Church a Pater Noster for four voices, with organ. His library purchased, in 1852, by Lowell Mason (see above, this section), who later donated the volumes to Yale College.

RINEHART, THOMAS FRANKLIN (1860-?).

RITTER, PETER (1763-1846). German. Kapellmeister an Mannheim (1803). Composed the popular hymn (translated as) "Lord of glory."

ROBERTS, JOHN VARLEY (1841-1920). British. Organist at St. John's, in Farsley, near Leeds--appointed in 1853 at age twelve; organist at St. Bartholomew's, Armley (1862-1868); organist and choirmaster of the parish church at Halifax (1868-1882); elected organist at Magdalen College, Oxford, in 1883, and there served until 1919. Founded the University Glee and Madrigal Society (1884). Organist of

St. Giles, Oxford (1885-1893). Published Practical Method of Training Choristers (1898, 1900, 1905).

ROBERTS, ROBERT (1863-?).

ROE, JOHN EDWARD (1838-1871).

RONTGEN, JULIUS (1855-1932). German. A professor of the Conservatorie at Amsterdam (1888-1916) and then its director (1918-1924). Conductor of the Society for the Advancement of Musical Art. Wrote a Fantasie fur Klavier und Violine; Nordische Ballade; and Hollandisches Volksleben.

ROOT, GEORGE FREDERICK. See in Section B above.

ROSENMULLER, JOHANN (1619-1684). German. Published, 1648, 1652-1653) Kernspruche, issued in two parts, each consisting of twenty Latin and German motets on Scriptures and other Church texts, for three to seven voices. Organist at the Nikolaikirche (1651-1655); left Germany for Venice. Kapellmeister at Wolfensbuttel (1674-1684).

ROSSINI, GIAOCHINO ANTONIO (1792-1868). Italian. This eminent opera composer experienced, early in his life, the playing and singing of church music. Composed his Stabat Mater in 1832, in addition to a number of smaller liturgical pieces and at least sixteen cantatas.

ROUSSEAU, JEAN JACQUES (1712-1778). French. The noted philosopher and writer taught himself music. Published his Dissertation sur la Musique Moderne in 1743; composed two opersa and wrote a number of articles on music for the Encyclopedie.

SANKEY, IRA DAVID (1840-1908). American. Known, prior to 1860, as a singer of songs; began to pursue evangelistic and gospel singing in 1871, when he joined Dwight Lyman Moody; toured with Moody between 1871 and 1899, traveling throughout America and Great Britain. Published Sacred Songs and Solos (1873), Gospel Hymns, 1-6 (1875-1891), Winnowed Songs and Solos (1890). Wrote The Story of the Gospel Hymns (1906).

SCHEIN, JOHANN HERMANN (1586-1630). German. Chorister in the chapel of the Elector of Saxony, at Dresden; studied theology and philosophy at Leipzig. Music director at the court of the Duke Johann Ernst of Saxe-Weimar (1613-1615); cantor at St. Thomas's Church and School, Leipzig (J.S. Bach's church) from 1615 to 1630. Edited the Lutheran hymn book, Cantional, oder Gesangbuch Augsburgischer Confession (Leipzig, 1627), and published Musica Divina, a collection of motets.

SCHNEIDER, FRIEDRICH JOHANN CHRISTIAN (1786-1853). German. Court conductor at Dessau (1821). Wrote text books and composed fifteen oratorios, including the noted Das Weltgericht.

SCHOLEFIELD, CLEMENT COTTERILL (1839-1904). British. Ordained in 1867 and served Anglican curacies at Hove, near Brighton, and St. Luke's in Chelsea. Chaplain of Eton College (1880-1890); vicar of Holy Trinity, Knightsbridge (1890-1895).

SCHOP, JOHANN (1600-1664). German. Entered the court orchestra at Wolfenbuttel (1615); music director at Hamburg (1644) and Ratsmusikant in 1654. Wrote hymn tunes for the divine odes of his friend and fellow townsman, Johann Rist.

SCHULTHES, WILHELM AUGUSTUS FERDINAND (1816-1879). German. Director of the choir at the Brompton Oratory (1852-1872).

SCHULTZ, JOHANN ABRAHAM PETER (1747-1800). German. Assisted Johann Kirnberger and Johann Sulzer with the music articles for their General Theory of Fine Arts; edited Kirnberger's Treatise on Pure Composition. Director of the French Theatre at Berlin (1776) and director of music in the household of Prince Henry of Prussia, at Reinsberg (1780). Director of music to the Danish court at Copenhagen (1787).

SCHUMANN, ROBERT (1810-1856). German. This most prominent composer produced a Missa Sacra, Requiem Mass, and a number of shorter pieces later adapted to hymns for worship in the church.

SCOTT, CLARA H. (1841-1897).

SCOTT-GATTY, ALFRED (1847-1918). British. Garter Principal King of Arms (1904), Rouge Dragon Pursuivant of Arms at the College of Heralds (1880), York Herald (1886). An amateur musician and composer, he founded the Magpie Madrigal Society in 1886.

SELLERS, ERNEST O. (1869-1952). American.

SEWARD, THEODORE FREELINGHUYSEN (1835-1902). American. Organist and teacher at New London, Connecticut, and at Rochester, New York-- all prior to 1860. Went to New York City in 1862. Music supervisor at Orange, New Jersey (1870) and director of the Jubilee Singers of Fisk University, Nashville, Tennessee. Edited The Musical Pioneer (1867), The Musical Gazette (1881), The Tonic Sol-Fa Advocate, and Musical Reform (1886).

SHAW, MARTIN EDWARD FALLAS (1875-1958). British. Studied at the Royal College of Music; conducted for Eileen Terry and Isadora Duncan. Organist and director of music at St. Mary's, Primrose Hill; at St. Martin-in-the-Fields; and at the Guildhouse, London. Published Additional Tunes in Use at St. Mary's, Primrose Hill (1915). A founder of the Plainsong and Medieval Music Society. Musical editor, with Ralph Vaughan Williams (see below, this section), of the Songs of Praise; editor of The English Carol Book and The Oxford Book of Carols (1928),

SHEPPARD, FRANKLIN L. (1852-1930).

SHERWIN, WILLIAM FISK (1826-1888). American. Studied music at Boston under Lowell Mason (see above, this section); became a teacher of vocal music in Massachusetts; Hudson, New York; Albany, New York; New York City. Composer of carols and hymn tunes for Sunday schools; associated with Robert Lowry (see above, Section B) in the preparation of Bright Jewels, a collection of songs and hymns for Sunday schools.

SHIELD, WILLIAM (1748-1829). British. Leader at theatres and concerts at Sacrborough; his first composition was an anthem for a new church at Sunderland. Produced and wrote operas for the Haymarket and Covent Garden, London. Appointed master of the King's music in 1817, after which he became a prolific composer of popular song pieces.

SHOWALTER, ANTHONY J. (1858-1924).

SHRUBSOLE, WILLIAM. See in Section B above.

SIBELIUS, JEAN (1865-1957). Finnish. Taught at the Philharmonic Orchestra School, Helsingfors (1893-1897); received (1897-1907) an annual grant from the Finnish government, which allowed him to devote himself to composition. His religious works include Musique Religieuse (1927) and Five Christmas Songs (1895).

SILCHER, FRIEDRICH (1789-1860). German. A noted composer of songs; taught at Stuttgart (1817); music director at Tubingen University (1817-1860). Edited a text for harmony and composition (1851).

SIMPSON, ROBERT (1790-1832).

SKINNER, T. STANLEY (fl. 1917-1928). American. Head of the Department of Music at Drury College, Springfield, Missouri (from 1917).

SMART, HENRY THOMAS (1813-1879). British. Initially a trial lawyer who turned to music. Organist at the Parish Church, Blackburn; at St. Giles, Cripplegate; at St. Philip's, Regent Street; at St. Luke's, Old Street; at St. Pancreas--all in London. Blind from 1865. Composed a Credo, several hymn tunes, three cantatas, and one oratorio. Edited the music for The Presbyterian Hymnal, published by the United Presbyterian Church in 1876.

SMITH, DAVID STANLEY (1877-1949). American. Taught in, and then became the head of, the Yale University School of Music. Organist at New Haven, Connecticut, churches; a consistent composer of orchestral music.

SMITH, HENRY PERCY (1825-1898).

SMITH, ISAAC (1734-1805). British. A precentor to the Alie Street Meeting House, Goodman's Field, London. Composed and published psalm tunes; compiled A Collection of Psalm Tunes in Three Parts, to which are added 2 Anthems and 2 Canons (1770).

SMITH, JOHN STAFFORD (1750-1836). British. Organist, singer, composer. His song, "Anacreon in Heaven," adapted to "The Star Spangled Banner." Assisted Sir John Hawkins with The History of Musick (completed in 1776); published A Collection of English Songs (1779) and

Twelve Chants Composed for the Use of the Choirs of the Church of England. Lay vicar of Westminster Abbey (1786); organist of the Chapel Royal and master of the children there.

SMITH, SAMUEL (1821-1917).

SNOW, LEVI FRANKLIN (1839-1876).

SOHREN, PETER (1630-1693). German. Kantor in Leichman's Church, Elbing (1674-1675); kantor to Durschau, then back to Elbing at his former post. Edited Johann Cruger's Praxis Pietatis Melica (1668); published his own Musikalischer Vorschmarck der Jauchzenden Seelen in Ewigen Leben (1683).

SOUTHGATE, THOMAS BISHOP (1814-1868).

SOWERBY, LEO (1895-?). American. Taught theory at the American Conservatory, Chicago; organist at the South Congregational Church, Chicago; composer of symphonic works and organ music.

SPILMAN, JONATHAN E. (1835-?).

SPOHR, LOUIS (1784-1859). German. Eminent violinist, conductor, composer, and teacher. A member of the Ducal Orchestra; toured extensively throughout Europe; introduced into England the practice of conducting the orchestra with a baton.

SPRATT, ANN BAIRD (1829-?).

STAINER, JOHN (1840-1901). British. Chorister at St. Paul's (1847-1856) and temporary organist there. Organist of St. Benet and St. Peter's, Paul's Wharf (1854-1856); first organist at St. Michael's in Tenbury (1856-1869); organist of Magdalene College, Oxford, and then of the University (1859-1872). Succeeded, in 1872, Sir John Goss as organist of St. Paul's Cathedral. Professor of Organ and Principal, National Training School for Music; organist of the Royal Choral Society; government inspector of music in the training schools; Professor of Music at Oxford. Wrote The Music of the Bible; A Treatise on Harmony; a cantata entitled The Crucifixion; edited the first edition of The Church Hymnary.

STANLEY, SAMUEL (1767-1822). British. Leader of the singing at Carr's Lane Meeting House, Birmingham (1789-1818); leader of the singing at Steelhouse Lane, Birmingham (1818-1822). Published Twenty-Four Tunes in Four Parts; Nineteen Psalms, Hymns and Charity Hymn Tunes; Sacred Music, comprising Two New Psalm and Hymn Tunes; Psalm and Tunes (in three books).

STATHAM, FRANCIS REGINALD (1846-?_. British.

STATHAM, HENRY HEATHCOTE (1839-1924). British. Honorary organist at Canon Barnett's Church, St. Jude's, Whitechapel. Wrote The Organ and Its Position in Musical Art and My Thoughts on Music and Musicians. A performing organist of considerable reputation.

STEBBINS, GEORGE COLES (1846-1945). American. A singing evangelist and father of the New York organist, George Waring Stebbins (1869-1930).

STEFFE, JOHN WILLIAM (fl. 1852). American. Little known beyond his composition of the tune to accompany "The Battle Hymn of the Republic."

STEGGALL, CHARLES H. British. Organist at Christ Church, Maida Hill; of Christ Church, Lancaster Gate; of Lincoln's Inn Chapel. Principal professor of the organ at the Royal Academy of Music; one of the founders of the Royal College of Organists; succeeded William Henry Monk (see above, this section) as the musical editor of Hymns Ancient and Modern.

STEWART, ROBERT PRESCOTT (1825-1894). Irish. Organist of Christ Church Cathedral, Dublin (1844); organist of Trinity College, Dublin (1844); conductor of the University of Dublin Choral Society, beginning 1846; vicar-choral of St. Patrick's Cathedral (1852)1 professor of theory and music at the University of Dublin (1861); professor of theory in the Royal Irish Academy of Music (1872); conductor of the Dublin Philharmonic (1873). Edited the Irish Church Hymnal (1876).

STOCKTON, JOHN HART (1813-1877). American. His hymn tunes appeared, originally, in Ira David Sankey's (see above, this section) Sacred Songs and Solos (1878).

STOKES, WALTER (1847-?).

STORER, HENRY JOHNSON (1860-1935).

STRATTNER, GEORG CHRISTOPH (1650-1705).

STUTSMAN, GRACE MAY (1886-?).

SULLIVAN, ARTHUR SEYMOUR (1842-1900). British. Chorister of the Chapel Royal (1854); organist of St. Michael's, Chester Square; organist of St. Peter's, Onslow Gardens. Musical director and professor of composition at the National Training School of Music (1876); conductor of the Glasgow Choral Union (1875-1877); conductor of the Covent Garden Promenade Concerts (1878-1879); conductor of the Leeds Festival (from 1880); conductor of the Philharmonic Society (1885-1887). Contributed hymn tunes to The Hymnary; musical editor of Church Hymns.

SUMNER, JOHN B. (1838-1918). American.

SWAN, TIMOTHY (1758-1842). American. Began teaching psalmody about 1775; published tune collections (from 1875). Published Federal Harmony (1785, 1792), Songster's Assistant (1800), New England Harmony (1801), Songster's Museum (1803)

SWEETSER, JOSEPH EMERSON (1825-1873). American. Edited, with George Frederick Root (see Section B above), A Collection of Church Music (New York, 1849).

SWENEY, JOHN R. (1837-1899). American. A prolific writer of gospel tunes for evangelical meetings and Sunday schools.

SWIFT, JAMES FREDERICK (1847-1931).

TALLIS, THOMAS (1510-1585). British. Organist of Waltham Abbey; gentleman of the Chapel Royal. Obtained (1575-1576), with William Byrd, letters patent to print music and ruled paper. Composed preces, responses, and litany for the Anglican choral service. Later wrote a motet, Spem in alium non habui; published, with Byrd, Cantiones quae ab argumento Sacrae vocantus.

TANS'UR, WILLIAM (1706-1783). British. Teacher of psalmody; settled in St. Neots as a bookseller and teacher of music. Published A Compleat Melodie, or, The Harmony of Sion (1734); Heaven on Earth, or, The Beauty of Holiness (1738); Sacred Mirth, or, The Pious Soul's Daily Delight (1739); The Universal Harmony, containing the Whole Book of Psalms (1743); The Psalm-Singer's Jewell, or Useful Companion to the Book of Psalms (1760); Melodia Sacra, or, The Devout Psalmist's Musical Companion (1771); A New Musical Grammar, or, The Harmonical Spectator (1746); The Elements of Musick Displayed (1772); Poetical Meditations (1740).

TAYLOR, VIRGIL CORYDON (1817-1891). American. Published Sacred Minstrel, or American Church Music Book (1846); Choral Anthems (1850).

TENNEY, JOHN H. (fl. 1885-1895).

TESCHNER, MELCHOIR (1584-1635). Polish (Silesian). Lutheran cantor at Fraustadt, Silesia; pastor of the Oberprietschen, near Fraustadt.

THOMAS, EDITH LOVELL (1878-?). American.

THOMAS, RHYS (1867-1932).

THOMPSON, ROBERT GEORGE (1862-1934).

THOMPSON, VAN DENMAN (1890-?).

THOMPSON, WILL LAMARTINE (1847-1909).

TIDDERMAN, MARIA (1837-1911).

TILLMAN, CHARLES D. (1861-1943).

TINDLEY, CHARLES A. (1856-1933).

TOMER, WILLIAM GOULD (1832-1896).

TOURJEE, LIZZIE ESTERBROOK (1858-1913). American.

TOURS, BERTHOLD (1838-1897). Dutch. Resident of London from 1861. Organist of the Swiss Church, Holborn (1862); musical advisor and editor to Novello and Company (1878).  Composed hymn tunes, anthems, and services for the Anglican Church.

TOWNER, DANIEL BRINK (1850-1919).  American.  An associate of Dwight Lyman Moody; head of the Music Department at Moody Bible Institute; more than two thousand hymn tunes attributed to him.

TOZER, AUGUSTUS EDMONDS (1857-?).  British.  Wrote hymns and hymn tunes for the Roman Catholic Church.  Edited Catholic Hymns with Accompanying Tunes, being a Musical Edition of St. Dominic's Hymn Book (London, 1885; enlarged edition 1901); Catholic Church Hymnal (London, 1905).

TUCKER, ISAAC (1761-1825).

TUCKERMAN, SAMUEL PARKMAN (1819-1890).  American.  Organist at Boston (1840-1849, 1853-1856); organist at Trinity Church, New York (1864-1890).  Published The Episcopal Harp (1840), Cathedral Chants (1858), The Trinity Collection of Church Music (1860), Original Hymn Tunes (1875).

TULLAR, GRANT COLFAX (1869-1950).

TURLE, JAMES (1802-1882).  British.  Chorister at Wells (1810-1813); organist at Christ Church, Blackfriars (1819-1829); organist at St. James's, Bermondsey (1829-1831); organist and master of the choristers at Westminster Abbey (1831).  Joint editor of the People's Music Book (1844); edited Psalms and Hymns (1862) and a collection of his own hymn tunes, published in 1885.

TURNER, HERBERT B. (1852-1927).

TYE, CHRISTOPHER (1508-1572).  British.  Master of the choristers, Ely Cathedral (1541-1542); rector of Doddington-cum-March-, Isle of Ely (1560); rector of Newton-cum-Capella and of Little Wilbraham, Cambridge.  Published The Acts of the Apostles, translated into Englyshe Metre. . .with Notes to eche Chapter, to synge, and also to play upon the Lute (1553).

UFFORD, EDWIN S. (1851-1929).

UGLOW, JOHN JAMES (1814-1894).  British.  A chorister of Gloucester Cathedral and a pupil of Sigismund Neukomm (see above, this section).  Spent most of his life in Cheltenham.

VAIL, SILAS JONES (1818-1884).

VENUA, FREDERICK MARC ANTOINE (1788-1872).

VINCENT, CHARLES JOHN, JR. (1852-1934).

VULPIUS, MELCHOIR (1560-1615).  German.  Cantor at Weimar (1600); composed tunes published in collections edited by him--Ein Schon Geist-
lich Gesangbuch (1604, 1609).


WADE, JAMES CLIFFT (1847-?).

WADE, JOHN FRANCIS (1711-1786).  British.  A copyist of plain-chant and
other music at Douai, in France; also taught music there.

WAINWRIGHT, JOHN (1723-1768).  British.  Settled in Manchester (1746)
and led the singing at the Manchester Collegiate Church (now Manchester Cathedral.  Organist of Stockport Parish Church (1750). Published A Collection of Psalm Tunes, Anthems, Hymns and Chants in
1765.

WALCH, JAMES (1837-1901).  British.

WALKER, EDWARD CHARLES (1848-1872).  British.

WALKER, WILLIAM ( 1809-1875).  American.  Edited The Southern Harmony
(1835).

WALLACE, WILLIAM VINCENT (1814-1865).  Irish.  Composer of popular operas; organist and violinist; performed throughout the world.

WALTER, SAMUEL (b. 1916).  American.

WALTER, WILLIAM HENRY (1825-1893).  American.

WALTON, JAMES GEORGE (1821-1905).

WARD, SAMUEL AUGUSTUS (1847-1903).

WARREN, GEORGE WILLIAM (1828-1902).  American.  Organist at St. Peter's,
Albany, New York (1846-1858); organist at Holy Trinity, New York
(1850-1860); organist at St. Thomas's, New York (1870-1902).  Edited Warren's Hymns and Tunes, as sung at St. Thomas's Church, published in 1888.

WARTENSEE, XAVIER SCHNYDER VON (1786-1868).  Swiss.  Directed the department of singing at the school of Heinrich Pestalozzi at Yverdon
(1815-1817); taught music at the Engelmann Institute for Young La-
dies at Frankfurt (1817-1844).

WATHALL, ALFRED GEORGE  (fl. 1905).

WATSON, LAWRENCE WHITE (1860-1927).

WEBB, GEORGE JAMES (1803-1887).  British.  Organist of a church at Fal-
mouth; emigrated to the United States in 1830; organist of the Old
South Church, Boston (1830-1837); professor of the Boston Academy
of Music.  Belonged to and wrote music for the Church of the New
Jerusalem (Swedenborgian).

WEBBE, SAMUEL (1740-1816). British. A prolific composer of unaccompa-
nied vocal music; secretary to the Catch Club and librarian of the
Glee Club; a Roman Catholic who served as organist of the chapel of
the Sardinian Embassy, London.

WEBSTER, JOSEPH PHILBRICK (1819-1875). American.

WEBSTER, LORIN (1857-?).

WEBER, CARL MARIA VON (1786-1826). Austrian. The contributions of this
most noted and influential composer of the nineteenth century to
the area of church music comes, principally,in the form of adaptations from larger, secular pieces and from eight cantatas and two
masses.

WEEDEN, WINFIELD S. (1847-1908).

WEIMAR,GEORG PETER (1734-1800). German. Chamber musician and court kantor at Zerbst (1758); kantor at Kaufmannkirche, Erfurt (1763); music director at the Gymnasium (1774). Wrote a book of chorals for
the Protestant churches (published 1803).

WELLESLEY, GARRET COLLEY, EARL OF MORNINGTON (1735-1781). Irish. Founded the Academy of Music (1757); professor of music at the University of Dublin (1764); composed glees and madrigals. Father of the
noted Duke of Wellington.

WELLS, MARCUS MORRIS (1815-1895). American.

WESLEY, SAMUEL SEBASTIAN (1810-1876). British. Grandson of Charles
Wesley. Became an organist at age sixteen; served five parish
churches (including Leeds) and four cathedrals--Hereford, Exeter,
Winchester, Gloucester. Conducted the Three Choirs Festival, at
Gloucester; unsuccessful candidate (1844) for the Professorship of
Music at Edinburgh University. Published The European Psalmist--
a collection of 733 hymn tunes, 130 of which he, himself, composed.

WEST, JOHN ALLISON (1853-?).

WHITAKER, JOHN (1776-1847). British. Organist at St. Clement, East-
cheap. Contributed to The Seraph Collection of Sacred Music, published in 1818.

WHITE, EDWARD LITTLE (1809-1851). American. Published The Modern Harp
(Boston, 1846) and Harmonia Sacra (Boston, 1851)--both in association with John Edgar Gould (see above, this section)--and the Boston Sacred Harmony (1846).

WIANT, BLISS (1895-?).

WILKES, JOHN BERNARD (?-1882). British. Organist at Monkland, near
Leominster (1860); contributed to the first edition of Hymns Ancient and Modern (1861), through the efforts of his vicar (and the
editor of the collection), Sir William Henry Baker (see above, in
this section).

WILLCOX, JOHN HENRY (1827-1875). American. A graduate of Trinity College, Hartford, Connecticut (1849); organist in Boston; a specialist in organ construction and a writer of Catholic church music.

WILLIAMS, AARON (1731-1776). British. Music engraver and publisher of psalmody; a music teacher and clerk to the Scots Church, London Wall. Compiled The Universal Psalmodist (1770); New Universal Psalmodist (1770); Harmonia Coelestis (1775); Psalmody in Miniature (1778); Royal Harmony, or the Beauties of Church Music (1780).

WILLIAMS, RALPH VAUGHAN (1872-1958). British. Organist of South Lambeth Church (1896-1899); extension lecturer at Oxford; Professor of Music, Royal College of Music, London. Music editor of The English Hymnal and, with Martin Edward Fallas Shaw (see above, in this section), Songs of Praise.

WILLIAMS, ROBERT (1781-1821). Welsh. Blind basketmaker and musician.

WILLIAMS, THOMAS JOHN (1869-1944).

WILLING, CHRISTOPHER EDWIN (1830-1904). British. Organist of Blackheath Park Church; assistant organist of Westminster Abbey; organist at Her Majesty's Theatre (1847-1858); organist to the Foundling Hospital (1848-1879) and director of music there; organist of St. Paul's, Covent Garden (1857-1860); organist and director of music at All Saints,' Margaret Street (1860-1868); organist and chorus master to the Sacred Harmonic Society (1872); re-engaged as organist and master pianist of Her Majesty's Theatre (then moved to Drury Lane). Conductor of the St. Albans Choral Union.

WILLIS, RICHARD STORRS (1819-1900). American. Edited, in New York, The Musical Times and The Musical World. Compiled Church Chorals in 1850 and wrote Our Church Music (1855), the latter a discussion for pastors and worshipers.

WILSON, HUGH (1766-1824). Scottish. Led the psalmody in the Secession Church at Fenwick, Ayrshire; manager of the Secession Church at Duntocher and a founder of its Sunday school. Composer of the noted psalm tunes "Martyrdom" and "Caroline."

WINCHESTER, CALEB THOMAS. See above, in Section B.

WOODBURY, ISAAC BAKER (1819-1858). American. Member of a New England traveling glee club; editor of the New York Musical Review and The Musical Pioneer. Edited Anthem Dulcimer (1850); Liber Musicus (1850); Cythera; and New Lute of Zion.

WOODMAN, JONATHAN CALL (1813-1894). American. Teacher at Rutgers Institute and at Packer Institute; an oratorio singer at Boston, New York, and Brooklyn; sometimes associated with Lowell Mason (see in this section above).

WOOLER, ALFRED (1867-1937).

WORK, JOHN W. (1901-?).

WOSTENHOLM, MAURICE L. (1887-?).  American.

WYETH, JOHN (1770-1858).  American.  Published a <u>Repository</u> <u>of</u> <u>Sacred</u>
    <u>Music</u> --editions in 1810, 1813, 1820, 1834.

WYVILL, ZERUBBABEL (1762-1837).  British.  Organist and teacher of mu-
    sic at Maidenhead.  Published <u>Anthem, Two Hymns and Two Dismissions</u>
    . . .<u>for the General Thanksgiving, June 1, 1802</u>.


YOAKLEY, WILLIAM (1820-?).


ZEUNER, HEINRICH CHRISTOPHER (1795-1857).  Born in Saxony; came to Bos-
    ton in 1824.  Organist of Park Street Church and for the Handel and
    Haydn Society (1830-1837).  Went to Philadelphia in 1854.  Compiled
    the <u>American Harp</u> (1832) and <u>Ancient Lyre</u> (1842).

ZUNDEL, JOHN (1815-1882).  Born in Germany, where he trained as a vio-
    linist and organist; organist at St. Petersburg (1840-1847); came
    to New York in 1847, where he served as organist (1850-1855, 1858-
    1865, 1867-1878) at Plymouth Church, Brooklyn.  Wrote <u>A Treatise</u>
    <u>on Harmony</u> and edited <u>Psalmody</u> (1855).

# FIRST-LINE INDEX

Numbers refer to <u>entries</u>, not to pages.

A broken heart, my God, my King,
1346
A charge to keep, I have, 1548
A few more years shall roll, 137
A glory gilds the sacred page, 314
A mighty fortress is our God, 624
A sinner was wand'ring at eventide
1271
A song, I'll sing to you, 303
A stranger in the world below,
1549
A thousand oracles divine, 1550
Abba, Father, hear Thy child, 1551
Abide in me, O Lord, and I in Thee
1230
Abide with me! Fast falls the
eventide! 792
Above the clear blue sky, 263
Above the hills of time the cross
is gleaming, 1291
Abraham, when severely tried, 1552
According to Thy gracious word,
880
Again as evening's shadow falls,
773
Again returns the day of holy rest
824
Again the Lord of life and light,
62
Again the morn of gladness, 437
Ah, holy Jesus, how hast Thou of-
fended, 179
Ah, how shall fallen man, 1437
Ah! whither should I go, 1553
Alas! and did my Saviour bleed?
1438
Alas! what hourly dangers rise,
1191
All as God wills, who wisely heeds
1931
All beautiful the march of days,
1949

All creatures of our God and King,
417
All glory, laud, and honor, 958
All hail the power of Jesus' name!
1065
All nature's works His praise de-
clare, 1420
All people of the earth, 840
All people that on earth do dwell,
737
All praise to Him who dwells in
bliss, 1554
All praise to our redeeming Lord,
1555
All praise to the Lamb! accepted I
am, 1556
All praise to Thee, O King divine,
1300
All praise to Thee, my God, this
night, 730
All the way my Saviour leads me,
1380
"All things are ready," come, 849
All things are Thine; no gift have
we, 1932
All things bright and beautiful,
11
All my heart this night rejoices,
1961
All to Jesus I surrender, 1402
Alleluia! Alleluia! 1992
Almighty God, Thy word is cast, 256
Almighty Lord, with one accord,
1239
Almighty Maker of my frame, 1192
Almighty Spirit, now behold, 881
"Almost persuaded," now to believe
127
Alone Thou goest forth, O Lord,
1301
Always with us, always with us,
981

1157
Away with our sorrow and fear,
1576

Be is my only wisdom here, 1577
Be known to us in breaking bread,
883
Be no dismayed, whate'er betide,
816
Be present at our table, Lord, 258
Be still, and let the spirit speak
571
Be still, my soul: the Lord is on
thy side, 157
Be strong! 46
Be Thou my Vision, O Lord of my
heart, 233
Beams of heaven, as I go, 1287
Bear the cross, ye sons of men,
1414
Beauteous are the flowers of earth
371
Before Jehovah's awful throne,
1442
Before Thy mercy-seat, O Lord,
81
Begin, my tongue, some heavenly
theme, 1443
Behold a Sower! from afar, 521
Behold a stranger at the door! 540
Behold the Christian warrior stand
884
Behold the glories of the Lamb,
1444
Behold, the heathen waits to know,
1406
Behold the Saviour of mankind,
1918
Behold the servant of the Lord!
1578
Behold the sure Foundation-stone,
1445
Behold the throne of grace, 988
Behold the western evening light!
1059
Behold us, Lord, a little space,
438
Behold, what condescending love,
1061
Behold, what wondrous grace, 1446
Being of beings, God of love, 1579
Beneath our feet, and o'er our
head, 611
Beneath the cross of Jesus, 279
Beneath the forms of outward rite,
124

Beset by snares on every hand, 386
Beyond the smiling and the weeping
138
Bless the four corners of this
house, 544
Blessed assurance, Jesus is mine!
1381
Blessed be the dear uniting love,
1580
Blessed Jesus, at Thy word, 1962
Blessed Master, I have promised,
368
Blest are the pure in heart, 713
Blest are the sones of peace, 1447
Blest be the tie that binds, 474
Blest Comforter divine, 1163
Blest hour, when mortal man re-
tires, 1090
Blest Spirit, one with God above,
264
Blow ye the trumpet, blow, 1581
Bondage and death the cup contains
1138
Book of books, our people's stren-
gth, 355
Book of grace and book of glory,
805
Bound up on th' accursed tree, 858
Bread of the world in mercy broken
612
Break, day of God, O break, 224
Break forth, O beauteous heavenly
light, 1315
Break forth, O living light of God
1411
Break, new-born year, on glad eyes
break! 512
Break Thou the bread of life, 756
Breast the wave, Christian, 1186
Breathe on me, Breath of God, 583
Brethren in Christ, and well belo-
ved, 1582
Brief life is here our portion,
960
Bright and joyful is the morn, 885
Bright was the guiding star that
led, 36
Brightest and best of the sons of
the morning, 613
Brightly beams our Father's mercy,
128
Brightly gleams our banner, 1082
Broad is the road that leads to
death, 1448
Brother, hast thou wandered far,
277

768
O sons and daughters, let us sing!
   973
O, speed thee, Christian, on thy
   way, 1350
O Spirit of the living God,/In all,
   910
O Spirit of the living God,/Thou,
   1308
O splendor of God's glory bright,/
   From light, 267
O spelndor of God's glory bright,/
   O Thou, 180
O spread the tidings round, 161
O still in accents sweet and
   strong, 781
O Sun of righteousness, arise,
   1907
O tell me no more of this world's
   vain store, 501
O that I could my Lord receive,
   1780
O that I could repent!/O that I
   1781
O that I could repent,/With 1782
O that I knew the secret place,
   1518
O that my load of sin were gone!
   1783
O that Thou wouldst the heavens
   rend, 1784
O the bitter shame and sorrow, 864
O the depth of love divine, 1785
O the great joy that I find in His
   service, 243
O they tell me of a home far be-
   yond the skies, 30
O think of the home over there,
   688
O Thou eternal Christ of God, 759
O Thou eternal Victim, slain,
   1786
O Thou from whom all goodness
   flows, 603
O Thou God of my salvation, 1027
O Thou, in all Thy might so far,
   667
O Thou, my Saviour, Brother,
   Friend, 1351
O Thou, our Saviour, Brother,
   Friend, 1787
O Thou pure Light of souls that
   love, 254
O Thou that hearest prayer, 228
O Thou to whom, in ancient time,
   1069

O Thou, to whose all-searching
   sight, 1908
O Thou who all things canst con-
   trol, 1909
O Thou who art the Shepherd, 1152
O Thou who camest from above,
   1788
O Thou who driest the mourner's
   tear, 937
O Thou, who hast at Thy command,
   307
O Thou who hast our sorrows borne
   1789
O Thou, who hast spread out the
   skies, 528
O Thou, who in the olive shade,
   631
O Thou, who when we did complain,
   1790
O Thou, whom all Thy saints adore
   1791
O Thou, whose bounty fills my cup
   338
O Thou whose feet have climbed
   life's hill, 110
O Thou, whose filmed and failing
   eye, 1269
O Thou, whose hand hath brought
   us, 523
O Thou, whose mercy hears, 1207
O Thou, whose own vast temple
   stands, 201
O Thou, in whose presence my soul
   takes delight, 1243
O 'tis delight without alloy,
   1519
O turn ye, O turn ye, for why
   will ye die, 659
O valiant hearts, who to your
   glory came, 34
O what a mighty change, 1792
O what amazing words of grace,
   845
O what delight is this, 1793
O what, if we are Christ's, 54
O what shall I do my Saviour to
   praise, 1794
O when shall we sweetly remove,
   1795
O where are kings and empires now
   335
O where is now that glowing love,
   732
O where shall rest be found, 911
O who, in such a world as this,
   912

# COMPOSER AND
# TUNE-SOURCE INDEX

Numbers following names refer to entries, not to pages; those
numbers in parentheses refer to dates of publication.

# TUNE-NAME INDEX

Numbers refer to <u>entries</u>, not to pages.

Autumn, 57, 147, 1052, 1612
Ave Virgo Virginum, 963
Avison, 954
Avon, 5, 324, 1295, 1564, 1633,
    1681, 1918
Away in the Manger, 1314
Ayrshire, 1253, 1936
Azmon, 100, 353, 1256, 1450, 1452,
    1550, 1699, 1707, 1720, 1761,
    1764, 1766, 1772

Badea, 1674
Balerma, 288, 480, 708, 1104, 1521
    1661
Balm in Gilead, 1369
Bangor, 1301
Baptism, 670
Baptiste, 444
Barby, 104, 177, 1733, 1920
Barnabas, 1785
Barnby, 465
Barony, 806
Bartholdy, 197, 1618, 1886, 1910-
    1911
Barton, 73
Bath, 893
Battle Hymn of the Republic, 664,
    681
Be Still, 571
Beacon Hill, 812
Bealoth, 1823
Bear the Cross, 1414
Beatitudo, 1016, 1217, 1458, 1726,
    1851
Beecher, 92, 1755
Belleville, 332
Bells, 1354
Belmont, 81, 222, 240, 338, 442,
    620, 1128, 1493, 1603, 1764,
    1871
Beloit, 674, 676, 982, 1897, 1940
Beloved, 1243
Bemerton, 465, 1103, 1496, 1632,
    1767, 1907
Ben Rhydding, 1509
Benediction, 440, 1985
Benevento, 1007
Benjamin, 1802, 1820-1821
Bentley, 325, 826
Bera, 540, 1908
Bernard, 965
Bethany, 3
Bethel, 1043, 1047
Bethlehem, 187, 521, 644, 1252,
    1420
Beulah, 1091, 1873

Beyond, 138
Bishop, 1878
Blairgowrie, 559, 870, 872, 1157
Blessed Assurance, 1381
Blessed Home, 152, 790
Blumenthal, 533
Boardman, 436
Bolton, 873, 965
Bonar, 153
Bonaventura, 1184
Bonn, 1961
Bowring, 167
Bortniansky, 779
Boyce, 948
Boylston, 53, 145, 172, 474, 680,
    921, 1409, 1511, 1548, 1560,
    1562, 1565, 1727, 1867
Bracondale, 704
Bradbury, 1285
Brahms, 453
Bread of Life, 756
Bremen, 585, 1969, 1971
Brest, 990
Bridgman, 998, 1714, 1775
Bring Them In, 1268
Bringing in the Sheaves, 1153
Bristol, 166, 1545, 1922
Brocklesbury, 1249
Brocklesby, 229
Bromham, 593
Bromley, 498, 1811, 1850
Brookfield, 51, 675, 768, 955,
    1213
Brothers' Voices, 116
Browne, 1114
Bryn Calfaria, 1741
Bullinger, 368, 430, 588, 959
Burleigh, 217
Burlington, 232, 314, 328, 408,
    475, 933, 1219, 1599, 1622
Byefield, 1521
Byrd, 473

Caddo, 631, 846, 1952
Caersalem, 1954
Caithness, 5, 944
Caledonia, 1434
Calm, 1898
Calvary, 457
Cambridge, 100, 845, 993, 1208,
    1454, 1492, 1494, 1523
Camp, 1960
Campmeeting, 916, 1603
Can It Be Right? 1071
Candler, 1607
Canonbury, 333, 522, 591, 715, 768

# ADDENDA TO THE HYMNS

ABBEY, M.E.
2006. Life is like a mountain railroad,/With an engineer that's
brave
AMEH-265. Life's Railway to Heaven (Charles D. Tillman)

AKERMAN, LUCY EVELINA METCALF
2007. Nothing but leaves! the Spirit grieves/Over a wasted life
AMEH-537. Nothing but Leaves (Silas Jones Vail)

ARMITAGE, ELLA SOPHIA BULLEY
2008. O Lord of life, and love, and power,/How joyful life might
be
MSSH-181. East Hampton (Carl Fowler Price)

BARBAULD, ANNA LAETITIA
2009. Come, said Jesus' sacred voice,/Come and make my path your
choice
HMEC-344. Horton (Xavier Schnyder von Wartensee)
MH (1905)-257. St. Bees (John Bacchus Dykes)
MH (1935)-192. St. Bees (John Bacchus Dykes)

DENNY, SIR EDWARD
2010. Jesus wept! those tears are over,/But His heart is still the
same
HMEC-203. St. Joseph (H.H. Slatham)
AMEH-337. Regent Square (Henry Smart)

FABER, FREDERICK WILLIAM
2011. In the field with their flocks abiding,/They lay on the
dewy ground
MSSH-72. In the Field (Henry John Farmer)

HEWITT, ELIZA E.
2012. Sing the wondrous love of Jesus,/Sing His mercy and His
grace
AMEH-495. Sing the Wondrous Love of Jesus (Mrs. J.G.
Wilson)

HOFFMAN, ELISHA ALBRIGHT
2013. I must tell Jesus of my trials;/I cannot bear these burdens
alone
AMEH-511. I must Tell Jesus (Elisha Albright Hoffman)
2014. Where will you spend eternity?/This question comes to you
and me
AMEH-258. Tenney (John H. Tenney)

LOZIER, JOHN HOGARTH
2015. I am on the shining pathway,/Adown life's short'ning years

AMEH-532.  I Am on the Shining Pathway (Scots Air)

SKILTON, A.L.
2016.  No beautiful chamber,/No soft cradle bed
AMEH-272.  No Room in the Inn (E. Grace Updegraff)

UNKNOWN
2017.  O Lord, our Lord, in all the earth,/How excellent Thy Name!
MH (1966)-44.  Christus, der is mein Leben (Melchior
Vulpius)

WATTS, ISAAC
2018.  Great God, indulge my humble claims;/Be Thou my hope, my
joy, my rest
HMEC-419.  Wimborne (John Whitaker)

WESLEY, CHARLES
2019.  Join, all ye ransomed sons of grace,/The holy joy prolong
HMEC-947.  St. Martin's (William Tans'ur)
MH (1905)-576.  Winchester Old (George Kirbye)

BAKER, SIR HENRY WILLIAMS
2020.  On this day, the first of days,/God the Father's name we
praise
HMEC-91.  Dijon (Geneman evening hymn)

ONDERDONK, HENRY USTICK
2021.  The Spirit, in our hearts,/Is whispering, "Sinner, come"
HMEC-355.  Olney (Lowell Mason)
AMEH-24.  Greenwood (Joseph Emerson Sweetser)